Elisabetta Piazzesi

The Complete Illustrated
TUSCAN COOKERY BOOK

Starters; Sauces; Pasta, Soup and Rice Dishes; Meat; Fish;
Omelettes; Vegetables; Desserts, Cakes and Pastries.

TWO HUNDRED AND FIFTY TRIED AND TESTED RECIPES,
WITH ILLUSTRATIONS, ANNOTATIONS, VARIATIONS AND SUGGESTIONS.

With the collaboration of
Pedro Di Vito

BONECHI

The photographs in this book were taken specially by Dario Grimoldi at the Ristorante "Lo Strettoio". The photographs on pages 9 (at the top) and 129 are by Giuliano Valsecchi.
     The photographs of Tuscan monuments and landscapes on page 6 come from the Publishers' Archives.

Editorial conception: Casa Editrice Bonechi
Project and production: Paolo Piazzesi
Photos: Dario Grimoldi
Translated by Stephanie Johnson

Printed in Italy by Centro Stampa Editoriale Bonechi.

ISBN 88-8029-340-0

Preface

To Niccolò and Marco

"KING WILY HAD A DAUGHTER with the deplorable habit of biting her finger nails. One day, he told her that a prince was coming to the castle and would only touch food cooked by her... So it was that the princess placed herself before a kitchen table brimming with vegetables, meat, game and fruit and cooked. She went on cooking until she forgot all about her hands...". The fantastic colours of that table covered with multi-coloured food have always illuminated my memories. Indeed, at times I would be tempted to swear that everything began by reading a fairy story in that old book that I still guard jealously. I was born in the country, in a house where there was so much freedom and colour, fragrance and song, and I remember always feeling the urge to handle this flour, slice that bread, gather those vegetables. What a great occasion the oil pressing was and what fun the grape harvest, ending in joyous singing and roguish verse, all of us together at the wooden tables, in front of the soups, the beans and the meat which had just been roasted over the glowing charcoal fire....

Tuscany. My ancient, noble land, with its landscape gently "drafted" and moulded by Man around the original natural beauty which stands out in all its splendour. Here is the azure sea, there are the mountains and the hills with their green slopes, punctuated with dream villages.... An admirable balance, into which monuments and works of art are inserted as if they had always been there, without distorting or clashing with anything. Our cuisine mirrors all this; it expresses simplicity, strength, skill, tenderness and good taste. To appreciate that so much vitality is the consequence of authenticity, it is enough merely to consider the recipes, their style and their application, that capacity to hand them down integrally in their original spirit, adapting them the while to changing habits and needs. To be able to discern the geniality, it is enough to contemplate how little is needed to prepare dishes fit for a king. My mode of cookery is born of popular tradition, retrieving its very high cultural and gastronomical level, aesthetical rigour and respect for things, which allows them to be handled without savagery. Add to this the ancient skill and simplicity that have always distinguished Tuscan cookery from that of other regions. There are no sauces drowning the food or greasy, indigestible dressings. You will discover that every ingredient, even the humblest, participates in the harmonious whole as if it were a detail in a work of

ELISABETTA PIAZZESI'S INGRAINED PASSION was crowned in 1975 when she started "lovingly and patiently" (as she is wont to stress) to compound the refined, lavish dishes that she sets before the patrons of "Lo Strettoio". The restaurant is situated among the hills encircling Florence. From the terrace giving onto the unforgettable spectacle of Brunelleschi's *Cupola* and so many artistic wonders, one almost seems to touch this City of the Flower (the municipal emblem is the Lily). The "Strettoio" tables are decked out on the premises of the ancient olive press which belongs to the seventeenth-century villa "Le Lepricine", where the author lives together with her husband and children. Owing to the clever choice made over three centuries ago with regard to the aspect of the building and the thickness of the walls (a metre), the restaurant is cool in summer and warm in winter. Pride of place here has

the monumental olive press (the term *strettoio* stands for "screw press"), which used to protect and store the delicate gold of the Tuscan hills, that very fine, pure olive oil that on these pages irreplaceably plays the main role. Elisabetta rules in the kitchen, her mind on today's practicalities but her heart with tradition, in the spirit of the artisans of her land. Her recipes thrive on the masterly balance that is expressed in this book. On the one hand, there is the family fare, the great dishes for festive occasions, the humbler, every-day dishes and the skill of her mother and grandmother, because without love there is no really good cuisine. On the other hand, there is controlled creativity, indispensable to "freshen up" the taste of Tuscan cookery and to satisfy the demand for fare in step with our times. An expert sommelier, her husband Pedro is in charge of the superb wine list, the organisation and the reception of clients. While drawing up this book, which paints a truthful picture of their personalities and professionalism, both husband and wife collaborated in the choice and preparation of the recipes, checking, one by one, the ingredients, amounts, timing and procedures. They put their hearts into the making of the dishes and placed the premises, furnishings, themselves and their exquisite taste at the disposal of Dario Grimoldi, so that he could use his camera with skill just as if he were photographing top models in a sumptuous fashion parade.

art, exalting the flavour without blunting it. Such is the taste of our cuisine: more than a gastonomic canon, it is a way of life. Cooking is a civilised, cultured means of communication and Tuscan cuisine communicates grace and elegance.

All the recipes that you will find here have been specifically checked through, step by step. Each procedure intentionally follows along classic lines, using traditional Tuscan ingredi-

ents. Where these latter are hard to come by, I suggest relevant substitutions in the notes included with the recipe or in the suggestions to readers. Comments are generally intended to introduce variations, offer advice for the presentation of dishes or make suggestions to facilitate the preparation and cooking.

As well as to my children, the book is dedicated to those who like to enjoy themselves in company around the dinner table.

NOTES AND SUGGESTIONS TO READERS:

- THE RECIPES ARE ALWAYS CALCULATED TO SERVE FOUR PEOPLE (EXCEPT WHEN SPECIFICALLY INDICATED DIFFERENTLY).

- SALT AND PEPPER ARE NOT MENTIONED IN THE LIST OF INGREDIENTS, AS THEIR USE IS TAKEN FOR GRANTED. THE RECIPES STATE WHEN TO SEASON THE DISHES, BUT EACH COOK WILL ADJUST THE SEASONING TO PERSONAL TASTE. SALT IS, HOWEVER, MENTIONED AMONG THE INGREDIENTS AS FAR AS DESSERTS, CAKES OR BISCUITS ARE CONCERNED.

- WHERE MENTION IS MADE OF OIL, REFERENCE IS MADE EXCLUSIVELY TO THE BEST *EXTRA VERGINE* OLIVE OIL, THUS ENSURING THE COMPLETE SUCCESS OF THE DISHES. ANY FURTHER COMMENT IS SUPERFLUOUS.

- INSTEAD OF *VINSANTO*, A GOOD DESSERT RAISIN WINE WHICH IS NOT TOO SWEET MAY BE USED.

- TUSCAN BREAD CAN, AT A PINCH, BE SUBSTITUTED WITH ANY KIND OF BREAD, PROVIDED THAT IT IS UNSALTED, HAS NO FAT (WHETHER OIL OR BUTTER) AND IS NOT SPICED.

- MENTION IS MADE OF VARIOUS ITALIAN CHEESES. IF YOU CANNOT FIND THE "GENUINE ARTICLE", HERE IS A BASIC DESCRIPTION TO HELP YOU DECIDE ON WORTHY SUBSTITUTES:

    PARMESAN CHEESE IS THE HARD, DRY CHEESE KNOWN WORLD-WIDE AS A COMPLEMENT TO MANY DISHES AND NEEDING NO INTRODUCTION HERE;

    PECORINO IS A HARD OR SEMI-HARD SHEEP'S MILK CHEESE AND IS AVAILABLE AT VARYING STAGES OF RIPENING;

    FONTINA IS A FAT, CREAMY, MILD CHEESE FROM THE PIEDMONT REGION;

    MADE FROM EWE'S MILK, *RICOTTA* IS SOFT AND FRESH, HAVING THE TEXTURE OF COTTAGE CHEESE;

    THE BEST *MOZZARELLA* IS TRADITIONALLY A CURD CHEESE MADE FROM BUFFALO MILK AND SHOULD BE EATEN VERY FRESH, BUT OF NECESSITY, IT IS NOW MORE FREQUENTLY MADE FROM COW'S MILK.

- RED-SKINNED ONIONS IN ITALY ARE FAIRLY SWEET AND COULD PERHAPS BE COMPARED TO SPANISH AND BERMUDA ONIONS, WHILE ITALIAN WHITE-SKINNED ONES ARE MORE PUNGENT IN FLAVOUR.

- IF *CANNELLINI* BEANS ARE UNAVAILABLE, THEY CAN BE REPLACED BY HARICOT BEANS.

- WHEN REFERRING TO OVEN TEMPERATURES, THE FOLLOWING EXPRESSIONS ARE USED FOR THE SAKE OF BREVITY, WITH THE EQUIVALENT TEMPERATURES AS GIVEN IN THE CHART:

    - SLOW OVEN - 160°C
    - MEDIUM OVEN - 170°C
    - HOT OVEN - 180°C
    - VERY HOT OVEN - 200°C

Index

MEAT AND GAME

FISH AND AMPHIBIANS

OMELETTES

VEGETABLE DISHES

DESSERTS, CAKES AND PASTRIES

STARTERS AND SAUCES

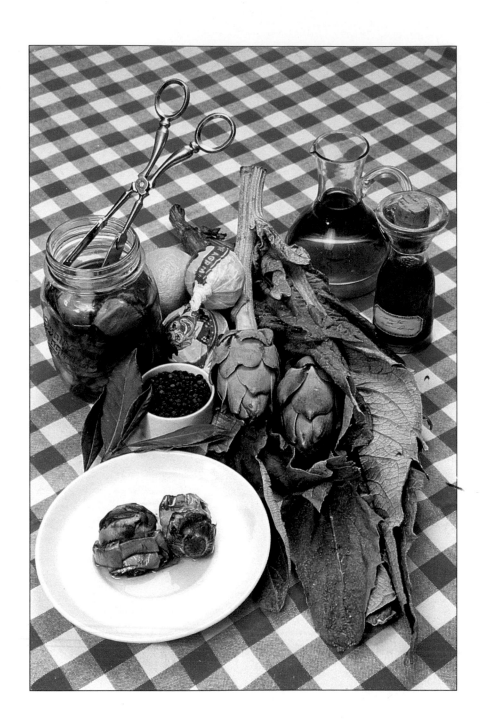

Aringa sott'olio

HERRINGS IN OIL

◆

- 2 SALTED HERRINGS
- 2 CARROTS
- 1 HEAD OF CELERY
- A FEW SMALL, PICKLING ONIONS
- OLIVE OIL
- CHILLI PEPPER

◆

PREPARATION TIME: 3/4 HOUR

HERRINGS TO BE SERVED in oil must not be smoked and should preferably be females with their roes, not males.

Bone the fish and rinse under running water. In a deep serving dish, lay the fillets on a bed of carrots, celery and fresh onions, all finely chopped.

Cover with olive oil and add one or two dried chilli peppers.

Leave to stand a while, a whole day even, before relishing them with white Tuscan bread.

———————

A PERSONAL TOUCH TO a traditional dish?

Boil some rather large potatoes. Allow to cool and cut into big, round slices. Cut up the herrings into small pieces (not too small) and simply serve on the potato rounds.

Baccalà in torta
SALT COD FISH CAKE

- 1 FILLET OF SALT COD, PREVIOUSLY SOAKED (SEE PAGE 133)
- TOMATO PULP
- 200G ITALIAN ARBORIO RICE
- KNOB OF BUTTER
- 1/2 L MILK
- 1 TABLESPOON WHITE FLOUR
- 1 CLOVE OF GARLIC
- OLIVE OIL

PREPARATION TIME: 1 1/2 HOURS

CUT THE SALT COD FILLET into chunks, coat with flour and deep fry in oil until golden on both sides. Remove the fish from the pan with the aid of a skimmer. Prepare a light tomato sauce in another pan with the oil, garlic and tomatoes. Add the fish. While this is bubbling away on the hob, make a béchamel sauce with the butter, flour and milk and add to the *baccalà* after draining off any excess oil from the tomato sauce. Once the rice is cooked (but the grains are still firm), mix everything together in a bowl, adding a pinch of chilli pepper. Butter and flour an ovenproof dish and bake in a medium oven for about 40 minutes.

WITHOUT ANY DOUBT, THIS IS an unusual way of presenting salt cod, a fish which is not sufficiently appreciated and is erroneously considered gastronomically trifling. On the contrary, it adapts to several modes of preparation, which are either unsophisticated (as in this recipe) or very refined (such as a *baccalà* mousse).

Carciofi sott'olio
ARTICHOKES PRESERVED IN OIL

- 10 SMALL GLOBE ARTICHOKES (MORELLINI, IF AVAILABLE)
- 1L WHITE WINE
- 1/2 GLASS RED WINE VINEGAR
- 2 LEMONS
- 10 BAY LEAVES
- WHOLE BLACK PEPPER
- OLIVE OIL

PREPARATION TIME: 1 HOUR

CAREFULLY CLEAN the artichokes, trim the tops and emerge in a saucepan containing water and a squeeze of lemon. Put the saucepan on the heat, adding the white wine, barely half a glass of vinegar, 2 bay leaves and 10 black peppercorns. When cooked, the artichokes must still be crisp. Drain well, leaving them upside-down to dry on a tea towel, for a whole day even. Put them in the appropriate jars, alternating with the bay leaves and a few peppercorns. Cover with good-quality olive oil and close the jars tightly. In this final phase, a chilli pepper or a pinch (and I mean just a pinch) of fennel seed can be added to your liking.

THESE LITTLE artichokes (see the illustration on the second page of this section) are one of my favourites for lending flavour to a nice rice salad or for giving the finishing touch to a cold side-plate.

Cipolle in agrodolce

SWEET-SOUR ONIONS

♦

- 1KG RED-SKINNED ONIONS
- 1 GLASS RED WINE VINEGAR
- 3 TABLESPOONS OLIVE OIL
- 1 TABLESPOON SUGAR
- PINCH OF SALT

♦

PREPARATION TIME: 3 HOURS

CUT THE ONIONS into segments and blanche for a few minutes (in a pressure cooker, if preferred), until all the juices have run out.

Place in a pan (traditionally, you carry on with the same one as before), add all the other ingredients together in one fell swoop, put over a low flame ... and wait. While waiting, frequently stir the mixture, which will, little by little, change consistency and colour.

Three hours are necessary for good results (which, of course, do also depend on the onion type).

WE ALL IMMEDIATELY THINK of the commonplace white, cocktail onions commercialised on television and when a plate piled high with a dark and mysterious mixture is put before us, we are a little disconcerted.

Just try them and in this dish you will savour all the patience, experience and simplicity of Tuscan cuisine. Here we go again, talking about patience and time....

By the way, this is how I met my husband; as a young girl I entered the restaurant kitchen and discovered him in the act of tasting the *cipolline in agrodolce*. I was captivated (not only by my husband-to-be, but also by the baby onions). So it is that I have continued to cook that ancient and curious dish, that onion concoction which requires so much time.

A particular touch can be lent by eating them with fresh ricotta, ewe's milk cottage cheese: an unusual combination to dazzle and delight your guests. My husband relishes them with a good, young Chianti... How the memories flood back!

Crostini alla beccaccia

WOODCOCK CROUTONS

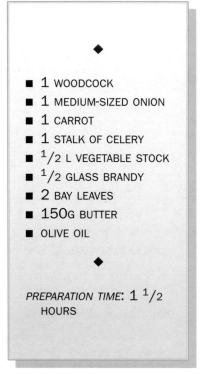

◆

- ■ 1 WOODCOCK
- ■ 1 MEDIUM-SIZED ONION
- ■ 1 CARROT
- ■ 1 STALK OF CELERY
- ■ $1/2$ L VEGETABLE STOCK
- ■ $1/2$ GLASS BRANDY
- ■ 2 BAY LEAVES
- ■ 150G BUTTER
- ■ OLIVE OIL

◆

PREPARATION TIME: 1 $1/2$ HOURS

LEAVE THE WOODCOCK until sufficiently mature. Pluck it, singe it, but, if you want to get the best out of it, do not draw it. Finely chop the vegetables and, with the 2 bay leaves, fry gently for a few minutes in 3 tablespoons of oil. Add the woodcock, sousing it with the brandy. Allow to cook for about 40 minutes over a moderate flame, keeping the pan covered and adding the stock from time to time. Remove the woodcock from the heat and carefully bone, without discarding anything. Bring up to the boil again. Remove the bay leaves, pass the lot through the grinder and whisk the butter in until the mixture is smooth and consistent. This is a delicacy for serving on toasted bread, moistened with a drop of brandy.

WOODCOCK (*Scolopax rusticola*) are traditionally most prized by hunters. Difficult to shoot, their flesh is very delicate on account of the quality of their diet.

They are not easy to find, as, unlike quails and pheasants, they cannot be bred. Our heart-felt advice to anyone coming into possession of a woodcock is to prepare these excellent croutons without hesitation, because the chance of savouring them again will not come by too soon.

Crostini alle anguille

EELS ON TOAST

◆

- ■ 200G EELS
- ■ BUNCH OF SWISS CHARD
- ■ 2 TOMATOES
- ■ PARSLEY AND GARLIC
- ■ WHITE WINE
- ■ OLIVE OIL

◆

PREPARATION TIME: $3/4$ HOUR

CHOP THE GARLIC and chard and brown in 4 tablespoons of oil in a saucepan.

Add the peeled tomatoes (they must be fresh and ripe), the eels cut into segments (it is imperative that these be small, so be sure your fishmonger gets your order in good time) and the parsley.

Moisten with half a glass of white wine and let it evaporate, so just the flavour remains.

Simmer gently until the meat of the eels disintegrates, making a thick sauce.

The sauce is then spread on rounds of toasted bread sprinkled with white wine.

Crostini ai fegatini

CHICKEN LIVERS ON TOAST

◆

- 300G CHICKEN LIVERS
- A LITTLE STOCK
- 1 RED-SKINNED ONION
- 1/2 GLASS VIN SANTO (OR SHERRY)
- 50G CAPERS
- SLICES OF WHITE BREAD
- OLIVE OIL

◆

PREPARATION TIME: 3/4 HOUR

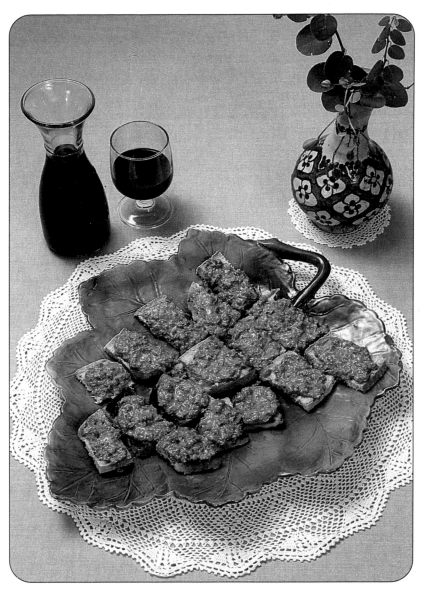

AMONG THE NUMEROUS TYPES of crostino, this one reigns supreme in Tuscan cuisine, owing to its fame and wide circulation. Nowadays, *crostini* with chicken livers are the most commonly found, especially on celebration days, and they are held to be the most classic examples in Tuscan cooking. Some people offer toast with chicken livers and spleen (one simple but efficacious recipe is to cook the livers first, the spleen being added a few minutes later). However, each cook adds, on her own initiative, either classic ingredients (such as anchovies) or more fanciful ones (indeed, I bet you won't find your neighbour using the same recipe). The recipe that I have given you, at any rate, is considered to be the classic one and the one which I like best of all.

TRIM THE LIVERS CAREFULLY, removing all traces of gall bladder. Rinse under the tap and leave to drain. Slice the onion finely and sauté in a pan with 2 tablespoons olive oil. When it begins to become translucent, add the livers. While cooking, gradually sprinkle in the vinsanto and season with salt and pepper. Cook over medium heat for half-an-hour. Finally add the capers, squeezed of all their vinegar. Chop up the sauce or, better still, pass through the mincing machine. Toast some slices of bread and sprinkle with just a little stock. Spread a portion of the mixture on each slice and serve. This is also good eaten cold.

Crostini di coniglio
RABBIT ON TOAST

- ■ 1/2 RABBIT (THE FORE QUARTERS)
- ■ 1 WHITE-SKINNED ONION
- ■ 1 CARROT
- ■ CELERY
- ■ 1/2 GLASS MILK
- ■ OLIVE OIL
- ■ CHILLI PEPPER
- ■ SLICES OF WHITE BREAD
- ■ PARSLEY

PREPARATION TIME: 1/2 HOUR

ONCE UPON A TIME, families used to throw nothing away and, in order to exploit the forequarters of a rabbit (that is, the least fleshy part from where it is more difficult to strip off the flesh), it was common use to finely chop some carrot, a white-skinned (pungent) onion and a little celery and brown them in a little oil in a pan. Do this, then add the forequarters of the rabbit (jointed), cover with milk and leave to simmer for about 40 minutes.

Draw the meat off the heat, leave to cool and bone the animal. Mince roughly. Return to the pan and cook slowly for a further 10 minutes, with the addition of some chilli pepper and salt to taste.

Serve the mixture on toast, dredged with chopped parsley to enhance the flavour and lend a touch of spring to the *crostini*.

Crostini di milza
SPLEEN ON TOAST

- ■ 300G CALF'S SPLEEN
- ■ 1 RED-SKINNED ONION
- ■ 80G BUTTER
- ■ 1 GLASS BRANDY
- ■ 4 ANCHOVY FILLETS
- ■ 2 RIPE TOMATOES

PREPARATION TIME: 3/4 HOUR

CHOP THE ONION and sauté in the butter in a pan. Skin and crush the spleen and place in the pan, together with the tomatoes and a pinch of salt and pepper. Simmer over gentle heat for half-an-hour. Add the brandy and the well-rinsed, boned anchovies. Reduce the mixture to a pulp over a low flame for a further 10 minutes, stirring frequently with a wooden spoon to blend thoroughly. Heap generously on rounds of toasted bread and the *crostini* are ready.

MY RECIPE FOLLOWS FAMILY memories (when my grandmother skinned the spleen, removing the pulp by scraping the meat off with the back of a knife). Accordingly, the customary capers and wine (red for some, white for others) have been replaced with tomatoes and brandy. Every housewife or cook, whether professional or amateur, has always added (or withheld) certain ingredients, in order to make any type of *crostini* (never lacking at festive Florentine tables) more personal and enjoyable.

Crostini col vinsanto

VINSANTO CANAPÉS

◆

- 300G CHICKEN LIVERS
- 2 GARLICKY SAUSAGES
- 1 ONION
- SPRIG OF ROSEMARY
- $^1/_2$ L VINSANTO (OR MEDIUM-DRY SHERRY)
- SLICES OF BAGUETTE-TYPE BREAD
- OLIVE OIL

◆

PREPARATION TIME: 1 HOUR

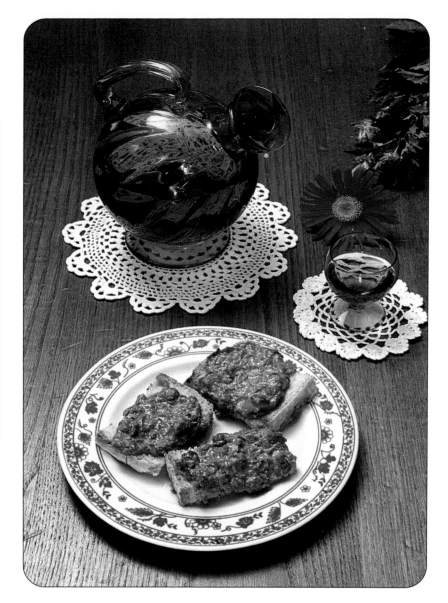

ALLOW ME TO SUGGEST, for a change, that this preparation does not need Tuscan bread, but rather the French baguette type, round in shape, with a softer texture to it.

Vinsanto can be found behind every threshold in Tuscany, and, to borrow an old Italian adage, it is like parsley: it turns up everywhere, in every "pie", from the antipasto to the dessert.

It adapts to thousands of uses: it can be drunk, poured or sprinkled, particularly when the occasion is special.

There was a time when these flavoursome, dainty and auspicious *crostini* would never be missing at any wedding feast.

SLICE THE BREAD into many rounds to be dipped into the vinsanto. Place the slices on a serving dish. Sauté the chopped onion in a pan with a trickle of oil. Crumble the sausages in your hands and add to the onion when it is half cooked, keeping the pan over low heat for a quarter-hour. Rinse the livers carefully under the tap and add to the pan, together with the other ingredients. Continue cooking for half-an-hour over gentle heat, seasoning with salt, pepper and the sprig of rosemary. Discard the herb and put everything through the grinder. Serve the mixture on the bread rounds and offer to your family or guests.

Crostini di polenta

CORNMEAL SLICES WITH SAUSAGES

◆

- 300G CORNMEAL
- 1 RED-SKINNED ONION
- 2 SPRING ONIONS
- 2 TOMATOES
- 3 SAUSAGES
- OLIVE OIL

◆

PREPARATION TIME: 1 HOUR

MAKE A FAIRLY THICK PORRIDGE, stirring with a wooden spoon over a low flame for about 40 minutes.

Separately, sauté the onion with the spring onions in a trickle of oil in a pan.

Add the crumbled sausages and raise the heat to cook the mixture through. Add the coarsely-chopped tomatoes and allow to reduce appreciably.

Place the cooked cornmeal on a pastry board (or else in a rectangular oven tray which is much more practical) and leave to cool.

Cut into rectangles which are not too thin and deep fry them in oil.

When they are very crisp and golden, liberally spread the mixture over them and serve hot.

THESE TASTY CROSTINI are for serving up especially in the winter, when the frying and consumption of a hot dish do not require too much of an effort. Not everybody manages to fry polenta without it crumbling. There is a trick and, like all tricks, it is simple. Everything depends on letting the cornmeal slices colour nicely on each side before turning them and on maintaining a high oil temperature.

Many qualities of cornmeal are available on the market nowadays, from coarse *Bramata* to very finely ground *Monte Amiata*.

I myself do not much care for the coarse type because the mixture turns out heavy and rather too "rough-and-ready" for me. For this *crostino*, I would use a medium-ground, bright yellow flour which has not been mixed with other starches.

Crostini di polmone

STEWED LIGHTS ON TOAST

- 300G LIGHTS
- 1/2 RED ONION
- 1/2 CARROT
- 1 STALK OF CELERY
- CAN OF PLUM TOMATOES
- STALE BREAD
- OLIVE OIL

◆

PREPARATION TIME: 1 HOUR

BROWN THE CHOPPED ONION, together with the more coarsely-chopped carrot and celery, in 4 tablespoons of oil in a large saucepan. Add the lights. Slow, lengthy cooking is needed because lungs tend to get tough at first (don't give up - it is quite normal for this ancient dish!). Then, little by little, they soften up and become as tender as when they were bought. Complete the cooking as for a normal stew.

Use the knife specially designed for dicing the lungs (or put through a modern mincer), heat it up for a moment in its sauce and serve over toasted bread (home-made, white bread is better) sprinkled with vinsanto (or sherry).

UNFORTUNATELY NOWADAYS WE overlook these economical, tasty dishes of old. With their being quite economical, lights are usually degraded to cat food (presuming that the feline race, spoilt by the sophisticated advertising of the food earmarked for them, avail themselves of it!). Among other things, lights are suitable for those who do not want to put on too much weight, as it has a limited nutritive power (today the expression is "value in calories") and an excellent flavour.

Donzellette alla salvia

SAGE-FLAVOURED CLAM FRITTERS

- 100G CLAMS (SHELLED AND CLEANED)
- 3 TABLESPOONS WHITE FLOUR
- A FEW SAGE LEAVES
- 2 GLASSES MILK
- 3 CLOVES OF GARLIC
- OLIVE OIL

◆

PREPARATION TIME: 1 HOUR

MAKE A COATING BATTER with the flour and milk and add the finely-chopped sage.

Clean and scald the clams in a saucepan over fierce heat, together with 3 cloves of garlic and a trickle of oil. Drain and season with salt and pepper.

Toss the clams into the batter and set aside for half-an-hour.

Deep fry the *donzellette* (literally "damsels") in boiling oil, the correct quantity for each being one tablespoon of the batter. Turn them carefully until they are golden on both sides.

They are good only when eaten piping hot, crisp and aromatic, with the clams as a tasty surprise.

— 21 —

Fette col cavolo nero

TOAST WITH KALE

- **2** BUNCHES OF DARK GREEN CABBAGE OR KALE
- STALE BREAD
- OLIVE OIL
- FRESHLY GROUND PEPPER
- LEMON
- GARLIC CLOVES

PREPARATION TIME: $^1/_2$ HOUR

S IMPLE TO PREPARE, THE OUTCOME (as in the following recipe for *fettunta*) is generally acknowledged to be superb, not just by virtue of the very tasty ingredients used, but also because of that minimum but indispensable care taken during the preparation which justifies my drawing up a proper recipe.

Boil the cabbage or kale, stripped of its midribs, for about 20 minutes.

Toast some slices of bread (not too thinly cut) and rub a pared garlic clove over the surface. Serve the toast with the vegetable leaves still dripping water.

Liberally dress with olive oil, a little freshly-ground pepper and a sprinkling of lemon and salt. The flavour can be fully appreciated only if the dish is eaten very hot.

Fettunta

GARLIC TOAST

◆

- SLICES OF WHITE, ITAL-IAN-STYLE BREAD
- GARLIC CLOVES
- OLIVE OIL

◆

PREPARATION TIME: $^1/4$ HOUR

CUT FOUR SLICES of firm, crusty bread. Toast them over the fire (marvellous cooked over charcoal, but of course a modern gas or electric grill will do fine), rub a clove of pared garlic over both sides. Finally, drench in olive oil (only Tuscan, of the best quality), sprinkle over a pinch of salt and eat them while hot (cold *fettunta* is awful).

If you wish to enjoy *fettunta* as a first course, serve it enriched with red tomato slices laid on top, with a sprinkling of chopped basil.

AS SOON AS MY CHILDREN were a year old, their wise grandmother always advised giving them bread and olive oil at tea-time, heedless of pre-digested infant formulas and, more likely than not, of the dictates of a dietetics system rather too prone to TV commercials. And, indeed, she is quite right. Of course, good, simple things never go out of fashion (just like grandmothers)... In confirmation of the complete digestibility of this appetising and nutritious combination of bread and oil, let me also add that, when my husband's stomach craves for something light after some stressful bouts of work and after continual sips of wine (don't get the wrong end of the stick - he is a sommelier), he adjusts the balance of his worn-out bio-rhythms by partaking of meals based on bread and olive oil. It is a short step from this to the *fettunta* (literally an "oiled slice"), intended as an antipasto. The time for *fettunta* is November, with the newly-pressed *olio nuovo*, but it is also great in summer (served as an appetiser, at tea-time, when you like).

Fettunta al tartufo

TRUFFLES ON TOAST

◆

- 40G TRUFFLE
- 4 SLICES OF BREAD
- 1 CLOVE OF GARLIC
- OLIVE OIL

◆

PREPARATION TIME: $^1/4$ HOUR

THIS MORE SOPHISTICATED (and expensive) version is a kind of "variation on a theme", suitable for starting off a dinner among friends rather than backing up daily fare.

Slice the truffle paper-thin and place in a bowl with a clove of garlic and 3 tablespoons of olive oil. Work in with a fork to reduce it all to a delicious sauce.

Spread this on the slices of toast, season with a little salt and serve immediately.

Fiori fritti

ZUCCHINI FLOWER FRITTERS

◆

- ■ 10 FRESH ZUCCHINI FLOWERS
- ■ 2 EGGS
- ■ 150G WHITE FLOUR
- ■ OLIVE OIL

◆

PREPARATION TIME: 3/4 HOUR

A POPULAR VARIATION in preparing the batter, commonly followed in restaurants big and small, consists in using just the white of the egg and not the whole egg.

In this way, the batter is frothier and creates a spectacular effect by forming a kind of "cobweb" over the fries (a similar result can be obtained by adding half a glass of ale to the water).

I find, however, that the batter which I have indicated in my recipe is particularly suitable for zucchini flowers because it covers them with a light film, making them decidedly crisp and, at the same time, delicate in consistency.

THE ABSOLUTE FRESHNESS OF THE MINIATURE marrow flowers is fundamental to get good results. This means that it is a seasonal dish that you can only enjoy in the spring or summer months, whether you have the good fortune of growing your own or have to turn to the greengrocer.

Carefully remove the pistil and the small, green, external leaves.

Prepare a batter in the following way: lightly beat the egg with a pinch of salt, add the flour and whisk to remove all lumps. Now add water until a homogeneous, fairly liquid mixture is obtained. Set the batter aside to rest for about 30 minutes.

Dip the zucchini flowers into the batter, taking care to hold the flowers upside down for a moment to let the surplus drain off. Deep fry in boiling oil, turning them over cautiously with the aid of 2 forks. It is essential to serve them crisp and piping hot.

Fiori ripieni

STUFFED ZUCCHINI FLOWERS

◆

- 20 LARGE, FRESH ZUC-CHINI FLOWERS
- 200G LEAN RAW MINCED MEAT (OR ELSE BOILED OR STEWED MEAT)
- 100G BÉCHAMEL SAUCE (SEE RECIPE ON PAGE 87)
- COATING BATTER (SEE RECIPE ON THE PREVI-OUS PAGE)
- 2 EGGS
- PARSLEY
- OLIVE OIL

◆

PREPARATION TIME: $^1/_2$ HOUR

To make dishes of this type, fundamentally simple, requires, however, quite some time and especially patience and love.

I particularly like these delicious, decorative flowers because they remind me of marvellous summer days when I was little and of how exciting it was going into my grandfather's vegetable garden to pick those funny, delicate flowers which hid under the huge, prickly leaves and which would later appear on the table, mouth-watering amid a haze of steam.

W ASH THE FLOWERS THOROUGHLY; they must be very fresh and rather large. The stuffing is prepared by mixing the béchamel sauce into the minced leftovers from boiled or stewed meat or the raw minced meat. In the latter case, first sauté in a tablespoon of oil over a fierce heat for ten minutes, allowing to cool before adding to the béchamel sauce. Bind the filling with the beaten eggs, season with salt, pepper and a little chopped parsley. Get the frying pan ready, then open up the flowers with your fingers and fill them very carefully with the stuffing (about a tablespoon for each flower). Roll them in the batter and fry immediately. A tasty alternative to the forcemeat consists in using mozzarella cheese enhanced with the aroma of a boned, mashed anchovy. Cut up the mozzarella, add the anchovy, 2 tablespoons of béchamel sauce and a handful of stale bread which has been left to soak in milk and then squeezed thoroughly. Bind it all with a beaten egg and then fry the flowers in the usual way.

I Baccelli col pecorino

CHEESE AND BROAD BEAN SALAD

- ■ 2 KG FRESH BROAD BEANS (UNSHELLED)
- ■ SEMI-SOFT PECORINO (UNMATURED)
- ■ 1 BUNCH OF CATMINT OR BASIL
- ■ OLIVE OIL

PREPARATION TIME: 1/2 HOUR

TAKE A NICE BASKET OF BROAD BEANS (refer to the recipe for *baccelli stufati* to appreciate what we mean by *baccelli*), preferably small and fresh (you can tell they are fresh if, on snapping open the pod, they "sing", i.e. they make a sharp, cheerful sound). Shell (removing each foot-stalk), wash and place them in a saucepan with a trickle of olive oil, a bunch of basil (or catmint) and salt.

Cover and bring to the boil for a few minutes. Once cooked, they will appear "wrinkled" but must be *al dente* or crisp to the bite. Drain and leave to cool. In a vegetable dish, prepare parings of semi-soft, unmatured pecorino. Mix the baccelli with the cheese, pour in 2 tablespoons of olive oil and correct the salt.

To give a touch of colour, which is never amiss on the dinner table, add a handful of well-chopped *radicchio rosso* and a bunch of radishes cut into rounds.

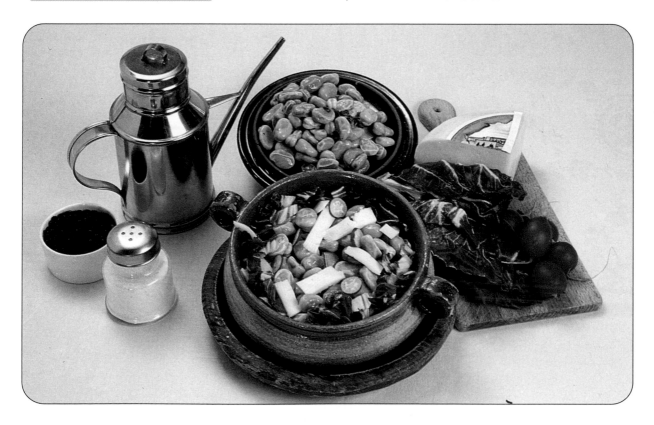

Lingua all'arancio

TONGUE WITH ORANGE

♦

- 1 SMALL CALF'S TONGUE
- 1 GLASS RED WINE VINEGAR
- ZEST (PITHLESS) AND JUICE OF 2 ORANGES
- OLIVE OIL

♦

PREPARATION TIME: 2 HOURS

ALTHOUGH TONGUE is generally used in the guise of a substantial main dish or is traditionally served on a platter with boiled meat, I suggest using this recipe as an *antipasto* because the orange marinade lends it a fresh, appetising flavour that is more suitable for the light, elegant impact of an entrée.

Wine does not usually go very well with vinegar-based preparations, but nevertheless, in this case there is a substantial meat component, so my husband, strong in his experience as a sommelier, proposes all the same washing down this very delicate dish with a young, light Chianti.

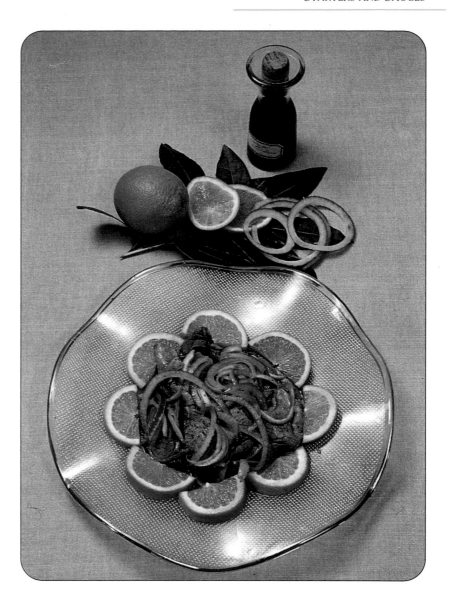

BOIL THE TONGUE, with some root vegetables, in plenty of water. The cooking time depends on the size. Draw off the heat when cooked through thoroughly (to test this, pierce the back part with a fork; the tongue will not bleed if cooked, but if it does bleed, return to the heat), skin at once (even if your fingers get burnt!) and leave it to cool completely. Then slice very thinly. Prepare the marinade in a separate dish with the finely-shredded orange peel, the juice and the vinegar and lay the tongue slices down, smothering them in olive oil and seasoning with salt and pepper. Set aside to allow the tongue to become impregnated with the flavours, turning the slices carefully from time to time.

Marmorizzato di lepre

MARBLED HARE

♦

- 1 SMALL HARE
- 400G PORK
- 200G VEAL
- 200G RAW PROSCIUTTO
- 200G CORNED TONGUE
- 100G WHITE TRUFFLE
- 80G SHELLED PISTACHIO NUTS
- 1/2 L DRY MARSALA
- 10G THYME
- 2 RED-SKINNED ONIONS
- 10G CLOVES
- 1L ASPIC JELLY
- 200G LARD
- 100G BUTTER

♦

PREPARATION TIME: 3 HOURS

BONE THE HARE CAREFULLY, putting the liver aside for a different dish. Indications regarding the size of the animal and its preparation for culinary use can be found at the bottom of the recipe on page 100.

Dice minutely and place in a large bowl. Also dice the boned pork, the veal and the raw ham. Mix the various meats using your hands, adding the onions studded with the cloves, salt and pepper.

Douse with Marsala. Leave the marinade to stand overnight.

The following morning remove the solid ingredients and put them in a sieve until all the liquid has run off. In a large casserole, brown the chopped onion in 50g of butter. Then add the meat and cook over a moderate flame for about an hour, basting with a little stock as the cooking liquid is absorbed.

Allow to cool and then add the finely-shredded corned tongue, the truffle cut into paper-thin slices and the roughly-chopped pistachios.

In a pan prepare the aspic jelly with a litre of water and the relative quantity of powdered gelatine, adding half a glass of Marsala. Leave until almost set and pour a half-inch layer into the bottom of a pâté mould.

Place in the refrigerator to set. Carefully add the mixture and the remaining aspic jelly, which must still be liquid, to cover the lot.

Chill in the refrigerator for at least 2 hours and serve with an accompaniment of butter curls and toast.

THIS STARTER IS ORIGINAL and very effective. The *marmorizzato* is proposed as a triumph of Tuscan aromas, with the hare taking pride of place. This recipe is, in many aspects, innovative. It knits together flavours which are typical of our culinary traditions in an unusual way (as is the presentation, too), so as to demonstrate (if there were any need) that Florentine gastronomy comes second to none as regards delicacy. This dish will be appreciated by the palate, but by the eyes, too, on account of the elegant play of marbling and light which enhances the surface. The long preparation will thus repay you well, without doubt, and success is assured the moment it arrives at the table, borne on a platter garnished with radishes and carrot curls, accompanied by a burst of applause.

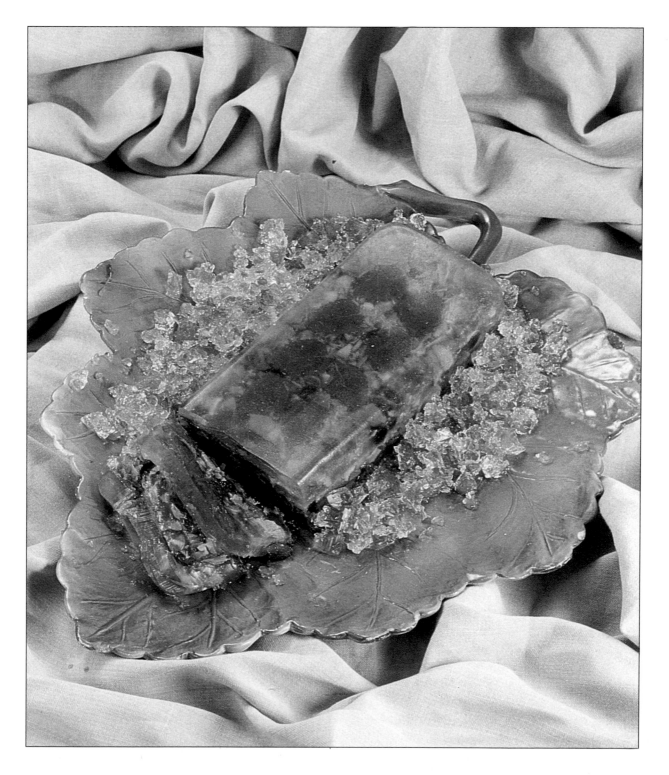

Pan di fegati
LIVER BREAD

◆

- 600G CHICKEN, CALF'S AND PIG'S LIVER
- A FEW BAY LEAVES
- HALF A LARGE LOAF OF STALE BREAD
- 5 WHOLE EGGS
- $^1/_2$ GLASS BRANDY
- 1 GLASS MILK
- A GENEROUS KNOB OF BUTTER

◆

PREPARATION TIME: 2 $^1/_2$ HOURS

THIS VERY REFINED *antipasto*, typical of our traditions (like the other breads which follow) is not really likely to crop up on daily family menus or even in restaurants, as it is the prerogative of gastronomic establishments of a certain tenor.

This dish can even be served cold, surrounded, perhaps, by some roughly-chopped aspic jelly to give it sparkle and appease the eye.

It is, in fact, a major dish which creates a fine effect and adapts to feast days.

SOAK THE BREAD, crustless, in the milk, then squeeze it well. Trim the liver pieces, cut them up and place with the butter, salt and pepper in a casserole over medium heat for about half-an-hour. Souse with the brandy, allow to evaporate and draw off the heat. Crumble the well-squeezed bread and add to the beaten eggs. Put the liver through the mincer and reduce it to a homogeneous paste. Carefully add the other ingredients.

Lay the bay leaves on the bottom of a rectangular, ovenproof dish to line it uniformly. Slowly pour in the mixture and cook in a *bain-marie* in a moderate oven for about 2 hours. Take it out of the oven, loosen the edges from the dish with the appropriate spatula and leave it to cool (but not completely). Turn it out onto a serving dish.

Pane alle erbe

HERB BREAD

◆

- 500G FLOUR
- 30G FRESH YEAST
- 1 TEASPOON EACH OF SALT AND SUGAR
- 1 GLASS MILK
- A BUNCH OF MINT, DILL, BASIL AND SHEEP'S SORREL
- 50G BUTTER
- 2 EGGS

◆

PREPARATION TIME: 1 ¹/2 HOURS

HEAP THE FLOUR INTO a "volcano" on the table, dissolve the yeast in the lukewarm milk and pour into the "crater" in the centre, together with the sugar and salt. Knead the dough with floured hands, shape into a ball and leave to rest for half-an-hour, covered with a tea towel. Clean the herbs, discarding the stems and blemished leaves. Rinse under the tap and spread out on a dry cloth which will then be rolled up to squeeze the moisture out. Shred very finely in the mincer. Lightly beat the egg, add the melted butter and the herbs, amalgamating them well into the other ingredients with the aid of a whisk. Add this mixture to the risen dough. Knead once more, adding, if necessary, 1 or 2 tablespoons of milk (never cold). Continue to knead until you can feel the dough soft and smooth. Place the dough in a greased loaf tin and pop into the oven at 200°C for 35 minutes. Allow to cool and serve as an original complement to the bread basket. It befits an important occasion.

Pane alle olive

OLIVE BREAD

◆

- 500G FLOUR
- 2 GLASSES MILK
- 200G GARLICKY BLACK OLIVES AND SPICED GREEN OLIVES
- 20G DRIED YEAST
- BUTTER
- OLIVE OIL

◆

PREPARATION TIME: 2 HOURS

PIT THE OLIVES and chop finely in the grinder. Blend with 2 tablespoons of olive oil in a small bowl and set aside for ten minutes. Heap the flour, mixed with the dried yeast, on the table, make a well in the centre and gradually add the chopped olives and spoonfuls of milk. With your fingers (floured if necessary), work the dough thoroughly, kneading it vigorously.

Continue until you obtain a homogeneous, soft paste and put it to rise in a greased loaf tin, covered with a tea towel. Leave for three quarters-of-an-hour to allow it to rise. Place the bread in an oven, pre-heated to 170°C, and bake for 1 ¹/2 hours.

Turn out when lukewarm and slice when cold.

Panzanella
Bread Salad

◆

- 1 LARGE LOAF OF WHITE BREAD, STALE
- 1 LARGE RED-SKINNED ONION
- 2 LARGE SALAD TOMATOES
- ABUNDANT BASIL
- OLIVE OIL

◆

PREPARATION TIME: $^1/_2$ HOUR

LITTLE ELSE IS NEEDED beside some stale white bread. Slice thickly and put to soak in a basin of water. Finely slice the onion and 2 tomatoes into a dish and add 2 handfuls of chopped basil. Squeeze the bread dry (therein lies the secret), add to the vegetables, plus olive oil, vinegar, salt and pepper. Stir to combine all the ingredients thoroughly.

IT IS A VERY SIMPLE DISH, but the bread absolutely must be stale and well-squeezed. *Panzanella* is also very good if eaten straight out of the refrigerator, especially in the summer. Of course, there are other versions (some rather complicated) and most of them require the addition of cucumber. It may be that I do not much appreciate this vegetable, or it may be that *panzanella* has always been made in this way in our household. At the most, I can suggest adding aromatic herbs such as catmint or savory.

Panzanella "della padrona"
The Landlady's Bread Salad

◆

- 1 LARGE LOAF OF BREAD
- 2 RED-SKINNED ONIONS
- 6 RIPE TOMATOES
- 100G TUNA FISH
- 6 EGGS
- 1 SPRIG OF BASIL
- OLIVE OIL

◆

PREPARATION TIME: $^1/_2$ HOUR

SLICE THE STALE BREAD thickly and soak in water. Squeeze it very well and place in a vegetable dish. Slice the onions and tomatoes finely and flake the drained tuna fish. Add, together with the chopped basil leaves. Boil the eggs for about eight minutes. Allow to cool and slice into rounds, only to be added at the last minute to this *panzanella*, which you will already have seasoned with salt, pepper and plenty of olive oil. Decorate the dish with the egg and red tomato rings, alternating them with basil leaves.

THIS *PANZANELLA* - also free of cucumber, for my personal taste - is called "della padrona" to distinguish it from the other, because the ingredients such as eggs and tuna fish (the latter especially) were once too expensive for the means of a poor peasant.

Pesce finto

MOCK FISH

- **500G** YELLOW, MEALY POTATOES
- **1** TABLESPOON OF TUNA FISH IN OLIVE OIL
- **2** TABLESPOONS OF MAYONNAISE
- **10** PICKLED GHERKINS
- **1/2** SWEET RED PEPPER
- **1** BLACK OLIVE

PREPARATION TIME: **1** HOUR

THIS RECIPE DOES NOT merely require the basic ingredients, but also a lot of imagination…. Boil the potatoes until they crumble easily and mash them with a fork. When they have cooled down, add the tuna fish (previously drained of oil), the mayonnaise (home-made with lots of lemon). Mix everything together. Season with salt and pepper and then … have fun! Take a long, oblong or round platter; it does not matter which as the "fish" will take on the shape you wish to give it.

Take the mixture in your hands - it's like becoming children again - and make the shape of a fish. Slice the pickled gherkins horizontally into quite thin rounds. Starting from the fish's tail, lay them one over the other to create the scales of the fish, then, with the red sweet pepper, make a nice smiling mouth and a long, majestic tail. The black olive forms the mischievous eye.

IF YOU NEED TO KEEP IT in the fridge for serving at an important soirée, brush it over with aspic jelly (it is easy to make up, with the addition of a whiff of brandy).

— 33 —

Pomodori ripieni
RICE-STUFFED TOMATOES

◆

- 4 FAIRLY RIPE TOMATOES
- 200G ITALIAN ARBORIO RICE
- 100G MOZZARELLA CHEESE
- 1 EGG
- 1 SPRIG OF BASIL
- 100G BUTTER
- GRATED PARMESAN CHEESE
- OLIVE OIL

◆

PREPARATION TIME: 3/4 HOUR

CHOOSE FOUR QUITE LARGE tomatoes and slice them horizontally just slightly above the "equator", setting the "lid" aside. Carefully scoop out the insides, seeds and all. Meanwhile, boil the rice in salted water and drain off not quite all the liquid while the rice grains are still firm and *al dente*.

Place in a bowl and leave to cool. Add the mozzarella, crumbling it in your hands, a sprig of chopped, scented basil, salt, a bare sprinkling of pepper and, finally, a lightly-beaten egg. Also add the tomato lid, cut into pieces, and mix all the ingredients thoroughly. Carefully fill the tomato shells with this mixture. Dust liberally with grated Parmesan.

Grease an oven-proof dish, arrange the tomatoes in it after drizzling a thin stream of oil over each one, together with a knob of butter.

Put into a hot oven for about twenty minutes. They are good eaten either cold or hot.

Roventini

BLOOD SAUSAGES

THIS DISH, WHICH HAS ALWAYS, since I was very little, stirred up strange feelings in me, is linked to the memory of Grandfather Luigi and his lovely shop in Via Calzaioli, around the corner from Palazzo Vecchio, with its high wooden shelves scrupulously polished and the smiling assistants dressed in black satin and lace. My grandfather, with his unfailing and winning smile, owned one of the few shops where lavish hand-made lace, rosettes, ribbons and fabulous flags were on sale. Even today, traditional Florentine traders remember the Piazzesi family's fine shop. Well, this elegant gentleman went wild for *roventini* (and for game) and more than once did he try to persuade his young granddaughter to taste those dark, savoury buns which you could hardly call inviting. Luckily, you learn to appreciate good things as you grow up.

- ◆
- ■ 50G FLOUR
- ■ 1L BLOOD FROM A RECENTLY BUTCHERED PIG
- ■ OLIVE OIL
- ◆

PREPARATION TIME: $^{1}/_{2}$ HOUR

WELL THEN, THE PROCEDURE is simple but it can turn delicate hearts and stomachs. Apart from anything else, there is no way that your handling of the dense pig's blood can be avoided.

Just pluck up courage, take a deep breath and roll up your sleeves!

Add a little flour before the blood coagulates, stir vigorously, season well with the "migliacciole" herbs and make thin fritters which are cooked in 2 tablespoons of olive oil in a heated pan.

They cool down very quickly. Turn them, let them dry on both sides and serve them with a dusting of cheese (pecorino or Parmesan).

THIS RECIPE HAS ITS ROOTS IN THE MOST ANCIENT of culinary traditions, when really every single part of an animal, including its very nutritious blood, was used up to stave off hunger. Besides, as I have underlined in other parts of the book, it is a peculiarity of Florentine cuisine to persevere creatively with the use of those ingredients which, given their low cost, one used to have to exploit. So it is that we have preserved those culinary artifices which long experience had "cooked up" to lend the dishes appeal and skilfully exalt their flavours.

This Florentine speciality has almost fallen into disuse today and is fated to sink into oblivion (except for those like me who are nostalgic). If you want to try it out, fresh pig's blood is needed, which your butcher (at whatever latitude he may be) should easily be able to procure for you in good time.

The typically Florentine expression "spezie migliacciole" refers to the herb assortment of a twig of rosemary and a pinch of fennel seeds. The name comes from "migliaccio", the popular appellation for the chestnut flour cake (or *Castagnaccio*, please see page 168) where these herbs are used.

Tondone all'alloro
BAY LEAF PANCAKES

◆

- 100G FLOUR
- 6 BAY LEAVES
- 1 GLASS WATER
- OLIVE OIL

◆

PREPARATION TIME: 3/4 HOUR

BAY LEAF PANCAKES were meant to "pad out" dinner by completing it and, in some cases, even substituting bread.

The recipe is very simple, but, like most Florentine concoctions, its execution requires time, patience, no hurrying (or "furia" as the Florentine expression has it) and the usual splattering of love.

So then! Finely chop the scented bay leaves (discard those which are nice and young, but which have no aroma). In a bowl, whisk up a thick batter with the white flour gently mixed into the water (be careful of lumps: that is why a whisk is the best thing).

Add the chopped bay leaves and allow the mixture to stand for at least half-an-hour before ladling it into a nice and hot, greased baking pan, letting the *tondone* turn golden brown on both sides.

This is good either hot or cold.

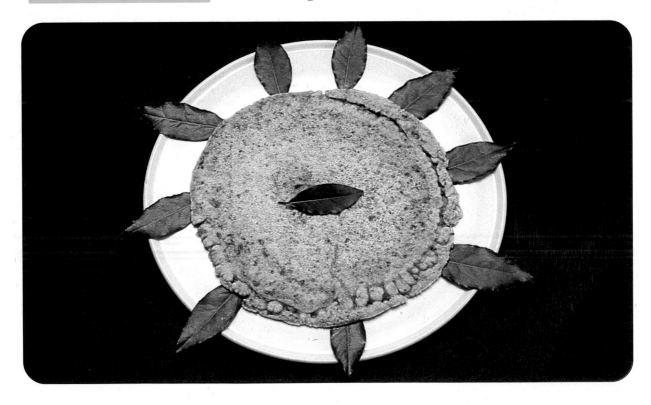

Tonno con cipolla e fagioli

TUNA FISH WITH BEANS AND ONION

♦

- 800G FRESH *CANNELLI-NO* OR SMALL HARICOT BEANS (300G IF DRIED)
- 2 MEDIUM RED-SKINNED ONIONS
- 200G TUNA FISH IN OLIVE OIL
- OLIVE OIL
- SALT AND PEPPER

♦

PREPARATION TIME: 1 HOUR

BOIL THE BEANS FOR FORTY minutes if they are fresh, or for 2 hours if they are dried and have previously been soaked for half an hour. For the correct procedure for cooking beans, please see the relative recipe.

Cut the onion up finely and add to the tuna fish (that you will have flaked in your hands) in a bowl. Add the cold, well-drained beans. Season with olive oil, salt and freshly-ground pepper.

THIS DISH CAN REALLY ONLY be eaten cold (which means neither hot nor warm, but definitely not straight out of the fridge either), so it is just right for the warm season, though the Florentines welcome it in any weather.

In its sublime simplicity, it calls to mind the old taverns which used to cram every corner of our historical centre and which have now practically all disappeared.

It is a dish which, talking about memories, evokes many pleasant pictures of me on my father's knee, with him laughing at the faces I made on tasting the onion!

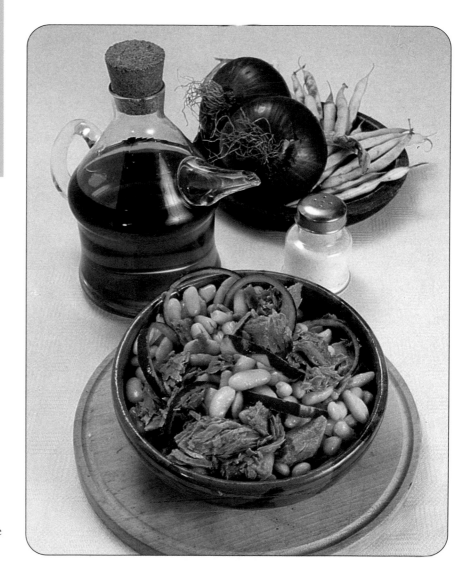

Torta di ceci

CHICKPEA PIE

- ■ 800G CHICKPEA FLOUR
- ■ 10 TEASPOONS OLIVE OIL

PREPARATION TIME: 3 $^1/_2$ HOURS

BRING 3 LITRES OF WATER to the boil, with a pinch of salt, in a large saucepan. As soon as boiling point is reached, draw off the heat and sprinkle in the chickpea flour, stirring carefully with a wooden spoon.

Return the pan to gentle heat and keep the porridge simmering for at least 3 hours, stirring continually. Pass it through a sieve (it must be absolutely smooth and free of lumps), adding all the oil little by little. Pour into a greased, shallow baking tray and place in a slow oven for half-an-hour. Remove from the oven when the surface has browned, grind some pepper over the top and set aside.

It is excellent whether served cold or warm. To impart a pleasant, appetising aroma, add some rosemary leaves before placing in the oven.

Salumi con frittatine

PLATTER OF SALAMI WITH OMELETTES

- ■ 100G TUSCAN RAW PROSCIUTTO
- ■ 100G TUSCAN SALAMI
- ■ 100G FINOCCHIONA (TUSCAN SALAMI WITH FENNEL SEEDS)
- ■ MIXED PICKLES AND VEGETABLES IN OIL
- ■ 6 WHOLE EGGS
- ■ BASIL
- ■ OLIVE OIL

PREPARATION TIME: $^1/_2$ HOUR

THIS DISH MUST BE presented on a platter to show off the cold meat slices to advantage, with the pickles and vegetables in oil in alternation. The perfect moment for serving it is in summer. It is ideal for a one-pot meal. If served together with spleen or chicken liver *crostini*, it becomes the classic Tuscan hors d'oeuvre. A delicious variation could take the form of little salami omelettes, alternated with chopped basil, piled up into pyramids. Put the cured meats, either together or separately, through the mincer and collect in a bowl. Mix thoroughly and add the beaten eggs. Make small omelettes, about 4 inches in diameter, and as each one is ready, sprinkle a little basil over and heap them up one on top of the other. They can be eaten either hot or cold. This dish is an original creation and the way it is presented is indeed unusual. It could be a real surprise for your family and many of your friends.

Pommarola
TOMATO SAUCE

◆

- **2** KG RIPE TOMATOES
- **2** ONIONS
- **1** CARROT
- **2** CELERY STALKS
- OLIVE OIL

◆

PREPARATION TIME: **2** HOURS

WASH THE TOMATOES, cutting out any blemished parts. Chop roughly and place in a large saucepan with the other vegetables, chopped. Heat slowly to boiling point over a moderate flame. Periodically, skim off the excess juices with a ladle (this will depend on the quality and ripeness of the tomatoes), leaving only the red, juicy pulp of the tomatoes to cook along with the other vegetables. When the mixture has broken up, lower the flame and drizzle a thin stream of oil into the pan, adding a pinch of salt. Continue cooking for twenty minutes. Then leave to stand a little and pass the sauce through a vegetable mill. Allow to cool completely and pour into air-tight jars. If in season, a sprig or two of basil could be added during the cooking stage, while a few whole, fresh leaves are placed in each jar to remind you of summer through the encroaching winter, which will be less tedious if brightened up with the aromas and colours of summer entrapped in your little jars.

"Florentine" tomatoes (i.e. those tubby, rather ungainly ones which are a bit like apples in shape, or rather, like miniature pumpkins) are the ones I would use, because they are sweet and rich in juicy pulp. I hold that they are highly suitable for making a sauce, even more so than the canonical Neapolitan plum tomatoes, all smooth and roughly olive-shaped. If you do not live in Florence or round about, you will have to find something suitable in replacement of my adored "fiorentini".

Salsa alla toscana

TUSCAN SAUCE

◆

- 50G LARD
- 1 ONION
- 1 STALK OF CELERY
- 1 CARROT
- 50G COOKED HAM
- ONE *BOLETUS EDULIS* MUSHROOM
- $^{1}/_{2}$L MEAT STOCK
- KNOB OF BUTTER
- OLIVE OIL

◆

PREPARATION TIME: 1 HOUR

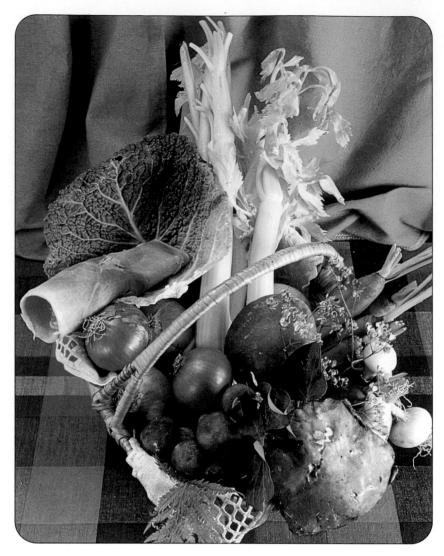

MELT THE LARD in a saucepan and add the finely-chopped onion, celery and carrot.

When all the vegetables are lightly coloured, add the ham cut into strips, with the fat discarded. Stir and season with salt and pepper.

Now add the *boletus edulis* mushroom (carefully wiped clean of all dirt with a damp cloth and sliced paper thin), and the half-litre of stock. Simmer gently for 15-20 minutes, stirring frequently with a wooden spoon to blend all the ingredients really thoroughly.

Skim off the fat and sieve the sauce. Return to very low heat and, if necessary, add a knob of butter to bind the sauce together.

THIS SAUCE IS EASY to make and delicious to taste. It is an excellent accompaniment for boiled meats and cooked vegetables.

It can, however, also be served as a spread on rounds of toast which have been sprinkled with a drop of "vinsanto" (or else medium-dry sherry).

Salsa verde
GREEN SAUCE

◆

- BUNCH OF PARSLEY
- 100G PICKLED CAPERS
- 3 EGGS, HARD-BOILED
- A PINCH OF THYME
- 1-2 TABLESPOONS OF RED WINE VINEGAR
- OLIVE OIL

◆

PREPARATION TIME: $^1/_2$ HOUR

RINSE THE PARSLEY and chop all ingredients finely after draining the capers of their preserving liquid. Place the ingredients in a bowl with 4 tablespoons of olive oil, the vinegar and a pinch of thyme, going easy on the latter because its strong flavour tends to smother the other ingredients. Blend the sauce well by stirring and correcting the quantity of vinegar. Serve with boiled meat or as a tasty spread on rounds of fresh, untoasted bread.

Salsa Estate
SUMMER GREEN SAUCE

◆

- BUNCH EACH OF CATMINT, PARSLEY, MINT AND BASIL
- 2 EGGS, HARD-BOILED
- 100G BUTTER
- 1 LEMON

◆

PREPARATION TIME: $^1/_2$ HOUR

USE ONLY THE LEAVES of the herbs, which are to be rinsed under the tap and dried in a clean tea towel. Shell the eggs and combine the ingredients in an electric blender, binding with the butter (softened at room temperature) and a few drops of lemon juice. Season with salt and pepper, taking care not to overpower the delicate aromas of the herbs. This is excellent served with meat, even grilled, or boiled vegetables, particularly potatoes.

THERE ARE UMPTEEN variations of this sauce. The recipe I have just described is apt for the summer season, when wild mints can easily be found on the roadside in country lanes, or else in a good greengrocers for those who are not so expert.

Sugo d'olive

OLIVE SAUCE

◆

- 100G SWEET BLACK OLIVES
- 100G GREEN OLIVES IN THEIR SEASONING LIQUID
- 100G GARLICKY GREEN OLIVES
- 50G GARLICKY BLACK OLIVES
- 4 RED-SKINNED ONIONS
- 2 CLOVES OF GARLIC
- 1L TOMATO PURÉE (OR THE EQUIVALENT OF CANNED TOMATOES)
- OLIVE OIL
- CHILLI PEPPER

◆

PREPARATION TIME: 2 HOURS

CHOP THE ONIONS ROUGHLY and brown in 8 tablespoons of olive oil in a saucepan.

Meanwhile carefully pit both green and black olives, cut into reasonably-sized pieces and add to the onions when these have turned golden.

Cook gently over medium heat for about a quarter-hour, stirring with a wooden spoon, so that the olives are fully blended with the onions.

Then add the tomato purée or canned tomatoes. Continue cooking over medium heat, stirring frequently, and season with salt and lots of chilli pepper. Simmer for about an hour.

This delicious sauce is perfect with short pasta, particularly *pennette* and *rigatoni*, which combine with it better because, as both types are shaped like small tubes, the sauce is trapped inside besides coating the outside.

PASTA, SOUP AND RICE DISHES

Un buon brodo...
A GOOD STOCK

◆

- ❷ 300G SILVERSIDE
- ■ $1/4$ COCKEREL (NOT BATTERY-REARED)
- ■ $1/2$ OX TONGUE
- ■ VEAL KNUCKLEBONE
- ■ 1 ONION
- ■ 1 CARROT
- ■ 1 HEAD OF CELERY
- ■ SMALL BUNCH OF PARSLEY

◆

PREPARATION TIME: $2 1/2$ HOURS

PUT ALL THE MEAT in a large saucepan with 4 litres of cold water. Add the uncut vegetables and parsley and bring to the boil. Keep simmering over medium heat for at least 2 hours until the meat is cooked. Remove the pieces of meat (the tongue is to be skinned immediately) and pass the stock through a fine-meshed sieve. Remember that, if you wish to serve the meat as a main dish, it absolutely must be added to boiling (and not cold) water, so that the heat sears the surface preventing all the flavour from seeping out into the stock.

A NICE BOWL OF CONSOMMÉ is always acceptable (but particularly so in winter) to start off an elaborate meal on an important occasion. The addition of white meat "rounds off" the flavour splendidly. If you add a shin, you will get a very dense broth which, filtered several times and left to chill in the fridge, can be used to accompany the boiled meats in the form of a tasty aspic jelly. Finally, it must be remembered that, if you wish to keep the stock for a few days, the vegetables must first be removed, otherwise the process of deterioration would be accelerated.

Le pappardelle
BROAD, FLAT NOODLES

◆

- ■ 500G WHITE FLOUR
- ■ 5 WHOLE EGGS

◆

PREPARATION TIME: $1 1/2$ HOURS

PLACE THE FLOUR in a mound on a pastry board. Hollow out a well in the middle and break 5 eggs into it. Work them in systematically and patiently until you obtain a nice, homogeneous dough which you will knead with your hands for a few minutes, finally shaping it into a ball. Set aside for an hour to rest before rolling out. When the dough is rolled out to the desired thickness, cut it into strips $1 -1/2$ inches in width. Serve it only just cooked (it must be *al dente*, still firm to the tooth) together with a tempting duck or hare ragù sauce. This type of pasta adapts well to being added to country-style soups, such as those based on pulses.

Acquacotta
TOMATO AND BREAD SOUP

- ◆ 3 RED-SKINNED ONIONS
- ◆ 1 YELLOW SWEET PEPPER
- ◆ 1 STALK OF CELERY
- ◆ 3 RIPE TOMATOES
- ◆ STALE WHITE BREAD (8 SLICES)
- ◆ 3 WHOLE EGGS
- ◆ OLIVE OIL

◆

PREPARATION TIME: 1 $^1/_2$ HOURS

CUT UP THE ONIONS, pepper and celery. In a frying pan, sauté the onion in oil until golden, then add the pepper, celery and the tomato pulp and leave to cook slowly for about an hour. Transfer everything to a casserole (preferably in earthenware) and add about a litre of water. Leave to boil about ten minutes more. Meanwhile, set out some soup bowls with slices of toast laid on the bottom, fill with the acquacotta and the eggs which you have just beaten. Leave to stand for a moment, then serve.

THE ELDERLY LADY who provides me with freshly-laid eggs seems to have stepped out of an antique print: she is all wrinkles with a large handkerchief on her head.

We have a proverb which runs, "A newly-laid egg is worth a ducat".

My version of *acquacotta*, a dish originating in the Maremma district of Tuscany, is extremely simple as regards the ingredients and the preparation.

There are more complex and "spectacular" recipes, but I truly believe that mine has the merit of being delicious, yet not too laborious.

Carabaccia

ONION SOUP

◆

- 1KG ONIONS
- 150G PEAS AND OTHER GARDEN VEGETABLES
- 1 HEAD OF CELERY
- 1 CARROT
- $^1/_2$L OF CHICKEN STOCK
- WHITE BREAD
- 1 GLASS WHITE WINE
- OLIVE OIL
- PARMESAN CHEESE

◆

PREPARATION TIME: 1 HOUR

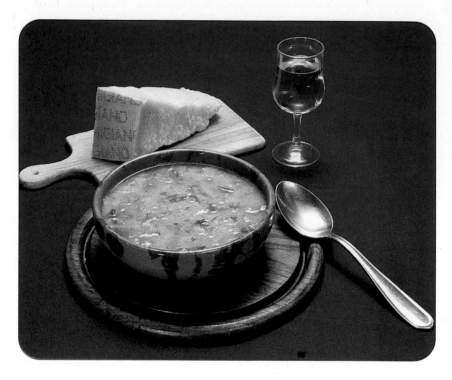

CHOP THE CELERY, carrot and onion up finely, and cook in a casserole (preferably one in earthenware) with 6 tablespoons of oil.

Sauté gently for about 40 minutes until the vegetables have completely expelled all their liquid.

Then toss the peas into the casserole and finish cooking.

Toast the bread, dunk it in boiling water and, after laying it in the bottom of each diner's soup bowl, pour over the *carabaccia*, finishing off with a liberal dusting of Parmesan cheese.

OVER THE YEARS, the original recipe of this delicious soup has been modified and simplified (indeed, during the Renaissance period, almonds, sugar, cinnamon and vinegar were added to it).

One could say that this operation of "rationalisation", which goes back centuries and which has been carried out with very many (if not all) dishes belonging to our culinary traditions, has amply succeeded in sharpening the flavour and aroma of the onions and other vegetables in the *Carabaccia*.

The result is a dish which can confidently compete with any *soupe à l'oignon*.

To the "modern" recipe requiring the peas to be pre-cooked (with a part then left whole and a part sieved), I prefer this very personal interpretation of mine, which adds the peas whole as cooking proceeds.

As a final touch, I suggest dunking the bread not just in pure, hot water, but in water to which a glass of white wine has been added, to lend more aroma to this ancient dish and to finish it off nicely.

Cibreo

CHICKEN GIBLET CASSEROLE

◆

- 400G CHICKEN LIVERS
- COCK'S TESTES AND COMBS, HEN'S UNLAID EGGS
- 3 EGG YOLKS
- 50G BUTTER
- 1 ONION
- WHITE FLOUR
- 1/2 GLASS STOCK
- 1 LEMON
- 3-4 SAGE LEAVES
- GINGER

◆

PREPARATION TIME: 1/2 HOUR

BROWN THE FINELY-CHOPPED onion in the butter in a casserole. As soon as it starts to colour, add the giblets. These will consist of the livers well-trimmed of any bile, the cock's testes and the combs previously scalded, skinned and rolled in flour, but not the unlaid eggs which will only be added at the end. Cook over gentle heat, every now and again sprinkling with stock.

When cooked (i.e. after about 20 minutes), take the casserole off the heat, beat the egg yolks with the lemon in a separate bowl and immediately pour onto the giblets. The *cibreo* is technically prepared like a fricassée, but I suggest without hesitation serving it as a first course, considering its incomparable delicacy. It must be served steaming hot and eaten at once.

THE TUSCANS, AND NOT they alone, refer to the small, flavoursome cock's testes with the name of *fagioli* or beans. Your butcher may not have all the necessary ingredients to hand: indeed, more than one cock and one hen are needed to provide a sufficient quantity of combs, wattles, *fagioli* and those delicious unlaid eggs, creamy yellow in colour, which can be found still shell-less in the ovaries of hens.

So, give him ample notice if you wish to experiment with this traditional, once-so-popular fricassee which has today sunk into oblivion. Afterwards you can lick your lips, as this is a dish fit for a king.

This latter fact is suggested by etymology, because the Italian term *cibreo* derives from the curious Latin form (*zin*)*gib*(*e*)*reus*, which means "made with ginger", crossed with *regius*, "fit for a king".

Crespelle fiorentine

FLORENTINE SAVOURY CRÊPES

■ *THE FILLING:*

■ 200G VERY FRESH RICOTTA OF GOOD QUALITY OR COTTAGE CHEESE

■ 2 EGGS

■ 200G SPINACH

■ A HANDFUL OF GRATED PARMESAN CHEESE

■ PINCH OF NUTMEG

■ THE *CRÊPES:*

■ 60G WHITE, SUPERFINE FLOUR

■ 2 EGGS

■ 1 GLASS MILK

■ 20G BUTTER

◆

PREPARATION TIME: $1\,^1/_2$ HOURS

FIRST OF ALL, cook the spinach, squeeze out all the liquor and put in a bowl together with the ricotta and Parmesan cheeses and a grating of nutmeg. Stir well to combine all the ingredients uniformly into a homogeneous mixture.

Then prepare the batter for the *crespelle*, first incorporating the eggs and salt into the flour, then adding the melted butter and the milk. Leave the mixture to stand for at least half-an-hour.

When the crêpes are cooked (in practice they are thin omelettes, fried in a little butter in a small frying pan until set on both sides), spread a little of the cheese and spinach stuffing over each one and roll them up like mini Swiss Rolls.

Grease an oven dish, cover the *crespelle* with béchamel sauce (please see page 87) and dredge with plenty of Parmesan cheese.

If you like, you can even dot with a few splatters of home-made tomato sauce (see relevant recipe). Bake in a hot oven for 20 minutes.

SIMPLE AND TASTY as they are, these crêpes are, unfortunately, served up nowadays in several ways which are not always correct. At any rate, the original recipe for these so-called "grandmother's kerchiefs" is the one I have described. The only valid variation could be to add aromatic herbs mixed into the spinach to make the crêpes still more delicate. This would only be in summer, however, when the aromas are at their keenest.

Ginestrata

EGG AND VINSANTO BROTH

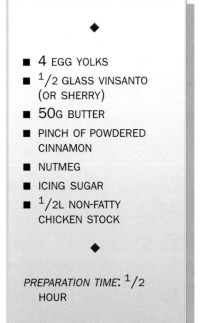

- ◆
- ■ 4 EGG YOLKS
- ■ ¹/2 GLASS VINSANTO (OR SHERRY)
- ■ 50G BUTTER
- ■ PINCH OF POWDERED CINNAMON
- ■ NUTMEG
- ■ ICING SUGAR
- ■ ¹/2L NON-FATTY CHICKEN STOCK
- ◆

PREPARATION TIME: ¹/2 HOUR

I N A BOWL, WHISK the egg yolks together with the vinsanto, stock, cinnamon and a suggestion of nutmeg.

Sieve the mixture and pour into a saucepan to which the butter and a pinch of salt have been added.

Cook gently for about a quarter-hour, stirring continuously with a wooden spoon until it thickens. The *ginestrata* is now ready.

Serve in dessert or soup bowls and dust with icing sugar.

ALLOW ME TO DRAW your attention to the freshness of the eggs. They should have been freshly-laid that day, so try and get them directly from someone who keeps free-range hens.

Only using eggs with a brightly coloured yolk can you get a nice, lively *ginestrata*, yellow like the flower (the common broom or *Genista*) from which it gets its name. Do not be alarmed by the simultaneous presence of both sweet and savoury spices and aromas. It is a trait of the noblest dishes of the Tuscan culinary tradition to artistically pair sweet with sharper flavours. Taste it, and you will recapture ancient, forgotten flavours.

Gnocchetti di pane

BREAD DUMPLINGS

- ◆
- ■ 250G STALE BREAD
- ■ ¹/2L MILK
- ■ 1 EGG
- ■ 250G FLOUR
- ■ 100G BUTTER
- ■ 2 CLOVES OF GARLIC
- ■ GRATED PECORINO CHEESE
- ◆

PREPARATION TIME: 1 ¹/2 HOURS

B REAK THE BREAD into pieces and place with the milk in a bowl. With the aid of a wooden spoon, make a mush and add the beaten egg, a pinch of salt and pepper. Sprinkle the flour in lightly, quickly stirring the mixture until thick. Put aside to stand for an hour.

Cook the *gnocchi* by dropping them, one by one, into a saucepan with plenty of salted water. Use two wetted teaspoons to help yourself with (a small amount is picked up with the first and scraped off with the second). Meanwhile, melt the butter with the garlic. Using a slotted spoon, strain off the dumplings after 5 minutes. Place in a heated serving bowl and drizzle the garlic-flavoured butter over. Serve with a mild pecorino cheese (roughly grated separately).

Gnocchi
POTATO DUMPLINGS

◆

- 1KG POTATOES
- 250G WHITE FLOUR
- 2 EGGS

◆

PREPARATION TIME: 1 HOUR

PUT THE POTATOES in cold water and bring to the boil. They can be peeled before cooking, if you prefer, to avoid having to handle them when they are boiling hot, but you should be aware that in this way they will not keep their mealy consistency. In general, this goes without saying.

Boil them for half-an-hour over medium heat, drain, peel (protect your hands with a tea towel so as not to get scalded) and mash them. Place on a pastry board or on top of the kitchen table.

Blend in the flour a little at a time (not all in one fell swoop), one whole egg, one egg yolk and a little salt.

Work the mixture in your hands until you get a soft pap (be careful that it does not stick to your fingers; if it does, add yet more flour to the mixture, sprinkling it in lightly and progressively mixing it in).

Shape the dough into long sticks that you will cut at an angle into half-an-inch-long strips. As you work, put them on a tea towel and dust with flour.

Boil in lightly-salted water, drain and pour a meat sauce over, or else, quite simply, sage-flavoured butter.

In any case, always dredge liberally with freshly-grated Parmesan cheese before serving at table.

Minestra con le patate

POTATO SOUP

- 600G POTATOES
- 1 RED-SKINNED ONION
- 1 CARROT
- 1 STALK OF CELERY
- 2 RIPE TOMATOES
- GRATED PARMESAN CHEESE
- WHITE TUSCAN BREAD
- $^1/_2$ GLASS WHITE WINE
- OLIVE OIL

PREPARATION TIME: 1 $^1/_2$ HOURS

IN A SAUCEPAN, PUT the potatoes in chunks together with the other vegetables in 6 tablespoons of oil. Bring gently to the boil and then add about a litre and a half of water, salt, pepper and the white wine.

Simmer for about an hour, adding 2 tablespoons of oil half-way through.

Pass through the vegetable mill and return to the heat for twenty minutes more.

Toast the bread slices, dice (if you wish, the bread cubes can be fried in olive oil) and put a handful in each person's plate.

Dust generously with Parmesan cheese.

THIS SIMPLE SOUP can also be served as a complete meal, with the addition of short pasta and consequently more liquid.

However, I think that it is better consumed just as the original recipe states, re-interpreted by me with the addition of white wine, which makes for a still more delicate flavour.

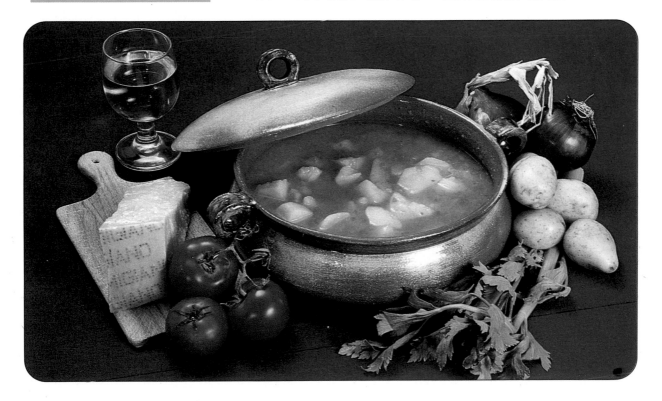

Minestra di ceci e peperoni

CHICKPEA AND PEPPER SOUP

◆

- 300G CHICKPEAS
- 200G SMOKED BACON
- 1 RED-SKINNED ONION
- 1 RED SWEET PEPPER AND 2 GREEN
- 1 CARROT
- 2 POTATOES
- 3 RIPE TOMATOES
- 2 BAY LEAVES
- A LITTLE SAVORY
- 1 CLOVE OF GARLIC
- PARSLEY
- OLIVE OIL

◆

PREPARATION TIME: 3 HOURS

SOAK THE CHICKPEAS overnight in cold water with a tablespoon of bicarbonate of soda and one of coarse sea salt.

Rinse thoroughly in cold, running water, then place in luke-warm water in a saucepan and heat. Add strips of bacon, the bay leaves and the savory.

Cover and cook slowly for 2 hours.

Put the finely-chopped onion in a saucepan and sauté in 6 tablespoons of oil.

As soon as it turns a golden colour, add the diced potatoes, the peppers (washed, seeded and cut into strips), the finely-chopped carrot and the tomatoes in chunks. Bring to the boil and cook for a quarter-hour over moderate heat, constantly stirring with a wooden spoon.

The moment the chickpeas are cooked, pour the prepared sauce into them, stirring gently.

Serve in soup bowls with a sprinkling of chopped parsley on top.

This fine soup, indeed distinctive on account of the original *concordia discors* of its flavours, is only good when served piping hot.

Minestra di centopelle

PSALTERIUM SOUP

◆

- **600**G PSALTERIUM
- **1** RED-SKINNED ONION
- **2** CARROTS
- **1** STALK OF CELERY
- **150**G BACON
- **¹/4** SAVOY CABBAGE
- **2** RIPE TOMATOES
- SAVORY
- OLIVE OIL

◆

PREPARATION TIME: **2** HOURS

IN A FRYING PAN, brown the chopped onion, carrot and celery and diced bacon in 6 tablespoons of oil until a nice golden colour. Add the psalterium cut into thin strips and stir well over fierce heat for a few minutes. Cover with about 2 litres of hot water and add the peeled tomatoes and the shredded cabbage. Season with savory and cook slowly for an hour-and-a-half, serving the soup nice and hot.

THE TERM "PSALTERIUM" or "manyplies" (*centopelle*) stands to indicate the omasum, a compartment of the stomach of ruminants lying between the reticulum and the abomasum. These names reflect the similarity of its folds to the white pages in a book or the large number of "plies" or folds of its membrane. It is wise to buy the psalterium pre-cooked, otherwise you will have to go through the laborious, unpleasant, smelly business of boiling and cleaning it. Offal is still included in the Tuscan diet, so we do not have difficulty in finding psalterium here. If substituted with tripe, the amount of tomato must be increased, while less water is needed. Dust the plate liberally with grated Parmesan cheese.

Minestra di farro

EMMER SOUP

◆

- **400**G EMMER
- ONION AND CELERY
- **100**G DRIED *CANNELLINI* BEANS
- **2** RIPE TOMATOES
- **100**G RAW *PROSCIUTTO*
- STALE BREAD
- OLIVE OIL

◆

PREPARATION TIME: **2** HOURS

SOAK THE BEANS in cold water for 10 hours. Cook for 45 minutes. Chop up the onion and sauté, together with the celery cut into short lengths, in 4 tablespoons of oil. Add a third of the beans (mashed with a little of the cooking liquor), the diced raw ham and the peeled tomatoes. Return to the heat for 10 minutes and add the emmer (after a 20-minute soaking) and the remaining whole beans. Cover with water, season and boil for an hour. Serve boiling hot over toast or with butter-fried bread croûtons.

TO EXALT THE FLAVOUR of this dish, substitute the *cannellini* beans for more "aggressive" *borlotti*, which may be eaten lukewarm in the summer, garnished with a trickle of olive oil. Here is an ancient dish, known also to the Pharaohs, mentioned in the Bible and given to bridal couples in ancient Rome as a gift.

Minestra di latte
MILK SOUP

◆

- 1L MILK
- 50G WHITE FLOUR
- 50G BUTTER
- 30G PARMESAN CHEESE
- 4 EGG YOLKS
- PINCH OF SALT

◆

PREPARATION TIME: 40 MINUTES

MELT THE BUTTER in a saucepan, work in the flour and, as soon as it begins to colour, slowly pour on the milk (which must be of room temperature, not straight out of the fridge). Let the sauce simmer gently for 20 minutes, stirring continuously.

To prevent the mixture from sticking to the sides, better to cook it in a *bain-marie*. When cooked, add the well-beaten egg yolks and Parmesan. Serve the soup really boiling hot (especially when the wind howls outside the door and a storm rages), with threads of melted Parmesan which will form on stirring the soup repeatedly.

Try and get your milk fresh from the cow (even if it means getting to know one personally!) and you will notice how this simple soup changes flavour completely, giving you an unforgettable taste which you could not hope to find in the same soup made with the very healthy - but rather insipid - milk offered by our central dairies.

Minestra di seccherelli
BREAD SOUP

◆

- 250G DRY BREAD
- 1L REDUCED MEAT STOCK
- 2 EGG YOLKS
- 50G GRATED PARMESAN
- 1/2 GLASS DRY MARSALA

◆

PREPARATION TIME: 1/2 HOUR

THE TERM "SECCHERELLI" indicates the dry left-overs from the bread bin which - provided that it is strictly unsalted Tuscan - are put to an unusual and very agreeable use.

PUT THE STALE BREAD in a canvas bag and crush it vigorously with a meat tenderiser, beating away until the bread is broken into fragments. Warm up a litre of meat stock and toss in the freshly-beaten egg yolks, then the bread chips, bringing just to simmering point before drawing off the heat and vigorously stirring the soup with a wooden spoon.

Add the Marsala to taste and finally the Parmesan. Serve the soup nice and hot, being careful, however, not to let it boil.

Minestra di porri

LEEK SOUP

♦

- ■ 1KG LEEKS
- ■ 2 TABLESPOONS WHITE FLOUR
- ■ $1/2$L STOCK
- ■ TUSCAN BREAD
- ■ PARMESAN
- ■ OLIVE OIL

♦

PREPARATION TIME: 1 $1/4$

THERE USED ALSO to be pine-nuts in the traditional, age-old recipe, to be added along with the Parmesan before baking, probably to give it a summer touch. This recipe is characteristic of St Lawrence's feast day on 10 August, a date which the Florentines particularly cherish, full of Medicean reminiscences as well as being known as the night of falling stars. It would even seem that this dish was so loved by Lorenzo the Magnificent's fellow citizens that they forgot all about the poor martyr roasted on the grid-iron and instead called that day the "Festa della porrea" (this possibly gave rise to the Italian term "purea" and subsequently to their "purè").

TRIM THE LEEKS, slice and cook gently in 6 tablespoons of oil in a pan. Be careful not to fry them, but let them cook slowly, turning them often with a wooden spoon.

When they are cooked, remove from the heat and add the flour, little by little, stirring continuously until the flour has been completely absorbed.

Pour on the stock (not boiling) and leave to cook over medium heat for another half-hour, until the leeks disintegrate.

Toast 6 slices of Tuscan bread, place in a baking dish, cover with the leek mixture and dust generously with grated Parmesan.

Bake in a hot oven for about 10 minutes.

— 55 —

Minestrone
VEGETABLE SOUP

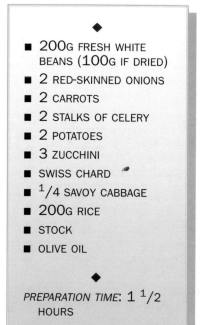

- 200G FRESH WHITE BEANS (100G IF DRIED)
- 2 RED-SKINNED ONIONS
- 2 CARROTS
- 2 STALKS OF CELERY
- 2 POTATOES
- 3 ZUCCHINI
- SWISS CHARD
- 1/4 SAVOY CABBAGE
- 200G RICE
- STOCK
- OLIVE OIL

PREPARATION TIME: 1 1/2 HOURS

F RY THE ONION, finely-chopped, and the other vegetables, diced, in 8 tablespoons of oil over medium heat, stirring often with a wooden spoon.

Keep the saucepan covered so that the vegetables 'sweat' in their own juice as long as possible. As soon as you see that the juice seeping out is no longer sufficient, add enough water to completely cover them. Leave to cook slowly for about an hour, with the lid on, seasoning with salt and pepper.

Then add the rice and boiling water to submerge everything again. Stirring frequently, simmer gently for another 15 to 20 minutes.

IF MADE WITH RICE, the *minestrone* is really only good served hot, but if you substitute the same amount of *maccheroncini* or *pennette* (both very short kinds of pasta), it is excellent eaten cold (on a summer's evening perhaps), with a nice bunch of fresh, fragrant basil finely chopped over your soup plate.

Minestrone con riso e fagioli
VEGETABLE SOUP WITH BEANS AND RICE

- 200G RICE
- 700G BEANS (300G IF DRIED)
- 5 RIPE TOMATOES
- 1 RED-SKINNED ONION
- 1 STICK OF CELERY
- CHILLI PEPPER PASTE
- CATMINT

PREPARATION TIME: 2 HOURS

C OOK THE BEANS in a pan with 2 litres of water for 40 minutes (2 hours if you use soaked dried beans). Meanwhile, sauté the chopped onion and celery in 6 tablespoons of olive oil. As soon as the onion colours, add the peeled tomatoes (canned ones are fine as an alternative) and leave to cook for another 10 minutes. When the beans are cooked, pour the sauce over them, season with salt and slowly add the rice, stirring with a wooden spoon. Simmer over low heat for about half-an-hour, stirring frequently and adding the chilli pepper paste last thing.

This delicious, traditional soup is served hot, seasoned with olive oil and a sprinkling of catmint in season (otherwise, use finely-chopped, fresh parsley).

Minestrone con la salvia

VEGETABLE SOUP WITH SAGE

♦

- 250G FRESH (OR DRIED) *BORLOTTI* BEANS
- 100G *PAPPARDELLE*
- A HANDFUL OF DRIED *BOLETUS EDULIS* MUSHROOMS
- A CLOVE OF GARLIC
- A BUNCH OF CHOPPED SAGE
- 1 RIPE TOMATO
- OLIVE OIL

♦

PREPARATION TIME: 40 MINUTES

IN A LARGE SAUCEPAN, brown the garlic, sage and mushrooms (previously soaked in luke-warm water) in 3 tablespoons of oil.

Add the tomato, the cooked beans (you will remember to soak them first if they are dried, won't you?), mashed in a vegetable mill, and their cooking water.

Season with salt and pepper and add the *pappardelle*. Cook gently until the soup is thick and tasty.

This should also be served with a trickle of crude olive oil as a final touch.

OTHER TYPES OF PASTA could take the place of the *pappardelle*, i.e. *maccheroncini* or small ribbed *penne* (*pennette rigate*), so long as they are made of durum wheat.

If the soup is cooked in less water, you will obtain a "ragù" to serve over a dish of pasta. This is a slightly more modern interpretation of an ancient peasant dish which was, of course, once eaten as a complete meal, but its "heaviness" may not be appreciated nowadays.

Pappa al pomodoro

TOMATO BREAD SOUP

◆

- 250G STALE, WHITE TUSCAN-STYLE BREAD
- 1L WATER OR HOT VEGETABLE STOCK
- 600G RIPE TOMATOES (I USE FLORENTINE)
- 4 LARGE CLOVES OF GARLIC
- OLIVE OIL
- BUNCH OF SCENTED BASIL

◆

PREPARATION TIME: $^3/4$ HOURS

I ADORE THIS DISH. I am horrified if it is proposed in the winter (where to find the scented basil and the ripe tomatoes which are essential for its successful outcome?) I realise that outside Tuscany, abroad especially, you cannot be so fussy. But my advice is to try and get as close as possible to the same quality of ingredients and the same preparation techniques described by me. Some people suggest leeks as a substitute for the garlic, others sieve it all before serving with crude olive oil. I hold that the basic recipe that I am presenting is the most balanced. By the way, it is delicious either hot or cold, but never dredged with Parmesan cheese.

FOR PERFECT RESULTS, assemble all the ingredients first because, though simple, this dish needs both very little cooking and a speedy preparation with no interruptions or changes of mind and mistakes are not allowed.

In a large saucepan, sauté the garlic gently in 4 tablespoons of olive oil. As soon as it turns golden, toss in the peeled tomatoes and a nice bunch of basil, all roughly chopped, and finally the thickly-sliced bread. Bring to the boil for a moment, adding the water or (if you like a smoother, fuller flavour) the vegetable stock so that you get a dense mush without the bread disintegrating.

Be careful, however, of the amount of juice exuded by the tomatoes; it does not go without saying that you absolutely must add all the liquid, be it water or stock.

Season with salt and pepper. That's all! Lift the lid and you will savour all the aromas of summer: close your eyes and you will see the blue Italian sky and will hear the cicadas drone.

Pappardelle
WITH RABBIT SAUCE

- 1 RABBIT OF ABOUT 1,200 KG
- ONION, CARROT, CELERY
- 3 RIPE TOMATOES
- A LITTLE SAVORY
- PARSLEY
- 300G PAPPARDELLE (BROAD, FLAT NOODLES)
- OLIVE OIL

PREPARATION TIME: $1\frac{1}{2}$ HOUR

RINSE THE RABBIT and joint, leaving aside the liver. In a pan, brown the chopped onion, carrot and celery in 6 tablespoons of oil. When it has coloured, throw in the rabbit joints and sauté over medium heat for 15 minutes. Turn the pieces over frequently with a wooden spoon. Add the peeled tomatoes and the roughly-chopped liver, salt, pepper and savory. Simmer the rabbit in its sauce for half-an-hour over a moderate flame. Draw off the heat and remove to a dish to cool. Bone and chop up the meat with a *mezzaluna*. Return to the cooking juices to boil. Use this delicacy to pour over *pappardelle* (home-made if possible) which become better impregnated with the sauce. Serve boiling hot, garnishing the tureen with sprigs of fresh parsley which you will also chop finely over the pasta.

Pappardelle
WITH DUCK SAUCE

- $\frac{1}{2}$ DUCK, WITH HEART AND LIVER
- 400G TOMATOES
- ONION, CARROT AND A STICK OF CELERY
- PARSLEY
- WHITE WINE
- GRATED PARMESAN
- OLIVE OIL

PREPARATION TIME: $1\frac{1}{2}$ HOURS

GENTLY FRY THE CHOPPED vegetables, with the exception of the tomatoes, in 6 tablespoons of oil, then toss in the jointed duck (plucked, drawn, cleaned out, wiped and singed as usual). Brown, then add the white wine. Cover and leave to cook for 15 minutes. Add the tomatoes (canned ones are fine), cook a further hour over low heat. Remove the duck from the pan, bone it as soon as possible and return the meat to the sauce with the roughly-chopped liver and heart. Bring to the boil once more and season with salt and pepper. Cook the *pappardelle* in salted, boiling water until *al dente* (about 10 minutes), serve with the steaming sauce poured over and dust with grated Parmesan. Alternatively, sprinkle a handful of fresh, finely-cut chives over the *pappardelle* and, in season, garnish each plate with chive flowers.

Pappardelle
WITH HARE SAUCE

◆

THE HARE SAUCE:
- 1 SMALL, YOUNG HARE WITH HEART, LIVER, LUNGS, ETC.
- 2 CARROTS
- 1 ONION
- CELERY
- PARSLEY
- RED WINE
- OLIVE OIL

THE PAPPARDELLE:
- 400G SUPERFINE WHITE FLOUR
- 3 WHOLE EGGS
- A TABLESPOON OLIVE OIL

◆

PREPARATION TIME: 1 ^{1}/2 HOURS

AS I HAVE ALREADY stated and will repeat with reference to dishes involving this wild, engaging little nibbler, this recipe today can only be attempted by those few who manage to come by a sufficiently-matured, fresh hare (and not frozen or imported as almost always is the case). Whether it is because the hunting of them of them is limited or even forbidden by law, or whether it is because this species is now scarcely encountered on our territory, this dish has become a choice delicacy of gourmands of Tuscan cuisine.

PREPARE THE *PASTA* with the flour, the whole eggs and the olive oil (which is missing from the "ordinary" *pappardelle* recipe). Work it in your fingers and roll it out. Leave to dry out and cut it into long strips an inch wide. To make the sauce, use only the forequarters of the hare. The hindquarters, more of a delicacy, can be roasted or cooked in *dolce e forte* (a strong, sweet sauce). Collect all the animal's blood because you will need it in substitution of the tomatoes (this is how they used to make this and other dishes before 1492).

Joint and add to the pan where the onion is browning in the oil. Over a slow flame, let the juices run out of the meat and add the parsley and other vegetables with the chopped offal. Allow the flavours to blend and then douse with red wine and the blood and reduce. Remove the hare joints from the pan and bone them. Return the boned meat to the sauce and leave it to cook for a few minutes more. Boil the pappardelle in salted water until cooked but firm to the bite and serve very hot, generously seasoned with the sauce, and sprinkle over some grated Parmesan.

Passata di patate cogli zoccoli
MASHED POTATO WITH CHUNKS OF BREAD

- 600G POTATOES
- 1 1/2L MILK
- 50G BUTTER
- 2 SLICES STALE WHITE BREAD
- 80G PARMESAN
- OLIVE OIL

PREPARATION TIME: 1 HOUR

PEEL THE POTATOES, wash and cut into small chunks. Place in the milk in a pan and cook gently, constantly stirring and lowering the flame still further when the milk begins to the boil.

Leave to cook for half-an-hour, until the potatoes disintegrate into the milk, add the butter and then sieve the vegetables. Allow to stand a while, away from the heat. Break up the bread into chips and fry in very little oil, browning on all sides.

Spoon a full ladleful of the purée into each bowl, add a handful of the fried bread croutons and dust with plenty of grated Parmesan. Serve at once.

Pasta e fagioli
BEANS AND PASTA

- 200G *RIGATONI* (SHORT, RIBBED NOODLES)
- 700G *CANNELLINI* BEANS (300G IF DRIED)
- 2 CLOVES OF GARLIC
- 1 SPRIG OF SAGE
- 1 SPRIG OF ROSEMARY
- OLIVE OIL
- CHILLI PEPPER

PREPARATION TIME: 2 HOURS

COOK THE BEANS OVER gentle heat for 40 minutes (for an hour-and-a-half if they are dried, after soaking for 2 hours covered in water), with the herbs and garlic to lend flavour and aroma. Then, either sieve or pass through a vegetable mill, so as to eliminate the outer husks. Place the purée in a saucepan, season with salt, pepper and a little chilli pepper to taste. Cook the pasta in the purée and add a little water to finish cooking.

THIS FAMOUS "SOUP" absolutely must be served hot with a "C" trickled over the surface in olive oil. The original recipe advises cooking the beans in an earthenware pot in a slow oven for several hours (about 3). I find, however, that excellent results are obtained if the ancient recipe is streamlined and adapted to modern rhythms, unfortunately faster and more pressing even in the kitchen.

Pennette delle colline di Firenze
PENNETTE FROM THE HILLS OF FLORENCE

◆

- 400G *PENNETTE* (VERY SHORT, PASTA "STRAWS")
- 300G LEAN MINCED BEEF
- 200G FRESH EWE'S MILK RICOTTA
- 1L HOME-MADE TOMATO SAUCE
- ONION, CARROT, CELERY
- SPRIG OF BASIL
- 1 GLASS WHITE WINE
- PARMESAN CHEESE
- OLIVE OIL

◆

PREPARATION TIME: 1 1/2 HOURS

CHOP UP THE VEGETABLES (except the tomatoes) and place in a pan with 6 tablespoons of oil. When they begin to colour, add the mince and raise the flame so that the meat browns and absorbs the flavours well. Stir with a wooden spoon and add the tomato sauce and whole basil leaves, season with salt and pepper and sprinkle the white wine over. Cook the sauce for an hour over very gentle heat, stirring now and then with a wooden spoon.

Meanwhile, boil the *pennette* (preferably ribbed; better for "picking up" the sauce) until they are *al dente*, drain and place in a tureen where you will have crumbled in the ricotta. Pour the sauce on top and stir well to combine all the ingredients. Serve with plenty of grated Parmesan and garnish with freshly-picked, scented basil leaves.

TALKING ABOUT BASIL, don't fret (especially those of you in colder countries), as it can be found everywhere nowadays, both in grocers selling early produce and in delicatessens. It may be dried; not the same thing, but it is better than doing without altogether.

Polenta coi ciccioli
CORNMEAL WITH SAUSAGES

◆

- 300G SAUSAGES
- 300G CORNMEAL
- 150G *CICCIOLI* (SCRAPS OF RENDERED PORK FAT)
- GRATED PARMESAN AND *PECORINO* CHEESES
- 50G BREADCRUMBS
- OLIVE OIL

◆

PREPARATION TIME: 2 HOURS

PRICK THE SAUSAGES and brown in a little oil. Raise the heat a little while, then lower it, adding a glass of water and cook slowly for half-an-hour. Allow to cool. Cut the sausages into pieces and bring to the boil in 1 1/2 litres of water seasoned with salt and pepper. As soon as boiling point is reached, remove from the heat and add the cornmeal, stirring to avoid lumps forming. Return to the heat and cook slowly for 45 minutes, stirring frequently. Just 5 minutes before the end, pour in the *ciccioli* and stir again. Draw off the heat and add the cheeses and the chopped parsley, stirring carefully. Butter an ovenproof dish and sprinkle with dried breadcrumbs. Pour in the polenta and bake in a very hot oven for 20 minutes until a golden crust has formed.

Polenta col cavolo nero

CORNMEAL AND KALE

- 300g CORNMEAL FLOUR
- 2 BUNCHES OF TUSCAN 'BLACK' CABBAGE OR KALE
- OLIVE OIL
- BACON

PREPARATION TIME: 1 $^1/_2$ HOURS

FOR ABOUT 20 MINUTES, cook the wrinkled leaves of the 'black' cabbage (actually dark green), but kale or collard will be fine, which will previously have been rinsed in running water and the midribs stripped off and discarded. Drain, preserving the cooking liquor. Into the latter you will gradually pour the cornmeal flour and let it cook slowly for about 40 minutes, stirring constantly with a wooden spoon so that unpleasant lumps do not form. In another pan, fry the diced bacon. When reduced, add the cabbage. When the *polenta* is almost ready, add the cabbage and bacon and serve immediately, if you like it hot.

Otherwise, when it has completely cooled down after transferring to an ovenproof dish, cut it up into half-inch slices and put under the grill.

Polenta pasticciata

CORNMEAL PIE

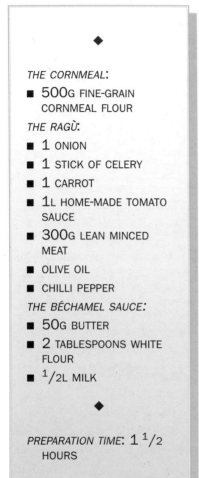

◆

THE CORNMEAL:
- 500G FINE-GRAIN CORNMEAL FLOUR

THE RAGÙ:
- 1 ONION
- 1 STICK OF CELERY
- 1 CARROT
- 1L HOME-MADE TOMATO SAUCE
- 300G LEAN MINCED MEAT
- OLIVE OIL
- CHILLI PEPPER

THE BÉCHAMEL SAUCE:
- 50G BUTTER
- 2 TABLESPOONS WHITE FLOUR
- $^1/_2$L MILK

◆

PREPARATION TIME: 1 $^1/_2$ HOURS

IN A LARGE PAN, SAUTÉ all the finely-chopped vegetables with 4 tablespoons of oil. Stir frequently with a wooden spoon for about 10 minutes over low heat, then add the minced meat, raise the flame a little and brown. After about 20 minutes, add the tomato sauce, salt, pepper and a teaspoon of chilli pepper paste.

Continue cooking very gently and in the meantime prepare the polenta.

Bring two litres of water to the boil, draw off the heat and, with the aid of a wooden spoon or, even better, of a whisk, shower in the cornmeal flour, stirring continuously so that lumps do not form.

Return to very low heat for about 40 minutes and, meanwhile, prepare the béchamel sauce.

Finish cooking the *polenta*, turn it out onto a pastry board (make sure that it is no thicker than $^1/_2$ inch) and allow to cool, while the meat sauce is simmering away.

Cut into squares and arrange a layer in a large, buttered ovenproof dish. Alternate a layer of polenta with 5 tablespoons of ragù and a handful of Parmesan cheese.

Continue in this way until the dish is full. Spread a generous ladle of béchamel sauce over the last layer, dredge with Parmesan and bake in a medium oven for half-an-hour, until a nice golden crust forms on top.

Ribollita

RÉCHAUFFÉ OF BREAD AND VEGETABLE SOUP

◆

- 1 FAIRLY LARGE RED-SKINNED ONION
- 2 CARROTS
- 1 STICK OF CELERY
- 4 POTATOES
- 10 ZUCCHINI
- 300G DRIED BEANS
- BUNCH OF SWISS CHARD
- 1 SAVOY CABBAGE
- 1 BUNCH OF TUSCAN 'BLACK' CABBAGE OR KALE
- TOMATO PURÉE
- 2-DAYS' STALE, TUSCAN, WHITE BREAD

◆

PREPARATION TIME: 2 1/2 HOURS

WHAT A LOT OF THINGS the famous (though rather poorly imitated) *ribollita* brings to mind! Few nowadays know how to cook it properly, because it requires a lot of love and time and, of course, simple but genuine ingredients. In my memory, my grandmother's dirge in particular stands out, "Seven things does this soup do: it uses up all left-over bread and quenches the thirst, it fills up the stomach and gives the tooth something to chew on, it aids sleep and the digestion, and it makes cheeks glow".

SOAK THE DRIED BEANS and cook over a slow flame. In a pan, gently fry the onion, sliced. Add the other vegetables, diced, with the exception of the cabbage, kale and beans which are added at a later point. When the vegetables have sweated out their juice, cover with hot water and then add all the cabbage and kale, shredded. Cover and simmer for an hour over medium heat. Add the cooked beans (some of them whole and some puréed), salt and pepper. Leave to simmer for another 20 minutes, stirring frequently because the beans tend to stick to the bottom of the pan. Add two or three tablespoons of tomato purée.

Slice the stale bread and, in an earthenware casserole, alternate layers of bread with the soup until the bread is well impregnated. Leave to stand for a day. To serve, remove the desired quantity from the casserole and heat it up or "re-boil" it as the name in Italian suggests.

Rigatoni strascicati

RIGATONI COOKED IN SAUCE

◆

- 350G RIGATONI
- 300G LEAN MINCED MEAT
- 1 RATHER LARGE RED-SKINNED ONION
- 1 STICK OF CELERY
- 1 CARROT
- 5 RIPE TOMATOES (OR $^1/_2$L HOME-MADE TOMATO SAUCE)
- OLIVE OIL

◆

PREPARATION TIME: $1\,^1/_2$ HOURS

FIRST OF ALL, prepare the meat sauce by chopping up all the vegetables (except the tomato) and browning them in 6 tablespoons of olive oil. When they have taken on colour, add the minced meat, raise the heat and cook over a medium flame for about 15 minutes, stirring frequently with a wooden spoon. Add the tomatoes or the purée, season with salt and pepper and leave to simmer very gently for an hour (but it is fine if you allow it to cook for longer), stirring with a wooden spoon from time to time. Cook the rigatoni in plenty of salted, boiling water and drain when the pasta is practically half-cooked. Put the ragù into a large saucepan, pour in the rigatoni and allow to finish cooking - the Italian term "strascicati" means "dragged through the sauce".

WHY RIGATONI AND NOT just plain penne? The reason is obvious: because the latter have a smooth surface, while the former are artistically ribbed and the meat sauce clings better. In Tuscan families, this dish forms the basis of the canonical repertory of any good housewife-cum-cook. Choosing it in restaurants, on the contrary, is not always a good idea because it is often interpreted rather too freely. It is excellent served the following day even, yet again "dragged" through the sauce, a small ladle of water being added this time (no butter, please).

Riso agli asparagi
ASPARAGUS RICE

- 350G ITALIAN ARBORIO RICE
- 2 BUNDLES OF ASPARAGUS
- 50G BUTTER
- 50G GRATED PARMESAN CHEESE

PREPARATION TIME: 1/2 HOUR

BLANCHE THE ASPARAGUS in a saucepan deep enough to accommodate it upright, fastened together,: be careful that it is not completely covered with water, but put the lid on the pan and make sure that steam does not escape from it while boiling (about 20 minutes). Drain the asparagus, reserving the water, then cut it up, ensuring that only the tender (not the stringy) part is used. Melt the butter in a pan and sauté, stirring frequently. Boil the rice in salted water, remove while still *al dente* and mix with the asparagus in the pan, adding half a ladleful of the liquor from the asparagus which you can allow to evaporate. Keep on the heat for a few minutes and serve the rice dredged with the cheese.

Risotto ai carciofi
ARTICHOKE RISOTTO

- 350G RICE
- 6 GLOBE ARTICHOKES
- 40G BUTTER
- 300G COOKED HAM
- 1 ONION
- 1 LEMON
- PARMESAN CHEESE
- RAISIN WINE
- PARSLEY

PREPARATION TIME: 1 HOUR

TRIM THE ARTICHOKES, discarding the tough leaves, and cut into thin wedges. Place in a bowl with water and the lemon. Chop up the onion and sauté slowly in the butter with the ham in strips. Add the artichokes, brown for 10 minutes, then add the rice and a glass of the raisin wine. Stirring with a wooden spoon, cook the rice over medium heat. Begin adding the boiling water (about three quarters of a litre). When the cooking is finalised (20/30 minutes), season with salt and pepper and, at the moment of serving, beat the rice, pouring in a handful of parsley and lots of grated Parmesan cheese.

I HAVE REPLACED the traditionally-used white wine with raisin wine which, to my taste, improves still further the delicate flavour of the artichokes and gives it a rather unusual fragrance all of its own.

Risotto coi fegatini
RICE WITH CHICKEN LIVERS

- 300G CHICKEN LIVERS
- 1 RED-SKINNED ONION
- 300G RICE
- HOME-MADE TOMATO SAUCE
- A LITTLE STOCK
- 100G BUTTER
- SPRIG OF SAGE
- PARMESAN CHEESE
- OLIVE OIL

◆

PREPARATION TIME: 1 HOUR

SAUTÉ THE FINELY-CHOPPED onion in 6 tablespoons of oil in a pan. When the onion begins to froth, pour in the rice, stirring gently but firmly with a wooden spoon and mixing it in well.

Now, over very low heat, add the tomato sauce (about half a litre will be necessary) and a glass of stock, letting it all cook very slowly for about 20 minutes, stirring the whole time.

In another pan, brown the thoroughly-rinsed and roughly-chopped chicken livers well in a knob of butter. After a quarter-hour, add to the rice and allow to boil gently a little more.

Season with salt and pepper and serve this classic Florentine risotto nice and hot, dredged with a mix of grated Parmesan cheese and chopped sage as a fragrant finishing touch.

Risotto nero
CUTTLEFISH RISOTTO

- 400G CUTTLEFISH
- 300G RICE
- 300G SWISS CHARD
- 1 SPRING ONION
- RAISIN WINE
- 2 CLOVES OF GARLIC
- OLIVE OIL

◆

PREPARATION TIME: 3/4 HOUR

CLEAN THE CUTTLEFISH thoroughly (discarding the bones, eyes and mouth, but reserving the ink sac) and chop roughly. Sauté the sliced onion and the garlic in the oil, add the cuttlefish and stir with a wooden spoon. Shred the chard, devoid of the midribs, and add. Cook for about half-an-hour over a slow flame. Sprinkle in the raisin wine and gradually incorporate the rice, adding boiling water as necessary. Last of all, add the sacs, beat for a few minutes and serve very hot. On special occasions, present the rice in a soup tureen surrounded by chard leaves which, together with the black rice, will form a pleasant chromatic contrast.

Spaghetti ai carciofi

SPAGHETTI WITH ARTICHOKES

- 6 GLOBE ARTICHOKES
- 400G SPAGHETTI
- 50G SLIVER OF COOKED HAM
- 100G BLACK OLIVES
- WHITE WINE
- 2 RIPE TOMATOES
- SAVORY
- 50G PARMESAN CHEESE
- OLIVE OIL

PREPARATION TIME: $1/2$ HOUR

CLEAN THE ARTICHOKES. Blanche for a few minutes in water acidulated with a squeeze of lemon. Drain and cut into wedges. Put 4 tablespoons of oil in a pan. Add the ham cut into strips and the roughly-chopped olives and put on the hob over a moderate flame for a few minutes. Moisten with the white wine and add the tomatoes. Season with salt and pepper, aromatising with savory leaves. Leave to cook over moderate heat for 10 minutes.

Boil the pasta (preferably spaghetti) until *al dente* and sauté with the artichoke sauce in a saucepan, as a final touch sprinkling grated Parmesan over. Serve on plates garnished with the artichoke leaves that you discarded because too tough, although they may be unblemished, and which you will have soaked in water with a squeeze of lemon so that they do not discolour.

Spaghettini al fagiano

SPAGHETTINI WITH PHEASANT AND CHIVE SAUCE

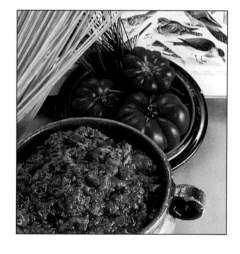

- 1/2 CLEANED PHEASANT
- CELERY
- 2 RED-SKINNED ONIONS
- 2 CARROTS
- TOMATO PURÉE
- CHIVES
- 400G SPAGHETTINI
- CHILLI PEPPER
- OLIVE OIL

PREPARATION TIME: 2 HOURS

SAUTÉ THE CHOPPED celery, onion and carrot in 2 tablespoons of oil. When sufficiently browned, add the pheasant, drawn and jointed, cover with a lid and cook slowly for half-an-hour. Remove the pheasant, bone and chop, being careful of little, spiky bones. Then replace it all in the saucepan, return to a higher flame for 10 minutes and stir. Add the purée (or else 4 or 5 roughly-chopped ripe tomatoes), salt and pepper and a generous teaspoon of chilli pepper paste. Leave to simmer gently for an hour. Boil the spaghettini and serve with the pheasant sauce and a sprinkling of chives, finely chopped at the last moment.

— 69 —

Tortelli

POTATO TORTELLI

THE PASTA:
- 500G FLOUR
- 5 EGGS

THE FILLING:
- 600G POTATOES
- 100G PARMESAN CHEESE
- NUTMEG
- GARLIC
- PARSLEY
- 1 RIPE TOMATO
- 1 EGG

PREPARATION TIME: 2 HOURS

THE PASTA, FIRST OF ALL. Heap the flour into a mound on the table and hollow out the centre into which you will break 5 whole eggs. With much care and patience, gradually work the eggs into the flour.

The result will be a slab of dough that you will shape into a ball and that you will leave under a tea towel to rest while you prepare the filling.

Boil the potatoes in their jackets (in this way they absorb less water). Chop up 2 cloves of garlic and a nice sprig of parsley. Add a ripe tomato, peeled and diced, a generous handful of Parmesan and a pinch of nutmeg to lend aroma.

Then mix it all with the peeled, mashed potatoes, adding salt and pepper and, last of all, a whole, lightly-beaten egg.

Roll out the dough and cut into strips 1 $^1/_2$ inches wide. Over half of these, spread 5 or 6 tablespoons of stuffing at well-spaced distances.

Cover each strip with another one of pasta and seal by pressing down well on the borders. Cut each strip into *tortelli* that you will place on a lightly-floured tea towel as you go.

Boil the *tortelli* in plenty of salted water, draining off the water when cooked but still firm to the bite. Make sure that the pasta is well-cooked in the thickest part. Serve them spread with a good meat sauce and sprinkled liberally with Parmesan cheese.

This is also delicious with just butter and sage, provided that there is always lots of Parmesan.

Zuppa alla contadina
TUSCAN PEASANT SOUP

◆

- 400G BREAD
- 500G BEANS
- 1 SAVOY CABBAGE
- 2 BUNCHES 'BLACK' CABBAGE OR KALE
- SWISS CHARD
- 1 RED-SKINNED ONION
- 2 CLOVES OF GARLIC
- CELERY AND PARSLEY
- 2 POTATOES
- 50G MILD *PROSCIUTTO*
- OLIVE OIL

◆

PREPARATION TIME: 2 HOURS

COOK THE BEANS in plenty of water, adding the raw ham cut into strips. Bring to a gentle boil and keep the pan covered over low heat. Meanwhile, chop up the onion, carrot, celery and garlic and place on the heat in a saucepan with 3 tablespoons of oil. Allow to colour, while you pick over and rinse the kale and chard (stripped of their midribs) and the Savoy cabbage, without its tougher external leaves. Put everything in the saucepan and allow the vegetables to sweat and exude their own liquor. Then douse them with a little cooking water from the beans and cook for 20 minutes over moderate heat. Pass most of the cooked beans through the vegetable mill and add to the green vegetables which will have almost completely collapsed by now. Add the remaining whole beans, seasoning to taste with salt and pepper. Toast the thickly-sliced bread and serve each slice dunked in a ladleful of soup that will have boiled over a medium flame for an hour altogether. This is excellent both hot and cold.

Zuppa di carni bianche
WHITE MEAT SOUP

◆

- 500G WHITE MEAT, COOKED AND MINCED
- MEAT STOCK
- STALE BREAD
- 30G BUTTER
- PARMESAN

◆

PREPARATION TIME: $1/4$ HOUR

WITH THE AID OF A *MEZZALUNA*, chop the chunks of boiled or roast meat left-overs, all scrupulously trimmed of bones and sinews. Dice everything up and place in a soup tureen.

Pour over the well-heated meat stock and dust with plenty of grated Parmesan cheese.

THIS IS MORE than a mere recipe, in fact, it seems to be a lesson in the art of making-do. Some colleagues would perhaps disdain to include it in their personal recipe books. But, on the spree the day after the Christmas festivities, when there were chicken, turkey and capon left-overs, how could one ignore this soup?

It was all finished off with chunks of bread fried in butter. It did not seem at all like drinking a soup made from the left-overs, but more like a delicacy, rich and aromatic, cooked then and there.

Zuppa del frantoio
OLIVE-PRESS SOUP

- ◆ -

- ¹/2L OLIVE OIL
- 500G RED KIDNEY BEANS
- 2 ONIONS
- 1 CARROT
- STICK OF CELERY
- 2 ZUCCHINI
- 500G TUSCAN 'BLACK' CABBAGE OR KALE
- 500G POTATOES
- 2 RIPE TOMATOES
- STALE BREAD
- SAVORY

- ◆ -

PREPARATION TIME: 1 ¹/2 HOURS

COOK THE BEANS for 40 minutes over low heat (2 hours if they are dried), then, reserving the water, sieve them, leaving aside two tablespoonfuls of whole beans. Brown the chopped onion, celery and carrot in 6 tablespoons of oil in a pan. When coloured, add the other vegetables, tomatoes included. Add the bean purée and a little savory, covering with the bean cooking liquor. Simmer for 10 minutes. Add the shredded cabbage or kale and cook gently for an hour with the lid on the pan, seasoning with salt and pepper. Add more water if necessary, checking that the minestrone is nice and dense and not too runny. Toast the slices of bread and alternate them in a tureen with the soup, drenching each layer with plenty of olive oil from the first pressing.

THIS RECIPE MAY APPEAR to be only an oily variation of an ordinary *ribollita*. But the name itself establishes the difference: the oil is the main ingredient of this soup. If it is "proper" *extra-vergine* olive oil, it is delicious. If the oil is less than perfect, well then...

Zuppa di cavolo nero
CABBAGE SOUP

- ◆ -

- 2 BUNCHES TUSCAN 'BLACK' CABBAGE OR KALE, 2 POTATOES
- ONION, CELERY AND CARROT, 4 TOMATOES
- 150G FRESH BORLOTTI BEANS (60G IF DRIED)
- STALE BREAD
- OLIVE OIL

- ◆ -

PREPARATION TIME: 2 HOURS

IF YOU USE DRIED BEANS, soak them for 2 hours. Brown the chopped onion in 6 tablespoons of oil in a saucepan. As soon as it begins to turn golden, add the diced vegetables and the peeled tomatoes (fresh or canned). Add a pinch of thyme to lend aroma, or take my advice and use savory. Cook for 10 minutes over medium heat, then add the beans and the *cavolo nero* or kale leaves, stripped of their midribs and roughly shredded. Cover the vegetables with one-and-a-half litres of cold water. Place the lid on the pan and cook over low heat for an hour and-a-half, seasoning with salt and pepper. Toast the slices of bread, arrange on the bottom of each soup bowl, pour over the minestrone and garnish with a trickle of oil in the shape of a "C". If you have fresh savory in flower, garnish each soup bowl with a sprig.

Zuppa di ceci e pane
CHICKPEA SOUP WITH GARLIC BREAD

♦

- 300g DRIED CHICKPEAS
- 1 SPRIG OF ROSEMARY
- WHITE ITALIAN-STYLE BREAD
- 1 RASHER OF BACON
- OLIVE OIL

♦

PREPARATION TIME: 2 HOURS

Soak the chickpeas (peas of the Mexican type would be better) in 2 litres of cold water in a saucepan, together with a teaspoon of bicarbonate of soda and a handful of coarse sea salt for 10 hours. Cook over a low flame for about an hour and a quarter, adding the bacon rasher half-way through. After that, sieve most of the chickpeas (careful of the husks which must be discarded completely) and keep the remaining whole peas to one side. Toast the slices of bread, rub both sides with garlic cloves and cut into cubes. Separately, heat several rosemary leaves (discard the woody stem) in a tablespoon of olive oil and when they soften up, toss into the soup to which you will have added the whole chickpeas.

Serve the soup with the garlic bread croutons and a trickle of olive oil in each bowl. Do not overdo it as regards the latter because that would make the soup too thick with a "heavy" flavour.

— 73 —

Zuppa di fagioli alla fiorentina

FLORENTINE BEAN SOUP

- 300G FRESH *CANNELLINI* BEANS (200G IF DRIED)
- 200G TUSCAN 'BLACK' CABBAGE OR KALE
- 4 VERY RIPE TOMATOES
- 1 ONION
- 1 CARROT
- 1 STICK OF CELERY
- 2 CLOVES OF GARLIC
- STALE BREAD
- PORK RIND
- 1 SPRIG OF ROSEMARY
- OLIVE OIL

PREPARATION TIME: 2 HOURS

HERE IS YET ANOTHER recipe based on olive oil and bread which allows umpteen variations. For example, there are some who add leeks to the onion, carrot, celery and garlic at the start, but I would prefer perhaps to "summon" the aid of savory, so easy to pick up at the side of a Tuscan country lane. (My advice to those who live elsewhere and could have difficulty in getting nice, aromatic savory is to treat themselves to a holiday in Tuscany and walk through the country to get a store of this precious herb!)

COOK THE BEANS with the cut-up pork rind in plenty of water. Meanwhile, finely chop the onion, carrot, celery and garlic and brown with the rosemary in lots of oil. Add half a glass of hot water and the tomatoes (or the equivalent amount of tomato paste).

When the beans are cooked (40 minutes if they are fresh or 2 hours if they are dried and have been previously soaked), sieve three quarters of them into the saucepan containing the root vegetables and also add the whole ones in their cooking liquid and the pork rind. Boil for another 10 minutes and the soup is ready. Arrange the slices of stale bread (if you like, toast them) in a soup tureen and pour over the soup. Leave to rest a short while and serve warm (but it can also be relished cold).

Zuppa di pane
BREAD SOUP

◆

- HAM BONE
- 400G SAVOY CABBAGE
- 3 ZUCCHINI
- 400G BREAD
- 200G POTATOES
- ONION, CARROT AND CELERY
- PARSLEY AND BASIL
- 600G BORLOTTI BEANS (300G IF DRIED)
- 200G TOMATOES
- OLIVE OIL

◆

PREPARATION TIME: 1 ¹/₄ HOURS

I N A SAUCEPAN, sauté the onion with the ham bone (or else with 50g of lard) in 6 tablespoons of oil. Cut the other vegetables into pieces, add the parsley and basil, too, and sauté very slowly.

After having cooked the borlotti beans (if fresh, they will need about 40 minutes in plenty of water, whereas dried ones, previously soaked in water, will need about 2 hours over very slow heat), sieve most of them, leaving a couple of tablespoonfuls whole.

Put the bean cooking water in the saucepan with the bone and the vegetables, add the beans (both the purée and the whole ones) and the roughly-shredded Savoy cabbage. Cook for about half an hour. Finally, add the very ripe tomatoes (I would prefer "Florentine" tomatoes).

Continue cooking for about another quarter-hour and serve the soup nice and hot on slices of stale, toasted bread, finishing off with a "C" in olive oil.

Zuppa di piselli
PEA SOUP WITH OLIVE OIL

◆

- 20 WHITE PICKLING ONIONS
- 2 CUPS OF STOCK
- 1KG SHELLED PEAS
- PARSLEY
- STALE, ITALIAN-STYLE BREAD
- OLIVE OIL

◆

PREPARATION TIME: 1 HOUR

S AUTÉ THE LITTLE WHITE onions in 4 tablespoons of oil. Add the stock, stirring with a wooden spoon.

When the onions are a golden colour, add the peas, parsley leaves and more of the stock. Make some bread chips to fry in 2 tablespoons of oil. Cook the soup over medium heat for three quarters-of-an hour, stirring and seasoning with salt and pepper.

Add the bread croutons last thing, stir rapidly and serve steaming hot, garnishing each soup bowl with fresh parsley sprigs.

Zuppa di ranocchi
FROG SOUP

- ◆
- ■ 12 GOOD-SIZED FROGS
- ■ 1 SMALL ONION
- ■ 1 SPRIG OF PARSLEY
- ■ 1 CARROT AND 1 STICK OF CELERY
- ■ 1 SMALL SPRIG OF BASIL
- ■ 5 RIPE TOMATOES
- ■ OLIVE OIL
- ◆

PREPARATION TIME: 1 HOUR

WASH THE FROGS, skin them, remove the head, feet and innards. Do take care when removing the gall bladder, or leave this operation to the fishmonger. Detach the thighs and put aside. In a saucepan, brown the chopped vegetables (not the tomatoes) and herbs in 4 tablespoons of oil. When they begin to colour, toss in the frogs and gently fry for about 10 minutes, stirring continuously with a wooden spoon. When the vegetables have been partly absorbed, add the roughly-chopped tomatoes. Boil for a further 10 minutes, if necessary adding a little water. Keep over gentle heat until the frogs disintegrate. Sieve the lot, transferring it to another saucepan where you will add the thighs, which have been cut into pieces after boiling and boning. If you wish, you can finish off the dish with toasted croutons of Tuscan bread which can also be well-rubbed over with garlic to taste. This is excellent only if served boiling hot.

Zuppa della puerpera
BREAD SOUP WITH WINE

- ◆
- ■ 4 SLICES OF STALE BREAD
- ■ 1 GLASS RED WINE
- ■ 50G CASTOR SUGAR
- ◆

PREPARATION TIME: $1/4$ HOUR

HEAT UP HALF A LITRE of water. Place the stale bread in large earthenware bowls. Douse with hot water until the bread breaks up, drain off the excess water, then sprinkle the red wine over and dredge with plenty of sugar.

I HAVE INCLUDED THIS SOUP among first course dishes, but it does not have to be eaten as such. It used to be prepared for nursing mothers with the aim of increasing their milk supply and used to get good results. I remember that, when my mother was nursing my brothers, she devoured it with might and main (though she always had a ready supply of the maternal food), under the complacent gaze of my grandmother who returned to the kitchen, oozing satisfaction. If there should not be any nursing mothers around, it really does not matter. Bread soup with wine is an excellent teatime snack for children, marvellous for replenishing physical and intellectual energy. However, don't exaggerate with the wine ....

MEAT AND GAME

Anteriore di torello farcito
STUFFED FOREQUARTERS OF BULLOCK

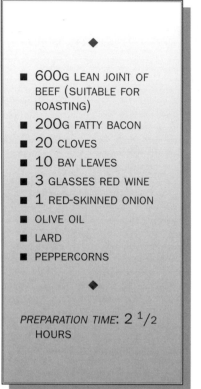

- 600G LEAN JOINT OF BEEF (SUITABLE FOR ROASTING)
- 200G FATTY BACON
- 20 CLOVES
- 10 BAY LEAVES
- 3 GLASSES RED WINE
- 1 RED-SKINNED ONION
- OLIVE OIL
- LARD
- PEPPERCORNS

PREPARATION TIME: 2 $^1/_2$ HOURS

MAKE A SERIES OF SMALL slits all over the beef into which you will insert a clove, a pinch of salt and a small bay leaf.

Cut the bacon into thin strips and roll them tightly around the beef ("larding" is the technical term), fixing them with toothpicks.

Chop up some bay leaves, mix with salt and ground pepper (or whole peppercorns) and roll the meat in this seasoning several times. Then leave the meat to stand and absorb the flavour for at least half-an-hour.

Slice the onion finely and fry it gently in 4 tablespoons of oil and a knob of lard in a large saucepan.

As soon as it begins to colour, add the meat, raise the flame and sear the surface for 5 minutes, frequently turning the meat over. Then lower the heat, add the wine (a full-bodied wine would be most suitable), cover with a lid and continue cooking over a moderate flame for two hours, if necessary adding hot water. Draw off the heat and wait at least half-an-hour before serving the beef, taking care to scrape up the meat juices in the bottom of the pan for spooning over the large carved slices of beef.

Serve with potatoes cooked among the ashes, or better still, wrapped in sheets of foil and baked.

I AGREE THAT THE GRAND-SOUNDING term "bullock" is only a memory of times gone by when "well endowed" beef was served at mammoth mediaeval and Renaissance banquets to symbolise strength and virility.

Of course, the same results can be obtained today with the best beef cuts (I do not believe that bulls are generally butchered young enough to be palatable), but at least let me exaggerate in the recipe - how can we ignore that virility has its appeal?

Arista
ROAST LOIN OF PORK

- ■ 1 ^{1}/2 KG OF LOIN OF PORK ON THE BONE
- ■ 2-3 CLOVES OF GARLIC
- ■ SPRIG OF ROSEMARY
- ■ OLIVE OIL
- ■ PEPPERCORNS

PREPARATION TIME: 2 ^{1}/4 HOURS

TAKE THE LOIN OF PORK (even if carving becomes more difficult, it absolutely must be on the bone because the taste is indisputably improved) and roll it in chopped rosemary, garlic, salt and pepper. If you like, you can score the meat with a knife and stick some peppercorns in the slits. Grease an oven tin, put in the pork and cook in a slow oven for a couple of hours. While cooking, the meat will exude a tasty gravy that you can cook potatoes in (but also turnips, Swiss chard, cabbage or spinach) to make an excellent, appetising side-dish. This is a dish fit for feast-days and is delicious even eaten cold, carved thinly and washed down with some good red wine.

IT USED TO BE THOUGHT (PERHAPS with someone's imagination working overtime) that the name derived from the Greek term *arista*, which, being a neutral plural, means "excellent things".

This superlative was presumably cried out by appreciative Greek guests during a sumptuous banquet held on the occasion of the Council of Florence in 1439, when prelates of the Roman Catholic and Greek Orthodox churches met.

But perspicacious scholars subsequently noticed the use of the term "arista" arising with a certain frequency on menus which were served to the Priors of Florence towards the middle of the fourteenth century. Whatever the truth, this roast pork represents without doubt one of the most important contributions of Florentine cuisine to universal gastronomy.

So delicious is it that it will be fully appreciated even without knowing the origin of the name - just try it and you will see

La Bistecca

BEEF STEAK

- ◆
- ■ 600-800G PIECE OF SIRLOIN STEAK
- ■ SALT AND FRESHLY-GROUND PEPPER
- ◆

PREPARATION TIME: $^1/4$ HOUR

ORIGINALLY KNOWN AS *carbonata* or "cooked over charcoal", the name *bistecca* comes from the English "beefsteak", which, apart from the fact that it has seized the upper hand, also has an aura of internationality, making it preferable. The success of Florentine beefsteak hangs for the most part on the quality of the meat, but without doubt on the cooking, too. I suggest using oxen of the Tuscan Val di Chiana breed, even though not easy to find. If the cut is right, the result is very good with other cattle stock (provided they have been reared properly). The *bistecca* must be an inch thick and be complete with its T bone, tenderloin and fillet. This precision is called for beyond the reaches of Tuscany (where it is simply called *Fiorentina*) as non-Tuscan butchers tend to proffer entrecôtes or rump steak instead of *bistecca*, the equivalent of visiting a neighbourhood primitive art exhibition instead of the Uffizi Gallery!

TAKE THE BEEF STEAK out of the refrigerator two hours beforehand, otherwise it will suffer in the cooking. Use a barbecue grill, with the charcoal glowing hot, but with no flame. Place the steak on the grill and keep over the fire for 5 minutes until a nice crust is formed. Turn it over (without piercing the meat) and repeat on the other side. The steak will remain over the fire just for the time needed to sear the surface well but keep it absolutely rare inside. Season with salt and pepper (better to use freshly ground pepper) and serve at once.

Relish it accompanied by a nice green salad or *cannellini* beans dressed in oil.

IF SOMEONE REMARKS that the animal proteins clash with the vegetable ones of the beans, making for a more strenuous digestion, well, my friends, sacrifices have to be made in life!

Americans visiting Florence order beefsteak thinking that it is closely related to the Texan T-bone steak. But there is a difference. Apart from the fact that our "Florentine" needs no cosmetic treatment, it is rightfully famous everywhere for its distinguishing characteristics: it is full of flavour (if cooked rare in the proper fashion), nutritious, pleasant on the eye and, apart from anything else, I am also convinced it is very good for the health. Do not deprive yourselves of the joy of eating it some time or other, perhaps in the open air in the summer, under the greenery of a pergola, washed down with our marvellous red wine. The memory will be indelible for you to savour in the grey days in store ahead.

Braciole col cavolo nero

PORK CHOPS WITH KALE

- 4 PORK CHOPS, ABOUT 150G EACH
- 4 BUNCHES TUSCAN 'BLACK' CABBAGE OR KALE
- 1 RED -SKINNED ONION
- 2 CLOVES OF GARLIC
- 1 GLASS LIGHT RED WINE
- WHOLE BLACK PEPPER
- OLIVE OIL

PREPARATION TIME: 50 MINUTES

TRIM THE LEAVES of the cabbage or kale, stripping them of their midribs, and rinse them. Cook in salted, boiling water for about 20 minutes. Drain well and chop with the aid of a *mezzaluna*, i.e. a double-handled rocking knife. With the garlic and finely-chopped onion, brown the chops on both sides in 4 tablespoons of oil in a saucepan, then add the red wine. Cover with the lid and cook over gentle heat for 15 minutes. Remove the meat from the pan and flavour the cabbage or kale in the gravy which has formed. Add the meat and return to the flame for another 10 minutes, stirring continually with a wooden spoon. Season with salt and pepper and serve nice and hot.

Variation: instead of the cabbage or kale, use turnip tops or broccoli, first blanched briefly in boiling water, then broken up and added to the meat.

A typical winter's dish, it likes to be accompanied by a good, sturdy red wine.

Braciole di vitella ai carciofi

VEAL CHOPS WITH ARTICHOKES

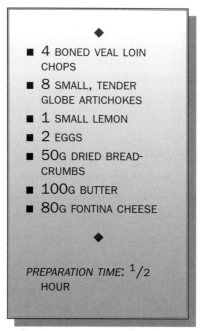

- 4 BONED VEAL LOIN CHOPS
- 8 SMALL, TENDER GLOBE ARTICHOKES
- 1 SMALL LEMON
- 2 EGGS
- 50G DRIED BREAD-CRUMBS
- 100G BUTTER
- 80G FONTINA CHEESE

PREPARATION TIME: $^1/_2$ HOUR

TRIM THE ARTICHOKES, removing the tougher outside leaves and the internal choke (if there is one). Place in a bowl of water lightly acidulated with a few drops of lemon.

Beat the meat briefly to flatten and allow to stand a while in the egg, beaten with a pinch of salt. Slice the artichokes paper thin.

Stuff each chop by covering about half of the meat with a little cheese and some artichoke slices. Fold over to make a parcel and press down well with your fingers. Dip first in the egg and then in the dried breadcrumbs.

Cook in butter with a pinch of salt and pepper for 15 minutes over medium heat, flipping the parcels over gently to brown them completely on both sides.

Serve the dish really hot, garnished with lemon slices and sprigs of parsley.

Braciole ripiene al tartufo

TRUFFLE-STUFFED VEAL CUTLETS

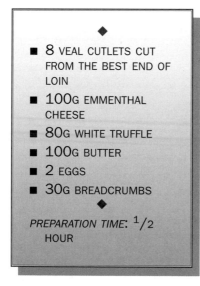

- 8 VEAL CUTLETS CUT FROM THE BEST END OF LOIN
- 100G EMMENTHAL CHEESE
- 80G WHITE TRUFFLE
- 100G BUTTER
- 2 EGGS
- 30G BREADCRUMBS

PREPARATION TIME: $^1/_2$ HOUR

BEAT THE MEAT OUT LIGHTLY and allow to stand a while in the egg, beaten with a pinch of salt. Clean the truffle by rubbing it delicately in a damp tea towel. Slice the Emmenthal and the truffle very thinly and distribute over the cutlets. Fold the sides over, pressing down carefully, then egg and crumb them. Shake the "parcels" to remove excess crumbs and fry in the butter over a medium flame, allowing to brown all over. Serve after cooking 15 minutes. They are excellent only if eaten very hot, together with cooked fennel bulbs heated in some butter in a saucepan.

BECAUSE OF THE COST, the ponderous decision of how much truffle to use is left to you. I can merely assure you that this recipe is delicious and that, of course, the more truffle there is ....

Braciole alla toscana

TUSCAN PEASANT STEAKS

- 4 SLICES OF STEAK (FROM THE TOPSIDE), ABOUT 150G EACH
- 500G CANNED TOMATOES
- 1 MEDIUM ONION
- 1 CARROT
- 1 STICK OF CELERY
- 1 GLASS WHITE WINE
- OLIVE OIL

◆

PREPARATION TIME: 1 HOUR 10 MINUTES

GENTLY SAUTÉ all the chopped vegetables (except the tomatoes) in 4 tablespoons of oil in a saucepan. When they begin to colour, add the beef slices (after beating them gently but systematically to tenderise them) and allow to brown, turning them with a wooden spoon. After a brief period of cooking, add the tomatoes (do not drain off all their liquid) and the white wine. Season with salt and pepper and cook for an hour over very gentle heat, with the lid on the pan. There is no need to worry about the length of cooking, so long as the flame is very low. At the end, the meat will be extremely tender and tasty (even if sautéed in a saucepan the following day).

If you have the patience to chop them up roughly with a *mezzaluna* once cooked and to replace them in their sauce for a further, brief cooking spell, you may use the mixture as a dressing for spaghetti or, better still, ribbed noodles, served dredged in Parmesan cheese.

WITH REGARD TO *BRACIOLE*, I think a marginal note is crucial, dealing with a traditional way of using up left-overs of this undisputed leading component of Italian family dinners (at least before the advent of hamburgers and frozen foods). When you find yourself making fried breaded escalopes, make a few extra ones. Keep aside those which are left over (if there are any as they are so good) for heating up that evening or the following day in home-made tomato sauce. Put the tomato purée, with a little oil and cloves of garlic in a pan over a flame. Let the flavours blend well, then immerse the escalopes for a few minutes to soften them up. Just great!

Cappone alla fiorentina

FLORENTINE CAPON

- 1 CAPON OF ABOUT 3KG
- 1 MEDIUM ONION
- 1 CARROT
- 1 STICK OF CELERY
- A PINCH OF SAVORY (FRESH IF POSSIBLE)
- GARLIC
- 2 SLIVERS RAW PRO-SCIUTTO
- 1 BAY LEAF
- 1 GLASS VINSANTO
- $^1/_2$L HOME-MADE TOMA-TO SAUCE
- $^1/_2$L STOCK
- STALE TUSCAN BREAD
- 2 KNOBS OF BUTTER
- OLIVE OIL

◆

PREPARATION TIME: 2 $^1/_2$ HOURS

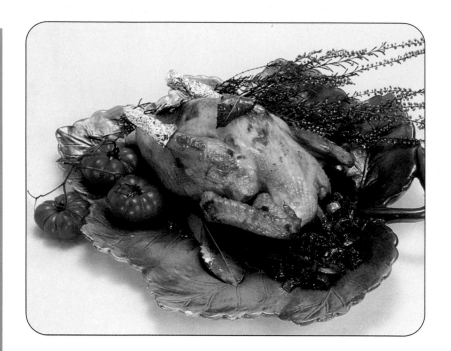

NOWADAYS, CAPONS are little exploited at meal times, indeed almost only for the Christmas festivities. It is the great size which makes them suitable for consumption when the company includes large numbers of relatives and friends. But if there is someone willing to satisfy their whim of eating this delicate dish in scantier company, well … two's company, three's a crowd.

CLEAN AND SINGE the capon, stud it with a few pieces of garlic, savory leaves, a bay leaf and a little salt. Truss the legs and place in 6 tablespoons of oil and a knob of butter in a saucepan, together with the chopped onion, carrot and celery. Brown over fierce heat, frequently basting both with the juices in the pan and the stock that you will have prepared separately (a bouillon cube will do fine).

Continue cooking the capon for half-an-hour, basting every now and then and shaking the pan so that nothing sticks. Add the shredded ham and allow to brown before adding the tomato sauce and a pinch of salt and pepper (remember that ham is salty) and cook over gentle heat for an hour and a half. Taste the gravy which forms and adjust to taste with the vinsanto. On celebration days, the capon is served up whole on a large dish. Or else it is jointed and arranged on large slices of toast, dipped in the gravy you get from boiling up the cooking juices (when the capon has been removed from the pan) with the addition of half a glass of stock, if necessary.

Cappone in agrodolce

SWEET-SOUR CAPON

- 1 SMALL CAPON
- 200G WALNUT HALVES
- 200G PITTED PRUNES
- 100G DRIED FIGS
- 100G PITTED GREEN OLIVES
- $1/2$L SOURED CREAM
- 2 GLASSES VINSANTO
- 1 TABLESPOON VINEGAR
- 150G BUTTER
- 10G CLOVES
- SALT AND PEPPER

PREPARATION TIME: $2\ 1/2$ HOURS

IN TUSCANY, THIS IS a triumphant Christmas dish. The original blending of the various flavours jazzes up dinner tables tired of the fowl invariably boiled. The dried fruit and the sour cream flavours marry perfectly.

If the latter is difficult to find, use a rather liquid (not thick) yoghurt. Garnish the platter with salad (preferably *radicchio rosso*) and the remaining green olives.

CLEAN THE CAPON by drawing, singeing, rinsing under the tap and cutting off the head and claws. Chop all the dried fruit in a bowl, breaking up the walnut halves and the green olives in your fingers, and season with salt, pepper and the cloves.

Mix well by hand, stuff the stomach opening of the capon and sew it up with kitchen string. Melt the butter together with the sour cream and the vinsanto in a large saucepan.

Add the capon, cover the pan and keep over medium heat for an hour and a half. Turn the capon over once only and baste frequently and carefully with its gravy. Should the liquid reduce too much, add a little hot water and a few teaspoons of vinsanto. When the fowl is cooked but very tender, place it on a serving dish and leave to cool for 15 minutes before jointing and serving it with its gravy, which you will have obtained by scraping the bottom of the pan and boiling the cooking juices over fierce heat. Remember to add a tablespoon of vinegar, but only at the last minute.

Capra e polenta

CORNMEAL AND GIGOT OF GOAT

◆

- 1KG GIGOT OF GOAT
- ^{1}/2KG CORNMEAL
- 3 CLOVES OF GARLIC
- ROSEMARY
- 3 OR 4 DRIED CHILLI PEPPERS
- 200G RIPE TOMATOES
- 1 GLASS RED WINE
- 1 GLASS STOCK
- 10 BAY LEAVES
- OLIVE OIL

◆

PREPARATION TIME: 2 ^{1}/2 HOURS

CUT THE GIGOT into chunks and place in a bowl with the red wine, rosemary, bay leaves, crushed garlic and the chilli peppers, plus a pinch of salt and pepper. Leave the meat to marinate for all the time the cornmeal is cooking. Place a saucepan over the flame with 2 litres of lightly-salted water. As soon as it boils, draw off the heat and sprinkle in the soft-grain (though not too finely-ground) cornmeal. Stir quickly with a wooden spoon as you pour in the cornmeal, trying to prevent lumps from forming. Return to low heat and let it simmer for three quarters of an hour, stirring continuously. In a saucepan, heat 6 table-spoon of oil and brown the meat. Pour the cooked corn-meal onto a tabletop or board and leave to cool.

Cook the meat in just the oil for a quarter-hour over medium heat. Add the filtered marinade and continue cooking with the addition of the stock and the tomato cut up small. Cover and cook the gigot for an hour over moderate heat.

Then slice the cornmeal and place on each individual plate, completing with the meat and the gravy. Eat boiling hot, washed down with a good, strapping red wine.

Cervello in salsa bianca

BRAINS IN A WHITE SAUCE

- ◆
- ■ ¹/₂KG CALF'S BRAINS
- ■ 100G BUTTER
- ■ 20G WHITE FLOUR
- ■ ¹/₂L MILK
- ■ 1 EGG
- ■ 50G DRIED BREAD-
  CRUMBS
- ■ SPRIG OF PARSLEY
- ■ SALT AND PEPPER
- ◆

PREPARATION TIME: ³/₄
HOUR

BLANCHE THE BRAINS briefly in hot water and skin, carefully removing the membrane which is rich in blood vessels. Rinse under a thin stream of cold, running water.

Cut up into about 10 nut-sized pieces and dip into the lightly-salted beaten egg, leaving for about 10 minutes. Roll in the dried breadcrumbs.

Melt the butter in a saucepan and fry the brain pieces over a slow flame for 20 minutes, turning them over carefully to cook them all over.

Prepare a rather liquid béchamel sauce by working 20g of flour into 30g of butter in a saucepan over the flame, blending in the milk.

Season with salt and pepper, add the chopped parsley and pour this sauce, boiling hot, over the very hot pieces of brain.

Finally, dredge the lot with finely-chopped parsley.

Chiocciole fiorentine

FLORENTINE SNAILS

SNAILS DO NOT DISAVOW their proverbial nature in this preparation either - time, patience and long intervals spent just waiting are needed. I mean, talking of slow food, there is no slower one than this in the preparation stage.

But not for any reason in the world must you deprive yourself of the pleasure of tasting this ancient, fragrant, delicious dish which demands love and a great deal of care in the making (as well as composure in the eating).

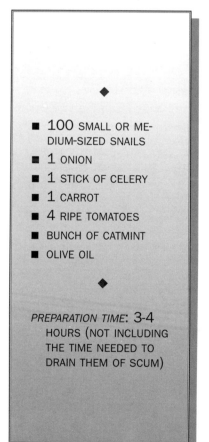

◆

- ■ 100 SMALL OR ME-
  DIUM-SIZED SNAILS
- ■ 1 ONION
- ■ 1 STICK OF CELERY
- ■ 1 CARROT
- ■ 4 RIPE TOMATOES
- ■ BUNCH OF CATMINT
- ■ OLIVE OIL

◆

PREPARATION TIME: 3-4
  HOURS (NOT INCLUDING
  THE TIME NEEDED TO
  DRAIN THEM OF SCUM)

CHOP UP THE ONION, carrot and celery and sauté in 4 tablespoons of oil in a saucepan. When sufficiently browned, add the snails. Raise the flame, cover the pan and cook for 10 minutes. Add the roughly-chopped tomatoes with the catmint, leaving it all to cook slowly for 3 hours. Stir the snails frequently and eat them hot, removing them from their shells with the help of the special two-pronged fork or quite simply with a long, pointed wooden cocktail stick.

THE SNAILS WHICH ARE the most suitable for eating should be gathered in spring or autumn when the ground is wetter. The bigger ones should be avoided in favour of the small and medium-sized. If possible, my advice is to get hold of cleaned-out snails, ready for cooking. Otherwise, follow this procedure: collect together the snails and put them in a covered basket to drain off all their slime and scum, leaving them with a bunch of lettuce leaves and some flour. After three days, wash them under running water, taking care to discard those which have died in the meantime (with a little patience, they are easy to recognise as they do not stick out their "horns") and adding a little vinegar to the water until all traces of slime have been flushed away. Continue in this way until there is no scum left. Only at the end of this lengthy, meticulous operation can the snails be relished in their full flavour. Incidentally, you might care to know that the ordinary aromatic herb called catmint is also known as catnip or wild mint.

Cinghiale in dolce e forte

WILD BOAR IN A SHARP, SWEET SAUCE

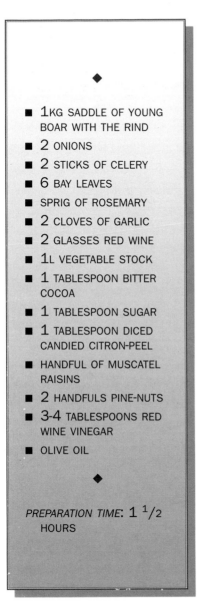

◆

- 1KG SADDLE OF YOUNG BOAR WITH THE RIND
- 2 ONIONS
- 2 STICKS OF CELERY
- 6 BAY LEAVES
- SPRIG OF ROSEMARY
- 2 CLOVES OF GARLIC
- 2 GLASSES RED WINE
- 1L VEGETABLE STOCK
- 1 TABLESPOON BITTER COCOA
- 1 TABLESPOON SUGAR
- 1 TABLESPOON DICED CANDIED CITRON-PEEL
- HANDFUL OF MUSCATEL RAISINS
- 2 HANDFULS PINE-NUTS
- 3-4 TABLESPOONS RED WINE VINEGAR
- OLIVE OIL

◆

PREPARATION TIME: 1 $^1/_2$ HOURS

THE MEAT OF THE BOAR should be mature, but fresh (and not from the freezer!), so order it in good time from your butcher. This beast is not hard for us to come by because it generally abounds in Italian woods and in Tuscany's Maremma district.

Marinate it overnight in red wine with the onion, celery, garlic and herbs to lend aroma and eliminate that unpleasant, gamy smell. Drain well and cut into pieces, removing the rind. Before beginning to cook the boar, put the raisins to soak in water for at least an hour.

Chop up all the marinade vegetables (herbs and garlic included) fairly roughly and heat in 6 tablespoons of oil. When they begin to colour, add the boar meat and, after a little while, also the wine, browning over medium heat for at least twenty minutes. Baste frequently with the vegetable stock and stir repeatedly with a wooden spoon so that the meat becomes impregnated with the vegetable flavours. Cook slowly for a further 40 minutes, trying it with a fork to judge if cooked. When satisfied, remove the meat from the pan.

In a separate saucepan, gently mix together the cocoa, sugar, citron-peel, the drained and dried raisins and the pine-nuts and heat over a very low flame until you get a creamy sauce which you will bind with 3-4 tablespoons of red wine vinegar and enough water to make it fairly runny. Then add this sauce to the gravy left in the bottom of the pan the boar was cooked in, blend and return to the heat for a minute along with the pieces of meat.

Serve at once.

THE SECRET OF THIS LONG preparation, which reveals sapid, age-old combinations, lies mostly in the final, very brief period when the meat is cooked in the sauce and also in the balance between the savoury and sweet flavours.

The freshness of the boar is indispensable, too, as is the quality of the vinegar. In cooking this recipe (but my advice holds good in general) do not hesitate to keep tasting the dish (despite the dictates of perverse modern tendencies). Only in this way can you obtain perfect harmony of the flavours which must characterise this delicacy. It demands skill in the kitchen and gives enormous satisfaction both to the cook making it and those tasting it.

Collo di tacchino ripieno
STUFFED NECK OF TURKEY

- 1 BONED TURKEY NECK
- 200G MINCED MEAT
- ONION, CARROT AND CELERY
- A HANDFUL OF BOTH BLACK AND GREEN OLIVES
- 1 EGG
- CHILLI PEPPER
- TRUSSING NEEDLE AND FINE STRING

PREPARATION TIME: 2 1/2 HOURS

SEW UP THE NECK at one end, stuff with meat, olives and egg well mixed together and flavoured with a pinch of chilli pepper. Sew up the other end. Wrap up tightly in a meat net and boil, together with the root vegetables and celery, in plenty of water over low heat for about two hours. Drain the neck when cooked and place on a dish. Place a weight along the entire length, so that all the cooking water is squeezed out. Leave to cool completely and serve sliced, perhaps accompanied with green sauce (p. 41) or a fragrant French dressing.

REGARDING STUFFED NECKS, Tuscan cuisine always uses chickens, the use of turkey in the kitchen being relatively recent.

But times change and we must adapt to them. Of course, consider that this American fowl is bulkier than its European cousin and there is, therefore, more to eat....

Coniglio alla cacciatora
RABBIT CACCIATORA

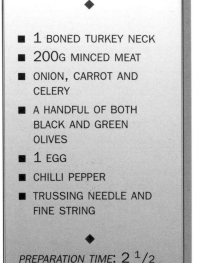

- 1 RABBIT, ABOUT 1/2KG IN WEIGHT
- ONION, CARROT AND CELERY
- WHITE WINE
- 4 RIPE TOMATOES
- GARLICKY BLACK OLIVES
- WHITE FLOUR

PREPARATION TIME: 1 1/4 HOUR

CLEAN THE RABBIT, joint and coat with flour. Sauté the chopped onion, carrot and celery in a saucepan with 4 tablespoons of oil. When it all begins to colour, throw in the rabbit, except for the liver which will be used elsewhere. Douse with the wine and cook for about 10 minutes over medium heat, stirring with a wooden spoon. Add the chopped tomatoes and the olives, correcting with salt and pepper. Cook for another 40 minutes over moderate heat.

THIS WAS ONE of Grandfather Luigi's favourite dishes. He, a keen hunter turned into a city dweller, expected his wife to provide it on feast days. This dish originated in the Romagna region of Italy where it was endowed with the aroma of nutmeg, being grated over it at the last minute and blended in with care.

Coniglio alla contadina
PEASANT RABBIT DISH

- 1 RABBIT, 1 $^1/_2$KG IN WEIGHT
- 1 RED-SKINNED ONION
- $^1/_2$KG RIPE TOMATOES
- ROSEMARY
- 2 CLOVES OF GARLIC
- WHITE WINE
- VEGETABLE STOCK
- OLIVE OIL

PREPARATION TIME: 1 $^1/_4$ HOURS

JOINT THE RABBIT AND rinse it. In a saucepan, brown the chopped onion and cloves of garlic in 4 tablespoons of oil. Add the rabbit joints, drained and dried, together with the liver cut into pieces. Raise the flame and pour the white wine over, lowering the heat when the liquid has evaporated. Cover with the lid and leave to cook over medium heat for about a quarter-hour. At this point, add the peeled, chopped tomatoes, the rosemary and also 5-6 basil leaves (if you like the fragrance and the season is the right one). Season to taste with salt and pepper. Cook for another 20 minutes, if necessary gradually adding the vegetable stock to maintain the mixture smooth.

Coniglio coi funghi
RABBIT WITH MUSHROOMS

- 1 RABBIT, ABOUT 1 $^1/_2$KG IN WEIGHT
- 3 *BOLETUS EDULIS* MUSHROOMS
- 80G WHITE FLOUR
- ROSEMARY, CHOPPED
- 2 CLOVES OF GARLIC
- 2 RIPE TOMATOES
- WHITE WINE
- VEGETABLE STOCK
- OLIVE OIL

PREPARATION TIME: 1 HOUR

RINSE AND JOINT THE rabbit. In a saucepan, sauté it (liver excepted) in four tablespoons of oil over medium heat for 10 minutes. Then remove from the pan and dust with the finely-chopped garlic and rosemary. Place it in a saucepan with 3 tablespoons of oil and cook for 10 minutes, dousing with the white wine. Now add the mushrooms in strips and moisten with a little vegetable stock. Add the tomatoes cut into pieces and bind with the flour dissolved in the vegetable stock. Cook gently for another half-hour and serve hot.

Coniglio coi baccelli

RABBIT & BROAD BEANS

◆

- A RABBIT, ABOUT 1.2KG IN WEIGHT
- 2KG BROAD BEANS, UNSHELLED WEIGHT
- 1 WHITE-SKINNED ONION
- 1 SPRIG OF BASIL
- 3 RIPE TOMATOES
- OLIVE OIL

◆

PREPARATION TIME: 1 1/4 HOURS

HULL AND TRIM the broad beans. Gently fry the finely-chopped onion in 3 tablespoons of oil in a saucepan. Cut the rabbit into about 10 portions, wash it and add to the browned onion. Sauté for 5 minutes over fierce heat, lower the flame and add the shelled broad beans, the peeled tomatoes, the basil, salt and pepper. Cook over medium heat with the lid on for about three quarters-of-an-hour, stirring carefully every now and again to blend in all the flavours. Serve very hot, with the broad beans on a separate plate.

Coniglio fritto

FRIED RABBIT

◆

- 1 RABBIT, ABOUT 1 1/2KG IN WEIGHT
- 2 EGGS
- 200G FLOUR
- LEMON
- OLIVE OIL

◆

PREPARATION TIME: 1 1/2 HOURS

RINSE THE RABBIT and cut into portions (about ten). Lightly beat the eggs in a bowl, toss in the rabbit pieces (except the liver) and leave to stand for an hour, after stirring it all with your fingers and adding a pinch of salt.

Then sprinkle in the flour until it is incorporated into the egg, turn the rabbit portions over again in this batter and deep fry in hot oil, adjusting the flame so that the meat cooks right through.

The fry will be ready after 20 minutes' cooking over slow heat. Serve up nice and hot with lots of lemon wedges.

Coniglio con le olive

RABBIT WITH OLIVES

◆

- 1 RABBIT, 1 $^{1}/_{2}$KG IN WEIGHT
- 3 CLOVES OF GARLIC
- DRY WHITE WINE
- $^{1}/_{2}$KG FRESH (OR CANNED) TOMATOES
- GARLICKY BLACK OLIVES
- OLIVE OIL

◆

PREPARATION TIME: 1 HOUR

WASH THE RABBIT, cut into about ten portions and brown in a saucepan with 2 cloves of garlic in 4 tablespoons of oil. Keep over fierce heat for 5 minutes, then add the wine and bring back to the boil. Add the tomatoes, black olives, salt and pepper. Leave to cook for 30 minutes over a medium flame. If you like, you can add the chopped liver together with the tomatoes. It is excellent served with boiled or mashed potatoes.

Coniglio in tegame

BRAISED RABBIT

◆

- 1 RABBIT, ABOUT 1.2KG IN WEIGHT
- 3 CLOVES OF GARLIC
- ROSEMARY
- WHITE WINE
- OLIVE OIL

◆

PREPARATION TIME: 1 HOUR

WASH THE RABBIT and divide into 12 pieces. Put in a frying pan with 3 cloves of garlic, 4 tablespoons of oil and the rosemary. Sear over a fierce heat for 5 minutes until the meat has turned brown, lower the flame and add the wine (tomatoes, too, if you wish). Season with salt and pepper. Cook for 40 minutes over medium heat, stirring. When you are ready to present it at the table, remove the garlic and rosemary and arrange on a serving dish. Add a couple of tablespoons of water to the pan, return to the heat, scrape the cooking juices off the bottom with a spoon and mask the rabbit with the resultant gravy. This dish is flavoursome, especially with boiled potatoes topped with the gravy.

Coratella

LAMB'S PLUCK

◆

- 600G LAMB'S PLUCK (TRACHEA, LIGHTS, HEART, LIVER, ETC.)
- GARLIC AND ROSEMARY
- WHITE WINE
- TOMATO PURÉE
- BLACK OLIVES
- OLIVE OIL

◆

PREPARATION TIME: 3/4 HOUR

CLEAN THE PLUCK well in vinegar and water. Cut into pieces and place over the heat with a clove of garlic, a twig of rosemary and 4 tablespoons of oil. Cover and brown over medium heat for 20 minutes. Add 2 tablespoons of home-made tomato sauce, the black olives, salt and pepper. Bring back to the boil and serve very hot.

Cuore alla griglia

GRILLED OX HEART

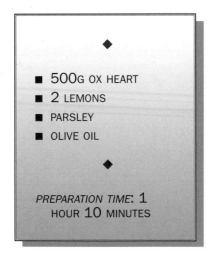

◆

- 500G OX HEART
- 2 LEMONS
- PARSLEY
- OLIVE OIL

◆

PREPARATION TIME: 1 HOUR 10 MINUTES

OX HEART IS VERY nutritious, cheap, quick to prepare and very pleasant, especially if you keep to the following instructions. Cut it up into roughly inch-wide strips and put into a deep bowl with plenty of olive oil, the juice of 2 lemons and lots of salt and pepper. Leave to stand in the marinade for an hour or more.

Heat the griddle on the hob and when it is hot, throw the strips of heart (thoroughly drained of oil) onto it. Let the heart splutter away, turning the pieces over with a fork. Five minutes are needed to cook it through properly. Serve immediately, nice and hot, with a sprinkling of parsley and a pinch of salt.

Fagiano alla toscana

PHEASANT, TUSCAN STYLE

◆

- A PHEASANT, ABOUT 1.3 KG IN WEIGHT
- 150G BACON
- SAGE
- OLIVE OIL

◆

PREPARATION TIME: 1 ¹/₄ HOURS

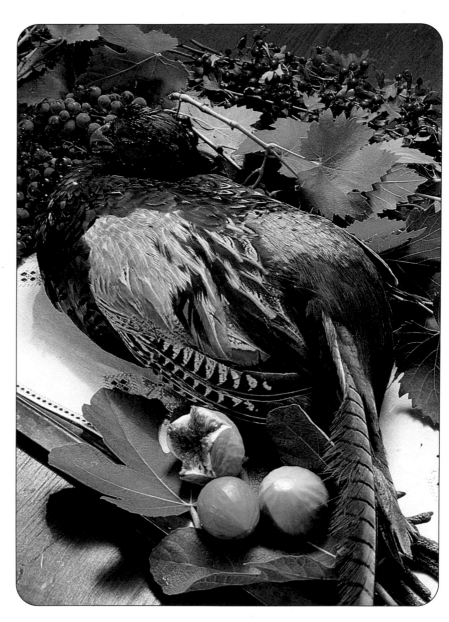

PHEASANTS THAT YOU FIND in the shops are often already ripened and drawn (i.e. deprived of internal organs). If this is not the case, remove the innards and leave the fowl to ripen for a week. (A little time is needed to bring the flavour out.) Pluck it with care (this is a lengthy operation which requires infinite patience!) Cut off the claws and head, singe and rinse it in water and vinegar. Now it is ready to be cooked. Thanks to its "trappings", this recipe enables us to appreciate the pheasant cock, even though his flesh is notoriously tougher than his mate's.

BARD THE PHEASANT with thin strips of bacon, after seasoning the inside well with salt and pepper. Truss with kitchen string, put in a baking tin with 4 tablespoons of oil and roast in a hot oven for at least 40 minutes. Baste frequently with the juices in the pan so that the meat does not dry out. When cooked, loosen the string and remove the bacon barding (chopped up, it goes into the juices in the pan to make the gravy). Divide the bird into portions and serve it hot, covered in gravy.

— 95 —

Faraona al vinsanto

GUINEA FOWL COOKED IN VINSANTO

- ◆ -

■ 1 GUINEA FOWL, ABOUT 1KG IN WEIGHT
■ 100G BUTTER
■ 1 CARROT
■ 1 STICK OF CELERY
■ 80G APPROX. RAW PROSCIUTTO
■ SAGE AND ROSEMARY
■ 2 GLASSES VINSANTO (OR MEDIUM-DRY SHERRY)
■ $^1/_2$L VEGETABLE STOCK
■ OLIVE OIL

- ◆ -

PREPARATION TIME: 1 HOUR

SINGE AND CLEAN the guinea fowl thoroughly and divide into about eight portions. Brown in a pan with 4 tablespoons of oil and 100g of butter, together with the finely-chopped carrot and the celery and the raw ham cut into short lengths.

Cook over moderate heat for about a quarter-hour. Then add the finely-chopped rosemary and sage and pour a glass of vinsanto over.

Season with salt and pepper to taste. As usual, keep a light hand with the salt because of the ham.

Cook for another ten minutes and add the second glass of vinsanto.

To impregnate the meat well with the flavour, turn it over carefully with the help of a wooden spoon.

If necessary, gradually add small amounts of vegetable stock until the pheasant is fully cooked. All-in-all, it will need about half-an-hour over medium heat. Serve masked with the gravy.

ALLOW ME JUST one word about *vinsanto*. It is a delicious, typically Tuscan, liqueur-like wine which is made in small, expensive quantities (at least, the "real" thing is) by letting the bunches of grapes dry on reed mats before crushing them. The must is then closed hermetically in special casks which have been subjected to lengthy seasoning and here it "matures", entirely out of the reach of air and light. For this reason, peasant families used to wall up the casks or bury them, bringing them back to the light of day even generations later and opening them to reveal an amber nectar to the wonder of onlookers, high in sugar content with a sweet, delicate flavour. As regards the name, some say it comes from its use in the Eucharist service. Perhaps this used to be true, but nowadays only more hastily-prepared wines, purpose-made and cheap, are found on the altar. They are, however, nothing to do with true vinsanto. If my memory does not fail me, some scholar mentions a different etymon in a "Storia di Firenze". At the banquets which took place during the Council of Florence in the period 1430 to 1439, it would seem that the erudite orthodox prelates participating were very appreciative of the food and wine offered to them. So, the story goes, one of them, on brushing his pious lips against the glass of vinsanto at the end of the meal (already finalised as regards the formula, but still waiting to be "baptised") exclaimed (I cannot tell you in which language), "But this is wine from Xanthos!", thus comparing it with one of the better-known and prestigious sweet wines from his part of the world. The Florentines present did not realise that the holy man was referring to the Greek island in the Mediterranean, but the assonance led them to believe that the prelate was assessing the wine as being so good that it should be made *santo* or holy and from that day on they began to call it thus. An unlikely story, maybe, but certainly less banal than the other one.

Fegatelli di maiale

TUSCAN PIG'S LIVER

◆

- 600G PIG'S LIVER
- 200G PORK NET (CAUL FAT)
- BAY LAUREL LEAVES
- LAUREL TWIGS FOR USE AS SKEWERS
- SLICED BREAD
- OLIVE OIL

◆

PREPARATION TIME: 3/4 HOUR

WASH THE PORK NET in luke-warm water. Cut the liver into 2-inch pieces and coat with the well-chopped bay laurel leaves, salt and pepper. Cut the net into squares big enough to wrap round the liver pieces. Impale them on the laurel twigs (cut in roughly 8-inch lengths), alternating a liver parcel with a slice of bread (preferably cut from the crusty part of the loaf) and separating them with a laurel leaf. Arrange the skewers in a meat tin with 5 tablespoons of oil and an additional pinch of salt. Cook in a medium oven for 20 minutes.

TAKE CARE in the cooking; if the liver parcels are left in the oven for too long, they will become tough.

I suggest using laurel twigs because they impart flavour to the meat from the inside.

Lastly, the bread…. You may use any kind of bread you like, but Tuscan-style bread is doubtless the most suitable. You see, our bread is nice and compact and, above all, it is not salted, so it will "back up" flavours without altering them. Indeed, it will bring the aroma out.

Fegato alla fiorentina

LIVER, FLORENTINE STYLE

◆

- 400G CALF'S LIVER
- 1 SPRIG OF SAGE
- 2 CLOVES OF GARLIC
- WHITE FLOUR
- OLIVE OIL

◆

PREPARATION TIME: 20 MINUTES

BE CAREFUL WHEN cooking the liver: the meat could become tough and leathery. A Tuscan saying goes, "Baccalà, liver and eggs; the longer they are cooked, the harder they become".

SLICE THE LIVER (it would be better to get the butcher to do this). Heat 2 cloves of garlic in a pan with 4 table-spoons of oil. When it begins to sizzle, add the slices of liv-er, dipped in flour seasoned with salt and pepper. Cook moderately for 10 minutes and serve nice and hot.

Fricassea rustica

VEAL IN A LEMON SAUCE

◆

- 800G VEAL STEWING STEAK
- PARSLEY
- 2 CLOVES OF GARLIC
- DRY WHITE WINE
- 2 EGG YOLKS
- 1 LEMON
- 100G BUTTER
- OLIVE OIL

◆

PREPARATION TIME: 1 ¹/2 HOURS

CUT UP THE STEAK and place in a frying pan with 3 table-spoons of oil, the butter, the parsley (tied in a bunch for easy removal) and the garlic. Cook over medium heat for 20 minutes, basting now and then with the wine. Remove the parsley and garlic and continue cooking an hour longer. Moisten with hot water, if necessary. Then draw the pan off the heat and remove the meat while it is still tender, but not rarely done. Beat the yolks with the juice of a lemon and pour it all into the gravy in the pan. Stir and, if necessary, sprinkle in a little hot water to bind, without returning the pan to the heat. Cover the meat with the sauce and serve.

HALF-WAY THROUGH the cooking, some cooks add a few dried mush-rooms, revived in hot water and then chopped. I approve, prov-ided, of course, that the mush-rooms are strictly *Boletus edulis*.

Insalata di trippa
TRIPE SALAD

- 500G TRIPE
- 1 WHITE-SKINNED ONION
- A FISTFUL OF BLACK OLIVES
- A FISTFUL OF SPICY GREEN OLIVES
- 1/2 RED SWEET PEPPER
- SPRIG OF PARSLEY
- 2 LEMONS
- OLIVE OIL

PREPARATION TIME: 20 MINUTES

CLEAN THE TRIPE thoroughly and cut into strips half an inch thick (or thinner, if you prefer).

Put in a bowl and add the pitted, roughly-chopped olives, the sweet pepper, finely shredded, the onion, cut into rings, and the parsley, chopped. Season with salt, pepper, oil and lemon juice.

THIS DELECTABLE SALAD is particularly appreciated in the summer because it is to be consumed cold.

Of course, everyone may add ingredients as they wish to give it a personal touch (e.g. fresh tomatoes in wedges), to round off the flavour (globe artichokes in oil) or to intensify it (e.g. basil leaves instead of the chopped parsley, either roughly torn up in your fingers or left whole as a colourful garnish).

Involtini di carciofi
ARTICHOKE ROULADES

- 8 SLICES OF BEEF (ABOUT 30G EACH)
- 50G RAW *PROSCIUTTO*, NOT TOO SALTY
- 3-4 GLOBE ARTICHOKES
- 4-5 RIPE TOMATOES
- WHITE WINE
- 2 CLOVES OF GARLIC
- 1 SPRIG OF SAGE
- OLIVE OIL

PREPARATION TIME: 3/4 HOUR

BEAT THE SLICES OF BEEF lightly to tenderise the meat. Trim the artichokes, removing the outside leaves and the choke, and slice them crosswise. Flatten the slices of beef and place on each one a slice of artichoke, a sliver of ham, salt and pepper, in that order.

Roll each one up tightly (they are also called "parcels") and secure with a toothpick. Put the roulades into a saucepan with 2 cloves of garlic, the sage and 4 tablespoons of oil and cook for a few minutes. Add half a glass of white wine, let it evaporate over fierce heat and drop in the roughly-chopped tomato (or else half a kilogram of canned tomatoes, drained), allowing to cook for another 20 minutes over a gentle flame.

Season with salt and pepper to taste and serve the roulades thoroughly hot.

Lesso rifatto

RÉCHAUFFÉ OF BOILED MEAT

◆

- 400G BOILED BEEF
- 2 WHITE-SKINNED ONIONS
- 300G CANNED TOMATOES
- A FEW BASIL LEAVES
- SPRIG OF SAGE
- OLIVE OIL

◆

PREPARATION TIME: $1/2$ HOUR

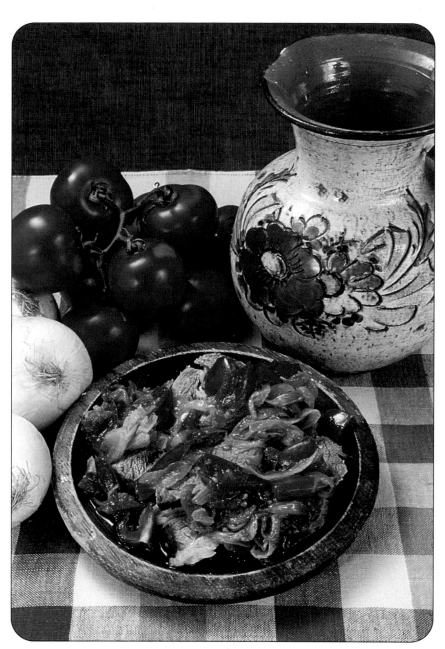

COOK THE FINELY-chopped onion gently in 4 tablespoons of oil in a saucepan. Do not let it colour, but allow it to retain its whiteness, covering with the lid and omitting salt.

Once the onions have withered somewhat, add the drained, chopped tomatoes, a little chopped basil and 3 whole sage leaves.

Cook for 10 minutes over moderate heat. Now add the sliced boiled meat and bring to the boil briefly to thicken the sauce. Season with salt and pepper. Serve the slices doused in the tasty tomato and onion sauce.

Lingua in dolce e forte

SWEET, SAVOURY TONGUE

- 1 OX TONGUE
- 2 RED-SKINNED ONIONS
- 2 CARROTS
- 2 STICKS OF CELERY
- CHOPPED PARSLEY
- 30G SWEET COCOA
- 30G PINE-NUTS
- 40G MUSCATEL RAISINS
- 30G CANDIED CITRON-PEEL
- RED WINE VINEGAR
- OLIVE OIL

PREPARATION TIME: 2 HOURS

IMMERSE THE TONGUE in plenty of cold water, put on the hob and boil for at least an hour, adding an onion, a carrot and a stalk of celery. Draw off the heat and skin while still hot. Transfer to a saucepan with the remaining vegetables, chopped, and 4 tablespoons of oil and cook with the lid on over a medium flame for a good 20 minutes. After that, prick the rear part of the tongue with the prongs of a fork and, if it bleeds, return to the heat until completely cooked. Remove from the saucepan and leave to rest on a plate, dousing with a little vinegar.

Meanwhile, prepare a sauce by carefully mixing the cocoa, pine-nuts, raisins and candied citron-peel and binding it all with 2 tablespoons of vinegar while still cold, if necessary adding 1-2 tablespoons of water.

Pour the mixture into the tongue cooking juices and return the pan to a gentle heat, stirring frequently with a wooden spoon. Taste so you can better judge the balance between the savoury and the sweet flavours (this mostly will depend on the amount of vinegar used) and keep on the flame just for the short time needed to blend all the ingredients well together. Draw the pan off the heat immediately so that the sauce does not separate out.

Allow the tongue to cool a little, carve it and serve with the sauce which is kept hot in a *bain-marie*.

This dish, a little complicated but truly sublime, has almost slipped into oblivion nowadays, but my father's eyes light up merely to hear it mentioned!

Lombatina ai funghi

LOIN OF VEAL WITH MUSHROOMS

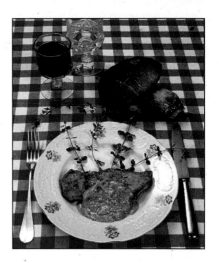

♦

- 4 LOIN OF VEAL CUT-LETS
- 2 *BOLETUS EDULIS* MUSHROOMS
- CATMINT
- 3 CLOVES OF GARLIC
- WHITE WINE
- WHITE FLOUR
- 50G MILD PECORINO CHEESE
- OLIVE OIL

♦

PREPARATION TIME: $^{1}/_{2}$ HOUR

FLATTEN THE CUTLETS, season with salt and pepper and leave to rest. Wipe the mushrooms over with a damp cloth. Slice thinly (stems included) and place on the hob, together with the garlic, catmint, 2 tablespoons of oil and a pinch of salt and pepper. Cook over medium heat for a quarter-hour and leave to cool. Slice the cheese and place in the centre of each cutlet along with a spoonful of the mushrooms. Fold the meat over into parcels, securing with a toothpick. Cook the meat in a frying pan with 2 tablespoons of oil for 10 minutes, seasoning lightly with salt. Transfer to a serving dish. Dissolve half a tea-spoon of flour in the cooking juices, add half a glass of white wine and allow to thicken, stirring over the heat. Mask the meat and serve immediately with sprigs of catmint.

Mozzarella in carrozza

MOZZARELLA IN A "CARRIAGE"

♦

- 1 MOZZARELLA CHEESE (ABOUT 300G)
- 8 SLICES OF BREAD
- 2 EGGS
- 2 TABLESPOONS MILK
- 200G FLOUR
- OLIVE OIL

♦

PREPARATION TIME: $^{1}/_{2}$ HOUR

IMMERSE THE BREAD devoid of crusts in a bowl where the egg has been beaten with the milk and a pinch of salt. Allow the bread to become well-impregnated, then cut the moz-zarella into 4 slices and sandwich each between two slices of bread. Dip first in the beaten egg, then in the flour, then once again in the egg, impregnating each side of the sandwich well. Fry in boiling oil. In order to make sure the sandwich is even-ly golden on both sides, adjust the heat and turn it over with two forks, being careful that the cheese does not leak out. The "carriage" (which comes from Naples, but has been cir-culating on Tuscan tables for a long time) is ready when the mozzarella begins to ooze out of the sides of the bread.

Lombatina con le olive

PORK CHOPS WITH BLACK OLIVES

- 4 PORK LOIN CHOPS, EACH ONE ABOUT 150G
- 2 CLOVES OF GARLIC
- 1/2L TOMATO PURÉE
- GARLICKY BLACK OLIVES
- ROSEMARY
- CHILLI PEPPER PASTE
- OLIVE OIL

PREPARATION TIME: 1/2 HOUR

THE CHOPS MUST HAVE a nice fatty border (if they are also on the bone, so much the better). Coat them with flour and cook them (with a piece of rosemary stuck into one side) in a frying pan with 4 tablespoons of oil. Keep over medium heat for a quarter-hour, being careful not to let them become tough and stringy.

Separately, in another pan, make a sauce by sautéing the garlic in 2 tablespoons of oil, throwing in the tomato and allowing to reduce. Lay the meat in the sauce, season with salt and pepper, add a little chilli pepper squeezed onto the tip of a teaspoon and cook over gentle heat for a few minutes. Then add the olives and turn the chops over in the sauce to absorb the flavours well.

Some advice? Do not skimp on the chilli pepper!

Pan ripieno con le rigaglie

GIBLET-STUFFED BREAD

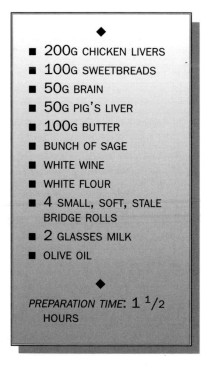

- 200G CHICKEN LIVERS
- 100G SWEETBREADS
- 50G BRAIN
- 50G PIG'S LIVER
- 100G BUTTER
- BUNCH OF SAGE
- WHITE WINE
- WHITE FLOUR
- 4 SMALL, SOFT, STALE BRIDGE ROLLS
- 2 GLASSES MILK
- OLIVE OIL

PREPARATION TIME: 1 1/2 HOURS

TAKE THE CRUMB out of each roll, cutting each lengthways and taking off the "lid". Douse the rolls in 2 cups of milk and leave to stand. Wash the giblets, cut them up roughly and brown in the butter in a saucepan with 2 or 3 sage leaves. Season with salt and pepper. Cook over medium heat for 10 minutes. Add the white wine, lower the flame, stir and continue cooking for another quarter-hour. Allow to cool a little, then chop finely (a *mezzaluna* is ideal here). Return the giblets to the saucepan, sprinkle some flour over, add a few tablespoons of water and cook over low heat for a few minutes. Season with salt and pepper, then spoon the giblet mixture into each roll. Arrange the *semellini* (this is how the Tuscans refer to their little, soft rolls made with oil) in a baking tin so that they are squashed up against each other. Drizzle over a trickle of olive oil and bake at 180°C. When the rolls are crisp, remove them from the oven, allow to rest just 5 minutes and serve them hot.

Peposo

PEPPERED STEW

- ■ 400G BEEF STEWING STEAK
- ■ 6 CLOVES OF GARLIC
- ■ 3 RIPE TOMATOES
- ■ 4 SLICES OF STALE TUS-CAN BREAD, TOASTED
- ■ SALT AND PEPPER

PREPARATION TIME: 2 TO 3 HOURS

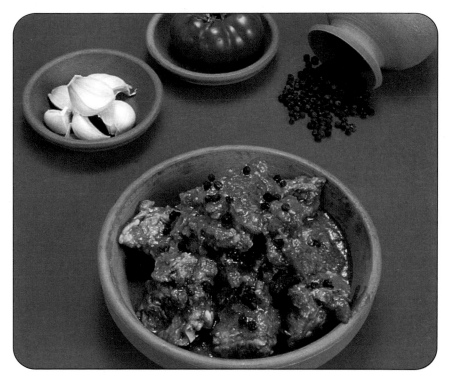

PLACE THE CUBED stewing steak in a deep saucepan with the chopped garlic and the tomatoes, skinned and roughly chopped. Season with salt judiciously and with as much pepper as you like (or peppercorns if you prefer). When I say "as you like", I mean a lot of pepper (the dish is not called *peposo* for nothing!), at least a full tablespoon. Pour in enough cold water to cover completely and cook very slowly, stirring from time to time. The dish will only be ready after some hours' cooking, two at least, maybe even three. Serve it all boiling hot over slices of toast. If the stew tends to dry out while cooking, add hot water so that the meat always has a little liquid to cook in.

HASTE IN THE KITCHEN is not in general an ingredient in the production of successful dishes, but, especially in this recipe, I should say that patience is indeed an essential element. In fact, *peposo* stew is indissolubly tied to the vigil watch of the furnace lads at Impruneta, in the hills behind Florence, who used to spend the whole night keeping an eye on the wood-fired ovens where the famous earthenware pots, bricks and vases were cooking. The cooking of *peposo* stew was then even lengthier than it is today, extending over even six to eight hours. The pots of stew were placed at the mouth of the furnace where the red terracotta was hardening and where the heat was low and even. Of course, nowadays, cooking times are shorter as the quality of meat available on the market does not need such long cooking. Pepper, which was at one time essential to cover strange flavours due to what could have been euphemistically defined as excessive ripening, today is merely an essential, irreplaceable component to give this great dish of Florentine tradition its exclusive flavour. You simply must try it if you want to say that you know something about the cuisine in these parts. If someone says to you, "After all, it is only a rather overcooked stew!", just point out (with a look of benevolent sympathy) that the difference between *peposo* and ordinary stew is the same difference between night (the night of the furnace lads) and day ....

Petto di fagianella

LITTLE BUSTARD HEN BREAST WITH GRAPES AND WALNUTS

TRY THIS RECIPE and then be objective - this is not a dish, it is a painting, the envy of the most beautiful Flemish still-lifes! It possesses all the softness, the tepidity and the clarity of the Tuscan autumn as soon as the summer heat fades. Just consider the ingredients: the velvety taste of the game bird, the warmth of the walnuts announcing the advent of the cold weather and the transparency of the grapes, imbued with the light of summer.

◆

- 1 LITTLE BUSTARD HEN, ABOUT 1.2KG IN WEIGHT
- 10 WALNUTS, SHELLED
- BUNCH OF WHITE GRAPES
- 50G BUTTER
- 1 GLASS SWEET VINSANTO
- 50G WHITE FLOUR
- $^{1}/_{2}$ GLASS MILK

◆

PREPARATION TIME: $^{1}/_{2}$ HOUR

WHY LITTLE BUSTARD HEN? (My love for this dish can be discerned in the adjective.) Because the flesh of the female, especially if young, is tenderer, assuring the success of the recipe. After cleaning the fowl (please see the recipe on page 95), cut out the breast and leave the rest of the bird for another recipe (perhaps you could stew it and then bone it to make a delicious sauce for spaghetti). Beat the breast (half-opened) to flatten evenly. Coat with flour and cook, together with salt and pepper, in 50g of butter for 5 minutes each side over medium heat. Baste frequently with half a glass of vinsanto. When the breast has coloured on both sides, place it on a serving dish. Blend half a teaspoon of flour into the cooking juices, add the remaining vinsanto and a little milk and return to a low heat, stirring continuously. Scrape the bottom of the pan with a spoon and add a dozen grapes (better if small) and the walnuts, shelled and crumbled in your fingers. As soon as the sauce thickens, correct for salt and pepper and mask the little bustard breast with it, garnishing the plate with vine leaves.

Petto di tacchino al tartufo

TRUFFLE-STUFFED TURKEY BREAST

- ■ ¹/₂KG TURKEY BREAST
- ■ 100G COOKED HAM
- ■ 40G MORTADELLA
- ■ 20G PARMESAN CHEESE
- ■ RAISIN WINE
- ■ 1 EGG
- ■ 20G WHITE TRUFFLE
- ■ 100G BUTTER
- ■ BREADCRUMB

PREPARATION TIME: 1 HOUR 10 MINUTES

CUT THE TURKEY BREAST into eight slices (not too thick). Beat them out and place in a bowl with 1 or 2 tablespoons of raisin wine and a little salt and pepper. Leave to stand for half-an-hour. Chop the ham and mortadella and add to two handfuls of breadcrumb previously soaked in milk and then pressed to squeeze the moisture out. Add the Parmesan cheese and the beaten egg. Combine by stirring the mixture well with a fork to and add the truffle, cut paper thin. Stuff the slices of turkey with the mixture, secure with a toothpick and cook them in butter in a pan over medium heat. Let the meat colour a little, turning it over on both sides, then baste with a liqueur glass of raisin wine and cook over a gentle flame for 20 minutes. Remove the meat from the pan and place on a serving dish. Put two tablespoons of water and one of raisin wine in the pan, raise the heat and scrape the bottom with a spoon. Spread the gravy over the meat and serve immediately. Applause!

Piccione alla diavola

DEVILLED PIGEON

- ■ 4 YOUNG PIGEONS
- ■ OLIVE OIL
- ■ SALT AND PEPPER

PREPARATION TIME: ³/₄ HOUR

REMOVE THE PIGEONS' necks and claws. Draw, singe and wash them, then beat a little to flatten. Brush liberally with oil, salt and very hot pepper. Allow the flavours to be absorbed, basting frequently for 10 minutes, at some distance from the heat.

Devilled pigeon cooked over a charcoal fire would be ideal, but a baking tin placed in a medium oven is fine. In this case, be sure to place a heavy saucepan lid on the pigeons and to turn them frequently so that they cook right through. Serve the birds well-cooked and doused in oil, having basted them while cooking with oil and lots of pepper. They are good hot, served with lettuce (the romaine or cos lettuce has greener, crisper leaves) or with boiled potatoes sprinkled with oil and freshly-ground pepper.

Pollastrina delicata

PULLET WITH A CREAM STUFFING

◆

- 1 SMALL CHICKEN, 1.2KG IN WEIGHT
- ^{1}/2L SINGLE CREAM
- 300G CHICKEN BREAST
- 2 EGGS
- 1 ONION
- 1 CARROT
- 1 STICK OF CELERY
- 1 SMALL TOMATO
- 400G ITALIAN ARBORIO RICE

◆

PREPARATION TIME: 2 HOURS

DRAW, SINGE AND WASH the pullet, removing the neck and claws. Save the liver and gizzard for other recipes.

Dry and season both inside and out with salt and leave to rest, wrapped in a dry tea towel. Then chop the chicken breast roughly, adding the lightly whipped cream, the salt and pepper.

Separately, beat the eggs and fold into the chicken breast mixture.

Stuff the chicken, sewing it up with kitchen string and being careful not to let the filling spill out.

Then, pour plenty of cold water into a roomy saucepan, add the vegetables (not the tomatoes) and place over moderate heat.

Wrap the chicken in a thin cloth that you will sew securely around the fowl, so that its delicate flesh will not break while on the boil.

I advise you not to use the nets on sale at butchers for this purpose because the strong tension of the elastic they are made from may end up cutting into the chicken flesh.

Carefully place the wrapped fowl in the pan and bring to the boil, leaving to cook for an hour and taking care that the flame is never too high.

Meanwhile, boil some rice in salted water, drain it absolutely *al dente* and serve as an accompaniment to the chicken that, once cooked, you will have untied with care and removed from the cloth it was wrapped in.

Make a bed of rice on a serving dish and lay the young chicken on top, garnish with segments of fresh tomato and serve with various sauces (not too piquant) such as, for example, a freshly-made Tuscan green sauce (the recipe is on page 41) or a light vinaigrette.

Pollo alla cacciatora

CHICKEN CACCIATORA

◆

- **1** CHICKEN, ABOUT 1 $^1/_2$KG IN WEIGHT
- **1** ONION
- **1** CARROT
- **1** STICK OF CELERY
- **4** RIPE TOMATOES
- A HANDFUL OF GARLICKY BLACK OLIVES
- WHITE FLOUR
- OLIVE OIL

◆

PREPARATION TIME: 1 $^1/_4$ HOURS

SINGE THE CHICKEN, wash it and draw it. Joint it (there will be about a dozen pieces if the chicken is nice and meaty) and coat with flour. Chop up the onion, carrot and celery and sauté in a saucepan with 4 tablespoons of oil, adding the chicken when the vegetables are on the point of turning golden. Brown for a few minutes over a high flame, turning the joints to impregnate the chicken with the vegetable flavours. Lower the heat and add the chopped tomatoes and olives. Correct for salt and pepper and leave to cook for 40 minutes, turning over the joints from time to time.

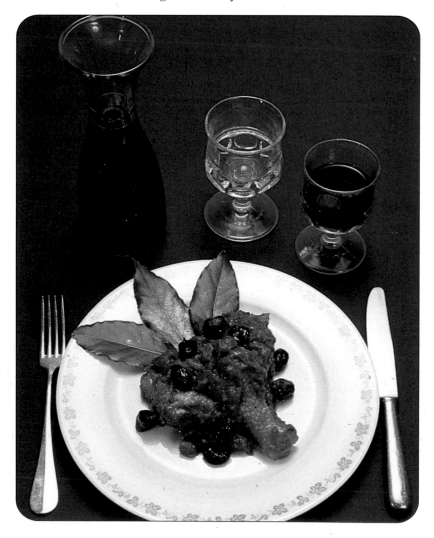

NOT INFREQUENTLY IS the preparation of this dish enriched with dried mushrooms (previously moistened in water).

I find, however, that the traditional recipe is the winning one as it does not mask the delicate flavour of the chicken meat.

With regard to the name, the origin of which is lost in the mists of time (can you really see hunters preparing such a delicacy with grace and patience?), any curiosity is bound to remain unsatisfied (at least here).

However, this is a dish that still today appears fairly frequently on Florentine and Tuscan tables, as it requires little fuss and the preparation time is short.

Pollo alla diavola

DEVILLED CHICKEN

- 1 CHICKEN, ABOUT 1KG IN WEIGHT
- BUNCH OF SAGE
- 1 LEMON
- OLIVE OIL

PREPARATION TIME: 1 HOUR

DOES THE TERM "DEVILLED" refer to all that pepper or to the fact that it is grilled over the flames of hell? If you do not have a barbecue with a charcoal fire, you could try with the grill on your cooker, but there is a difference!

CLEAN THE CHICKEN by removing the head, claws and insides. Wash and singe it. Open it like a book, cutting it along the breast bone, and flatten it evenly all over, dusting with salt, pepper and plenty of chopped sage.

Grill over the glowing charcoal for a quarter-hour on each side, basting with a brush dipped in olive oil and lemon. Serve hot, accompanied by lots of potato chips.

Pollo al mattone

CHICKEN UNDERNEATH A BRICK

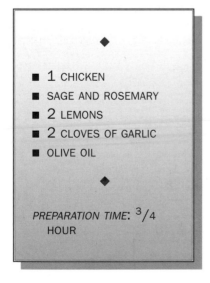

- 1 CHICKEN
- SAGE AND ROSEMARY
- 2 LEMONS
- 2 CLOVES OF GARLIC
- OLIVE OIL

PREPARATION TIME: 3/4 HOUR

CLEAN THE CHICKEN by drawing it, cutting off the claws and head, washing it and singeing it. Open it out like a book, cutting along the breast bone and beating it out, just like in the previous recipe. Chop the herbs finely (if you like, 2 crushed cloves of garlic can be added) and sprinkle over the chicken, brushing with oil. Place on the grill over a glowing charcoal fire. While cooking is proceeding over a nice, crackling fire, crush the chicken underneath a heavy clay brick. It should remain so for half-an-hour, during which time you will turn it frequently (without forgetting to baste it with oil and to season with salt and pepper) so that it cooks on both sides, every time covering it up again with the brick. Serve hot and sprinkle liberally with lemon juice.

Pollo fritto

FRIED CHICKEN

◆

- **1** SPRING CHICKEN
- **3** EGGS
- **250G** WHITE FLOUR
- OLIVE OIL

◆

PREPARATION TIME: **1** HOUR

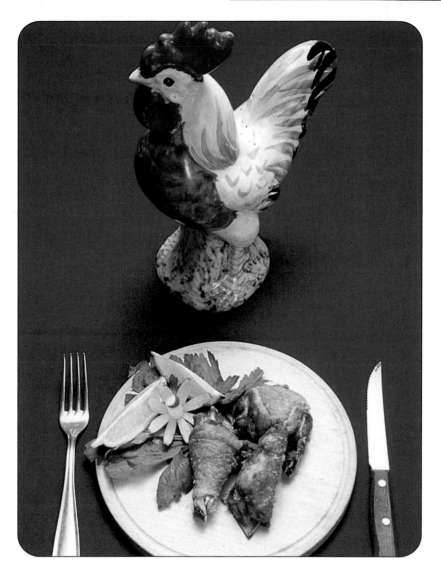

FRIED FOOD REPRESENTS one of the mainstays of Florentine culinary traditions. Indeed, there is a saying which goes like this, "Even an old shoe is good if fried", meaning that even the humblest strip of leathery meat can cut a figure if fried properly. Our cuisine reaches its acme with our mammoth fry-up of chicken, rabbit, brains, sweetbreads, zucchini, zucchini flowers and globe artichokes, all together, adding, if you wish, potatoes and onions. A real triumph for the eye and the palate - provided that the secret of our fry-up is known and respected (something we witness more and more rarely on both family and restaurant tables). It goes without saying that the secret is in the olive oil, in its quality and purity. Perfect for use in any preparation, whether cooked or uncooked, it is essential if you want a good, crisp fry.

C UT THE CHICKEN into small pieces, rinse and dry them. Beat the eggs in a bowl with a pinch of salt, and dunk the chicken pieces in it, leaving them to stand for about 20 minutes. Stir well from time to time so that the chicken is well-impregnated. When you are ready to fry, sprinkle the flour into the bowl and let the egg absorb it thoroughly. It is fundamental that each piece of chicken be well imbued with the mixture. Heat the oil (lots of it and strictly of olives) to the correct temperature in a large frying pan and fry the chicken in it for 20 minutes. Keep the flame low to start with, raising it towards the end to give that final golden colour which is indispensable when frying. Serve *in tavola* with lemon wedges as soon as you have drained off the oil.

Pollo in fricassea coi funghi

Chicken in a Lemon-Mushroom Sauce

- 1 CHICKEN, ABOUT 1KG IN WEIGHT
- 50G BUTTER
- 1 ONION
- 1 CARROT
- $^1/_2$ GLASS STOCK
- HANDFUL DRIED *BOLETUS EDULIS* MUSHROOMS
- 50G WHITE FLOUR
- 2 EGGS
- 1 LEMON
- OLIVE OIL

PREPARATION TIME: 1 HOUR

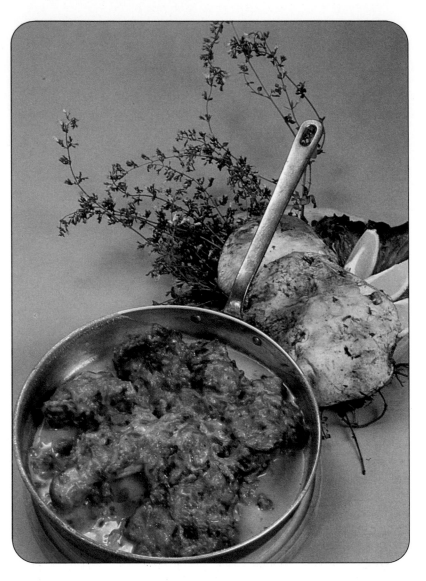

S OFTEN THE mushrooms for 20 minutes in half a glass of hot stock. Meanwhile, clean the chicken and joint into about 10-12 portions. Make a mirepoix of finely-chopped onion and carrot, sautéed in 2 tablespoons of oil and 50g of butter. Add the dried and floured chicken pieces. Turn them over, cover the pan and cook over medium heat for about half-an-hour. Then add the mushrooms. Cook some ten minutes more, stirring carefully. Remove the meat from the pan, beat the egg yolks together with the lemon juice and pour into the pan, strictly off the heat. Return the chicken to the pan and stir gently, binding the sauce with one or two tablespoons of hot water.

Serve this dish hot, with lots of creamy sauce. Remember that a fricassee cannot be re-heated and above all, remember to carry out the last operation off the heat.

Polpette 1
CROQUETTES OR RISSOLES I

- 300G LEAN MINCED MEAT (OR BOILED LEFT-OVERS)
- 1 GLASS OF MILK
- KNOB OF BUTTER
- 1 TABLESPOON FLOUR
- PARMESAN CHEESE
- 2 BOILED POTATOES
- PARSLEY
- 3 EGGS
- 250G DRIED BREAD-CRUMBS
- OLIVE OIL

PREPARATION TIME: $^1/2$ HOUR

SCALD THE MINCED MEAT briefly in a tablespoon of oil (this will not be necessary if it is boiled meat; it must, however, all be chopped up). Make a béchamel sauce with the milk, butter and flour and when it thickens, add to the meat in a bowl. Also add two tablespoons of grated Parmesan cheese, the potatoes (boiled and mashed with a fork), the chopped parsley and the three beaten eggs. Combine everything together well, form into little, smooth balls, flatten them a little and roll in the dried bread-crumbs. Fry in boiling oil, turning them over carefully so that they cook evenly. Place them on a sheet of brown paper on a serving dish and serve them up hot, garnished with wedges of lemon.

Polpette 2
CROQUETTES OR RISSOLES II

- 300G LEAN MINCED (OR BOILED) MEAT
- 2 EGGS
- 2 CLOVES OF GARLIC
- A LITTLE BREADCRUMB
- 1 CUP OF MILK
- 200G DRIED BREAD-CRUMBS
- OLIVE OIL

PREPARATION TIME: 40 MINUTES

STEEP THE BREADCRUMB in the milk for 10 minutes. Add chopped parsley and garlic to the meat, along with two whole eggs, salt and pepper, working it all in well. Then add the breadcrumb, with most of the moisture pressed out, and mix in thoroughly. Roll the mixture into little, round, close-packed balls, slightly flattened. Drop them into the dried breadcrumbs and fry in hot oil, browning them all over. If you have used raw minced meat, keepk the heat low so that they cook right through. They are also good eaten cold.

THE AUTHENTIC FLORENTINE custom is to complete the dish with a tomato sauce (4 tablespoons of olive oil, ripe tomatoes cut up small and 2 cloves of garlic cooked for 15 minutes). Put the already-fried croquettes into the sauce and return to the flame for another 5 minutes. Serve with boiled potatoes.

Polpettone
MEAT ROLL

- 300G LEAN MINCED MEAT
- 30G MORTADELLA
- 30G SALAMI
- 2 EGGS
- A LITTLE BREADCRUMB
- 1 GLASS OF MILK
- 200G FLOUR
- WHITE WINE
- OLIVE OIL

PREPARATION TIME: 1 HOUR

Soak the breadcrumb in the milk for 10 minutes. Separately mix the minced meat and the chopped salami and mortadella. Add the beaten eggs and the breadcrumb, first having pressed out the milk. Season with salt and pepper. Work the mixture into the shape of a dumpy sausage. Roll in flour and place in a wide pan with 6 tablespoons of oil. Cover and allow to brown over low heat. When an even, brown crust has formed, turn the roll over, pour in half a glass of wine and cook for 40 minutes. When the *polpettone* is ready, allow to cool a little before slicing it up and masking with the gravy left in the pan.

THE MEAT ROLL is good served cold in summer, but then it is better boiled rather than pot-roasted and served with mayonnaise and boiled vegetables. To cook the meat, the water should not be allowed to go beyond a slight rippling of the surface ("simmering point"), otherwise there is a risk of the mixture breaking up.

Poppa al pepolino
CALF'S UDDER WITH SAVORY SAUCE

- 4 HALF-INCH SLICES OF CALF'S UDDER
- FRESH SAVORY
- $1/2$L TOMATO PURÉE
- 2 CLOVES OF GARLIC
- 1 EGG
- 100G BREADCRUMBS
- OLIVE OIL

PREPARATION TIME: $1/2$ HOUR

Put the slices of udder in the beaten egg and leave for 10 minutes. Drain and coat with dried breadcrumbs. Fry in boiling oil in a frying pan, turning them to brown on both sides. Draw off the heat and dry on brown paper. Make a sauce by heating the cloves of garlic in 2 tablespoons of oil in a saucepan. When the garlic begins to sizzle, add the tomato purée and the savory, season with salt and pepper and reduce over moderate heat for 10 minutes. Place the slices of udder in the saucepan and return briefly to the boil. Finally, serve them nice and hot, masked with the savory sauce.

Quaglie coi fichi

QUAILS WITH BLACK FIGS

- 8 QUAILS
- 10 SMALL, BLACK FIGS
- 8 THICK BACON RASHERS
- 2 CHICKEN LIVERS
- 100G BUTTER
- 1 GLASS OF *GRAPPA* (ITALIAN *EAU DE VIE*)
- JUNIPER BERRIES

PREPARATION TIME: 1 HOUR

NOWADAYS ONE CAN buy quails already cleaned and singed, so they just need careful washing. Season with salt and pepper inside and out and leave to stand on a cloth. Remove the hard stalk from the black figs (nice and ripe and red on the inside) and chop roughly, whereas the chicken livers are chopped finely and added. Season with a pinch of salt and pepper. Stuff the quails with this mixture, adding a juniper berry to each one and seal with the bacon by wrapping it around the bird lengthways.

Use toothpicks to secure, if necessary, and arrange the quails in a meat tin with flakes of butter.

Make sure that the birds' wings are fixed underneath, so that they do not work free while cooking thus taking on a rather uninviting aspect! Bake in a hot oven for at least half-an-hour, basting with very little stock which is then replaced with *eau-de-vie* towards the end. When cooked, place the quail on a serving dish garnished with fig leaves (choose the smallest ones). Add a little flour and 2 tablespoons of *grappa* to the cooking juices in the meat tin and allow to heat through for a moment. Mask the quails liberally with the gravy and enjoy them especially in September, when figs are at the height of their flavour and the spent green of the fig leaves merrily offsets the blue of the late summer sky.

Quaglie sul crostone
CROUTE OF QUAILS

◆

- **8** QUAILS
- **8** THIN SLICES OF BACON
- **1** MEDIUM ONION
- **1** CARROT
- **$^1/_2$** STICK OF CELERY
- **3-4** BAY LEAVES
- DRY WHITE WINE
- **1** GLASS VEGETABLE STOCK
- KNOB OF BUTTER
- **1** TABLESPOON FLOUR
- STALE TUSCAN BREAD, TOASTED
- OLIVE OIL

◆

PREPARATION TIME: **1** HOUR

CLEAN AND SINGE the quails. Wrap each one in thin strips of bacon which, if necessary, can be secured with toothpicks.

Place in a frying pan with 6 tablespoons of oil and add the vegetables securely tied in a bundle for easy and complete removal when it is time to make the sauce. Season lightly with salt and pepper.

Sauté for about 25-30 minutes, gradually adding the white wine, always over a medium heat and without covering the pan.

Then remove the quails and the bundle of vegetables and add the butter off the heat (it will melt in the hot cooking juices), 1-2 tablespoons of stock and a tablespoon of flour to thicken the sauce. Return to the heat and correct for salt and pepper according to taste and, if necessary, thin the sauce with stock.

Toast the bread in the meantime and dunk in the stock. Arrange two pieces on each dinner plate and top each one with a quail, dousing it all with the sauce (nice and hot, please).

Serve with a garnish of bay leaves. Remember to remove the toothpicks from the quails before serving them....

Rognoni alla fiorentina
FLORENTINE KIDNEYS

◆

- 2 CALF'S KIDNEYS
- 100G BUTTER
- PARSLEY
- 100G DRIED BREAD-
CRUMBS

◆

PREPARATION TIME: 2
HOURS

SKIN THE KIDNEYS and rinse in cold, running water for at least half an hour (the reason is easy to appreciate; they must not start cooking beforehand). Remove the core with your hands and cut the kidneys lengthways. Heat the butter in a saucepan and when it froths throw in the kidneys, after having dried them well.

Cook them briefly, then draw off the heat and turn them in a mixture of chopped parsley, dried breadcrumbs, salt and pepper. Leave them for at least an hour to absorb the flavour well, then roll once more in the dried breadcrumbs and return them to the heat in the same saucepan, adding a knob of butter. Cook gently for at least 10 minutes. Serve very hot.

THE KIDNEYS ARE also very good grilled.

In this case, regulate the heat of the charcoal fire or the grill adjustment on your cooker so that they cook right through.

The meat is excellent if it comes out tender. If not, it will need some further cooking over a gentle heat.

Salsicce e fagioli
SAUSAGES AND BEANS

- 400G *CANNELLINI* BEANS
- 5 GARLICKY, WELL-SEASONED SAUSAGES
- SPRIG OF SAGE
- $^1/_2$L TOMATO PURÉE
- 3 CLOVES OF GARLIC
- OLIVE OIL

PREPARATION TIME: 1 $^1/_2$ HOURS

COOK THE BEANS for 40 minutes (2 hours if dried, after a 2-hour soaking). Cut the sausages into short lengths and cook in a pan with 2 cloves of garlic and the sage. Cook slowly, piercing them so that they cook right through. They should be cooked, but crisp, not boiled. At this point, add the tomato purée, season with salt and pepper and reduce over moderate heat for a further 10 minutes. Add the beans, draining them well and combine the flavours over gentle heat, stirring carefully with a wooden spoon.

SAUSAGES AND BEANS, a strapping, tasty combination, softened by the aroma of the sage, garlic and tomato, ideal for warming up a cold winter's evening.

But they are also very good eaten in the summer, served up in a buffet, for example, as the highlight among the cold meats, cheeses and quality wines....

Salsicce e uva
SAUSAGES AND GRAPES

- 6 LEAN, GARLICKY SAUSAGES
- BUNCH OF BLACK COOKING GRAPES
- 50G BUTTER
- 1 GLASS RED WINE

PREPARATION TIME: $^1/_2$ HOUR

MELT THE BUTTER in a saucepan. Cut the sausages to pieces (if you can get small, tasty, wild boar sausages, use about ten of them, moistened with a little water to help the cooking along) and brown over a moderate flame for 10 minutes. Swill with wine, add the grapes, bring briefly to the boil and serve nice and hot.

AT GRAPE HARVESTING time, the aroma of sausages cooked with grapes and wine wafted over the air, almost symbolically linking the ongoing harvest to the previous year's. There were huge, steaming pots on the wooden boards under the portico where everybody tucked in, dunking their bread in the sauce....

Sella con le mele

RABBIT WITH APPLES

- 4 SADDLES OF RABBIT
- 4 EATING APPLES
- 1 GLASS DRY WHITE WINE
- ROSEMARY
- 2 TABLESPOONS SUGAR
- 2 TABLESPOONS BRANDY
- OLIVE OIL

PREPARATION TIME: 3/4 HOUR

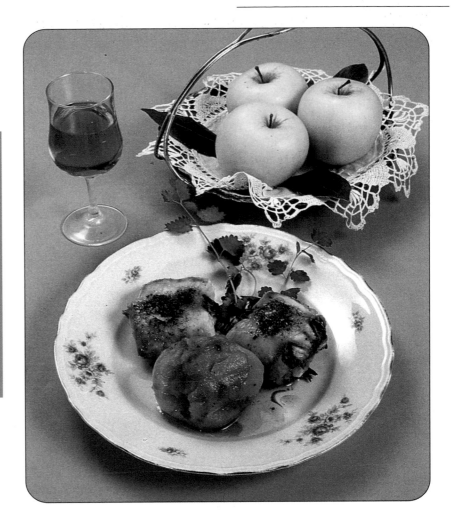

THIS DISH CANNOT BE found in "orthodox" Florentine recipe books. As if our gastronomy did not keep up with the times and did not continually enrich itself with new preparations and new ideas, due to the creative contributions of gourmets and as a consequence of the incessant modification of alimentary tastes and customs!

Let us therefore make room for a delicious novelty, especially if (as in this case) the delicate and masterly balance of the rabbit meat contrasted with the sugar and apples (a combination in honour of those anglobeceri or English expatriates who have loved and ennobled Florence so much) rightfully collocates it in the central groove of our higher and more authentic culinary tradition.

RINSE THE SADDLES and stud with rosemary, salt and pepper. Place in a casserole dish with 3 tablespoons of oil and bake in a hot oven for a quarter-hour. Peel and core the apples with the special implement, blanche for a moment in boiling water and add to the rabbit. Douse with brandy and return the dish to the oven for at least another 20 minutes.

Then, remove the well browned and golden rabbit and apples from the pot and arrange on a serving dish.

Put 2 tablespoons of sugar in the cooking juices left in the pot, allowing to dissolve over low heat and, when just about to caramelise, scrape the bottom well with a spoon and add the white wine.

Let this gravy thicken, binding if necessary with two drops of hot water. Mask the meat and the apples with the gravy and serve hot.

Spiedini alla fiorentina

FLORENTINE SPIT ROAST

- **300**G PIG'S LIVER
- **200**G LOIN OF PORK
- **100**G PORK NET (CAUL FAT)
- **3** GARLICKY SAUSAGES
- STALE BREAD
- SAGE AND BAY LEAVES
- OLIVE OIL

PREPARATION TIME: 3/4 HOUR

THESE SKEWERS WERE originally completed with lark, thrush, starling and chaffinch, almost impossible to find nowadays.

Well, not impossible if you are quite happy with just watching them fluttering or hopping around; what is difficult, to the chagrin of hunters and gourmands, is to track them down in a state of decease, ready for the pot.

I remember the fuss that was made in honour of my grandfather's companions in the shooting party when they returned from hunting, with the spit roasts browning in front of the fire while the fat dripped sizzling into the glowing charcoal.

Besides, autumn, hunters and spit roasts have always gone together as the poet Carducci says in his *Martinmas in the Tuscan Maremma.*

DIVIDE THE LIVER INTO 2-inch cubes. Rinse and soften the pork net in tepid water and cut into small squares for wrapping the liver pieces in. Cube the loin and sausages, as well. Cut the stale bread into fingers, preferably using the crusty side, which will toast nicely when cooked on the spit.

Thread the skewers, systematically alternating the ingredients, and always placing one leaf of bay and one of sage next to the meat cubes (in other words, a slice of bread, bay leaf, liver, sage, bread, bay leaf, loin of pork, sage and so on up the skewer). Season with salt and pepper.

Put the prepared skewers to turn on the spit in front of a fire, brushing frequently with oil. If you do not have a fireplace, use a slow oven, arranging the skewers in a roasting tin with a trickle of oil and only seasoning with salt and pepper when half cooked, at the moment that you turn them.

Stracotto
BRAISED BEEF

- 1KG SIRLOIN
- 1 MEDIUM ONION
- 1 CARROT
- 1 STICK OF CELERY
- 300G RIPE TOMATOES
- 1 GLASS RED WINE
- OLIVE OIL

PREPARATION TIME: 2 HOURS

PRESUPPOSITION: the sirloin should be larded as for roast beef. Season the meat with salt and pepper and put aside while you prepare a mirepoix with the finely-chopped vegetables. Sauté in a saucepan with 4 tablespoons of oil. When the mirepoix is nicely browned, add the meat, the tomatoes, salt and pepper and cook over strong heat for 10 minutes. Douse with red wine, lower the flame and proceed with cooking over low heat for about an hour-and-a-half.

THE MEAT MUST END UP a nice brown colour, well cooked, i.e. very tender, with a sauce that lends itself to serving with boiled or mashed potatoes. My mother-in-law usually increases the quantity of onions and reduces the tomatoes almost to nothing.

Perhaps this method is closer to the age-old recipe, when tomatoes had not yet crossed the Atlantic.

However, the secret lies above all in the cook's patience; she will dedicate herself with love and care, stirring the sauce and keeping the flame just right so that cooking is slow and gentle.

Stufato con peperoni e patate
STEW WITH SWEET PEPPERS AND POTATOES

- 600G STEWING BEEF
- 2 ONIONS
- CELERY AND CARROT
- 4 RIPE TOMATOES
- 2 YELLOW SWEET PEPPERS
- 2 POTATOES
- BASIL
- OLIVE OIL

PREPARATION TIME: 2 HOURS

CHOP THE ONION, celery and carrot up roughly and brown in 4 tablespoons of oil. When almost ready (a quarter-hour over medium heat), add the cubed meat and raise the flame a little. Stir with a wooden spoon and cook for 5 minutes. Add the tomatoes (or purée) and salt. Lower the heat and cover with the lid. Cook the stew slowly for an hour, stirring from time to time. Cut the potatoes, duly peeled and washed, and sweet peppers into quite large pieces. Add to the stew and cook with the lid on for a further 15/20 minutes over gentle heat. With a fork, try the meat. If cooked (an hour-and-a-half should be enough, if the quality of the meat is good), it will be very tender. Serve with a sprinkling of freshly-ground pepper and a little fresh, chopped basil to taste.

Stufato coi funghi

VEAL STEW WITH MUSHROOMS

- 1/2KG VEAL STEWING STEAK
- 1 SMALL ONION
- 2 CLOVES OF GARLIC
- SPRIG OF CATMINT
- 300G FRESH *BOLETUS EDULIS* MUSHROOMS
- 1/2L TOMATO PURÉE
- 1 GLASS VEGETABLE STOCK
- OLIVE OIL

PREPARATION TIME: 1 HOUR

CHOP UP THE ONION and garlic and place in a saucepan on the heat with 4 tablespoons of oil. Cube the stewing steak, each piece being the size of a walnut. When the onion begins to colour, add the veal and brown well over fierce heat for 5 minutes, stirring frequently with a wooden spoon. Add the stock and continue to cook over very low heat for a further 20 minutes. Meanwhile, clean the mushrooms thoroughly and slice them paper thin (include the stems, too, if they are unblemished). Now add the tomato purée and the mushrooms to the meat and aromatise with a sprig of catmint. Cook with the lid on for 20 minutes over medium heat, then serve the stew steaming hot. To test whether cooked well enough, prod the meat with a fork. It should feel very tender, otherwise boil the stew up a little more, if necessary adding a few tablespoons of stock. The stew is delicious if served with cornmeal which has been cooked slowly.

Tordi allo spiedo

THRUSH ON THE SPIT

- ■ 8 THRUSHES
- ■ 2 SAUSAGES
- ■ 200G PIG'S LIVER
- ■ 100G PORK NET (CAUL FAT)
- ■ SAGE AND BAY LEAVES
- ■ TUSCAN-STYLE BREAD
- ■ OLIVE OIL

PREPARATION TIME: 40 MINUTES

CLEAN THE THRUSHES (they are quite a task to find, but, with a little patience, not impossible). Thread them onto skewers, alternating with a slice of bread, a bay leaf, a piece of liver wrapped in caul fat, a piece of sausage, a sage leaf, a thrush, then beginning again with the bread and so on until the skewer has been filled up (it will have to be quite long to accommodate at least two birds with a reasonable number of all the ingredients in order).

Moisten each skewer with a brush dipped in oil, salt and pepper and cook on a spit for 20 minutes, basting frequently so that the ingredients do not dry out or char. If you do not have a spit, the kitchen oven is fine, regulated on moderate heat. Cook the skewers in a meat tin, with the oven door left ajar so that you can baste them often.

Tordi scappati

BEEF BIRDS

- ■ 8 SLICES OF BEEF, EACH WEIGHING ABOUT 30G
- ■ 8 SLIVERS NOT TOO SALTY HAM
- ■ 16 SAGE LEAVES
- ■ GLASS OF WHITE WINE
- ■ GLASS OF STOCK
- ■ KNOB OF BUTTER
- ■ 1 TABLESPOON FLOUR
- ■ OLIVE OIL

PREPARATION TIME: 1 $^1/_2$ HOURS

BEAT OUT THE SLICES AND LAY a sliver of ham and two little sage leaves on each one. Roll them up and secure each with a toothpick. Brown the roulades in 3 tablespoons of oil in a saucepan over moderate heat for a quarter-hour, gradually pouring the white wine over. Then add a pinch of salt and pepper (remember the salty ham) and moisten with 2-3 tablespoons of stock. Cook for about an hour, adding stock, if necessary. Serve the roulades with the gravy made by binding the cooking juices with a tablespoon of flour and a knob of butter.

EVEN THOUGH MENTION is made of *tordi* or thrushes in the title, they are, of course, "on the wing"! This is merely the way the Florentines have (as usual mocking and picturesque) of referring to beef olives which, at first sight, may even resemble chubby little birds, but which (luckily for us, as they are truly delicious) do not take flight… My grandmother used to cook her "birds on the wing" with the addition of a juniper berry in each roulade.

Trippa alla fiorentina
FLORENTINE TRIPE

■ 1KG TRIPE
■ 2 RED-SKINNED ONIONS
■ 2 CARROTS
■ HEAD OF CELERY
■ 1/2KG CANNED TOMA-TOES
■ PARMESAN CHEESE
■ OLIVE OIL

PREPARATION TIME: 2 HOURS

WASH THE TRIPE and cut it into finger-length strips. Make a mire-poix in 6 tablespoons of oil in a saucepan. Add the tripe and, stirring frequently with a wooden spoon, blend the flavours well. When, after 20 minutes' cooking, some of the liquor has seeped out of the tripe, add the drained tomatoes, salt and pepper and cook for another hour over moderate heat, stirring frequently. Serve the tripe hot, with the addition of Parmesan cheese.

A MORE LUXURIOUS version of this dish encompasses the addition of minced meat to the mire-poix which is a quarter-cooked before throwing in the tripe. I find that this variation makes the dish a little heavy (it is tasty enough on its own) and that the flavour of the minced meat does not marry well with tripe. However, this dish of ours, known the world over, is still today cooked in Florentine homes, seeing as the raw material, economical and of first-rate quality, is readily available.

Trippa al vin bianco
TRIPE COOKED IN WHITE WINE

■ 800G TRIPE
■ 4 CARROTS
■ 2 WHITE-SKINNED ONIONS
■ 250G BUTTER
■ 1L DRY WHITE WINE
■ CHOPPED PARSLEY

PREPARATION TIME: 2 1/2 HOURS

CHOP THE ONIONS and carrots finely into a roomy saucepan and sauté gently in the butter.

When golden, add the tripe, previously washed and shredded.

Cook for 2 hours over low heat, stirring frequently and gradually adding the white wine.

Season with salt and pepper and serve the tripe hot, with a dusting of Parmesan cheese.

I DISCOVERED THIS DISH thanks to my maternal grandmother who lived in the country and who, having but a few things to hand, used to splash out on wine to ring the changes and add more flavour to humble dishes, among which one was tripe.

Trippa con la zampa
TRIPE AND CALF'S FOOT

- 1KG TRIPE
- 1 CALF'S FOOT
- ONION, CARROT AND CELERY
- 500G TOMATOES
- VEGETABLE STOCK
- PARMESAN

PREPARATION TIME: 2 HOURS

BOIL THE CALF'S FOOT and cut into thin strips. Sauté the onion, carrot and celery in 4 tablespoons of oil. Wash the tripe and cut into finger strips.

When the vegetables turn golden in colour, add the tomatoes and cook for 10 minutes. Then add the tripe and the calf's foot and continue cooking over low heat for about an hour and a half, stirring often and regulating the salt and pepper.

If necessary, add the vegetable stock little by little, so that the tripe always has a watery sauce to cook in.

Serve nice and hot, dusting with Parmesan cheese at the last instant.

Trippa in fricassea
TRIPE IN A LEMON SAUCE

- 800G TRIPE
- 2 CLOVES OF GARLIC
- PARSLEY, TIED IN A BUN- DLE
- $^1/_2$L VEGETABLE STOCK
- 4 EGGS
- 2 LEMONS
- 150G BUTTER
- OLIVE OIL

PREPARATION TIME: 2 HOURS

WASH THE TRIPE and cut into inch strips. Put into a saucepan with the garlic, the parsley (tied in a bundle for easy removal), the butter and 3 tablespoons of oil. Cook over moderate heat for half-an-hour, allowing the tripe to exude its liquor. Stir frequently with a wooden spoon. Season with salt and pepper and cook a further hour, adding stock, if necessary. Take out the garlic and parsley and remove the tripe from the saucepan, draining off the cooking juices, half of which are to be discarded. Beat the egg yolks, adding the lemon juice and pour at once into the saucepan without returning it to the heat. Add the tripe. Still off the heat, stir the tripe in its sauce and serve. Garnish with segments of lemon and dust with chopped parsley.

Uccellini finti

VEAL BIRDS

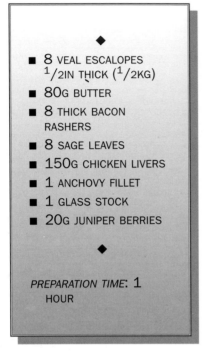

- ■ 8 VEAL ESCALOPES 1/2IN THICK (1/2KG)
- ■ 80G BUTTER
- ■ 8 THICK BACON RASHERS
- ■ 8 SAGE LEAVES
- ■ 150G CHICKEN LIVERS
- ■ 1 ANCHOVY FILLET
- ■ 1 GLASS STOCK
- ■ 20G JUNIPER BERRIES

PREPARATION TIME: 1 HOUR

CLEAN AND RINSE the chicken livers, chop up and sauté in the butter for 10 minutes. Soften up the veal escalopes with a meat tenderiser. Bone and rinse the anchovy, break it up in your fingers and add to the livers with the stock. Bring to the boil. Season with salt and pepper and add the juniper berries. Spread a tablespoon of the mixture over the veal slices. Roll them up and finish by wrapping them in the bacon rashers. Add a sage leaf to each and secure with two toothpicks. Arrange the veal birds in a square, heat-resistant dish and place on the hob for 15 minutes, until they colour nicely. Sprinkle with a tablespoon of stock and finish cooking over gentle heat for 10 minutes.

THESE USED TO BE rolled in lard, but I find that bacon imparts a good flavour to the dish, without making it too heavy to digest. Just like in the case of the "Tordi scappati" or "Birds on the Wing" which I mentioned previously, the name refers to the final aspect of the dish, which recalls little birds, particularly the chubby thrush.

Umido di rigaglie al tartufo

CHICKEN GIBLET STEW WITH TRUFFLES

- ■ 200G CHICKEN LIVERS
- ■ 100G COCKSCOMBS
- ■ 50G GIZZARDS
- ■ A LITTLE STOCK
- ■ 1 WHITE-SKINNED ONION
- ■ PARSLEY
- ■ 40G TRUFFLE
- ■ BURRO

PREPARATION TIME: 1 HOUR

CLEAN THE CHICKEN LIVERS (removing the gall bladder carefully), scald the cockscombs and rinse them. Scald the gizzards in boiling water, then cool them. Finely chop the onion and sauté in a knob of butter in a saucepan over low heat. Chop the giblets and throw them into the saucepan as soon as the onion turns golden. Add stock, chopped parsley, salt and pepper. Cook over a medium flame for 20 minutes, stirring with a wooden spoon. Warm 4 individual earthenware bowls, pour into each a portion of the giblets and slice some truffle very finely over the top. Serve hot, with toast and butter curls served on lettuce leaves.

THE GIZZARD IS the thick-walled stomach that birds have to grind hard food by muscular action. That of farmyard fowl is particularly well-developed, though not too hard, and is mild to taste.

Valigiette

STUFFED CABBAGE LEAVES

◆

- 1 SAVOY CABBAGE
- 400G LEAN MINCED MEAT (OR BOILED LEFT-OVERS)
- 1 CLOVE OF GARLIC
- 2 EGGS
- 1 TABLESPOON PARME-SAN CHEESE
- SPRIG OF PARSLEY
- 300G TOMATO PURÉE
- OLIVE OIL
- CHILLI PEPPER

◆

PREPARATION TIME: 1 1/4 HOURS

DISCARD THE EXTERNAL LEAVES (too woody) of a nice Savoy cabbage. Choose some lovely, big leaves with reasonably tender midribs, pull them off the main stem and cook in boiling salted water for 10 minutes. Drain one by one with the aid of a skimmer and lay them out to dry on a tea towel. Make the stuffing with the minced meat (or finely-cut boiled meat), the eggs, the garlic and the chopped parsley.

Combine the ingredients and heat over the flame for 10 minutes. Take a spoonful of the mixture and place on each cabbage leaf, which you will then wrap up tightly in your fingers to make firmly-closed parcels.

Arrange them in a saucepan with 8 tablespoons of oil and cook slowly for 20 minutes. Then add the well-drained tomatoes and, turning the "suitcases" over carefully, season with salt and pepper (or chilli pepper) to taste.

Cook for a further 20 minutes. These are very good eaten either hot or cold, perhaps sprinkled with some Parmesan cheese.

I CAN JUST PICTURE my mother-in-law's hands in the act of preparing the "suitcases" and pressing them a little to get the stuffing to stick to the leaves. On reading the recipe, some may wonder that I do not suggest binding the parcels with kitchen string, to be removed once cooked. Well, if you are careful, the well-wrapped parcels will stay hermetically closed!

Vitella, trippa e zampa

VEAL, TRIPE AND CALF'S FOOT IN A LEMON SAUCE

- 300G BEST END OF VEAL
- 1 CALF'S FOOT
- 1/2KG TRIPE
- 3 EGG YOLKS
- 2 CLOVES OF GARLIC
- 1 LEMON
- 1 TEASPOON SUGAR
- SPRIG OF PARSLEY
- 200G PEAS, SHELLED AND SWEET
- SMALL, FLOURY POTATOES
- 1 WHITE-SKINNED ONION
- 1 CARROT
- OLIVE OIL

PREPARATION TIME: 2 HOURS

ON TACKLING THE explanation of this recipe, I will assume that you have been provided with both the calf's foot and the tripe already cleaned and ready for use. Chop the onion and sauté in 4 tablespoons of oil in a deep saucepan. When it starts to colour, add the cubed veal, salt and pepper and cook over moderate heat. Scald the calf's foot in a saucepan with a carrot, an onion and a sprig of parsley for about half-an-hour. Leave to cool a little. Wash the tripe, cut into strips half an inch wide and place in a bowl where you will add the calf's foot, this also having been cut into strips. Cook the peas in very little water in a saucepan, adding a trickle of oil, a little lemon peel, a teaspoon of sugar, a pinch of salt, the garlic and a little chopped parsley. Cook over medium heat for 15 minutes - no longer, otherwise they might turn into a mush. Also put the potatoes in their skins in cold, lightly-salted water and bring to the boil for a quarter-hour. Drain with care and leave to cool wrapped in a cloth. When the veal is cooked (about three quarters of an hour will be needed) add the strips of tripe and calf's foot as well and boil more rapidly for ten minutes. Beat the egg yolks with the lemon juice separately and, off the heat, pour into the saucepan. Stir, always following the same direction.

Serve the meats with their sauce placing a spoonful of hot peas and one or two spoonfuls of warm, peeled potatoes on each dinner plate. Dust with chopped parsley.

THE COMBINATION OF TRIPE and calf's foot forms a "classic" dish in Florentine cooking, or rather it used to be so, though now this ancient dish is missing from family dinners and restaurant menus. This is a pity and I am not the only one to grieve; there are also many other authors of books about Tuscan cooking. It is a twofold pity, because this is an emblematic recipe of a cuisine where perhaps the principal concept lies in making delicacies out of simple, cheap ingredients (I like to think that the virtue of being able to extract the nice, good side of what is lowly or despised is, or used to be, a quality which is typically Tuscan and especially Florentine). I therefore bring to your attention this personal interpretation of a classic combination, which seems to me particularly successful in virtue of its association with veal, as well as complete thanks to the presence of the vegetables and also suitable for modern stomachs (a little more delicate and demanding than those of our forefathers) because of the preparation in fricassee. Its preparation is long and laborious, but, as the saying goes, per aspera ad astra.

FISH AND AMPHIBIANS

Anguilla al forno

BAKED EEL

- 1KG EELS
- 200G WHITE FLOUR
- 1 ONION, CARROT AND CELERY
- 1 GLASS OF RED WINE
- ROSEMARY
- OLIVE OIL

PREPARATION TIME: 1 HOUR

SKIN AND CLEAN the eel as described in the following recipe and cut into chunks. Chop the rosemary leaves up finely and add to the flour in which the pieces of eel are then well coated.

Chop the vegetables up together and spread on the bottom of a baking dish, laying the chunks of eel on top.

Bake in a medium hot oven for about 20 minutes, frequently basting with red wine.

Season with salt to taste and switch off the oven when cooked, but do not remove the dish until a further quarter-hour has passed.

THIS DELICIOUS EEL dish is truly a delicacy if you serve it at table with some nice, bright yellow polenta, made up of very fine cornmeal and cooked rather slowly.

Anguilla alla fiorentina

EEL FLORENTINE STYLE

- 1KG EEL
- 3 CLOVES OF GARLIC
- 100G DRIED BREAD-CRUMBS
- 6 SAGE LEAVES
- 1-2 GLASSES OF RED WINE
- OLIVE OIL

PREPARATION TIME: 2 HOURS

TAKE A KILOGRAM of fresh eel, preferably already skinned and cleaned. Otherwise, if this chore is up to you, here follows the procedure.

With a sharp knife cut into the skin under the head of the eel, pull it up and then, gripping it in a cloth (and holding the fish by the head), rip the skin off with one tug, as if it were a glove.

Draw the fish and eliminate the heads, then cut the eels into large segments.

Steep the chunks of eel in olive oil, salt and pepper for about an hour. Then, in a roomy ovenproof dish, sauté the sage and garlic quickly with 3 tablespoons of oil.

Coat the eel in breadcrumbs and place in the baking dish, adding the steep liquid. Finally, place in a hot oven for about 40 minutes.

Anguilla in umido 1
STEWED EELS I

◆

- ABOUT 1 KG EEL
- 1 WHITE-SKINNED, PUN-GENT ONION
- 2 CLOVES OF GARLIC
- 1/2 LEMON
- 1/2 GLASS WHITE WINE
- WHITE FLOUR
- 4 RIPE TOMATOES
- PARSLEY
- OLIVE OIL

◆

PREPARATION TIME: 1 HOUR

CLEAN THE EEL WELL, removing the head and tail and drawing the fish. Wash, cut into chunks and coat with flour. Fry the chopped onion and the cloves of garlic with 3 tablespoons of oil in a saucepan, then add the eels together with the white wine and the lemon zest. Cook with the lid on for about half-an-hour. Now you can add the tomatoes, peeled and chopped, leaving everything to cook over low heat for a further 10 minutes, stirring carefully. Serve the eels very hot with a sprinkling of parsley.

Anguilla in umido 2
STEWED EELS II

◆

- 1 KG RATHER SMALL EELS
- 1 ONION
- 1 STICK OF CELERY
- 1 CARROT
- PARSLEY
- 5 RIPE TOMATOES
- OLIVE OIL

◆

PREPARATION TIME: 1/2 HOUR

USE SEVERAL TENDER, smaller eels rather than one large one for this recipe. Once the fish has been cleaned, divide each into 2 or 3 chunks. Fry the chopped onion, carrot and celery in 4 tablespoons of oil. Add the eels and the tomatoes, roughly chopped, salt and freshly-ground pepper. Cover and leave to cook over gentle heat for a quarter-hour. Serve the eels hot, with a liberal sprinkling of parsley. A delicious variation is to finish cooking, allow to cool, then bone the eels, which you will cut into smaller pieces. Prepare a porridge with 2 litres of milk and 200g of semolina: when the milk boils, season with salt, stir in the semolina and leave to simmer gently for 10 minutes. In the meanwhile, bring the eels up to the boil again in the sauce they were cooked in. Place a ladleful of the porridge in each bowl and pour the sauce over, finishing off with grated Parmesan cheese.

Anguilla in fricassea
EEL FRICASSEE

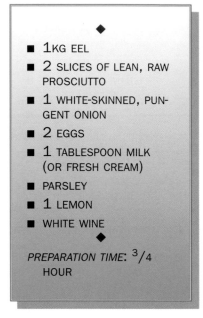

- 1KG EEL
- 2 SLICES OF LEAN, RAW PROSCIUTTO
- 1 WHITE-SKINNED, PUNGENT ONION
- 2 EGGS
- 1 TABLESPOON MILK (OR FRESH CREAM)
- PARSLEY
- 1 LEMON
- WHITE WINE

PREPARATION TIME: $^3/_4$ HOUR

DRAW AND SKIN the eel (please see page 130 for the instructions), cut into small segments and fry gently in a saucepan with 4 tablespoons of oil, the onion and the slices of ham cut into strips. Cook over moderate heat for 20 minutes. Add half a glass of wine and continue cooking another 15 minutes. Beat the egg yolks with a tablespoon of milk (or fresh cream) and a splash of lemon juice. As soon as the eel is cooked, remove from the heat and immediately pour the egg sauce into the pan. When everything has blended nicely, you know the dish is ready for serving.

PRACTICAL TRICK: if the sauce should separate, carefully add hot water, drop by drop, until the desired consistency is reached.

This dish is to be served hot and eaten straightaway, because the egg sauce tends to curdle on cooling and the eel consequently tastes heavier.

Baccalà coi porri
SALT COD WITH LEEKS

- 800G SALT COD, PREVIOUSLY SOAKED
- 6 MEDIUM LEEKS
- WHITE FLOUR
- 300G HOME-MADE TOMATO SAUCE
- OLIVE OIL

PREPARATION TIME: $^3/_4$ HOUR

BONE THE FISH. Divide into 4 chunks (or even 6), coat in flour and fry in very hot oil until golden on both sides. Drain the pieces on kitchen or brown paper. Rinse the leeks, cut into thin rings. Gently fry them for 10 minutes in 4 tablespoons of oil in a pan. The addition of one or two tablespoons of hot water may be necessary to finish off cooking. Add the fish, season with salt and pepper and simmer for a quarter-hour.

THIS DELICIOUS DISH is excellent served with *polenta*.

With reference to the ingredients, I wish to remark on the tomato sauce: most ancient recipes recommend it, whereas nowadays tomato tends to be excluded so as not to weigh down a dish which is rich on its own.

Baccalà alla fiorentina

FLORENTINE SALT COD

◆

- 800G SALT COD, PRE-VIOUSLY SOAKED
- 2 LEEKS
- 300G TOMATOES
- 4 CLOVES OF GARLIC
- PARSLEY
- WHITE FLOUR
- OLIVE OIL

◆

PREPARATION TIME: $^1/_2$ HOUR

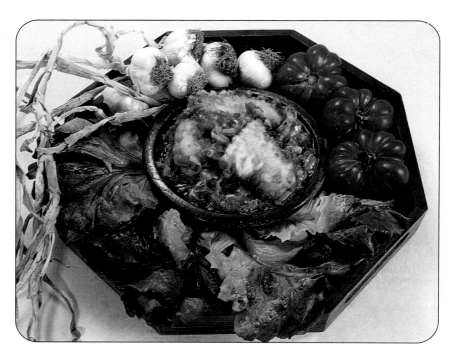

IT IS NOT DIFFICULT for Florentines to get hold of some good-quality *baccalà*.

Traditionally every Thursday, grocers put the salt cod to soak in zinc tanks supplied with running water, so that it is nice and tender on the Friday morning.

The cod is of the Labrador type which, though large, is at the same time tender.

It will doubtless not be difficult to find excellent salt cod abroad.

If you should have to do the soaking yourself, remember that this must go on for twenty-four hours and that it absolutely must take place under running water (a trickle is enough) so that all the salt gets rinsed away.

THE MOST CLASSIC of Florentine recipes for this fish lays down that a tomato sauce (remember to purée the tomatoes) is made with garlic and chopped leeks fried in 4 tablespoons of oil in a saucepan.

When the leeks take on a golden colour, add the tomatoes and cook slowly for about a quarter-hour. Cut the fish into at least 6 chunks, bone, coat with flour and deep fry in oil. Allow to colour on both sides over medium heat. Pat dry on brown or kitchen paper, then add to the sauce for a last, brief stewing. Sprinkle liberally with finely-chopped parsley.

A tasty, rather unusual alternative is to use the *baccalà* as a sauce for spaghetti or thin noodles. In this case, increase the amount of tomato sauce (from 300g to 500g or 600g) and, once the fish has been fried, flake it in your fingers (careful of any bones which may still be around!) and place in the sauce, with a good sprinkling of chilli pepper and parsley. The result will be a rather unusual dish of delicious spaghetti, fragrant and appetising.

Baccalà e ceci

SALT COD AND CHICKPEAS

◆

- 600G SALT COD, PRE-VIOUSLY SOAKED
- 300G DRIED CHICKPEAS (MEXICAN VARIETY)
- 1 TABLESPOON BICAR-BONATE OF SODA
- 1 TABLESPOON COARSE SEA SALT
- 1 LEEK
- OLIVE OIL

◆

PREPARATION TIME: 2 HOURS

THE PREPARATION of this classic dish starts the previous day. The chickpeas must be soaked overnight in cold water with one tablespoon of bicarbonate of soda and one of coarse sea salt (to prevent the husk from hardening). Then they are rinsed in running water and put in a saucepan full of water to cook over low heat for a couple of hours (the length of cooking depends on the type of chickpea). Taste them; if they are soft (but not disintegrated), then they are ready.

In a baking dish, gently fry the finely-sliced leeks in 2 tablespoons of oil, then add the cod fillets, boned and divided into about 6 portions. Bake in a medium oven for about 10 minutes. Now you can add the chickpeas with a little of their cooking water (to come to about half an inch up the sides of the dish) and return to the oven for a further 10 minutes. Serve nice and hot.

Baccalà marinato

MARINATED SALT COD

◆

- 800G SALT COD
- 100G HOME-MADE TOMATO SAUCE
- 2 CLOVES OF GARLIC
- PARSLEY AND ROSEMARY
- WHITE FLOUR
- RED WINE VINEGAR
- CHILLI PEPPER
- OLIVE OIL

◆

PREPARATION TIME: 3/4 HOUR

BONE THE FISH FILLET and cut into pieces. Coat with flour and deep fry in plenty of oil, browning on both sides. Place in a roomy bowl.

Gently fry the garlic separately in 3 tablespoons of oil, adding the rosemary, tomato sauce, parsley (leave the leaves whole) and vinegar (please make sure it is of good quality). Let it evaporate, if necessary adding cold water to balance the strong flavour of the vinegar. Leave the marinade to simmer over gentle heat for 10 minutes, seasoning with salt and chilli pepper (use dried peppers in this case; 3-4 will be enough). Leave to cool, then mask the fish in the bowl until completely smothered.

Leave to stand a whole day and serve as a tasty summer antipasto, together with large lemon wedges.

Baccalà fritto

FRIED SALT COD

- 800G SALT COD, PRE-VIOUSLY SOAKED
- 1 GLASS WHITE WINE
- 200G WHITE FLOUR
- CHOPPED PARSLEY
- OLIVE OIL

PREPARATION TIME: 3/4 HOUR

THE BRIEF INITIAL parboiling lightens the rather overpowering flavour of this fast Baltic fish, ensuring that, though fried, this dish is not the least bit heavy or indigestible.

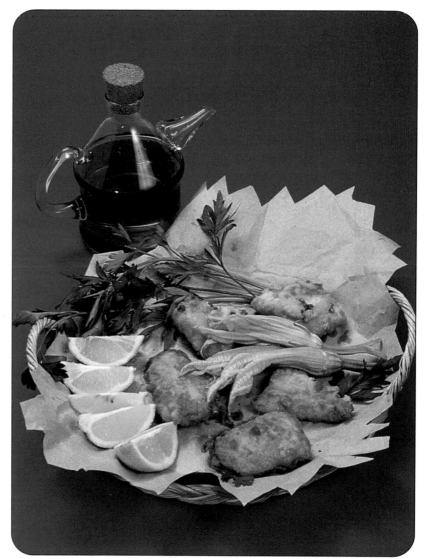

CUT THE BACCALÀ fillets into pieces and place them in a pan of cold water.

Put on the hob, taking the pan off as soon as it looks like boiling. Drain and pat the fish dry.

The batter is made in the following way: in a bowl, dissolve the flour in the white wine and enough water to obtain a soft, homogeneous mixture. Season with salt and chopped parsley.

Carefully dip each piece of cod into the batter and deep fry in really hot oil. When both sides are golden in colour, serve very hot, garnished with lots of lemon wedges and parsley sprigs.

Cacciucco

FISH SOUP

◆

- 1 ¹/₂KG ASSORTED FISH (MULLET, SCORPION FISH, SOLE, DOGFISH, MANTIS PRAWNS, SHELLFISH AND WHAT YOU WILL...)
- 1 GLASS WHITE WINE
- 500G TOMATO PASTE
- UNSALTED, STALE BREAD
- GARLIC
- OLIVE OIL
- PARSLEY TO TASTE

◆

PREPARATION TIME: 1 HOUR

THIS TASTY FISH SOUP, which, in deference to recent alimentary practice, I prefer to serve as a main course (or rather as a light luncheon dish) instead of as just the first course, is usually ascribed to the Livornese culinary tradition.

However, seeing that Livorno was founded by Florence, this exceptional recipe is, *tout court*, officially relegated to Tuscan culinary traditions.

The reason is also because nowadays, fortunately, one can find fresh fish in inland markets as well as in seaside ones.

WHEN CHOOSING THE FISH, do not turn your nose up at the cheaper and uglier varieties which, in fact, have a surprise in store for their excellent flavour. Clean and wash the fish (you could leave this chore up to the fishmonger). Brown the garlic in 4 tablespoons of oil in a large saucepan, add the powdered chilli pepper (the tip of a teaspoon) and the white wine. When the latter has evaporated, add the tomato paste and simmer for another 5 minutes over low heat. Add the fish, beginning with the variety needing the lengthiest cooking (dogfish), finishing up with that needing the least (mullet). Continue cooking over medium heat for a further quarter-hour, delicately moving the fish with the aid of a wooden spoon, so that the flavours of the sauce are absorbed well.

Toast some slices of bread and rub them liberally with garlic. Place one slice in each soup bowl, spoon over the *cacciucco*, smothering the toast in the "fish stock". Serve at once, with a sprinkling of parsley, if you wish.

Calamari inzimino

SQUID STEW

- 1KG SQUID
- 2 BUNCHES OF SWISS CHARD
- 2 CLOVES OF GARLIC
- 1 GLASS WHITE WINE
- BUNCH OF PARSLEY
- 200G HOME-MADE TOMATO SAUCE
- OLIVE OIL

PREPARATION TIME: 1 ¹/₂ HOURS

THE ORIGIN OF THE TERM *"inzimino"* is shrouded in mystery. The Italian dictionary does not help much, merely stating that it is a Tuscan term to describe a "dish prepared with a so-called *zimino* sauce", based on "vegetables (chard, spinach, parsley and garlic) and various seasonings and used in the preparation of fish dishes".

There is a suggestion that it derives etymologically from the Roman word *cuminum* or cumin.

But it is not clear what this dish has to do with cumin (or *kümmel*, used by the Germans to make a liqueur or flavour bread).

With all these variations we run the risk of straying off course.

Let us, therefore, leave our curiosity unsatisfied, as it will not impair the delicate flavour of this recipe.

STRIP OFF THE central midribs from the chard, rinse the leaves and cook in boiling water. Drain and squeeze the moisture out, putting to one side for the moment. Clean the squid (a chore that the fishmonger will happily undertake for you), removing the ink-sac and central rostrum. Slice the sac into rings and cut the tentacles into chunks. Fry the two cloves of garlic with 3 tablespoons of oil in a saucepan. When it colours, add the squid and white wine.

Put on the lid and simmer for 10 minutes over a low flame. Then add the chard (you can chop it up with a *mezzaluna*, rocker knife), salt, pepper and tomato sauce. Cover the pan and simmer over low heat for about 40 minutes.

You may indeed ask ,"Why squid, when the traditional recipe calls for cuttlefish?" Because squid are more delicate and tender. But, should you wish to try it with cuttlefish, I will not be the least perturbed.

Galantina di tonno
Tuna Galantine

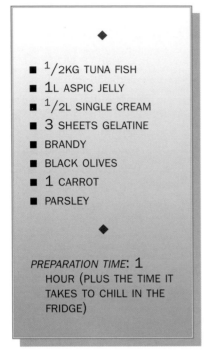

- 1/2KG TUNA FISH
- 1L ASPIC JELLY
- 1/2L SINGLE CREAM
- 3 SHEETS GELATINE
- BRANDY
- BLACK OLIVES
- 1 CARROT
- PARSLEY

PREPARATION TIME: 1 HOUR (PLUS THE TIME IT TAKES TO CHILL IN THE FRIDGE)

DRAIN THE TUNA. Prepare a litre of aspic jelly, adding half a glass of brandy at the final boiling stage. Pour an inch and a half of jelly into a loaf tin and allow to chill. Before it cools completely, slice the black olives, the carrot and a few parsley sprigs and lay over the aspic. Return to the fridge. Chop the tuna finely, whip the cream and add half an inch of boiling milk in which you will have dissolved the three sheets of gelatine (previously soaked in cold water). Stir it all quickly, season with salt and pepper and chill the mixture in the fridge.

Half-an-hour later the mousse will have thickened; take a flexible spatula and spread it over the aspic, shaping it so that there is room at the sides for pouring in the remaining aspic after a quarter-hour. Replace in the fridge for two more hours. Turn out, using a cloth dampened in hot water and placed under the tin (though just for a moment!).

Lamprede all'aceto
Lamprey in Vinegar

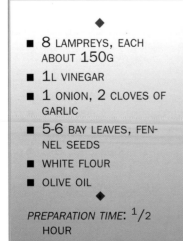

- 8 LAMPREYS, EACH ABOUT 150G
- 1L VINEGAR
- 1 ONION, 2 CLOVES OF GARLIC
- 5-6 BAY LEAVES, FENNEL SEEDS
- WHITE FLOUR
- OLIVE OIL

PREPARATION TIME: 1/2 HOUR

FINDING LAMPREY is not the easiest of tasks, but if you manage to, you will savour a delicious dish (if not, fall back on mullet).

Clean the lampreys, removing innards, fins and gills, but leaving the heads and tails on. Coat with flour and fry, then dry on brown paper. For the marinade, put the very finely-chopped onion in a bowl with the vinegar, 8-10 peppercorns and a pinch of fennel seeds. Leave to stand for 10 minutes, then pour into the pan where you fried the lamprey and simmer briefly. Place the fish on a platter, posing a bay leaf on each one. When the marinade is cool, pour it over and leave to rest for a whole day (indeed, this plate is cooked one day for the next).

Polpo marinato

MARINATED OCTOPUS

- ABOUT 1KG OCTOPUS
- 1 STICK OF CELERY
- 1 CARROT
- 2 BAY LEAVES
- 5 BLACK PEPPERCORNS
- WHITE WINE
- RED VINEGAR
- THIN-RINDED LEMON
- PARSLEY
- OLIVE OIL

PREPARATION TIME: ABOUT 3 HOURS

CLEAN THE OCTOPUS and place in a pan of cold water with the celery, roughly-chopped carrot, bay leaves, a glass of white wine and peppercorns. Cover and bring to the boil, then lower the heat. With the lid still on, simmer for an hour and a half. Do not attempt to eat immediately it is cooked, but allow it to cool in its stock. This is the secret to have your octopus tasty and tender. Cut it into pieces and place in a bowl. Sprinkle with oil, a glass of vinegar and some lemon juice, adding the zest, too, shredded and without any pith. Shake a little parsley over, but wait at least another hour before relishing it.

Polpette di baccalà

SALT COD CROQUETTES

- 600G SALT COD
- 2 ANCHOVIES
- 300G STALE BREAD
- 1 CUP MILK, 1 EGG
- GARLIC AND PARSLEY
- 200G DRIED BREAD-CRUMBS
- OLIVE OIL

PREPARATION TIME: 3/4 HOUR

SOAK THE BREAD in the milk. Put the salt cod in cold water, bring to the boil and then remove it from the heat immediately. Drain, dry, and bone carefully. Chop it up, together with the garlic, parsley and boned, rinsed anchovies. Whisk the eggs in a bowl and combine the bread (with all the water squeezed out), salt and pepper. Add the chopped salt cod and the other ingredients, stirring until well blended. Make little balls, roll them in the breadcrumbs and deep fry in oil.

THESE SUCCULENT little fish croquettes are good both hot or cold. They are an excellent summer dish when served cold, presenting a fine sight if shown off properly, on a tray decorated with lemon slices and green vine leaves.

Ranocchi alla fiorentina

FROGS FLORENTINE STYLE

◆

- 1KG FROGS
- 1 ONION
- PARSLEY
- 1 LEMON
- WHITE FLOUR
- 1 EGG
- 100G DRIED BREAD-CRUMBS
- 2 TABLESPOONS GRATED PARMESAN CHEESE
- OLIVE OIL

◆

PREPARATION TIME: 1 $^1/_2$ HOURS

CHOP THE ONION and parsley finely and sauté gently in a saucepan with 3 tablespoons of oil.

Previously, you will have skinned, drawn and washed the frogs at length under cold running water (even though, in this case, it is worth asking the fishmonger to take care of this, especially if you are soft-hearted and rather squeamish).

Put them in the pan for about 10 minutes to absorb the flavour of the onion mixture. You can, if you like, add the juice of half a lemon at this point.

Then, remove the frogs from the pan and put them to dry on kitchen paper or on ordinary brown paper.

Coat them in flour, dip into the beaten egg and finally roll in the breadcrumbs which have been mixed in with the Parmesan.

Lastly, deep fry in oil and serve very hot, together with slices of lemon.

Ranocchi fritti

FRIED FROGS

◆

- 1 KG SMALLISH FROGS
- 3 EGGS
- 200G FLOUR
- LEMON
- OLIVE OIL

◆

PREPARATION TIME: 1 $^1/_4$ HOURS

OBTAIN FROGS WHICH HAVE ALREADY BEEN CLEANED (otherwise, proceed as in the previous recipe) and rinse them at length in running water. Beat the eggs with the salt and a drop or two of lemon juice in a bowl, drop in the frogs and leave for about an hour.

Drain them, coat them in flour again and fry in plenty of boiling oil.

Salt the frogs well and serve with slices of lemon.

GETTING THE FROGS by oneself is quite a problem considering that they are caught at night and (in Italy, at any rate) our rivers are not all uncontaminated oases.

But if you manage to catch some in clear, healthy water, you will taste the difference compared to those bought at the market. You will be surprised how much more delicate and tender the flavour is.

Sogliole con spinaci

SOLES WITH SPINACH

♦

- 700G SOLE FILLETS
- 1KG SPINACH
- 1 GLASS WHITE WINE
- 100G BUTTER
- WHITE FLOUR
- $1/2$L MILK
- PARMESAN
- OLIVE OIL

♦

PREPARATION TIME: 1 HOUR

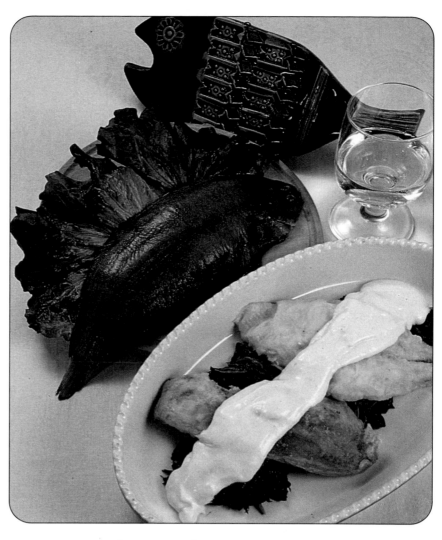

GET YOUR FISHMONGER to prepare the fillets. Coat them with flour and cook them with a knob of butter and a glass of white wine in a frying pan. Meanwhile, trim and rinse the spinach thoroughly and boil in very little water (almost nothing). Drain, squeeze the liquor out and heat with a knob of butter to lend flavour. Make a light béchamel sauce (with 50g flour, 30g butter and half a litre of milk). See the instructions on page 87.

Then, put the spinach in a buttered baking dish, lay the fillets of sole on top and cover with the béchamel sauce, sprinkling liberally with grated Parmesan cheese. Bake in a hot oven.

AS FOR MANY OTHER recipes of Tuscan cuisine, tradition lays down that nutmeg be used, especially in this one.

You may have noticed that I myself never include it in my recipes (except in those dishes "inherited" from my paternal grandfather).

In actual fact, I find it better suits the Romagnese tradition.

To my way of thinking it has an aroma which does not marry well particularly in this recipe, as it is too acrid and easily "recognisable" among the other more sober, light and delicate flavours.

Totanetti inzimino

BABY SQUID WITH CHARD

◆

- 800G SMALL, BABY SQUID
- 1KG SWISS CHARD
- 1KG CANNED TOMATOES
- 1 WHITE-SKINNED, PUNGENT ONION
- 3 CLOVES OF GARLIC
- OLIVE OIL

◆

PREPARATION TIME: 3/4 HOUR

ONCE YOU HAVE CLEANED the squid, sauté the garlic and chopped onion in 4 tablespoons of oil in a roomy pan. Meanwhile, boil the chard (stripped of the midribs) in plenty of water, keeping the lid on to maintain the nice green colour of the vegetable.

Drain and squeeze the water out.

Cut up the baby squid and place in the pan with the onion and garlic.

Sweat over moderate heat for about 10 minutes, until some liquor has seeped out of the vegetables.

Now add the tomatoes, bringing them to the boil for a very short while, and finally add the drained chard. Season with salt and pepper to taste, cover and cook over low heat for about a quarter-hour.

If you try the squid carefully on your fork, it should now taste tender. If not, it needs a little more cooking, obviously over low heat.

Trote gratinate

BAKED TROUT

◆

- 4 SMALL TROUT
- 2 EGGS
- 100G BUTTER
- 250G GRUYÈRE CHEESE
- MILK
- ROSEMARY
- CHOPPED PARSLEY
- DRIED BREADCRUMBS

◆

PREPARATION TIME: 3/4 HOUR

CLEAN AND WASH the trout well, scaling the fish carefully with the special knife.

Gently melt the butter in a frying pan without allowing it to smoke and cook the trout with the fragrant rosemary and parsley.

Then, transfer the trout to a baking dish, together with the cooking juices. Lightly beat the egg yolks in half a glass of milk with salt and pepper and pour over the trout in the baking dish.

Sprinkle with lots of finely-grated Gruyère cheese and a few dried breadcrumbs.

The trout is then placed in a medium oven to bake for a quarter-hour.

OMELETTES

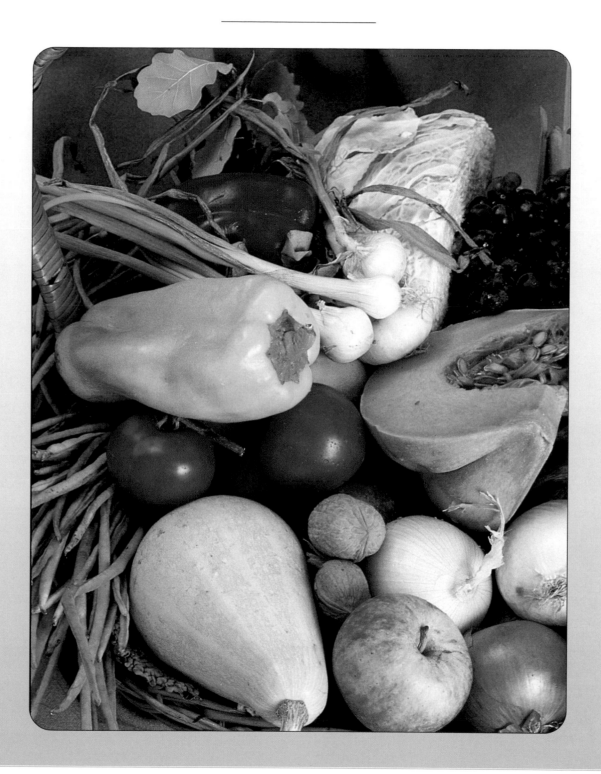

Frittata col cavolfiore

CAULIFLOWER OMELETTE

- 1/2 CAULIFLOWER
- 3 CLOVES OF GARLIC
- 3 EGGS
- OLIVE OIL

PREPARATION TIME: 3/4 HOUR

RINSE THE CAULIFLOWER and remove the heart (usually it is too tough and woody) and the external leaves with the exception of any tender, little ones. Cut it up and sauté gently in a frying pan with oil, chopped garlic, salt and pepper. Then add one or two tablespoons of water, cover and cook slowly for about 20 minutes. At the end, it should all be well-browned and cooked.

Lightly beat the eggs and pour over the cauliflower, which should be nice and hot. Allow to solidify somewhat, then turn the omelette over with the aid of the frying pan lid, so that it may colour on the other side, too.

Frittata con gli zoccoli

BACON OMELETTE

- 4 EGGS
- 200G BACON
- OLIVE OIL
- SALT AND PEPPER

PREPARATION TIME: 1/4 HOUR

SLICE THE BACON thickly, then cut into cubes. Place in a pan to brown and sizzle in a thin layer of oil. Lightly beat the eggs, adding a pinch of salt and pepper. Pour the mixture into the scorching pan, cook the omelette on both sides and serve piping hot, relishing it with bread baked in a wood-fired oven.

Thank heavens that here in Tuscany we can still get those nice loaves all fragrant and tasty, hiding small pieces of carbonised wood underneath.

Frittata di asparagi

WILD ASPARAGUS OMELETTE

- 1 BUNCH OF WILD ASPARAGUS
- 50G BUTTER
- 3 EGGS

PREPARATION TIME: $1/2$ HOUR

WILD ASPARAGUS which, with a little effort, can generally be found in the woods in Europe, is nowadays obtainable at the greengrocer's. Boil the asparagus, after removing the tough, woody part. Heat the tips in the butter in a non-stick frying pan. Stir over low heat for a few minutes to let the flavours blend. Lightly beat the eggs, add salt and a pinch of pepper. Raise the flame and, when the butter froths, throw in the eggs and allow to set, lowering the heat and pricking the omelette with the prongs of a fork. If you like, the inside of the omelette can be left "creamy", or else it can all be tossed over (with the help of the frying pan lid) so that it sets on both sides.

Frittata di vitalba

CLEMATIS SPROUTS OMELETTE

- A FEW SPROUTS OF OLD MAN'S BEARD
- 3 EGGS
- OLIVE OIL
- LEMON

PREPARATION TIME: $1/2$ HOUR

YOU NEED A NICE BUNCH of old man's beard (also known as traveller's joy). Rinse thoroughly under running water and scald for about 15 minutes in water acidulated with a segment of lemon to avoid discolouring (when picking the sprouts, be careful of your hands, too, otherwise they will also turn black). Drain them well and sauté gently for a few minutes with a tablespoon of oil in a non-stick frying pan. Lightly beat the eggs and pour into the pan, letting the omelette colour nicely on both sides. *Vitalbini* are the young shoots of the *Clematis odorosa* or *vitalba* which push forth in spring.

THIS CLIMBER CAN BE found almost everywhere, often twisted around the leaves of other trees. It has dark green leaves (used in general medicine and as a herbal remedy for the analgesic and depurative properties) and in season it produces panicles of little white, scented flowers. I prefer to brown both sides of the omelette instead of leaving it runny, because in this way the bitter flavour of the clematis is heightened without being smothered by the flavour of the egg. It is an old recipe, made infrequently for the more elderly, so you will surprise your family and friends by serving it up on a tray, surrounded by bunches of fresh clematis and segments of ripe tomato to create a lively colour contrast.

Frittata di cipolle

ONION OMELETTE

◆

- 6 RED-SKINNED ONIONS
- 2 TABLESPOONS OF OLIVE OIL
- 4 EGGS

◆

PREPARATION TIME: ¹/₂ HOUR

SLICE THE ONIONS into rings and sauté in a frying pan until golden. Beat the eggs with salt and pepper. Pour into the pan, raising the heat a little. Allow to set on one side, toss the omelette over and brown on the other side.

THIS IS EXCELLENT, either hot or cold. A delicious way of offering it, either as a complete light meal or as a starter, is to make some bread "chips" and cubes of omelette (thicker and more solid) and pumpkin (in winter) or melon (in summer), impaling them alternately on skewers.

Frittata di fiori di zucca

ZUCCHINI FLOWER OMELETTE

◆

- 500G ZUCCHINI FLOW-ERS
- 2 CLOVES OF GARLIC
- 6 NEWLY-LAID EGGS
- CATMINT
- OLIVE OIL

◆

PREPARATION TIME: ³/₄ HOUR

CLEAN THE ZUCCHINI FLOWERS, leaving the pistil intact, and tear them into pieces. Put a little oil in a frying pan with a handful of catmint and the garlic and scald the flowers slightly (they must keep their bright yellow colour). Allow to cool and add the beaten egg. Fry everything in a barely-greased frying pan and make a soft, light omelette.

ALTHOUGH CATMINT plays an important role in my recipe, I can assure you that the success of the dish is guaranteed even without that extra touch. Alternatively, use a pinch of thyme (even if dried), but only a pinch!

Frittata di pomodori verdi

GREEN TOMATO OMELETTE

◆

- 2 GREEN SALAD TOMATOES
- 3 EGGS
- OLIVE OIL

◆

PREPARATION TIME: $^1/_2$ HOUR

Rinse the tomatoes well and cut them into rounds horizontally, i.e. across their width. It is advisable to scrupulously remove the seeds, as well.

Coat the tomato slices with flour and deep fry in hot oil, turning them so that they are nicely browned on both sides.

When well-cooked (10 minutes will be needed for a good fry which is reasonably springy), place them in a baking dish and pour over the lightly-beaten eggs.

Put in a hot oven for about 5/7 minutes and serve the omelette very hot, but still a little runny in the centre (or else, if you like, leave the omelette in the oven a few moments more to cook right through and make the tomatoes nice and crisp).

Frittata di ricotta

RICOTTA CHEESE OMELETTE

- 200G EWE'S MILK RICOTTA (OTHERWISE COTTAGE CHEESE)
- 50G GRATED PARMESAN
- 6 EGGS
- 1/2 WHITE ONION
- 2 RIPE TOMATOES
- OLIVE OIL

PREPARATION TIME: 1/2 HOUR

WITH A WOODEN SPOON, work the *ricotta* (previously drained in cheesecloth) together with the Parmesan cheese in a bowl. Season with salt and pepper and leave to stand a while. Sauté the sliced onion with the chopped tomatoes in 2 tablespoons of oil for 10 minutes. Beat the eggs. Heat a non-stick pan, pour in a trickle of oil (the omelette will slip out more easily) and spoon over a ladle of the egg mixture. Cook the omelette slowly, prick it several times and draw off the heat without ever turning it over. Make 3 more omelettes in this way, filling the centre with the cheeses. Roll each omelette up and place these rolls in the tomato sauce. Heat over a high flame for a few moments and serve each omelette accompanied by its sauce.

MY GRANDMOTHER USED TO RECITE "butter from the cow, *cacio* (or hard cheese) from the sheep, *ricotta* from the goat", in the times when the ingredients were precisely those. It is not easy to find *ricotta* from goats nowadays, in fact it is more likely to be made from pure sheep's milk. However, be careful in June and July, the lambing season, when it is hard to find ewe's milk.

Frittatine verdi

SMALL SPINACH OMELETTES

- 600G FRESH SPINACH
- 6 EGGS
- 1/2 GLASS MILK
- OLIVE OIL
- 2 LEMONS

PREPARATION TIME: 1 HOUR

BOIL THE SPINACH in very little water, drain, cool and squeeze the liquor out. Pass through the mincer to reduce to a pulp. Beat 6 eggs and add the spinach, salt and pepper, stirring with a fork. Grease an omelette pan with a little oil and allow a ladle of the mixture to set over a moderate flame. Prick the omelette and turn it over. Let it dry on both sides, draw off the heat, roll it up in foil (just like a little sausage) and leave to cool. Continue until all the mixture has been used up. You will obtain about 6 little omelettes. Once they are cold, slice them and arrange around the serving dish like the rays of the sun, with a splashing of lemon juice. Garnish with lemon segments and serve as a side plate with boiled meats.

Tortino alla fiorentina

FLORENTINE OMELETTE

◆

- 300G SMALL, FRESH ZUCCHINI
- 4 WHOLE EGGS
- $^1/_2$ GLASS MILK
- PINCH OF MARJORAM
- OLIVE OIL

◆

PREPARATION TIME: $^1/_2$ HOUR

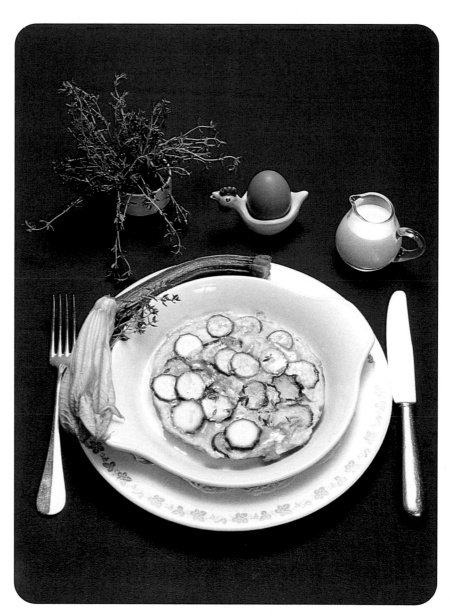

THIS TRADITIONAL Tuscan omelette is delicious especially in summer, when fresh zucchini can be used (those that "sing", or rather, make a cheerful sound, when rubbed against your hands). It also makes an excellent dish served cold the following day.

SLICE THE ZUCCHINI into rounds and sauté until golden in 2 tablespoons of oil in a frying pan.

Turn them over to brown on both sides. Lightly beat the eggs, adding the milk, salt and pepper. When the vegetables are well-cooked (they must cook slowly for about a quarter-hour), throw in the beaten eggs. Let the omelette set on one side, then, helping yourself with the pan lid, turn it over to brown on the other side. Serve the omelette dusted with a pinch of marjoram.

— 149 —

Tortino di carciofi

ARTICHOKE OMELETTE

◆

- 6 SMALL, TENDER GLOBE ARTICHOKES
- 5 FRESHLY-LAID EGGS
- WHITE FLOUR
- OLIVE OIL

◆

PREPARATION TIME: 1/2 HOUR

CLEAN THE ARTICHOKES and remove the stems. Cut them into thickish wedges, dredge with flour and fry in an ovenproof dish. When they are golden on both sides, pour the beaten egg over and lightly season with salt and pepper. Now it depends on your taste; if you like the omelette cooked well and not "creamy", bake in a hot oven for a few minutes, otherwise, enjoy it as it is, not completely set, but (to my way of thinking) fresher and more appetising.

Uova al pomodoro

TOMATO EGGS

◆

- 4 FRESH EGGS
- 2 VERY RIPE TOMATOES
- OLIVE OIL

◆

PREPARATION TIME: 20 MINUTES

FOR 10 MINUTES, cook the tomatoes in 2 tablespoons of oil in a small frying pan. Season with salt and pepper, break in the eggs and mix, taking care not to break the yolks. Add yet another pinch of salt and pepper and keep over the heat until the whites have set. Serve nice and hot.

VEGETABLE DISHES

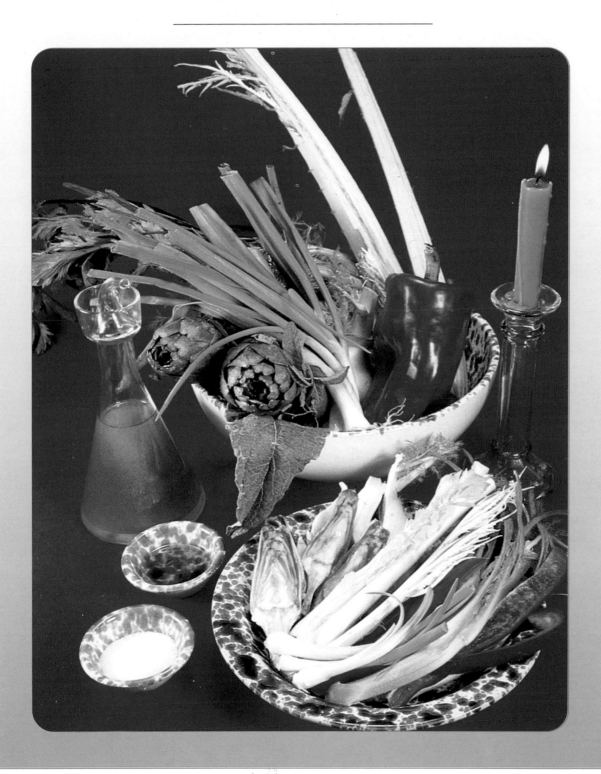

Asparagi fiorentini

ASPARAGUS, FLORENTINE STYLE

- 1KG GREEN ASPARAGUS
- 80G BUTTER
- 4 EGGS
- GRATED PARMESAN
- FRESHLY-GROUND PEP-PER

PREPARATION TIME: $^3/4$ HOUR

TRIM THE aspara-gus and scrape. Tie into bundles and place them carefully upright in a saucepan, pouring in enough cold water to cover the white part. Put on the lid and boil for a quarter-hour, without ever lifting the lid. Remove the vegetables from the pan and test their consistency; they must be cooked, but firm. Cut away the white part and place the green tips in a saucepan where you have melted a little butter. Sauté the asparagus over low heat for 5 minutes, turning them over with a wooden spoon. Dust liberally with Parmesan cheese, salt and pepper. Arrange the asparagus in a circle on a serving dish with the tips pointing inwards and serve with the eggs (one per person, fried separately) lying on the green tips.

Baccelli stufati

BRAISED BROAD BEANS

- 2KG FRESH BROAD BEANS
- 1 WHITE-SKINNED ONION
- 4 RED, RIPE TOMATOES
- BASIL
- OLIVE OIL

PREPARATION TIME: $^3/4$ HOUR

HULL THE BROAD beans. Sauté the onion in 4 table-spoons of oil in a saucepan until they are translucent. Add the beans, the peeled tomatoes cut into pieces, the basil, salt and pepper. Cover and cook slowly for half-an-hour, stirring with a wooden spoon. At the end, add a dash of chilli pepper paste.

WARNING: THE TERM *baccelli* is not used by the Florentines to mean the fresh, green fruit of the broad bean plant, but the tender, juicy seeds. Use large, ripe broad beans for this recipe rather than the little, tender ones, excellent for eating raw with pecorino.

Carciofi fritti
FRIED ARTICHOKES

◆

■ 6 GLOBE ARTICHOKES
■ 2 EGGS
■ 100G WHITE FLOUR
■ OLIVE OIL

◆

PREPARATION TIME: 3/4 HOUR

TRIM THE ARTICHOKES well and quarter (or divide into even more parts if the artichokes are very big, but bear in mind that the smaller and more tender the globes are, the better).

Plunge them into some water and lemon juice for a few minutes (some people suggest rubbing lemon along the knife blade before cutting the artichokes so that the cut edges of the vegetable do not discolour). Then drain and dry them.

Lightly beat the eggs in a bowl, dip the artichokes into the flour and drop them into the beaten egg, turning them round with your fingers. Finally deep fry them in boiling oil. Dry them on brown paper (or something similar), season with salt and serve nice and hot.

Carciofi ritti
UPRIGHT ARTICHOKES

◆

■ 6/8 GLOBE ARTI-CHOKES FOR FRYING
■ 2 CLOVES OF GARLIC
■ 1 BUNCH OF PARSLEY
■ 100G BACON
■ OLIVE OIL

◆

PREPARATION TIME: 1 1/4 HOURS

TRIM THE ARTICHOKES carefully, removing the tougher external leaves and breaking off the "heads" where attached to the stem, so that they can "stand up" easily.

Take a deep baking tin and arrange the artichokes upright in it. With your fingers, open the heads carefully and, among the leaves, place in each one, a mixture of crushed garlic, chopped parsley and the diced bacon, all seasoned with salt and pepper.

This having been done, 3 or 4 tablespoons of oil and half a glass of water are poured into the dish which is then covered and heated over a moderate flame for about 40 minutes. (The cooking time may vary, depending considerably on the quality and size of the artichokes.)

When nearly cooked, you can, if you wish, add tomato purée or, even better, 2 or 3 ripe tomatoes and a pinch of marjoram.

Cardi trippati

BRAISED CARDOONS

- ◆
- ■ 800G CARDOONS
- ■ 100G BUTTER
- ■ 1 WHITE-SKINNED ONION
- ■ 1 LEMON
- ■ 1 TABLESPOON WHITE FLOUR
- ■ GRATED PARMESAN CHEESE
- ◆

PREPARATION TIME: 2 ¹/₂ HOURS

PICK OVER THE CARDOONS (they should be small or medium-sized, the larger ones being stringy with too much waste), removing the external midribs with their fibrous parts. Cut the tender stems into rather long chunks and cut the hearts of the cardoons up small. Dip in water acidulated with lemon juice, as cardoons tend to darken. Boil in lightly-salted water, adding a tablespoon of white flour to help maintain the cardoons' nice white colour. Cook slowly for two hours. Slice the onion finely and sauté in butter until it turns golden. Then add the cardoons and gently brown for 10 minutes. Transfer to a baking dish that retains the heat (they are only good if eaten hot) and serve with Parmesan cheese.

Cavolo saltato

RÉCHAUFFÉ OF CAULIFLOWER

- ◆
- ■ 1 MEDIUM-SIZED CAULIFLOWER
- ■ 3 CLOVES OF GARLIC
- ■ 100G BLACK OLIVES
- ■ 200G CANNED TOMATOES
- ■ OLIVE OIL
- ◆

PREPARATION TIME: ¹/₂ HOUR

TRIM THE cauliflower, leaving any tender leaves. Parboil in salted water for 10 minutes, putting a piece of bread in the pan so that the whole house does not become impregnated with the smell. Drain, cool and divide into sprigs. Brown the garlic in 3 tablespoons of oil, add the cauliflower (chopped stem included) and sauté over medium heat. Pit and chop the olives and add to the pan with the tomato. Season with salt and pepper and cook for 10 minutes.

SOME RECIPES suggest the addition of sausages, onion and parsley to this dish, but I find it rather indigestible. Indeed, I would even prefer it without either olives or tomato, but quite simply boiled and reheated in the pan with oil and garlic.

Fagioli all'olio

BEANS IN OIL

◆

- ■ ½KG OF FRESH *CAN-NELLINO* OR *TOSCANELLO* BEANS
- ■ OLIVE OIL
- ■ FRESHLY-GROUND PEPPER
- ■ 4 CLOVES OF GARLIC
- ■ SPRIG OF SAGE

◆

PREPARATION TIME: **1** HOUR

IF YOU CAN, use fresh beans (if they are dried, soak them overnight in water, with the addition of a tablespoon of bicarbonate of soda), hull them and boil in a little salted water, barely enough to cover.

Cook over a low heat for three quarters-of-an-hour, strictly keeping the lid on the pan.

Serve hot, dressed with plenty of high-quality extra-vergine olive oil and with a grinding of pepper over the top (if it is to your liking).

IT IS NOT REALLY ALL that simple to cook the beans properly (if you have difficulty in tracking down the famous *toscanello* beans, do not despair because there are varieties of small, white beans which can easily substitute them). I remember my first experiences as a young, callow girl resulting in sad, mushy pulps or else with hard pieces wandering round the saucepan, with my mother and grandmother survey-ing it all with an interrogative air. You see, the secret of this simple, plain dish lies wholly in the cooking, which must be slow and gentle, unconditionally underneath a lid. That is all. The advice of the great gourmet Zenone Benini comes to mind; in his *Cucina di casa mia*, he states that "*i fagioli cuociono col bollire piano, e tappati*", explain-ing that the flame must be low because "during the cooking time, the beans should not stir. Heaven help us should they give chase to each other".

A plate of beans seasoned with good quality Tuscan oil, a nice slice of unsalted Tuscan bread and a good glass of wine - my husband says he would never tire of eating them! Try them in June in the Tuscan countryside, in the shade of a vine, and you will appreciate that here is the secret of our cuisine.

Fagioli all'uccelletto

BEANS WITH TOMATO SAUCE

♦

- 800G FRESH CANNELLI-NO BEANS (300G IF DRIED)
- 3 CLOVES OF GARLIC
- SPRIG OF SAGE
- 5 RIPE TOMATOES
- OLIVE OIL
- CHILLI PEPPER

♦

PREPARATION TIME: 1 ¹/₄ HOURS

BOIL THE BEANS, adding a tablespoon of oil (if they are dried, soak them first for 2 hours), removing from the heat while they are still *al dente*. In a casserole of terracotta (but steel will do), sauté the garlic and sage in 6 table-spoons of oil and add the peeled, roughly-chopped toma-toes. Reduce over medium heat for about 10 minutes, stir-ring with a wooden spoon. Add the beans with a little of their cooking water. Simmer over a low flame for a quarter-hour, add salt and pepper (or a little chilli pepper).

A CLASSIC OF Tuscan tradition, it discloses a masterly fusion of flavours in its simplicity. The ori-gin of the definition *"all'uccelletto"* remains shrouded in mystery, just like the names of so many other traditional dishes. The most likely conjecture is that it refers to the presence of sage, an essential ingredient when cooking little birds, in Italian *uccellini*. Strangely enough, Artusi (the foremost Italian cookery expert) was a fore-runner in recommending their use as a light luncheon dish; "These beans go very well with boiled meats, if you do not wish to eat them on their own". He first adds the beans and then the tomatoes, but I go my own sweet way.

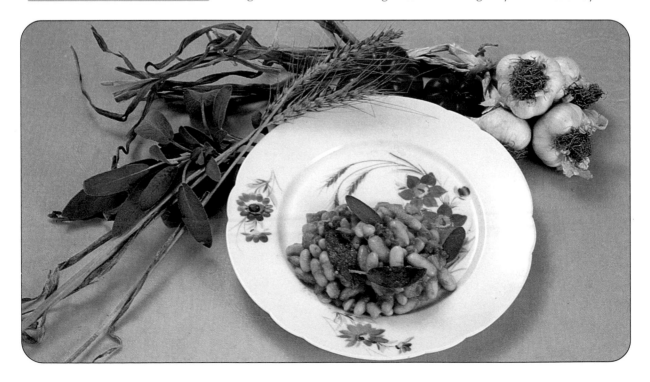

Fagioli al fiasco

BEANS IN A FLASK

◆

- 350G *TOSCANELLO* OR SMALL HARICOT BEANS
- SAGE LEAVES
- CLOVES OF GARLIC
- OLIVE OIL
- PEPPERCORNS

◆

PREPARATION TIME: 2 HOURS (MINIMUM)

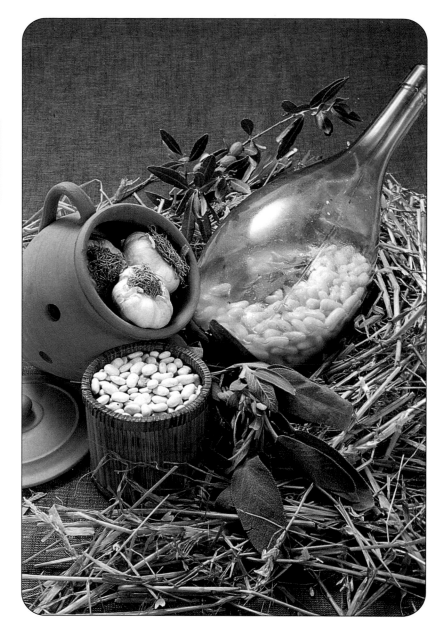

SOAK THE BEANS for about an hour in slightly tepid water. Drain them and drop them one by one (it is worth the trouble!) into a Chianti flask devoid of its traditional straw covering, along with the sage and 2 cloves of garlic. Add cold water and olive oil until the flask is full to the neck. Bung it with a wad of cotton wool so that the contents do not escape but excess steam can. If you have a fireplace, place the flask on a bed of ashes and embers so that it is partially covered. Too intense heat would cause the flask to explode, so do not put it too close to the roaring part of the fire. Make sure that the heat is always uniform.

If you do not have access to a wood fire, cook the beans by placing a rolled-up cloth on the bottom of a saucepan to form a kind of nest. Stand the flask on it upright and pour water into the pan so that the flask is almost completely covered. Bring to the boil and keep on the hob for 2 hours. Always remember to add hot water to the saucepan as it evaporates. *Fagioli al fiasco* are excellent hot or cold, seasoned, of course, with plenty of olive oil and freshly-ground pepper. They are delicious when served with fresh, thinly-sliced onions.

— 157 —

Piselli alla fiorentina

FLORENTINE PEAS

◆

- 1KG PEAS
- 100G FATTY BACON
- 1 LEMON
- 3 CLOVES OF GARLIC
- SPRIG OF PARSLEY
- 1 TEASPOON SUGAR
- 6 TABLESPOONS OLIVE OIL

◆

PREPARATION TIME: $^1/_2$ HOUR

HAVING SHELLED and rinsed the peas, cook them in a saucepan with the oil, the garlic in its "jacket" (i.e. do not remove the skin from each clove) and all the parsley.

Douse the peas with a little cold water and cook them with the lid on for a good quarter-hour. Add the diced bacon.

Bring the peas to the boil once more, adding the sugar, salt and a little pepper.

FOR A STILL FRESHER aroma, add pieces of pithless lemon zest to the first stage of cooking, or you can even leave it to the end, if you like.

These spring vegetables are always to be served hot. You will taste how the lemon zest imparts a flavour of freshness, exalting the delicate consistency.

Pomodori verdi fritti

FRIED GREEN TOMATOES

◆

- 4 GREEN SALAD TOMATOES
- 3 TABLESPOONS FLOUR
- BASIL
- 3 CLOVES OF GARLIC
- OLIVE OIL

◆

PREPARATION TIME: $^1/_2$ HOUR

WASH THE TOMATOES and cut them into half-inch slices. With extreme care, dip them in the flour so that the slices are well-coated on both sides.

Fry the floured tomato slices in boiling oil, turning them over gently so that they are well-browned on both sides.

They must be served very hot, liberally sprinkled with salt, garlic and chopped basil.

A SIMPLE, delicious dish for eating in the summer, perhaps with hard-boiled eggs in a green sauce (see recipe on page 41) and other mixed cooked or salad vegetables.

Salvia fritta
FRIED SAGE FRITTERS

- ◆
- ■ 2 SPRIGS OF LARGE-LEAFED SAGE
- ■ BATTER, OLIVE OIL
- ◆
- PREPARATION TIME: $1/2$ HOUR

THE LEAVES MUST BE UNBLEMISHED and aromatic. Rinse and dry them and make a thin batter to dip them into. Deep fry them in oil. Eat them crunchy, with a little salt. A variation: pieces of chopped, boned anchovy added as a filling between pairs of leaves which are then fried. My husband says they are to be served with white wine.

Sedani ripieni
STUFFED CELERY

- ◆
- ■ 1 HEAD OF CELERY
- ■ ABOUT 100G EACH OF MINCED VEAL AND PORK, LEG OF LAMB AND CHICKEN LIVERS
- ■ 50G EACH OF COOKED HAM AND MORTADELLA
- ■ 2 EGGS AND 2 YOLKS
- ■ 50G PARMESAN CHEESE
- ■ $1/2$L TOMATO PURÉE
- ■ WHITE WINE
- ■ ONION, CARROT AND CELERY
- ■ OLIVE OIL
- ◆
- PREPARATION TIME: $1 1/4$ HOURS

CHOOSE THE TENDEREST stalks, discarding the toughest ones and the leaves. Rinse and blanche for a few minutes in boiling water. Drain and place on a tea towel to dry. Mix the three types of meat with the chopped ham and mortadella in a bowl, adding the yolks and the grated Parmesan. Blend all the ingredients and stuff the celery, opening and flattening the stalks. Close each stalk carefully, dip in flour and then into the beaten egg and fry in 6 tablespoons of oil in a saucepan over low heat for 20 minutes, stirring. In a separate pan, make a mirepoix and add the chopped chicken livers together with a glass of white wine. Sauté for 10 minutes, then add the tomato purée. Place the stuffed celery stalks in this sauce, bring to the boil again and season with salt and pepper. Serve very hot.

THIS IS A DELICIOUS, substantial dish which presents the taste buds and the eyes with rare, luscious sensations. Give it to your guests, even the most finicky ones and your patience in the kitchen will be rewarded (indeed it requires quite some time to make).

Spinaci saltati

SAUTÉED SPINACH

- ◆
- ■ ¹/₂KG FRESH SPINACH
- ■ 3 CLOVES OF GARLIC
- ■ OLIVE OIL
- ■ LEMON (OPTIONAL)
- ◆

PREPARATION TIME: ³/₄ HOUR

WASH the spinach leaves carefully in plenty of water, making sure that the grit inside the folds of the leaves is removed.

Cook for 10 minutes with very little salted water in an uncovered saucepan (so that the leaves keep their bright green colour). Drain, leave to cool a little, squeeze in your hands and roll into little balls. Cut them up on a chopping board (a *mezzaluna* or double-handled, curved knife would help here) and toss into the oil in which the garlic has been gently sautéed. Let the spinach absorb the flavour well and season.

THIS IS EXCELLENT served with both boiled and roast meats. If you like, garnish with lemon.

Should you not appreciate the taste of garlic but only want the aroma, remove the cloves as soon as they start to colour, before tossing the spinach into the hot oil.

Zucchine pasticciate

ZUCCHINI RAGOUT

- ◆
- ■ 400G ZUCCHINI
- ■ 1 RED-SKINNED ONION
- ■ 100G CANNED TOMATOES
- ■ BASIL
- ■ 150G GRATED PECORINO CHEESE
- ■ OLIVE OIL
- ◆

PREPARATION TIME: ³/₄ HOUR

WASH and dry the zucchini, top and tail them and slice into thickish rounds.

Slice the onion into rings and cut the tomato into wedges. Put all the vegetables in a saucepan with 6 tablespoons of oil, sprinkle chopped basil over and season lightly with salt and pepper. Cover and cook for half-an-hour over gentle heat, stirring from time to time. Just before serving the zucchini boiling hot, dredge with pecorino and mix quickly to combine everything. This is an excellent side-plate to accompany boiled meats.

DESSERTS, CAKES AND PASTRIES

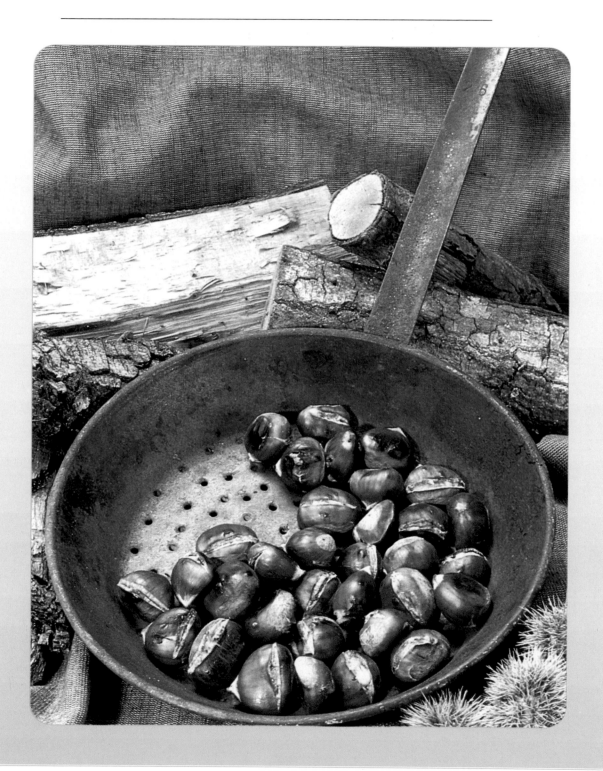

Anicini

ANISEED BISCUITS

◆

- 300G FLOUR
- 150G THIN HONEY
- 100G BUTTER, MELTED
- 150G CASTER SUGAR
- 30G ANISEED
- BARE PINCH BAKING POWDER
- 3 EGGS PLUS 2 EGG YOLKS
- ¹/2 CUP MILK

◆

PREPARATION TIME: 50 MINUTES

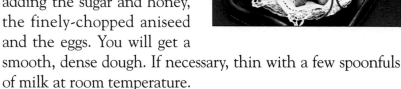

MELT THE HONEY and sugar in a small saucepan over quite a gentle heat, then leave to cool. Put the flour and baking powder in a bowl and mix briefly before adding the sugar and honey, the finely-chopped aniseed and the eggs. You will get a smooth, dense dough. If necessary, thin with a few spoonfuls of milk at room temperature.

Grease a shallow baking tin, pour in the mixture and cook in a moderate oven for half-an-hour. Allow to cool and cut into wide strips which you will then divide obliquely into biscuits.

Anicini should be eaten up fairly quickly as the honey tends to make them rubbery after a while.

Ballotte

BOILED CHESTNUTS

◆

- 1KG UNBLEMISHED CHESTNUTS
- 4 BAY LEAVES
- SPRIG WILD FENNEL

◆

PREPARATION TIME: 1 HOUR

PUT THE CHESTNUTS in a large saucepan with the bay leaves and the sprig of wild fennel and cover with plenty of cold water.

Simmer gently for at least an hour until soft, then drain.

DRAINED, PEELED and cooled, these can also be eaten with fresh ricotta (cottage) cheese and vinsanto (or sweet sherry). For centuries chestnuts were the main alimentary resource of the people living on the Italian Apennines, but today they are a treat.

Biscotti di Prato

PRATO BISCUITS

◆

- 500G WHITE FLOUR
- 400G SUGAR
- 250G ALMONDS
- 3 WHOLE EGGS AND 2 EGG YOLKS
- 1 BEATEN EGG
- 1 TEASPOON BAKING POWDER

◆

PREPARATION TIME: 1 1/2 HOURS

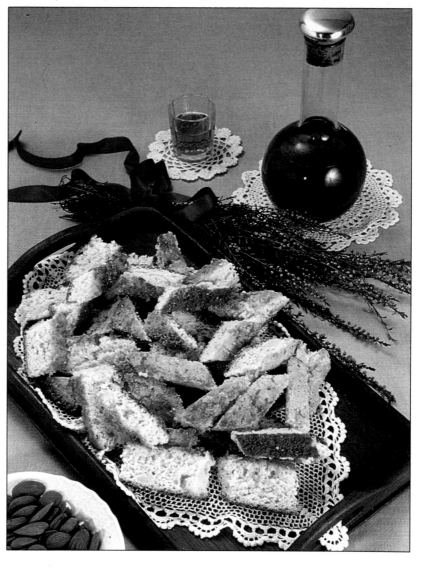

THOROUGHLY MIX all the ingredients (with the exception of the beaten egg) and knead. If necessary, add a few drops of milk, bearing in mind that the dough must be smooth but not sticky.

Shape into two stick loaves 4in wide and 12in long, brush with the beaten egg and dust with sugar.

Place on a baking tray lined with grease-proof or baking paper and cook in a low oven for at least an hour.

When the surface is crisp and golden, remove from the oven and, using a wide-bladed knife, cut the loaves obliquely into biscuits 1/2 in thick while they are still hot.

Once cold, these biscuits can be kept for a long time in an air-tight container, so that they do not lose their fragrance.

It is traditional to serve them together with a glass of vinsanto, into which they are dunked.

THERE ARE SOME VARIATIONS of this recipe, such as the one where the almonds are toasted in the oven before mixing into the dough, or the one recommending a pinch of saffron to give the biscuits a bright yellow colour. I think that my recipe - the most respectful of tradition - is ideal if you want biscuits with a balanced, pleasant flavour for relishing on any occasion.

Bomboloni
DOUGHNUTS

◆

- 300G WHITE FLOUR
- 50G BUTTER
- 20G YEAST
- 200G CASTER SUGAR
- 1 LEMON
- PINCH OF SALT
- OLIVE OIL

◆

PREPARATION TIME: 3 ^{1}/$_2$ HOURS

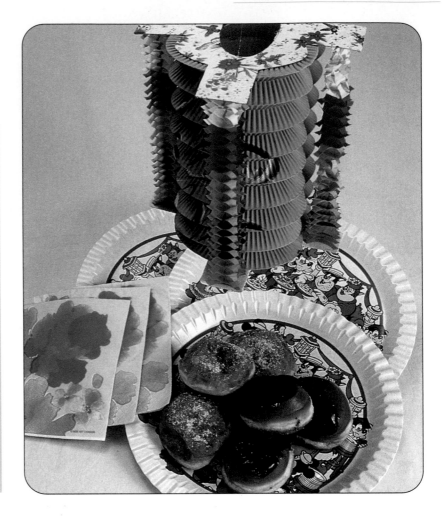

THEY ARE VERY GOOD just fried and served, but they are duly appreciated cold as well.
The best way of cooking them is filled with jam, confectioner's custard or chocolate. (The procedure is not very complicated: spoon the filling into a pastry bag with a small nozzle and stuff the doughnuts through a hole at the top of the disc of risen dough). If you form rings instead of discs, the result are what are commonly called "frati" or friars - reference to the tonsure of the brethren is evident. These are fried and sugared in exactly the same way as their paunchy counterparts.

HEAP THE FLOUR into a "volcano" with a crater in the middle, where you will put 2 tablespoons of sugar, the melted butter, the grated lemon zest, a pinch of salt and the yeast dissolved in half a glass of warm water. Work the dough in your fingers and form into a ball which you will put aside in a dry place for two hours, covered with a tea towel. Roll out the dough with a rolling pin until ^{1}/$_2$ in thick. Using a glass (or biscuit cutters), cut the dough into a number of discs that you will leave to rise again for another hour shrouded under a floured tea towel (scraps can be used up by kneading them again and proceeding as before). Deep fry them in hot oil, taking care to let them "float" so that they will cook without soaking up the oil (should they sink, the temperature is obviously too low). Turn them over to cook on the other side. Once fried, drain them and roll in the caster sugar.

Bruciate

ROAST CHESTNUTS

♦

■ 1KG CHESTNUTS (PREFERABLY CHOICE MARRONS)

♦

PREPARATION TIME: 20 MINUTES

CHESTNUTS COME in two types; ordinary ones and choice marrons. The former are small, dark and elongated, the latter being large and roundish, with a wavy, streaked outer skin. While ordinary chestnuts are fine for boiling, choice marrons are bigger and more flavoursome for roasting.

MAKE A SLIT in the skin (the Tuscans call it rather disturbingly "castrating") and place over a fierce heat in the special roasting pan with holes in the bottom, frequently turning the nuts over.

The fire really should be a log one, but, as not everyone possesses a fireplace, the kitchen hob will do.

When they are cooked and a little burnt (do not worry if the skins are somewhat charred) wrap them up in a length of woollen cloth and let them "stew" a little. Enjoy them while still scorching hot.

A tasty alternative is to soak them in a bowl of red vintage wine, once they are cooked and peeled.

Brutti ma buoni

ALMOND MERINGUES

♦

■ 4 EGG WHITES
■ 30G ALMONDS, PEELED
■ 30G HAZELNUTS, SHELLED
■ 50G VANILLA SUGAR
■ 100G BUTTER

♦

PREPARATION TIME: 1 HOUR

WHISK THE EGG whites until fluffy, gradually adding the sugar (never add it all at once if you do not want the mixture to collapse).

Toast the almonds and hazelnuts briefly in the oven, then chop roughly. Slowly add the nuts to the meringue mixture. Spoon small quantities onto a greased baking tray. Bake in a pre-heated, very slow oven for half-an-hour until you get little, crisp "mounds". Leave to cool and ... tuck in!

— 167 —

Castagnaccio
CHESTNUT CAKE

- ■ 200g CHESTNUT FLOUR
- ■ TUMBLER COLD WATER
- ■ 6 TABLESPOONS OIL
- ■ ROSEMARY
- ■ A HANDFUL EACH OF PINE-NUTS AND SULTANAS

PREPARATION TIME: 1 HOUR

STEEP THE SULTANAS IN HOT WATER. Pour the chestnut flour into a bowl where you have put 2 tablespoons of genuine olive oil.

Gradually add the cold water, stirring with a whisk to obtain a pouring mixture without lumps. Set the mixture aside for at least half an hour and, in the meanwhile, oil a shallow rectangular cake tin.

Heat 3 tablespoons of oil in a small saucepan and throw in the rosemary leaves for a short moment to flavour it.

Pour the mixture into the cake tin, sprinkle the pine-nuts and the well-dried sultanas over the top and drizzle over the rosemary-flavoured oil too, together with the rest of the oil.

Bake in the oven at 220°C for 30-40 minutes.

CASTAGNACCIO MUST BE of a nice brown colour with the top all wrinkled. The secret lies in the flour used; be cautious of flour on sale in October, because it is left over from the previous year. Genuine chestnut flour does not reach shop shelves before half-way through November, is mealy and sweet (indeed, the addition of sugar should not be necessary) and is good enough to eat raw.

Cenci
FRIED PASTRY TWISTS

◆

- 300G WHITE FLOUR
- 50G BUTTER
- 2 EGGS
- 1 TABLESPOON SUGAR
- 1 TABLESPOON MARSALA
- PINCH OF SALT
- 200G VANILLA SUGAR
- OLIVE OIL

◆

PREPARATION TIME: 1 1/2 HOURS

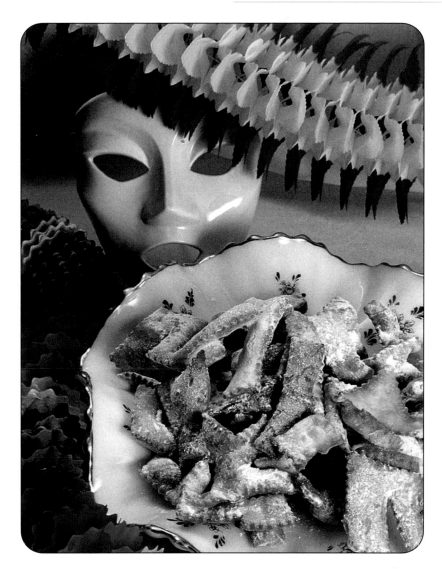

THESE PASTRY twists are good to eat either boiling hot or cold. They are consumed both at Carnival time (when they are customary in Tuscany) and also in the height of summer, even at a child's birthday party, seeing as they are not at all indigestible and are easy to make. Everyone makes his or her own slight modifications to the basic recipe or even to the shape (for example, some cooks tie the ribbons of dough before frying them or they clip the edges into fringes). Creativity is welcome, for the flavour of *cenci* is always appreciated.

MOUND THE FLOUR UP on a board and, in a hollow in the centre, place the butter (soft, not straight out of the refrigerator), the sugar, the eggs, a tablespoon of Marsala and a pinch of salt. Work the dough in your fingers until it is firm (add a little flour, if necessary). Cover and leave to "rest" for an hour in a dry place. Roll out the dough quite thinly and cut into strips about 2 inches by 4 (however, the size is up to you; it would appear that they are called cenci or "rags" precisely because they come in different shapes and sizes!). Deep fry in boiling oil. They are ready when they turn crisp and golden; be careful not to overcook and burn them. Drain and dust liberally with vanilla sugar.

Ciambellone
ORANGE RING CAKE

◆

- 150G BUTTER
- 2 EGGS, SEPARATED
- 200G FLOUR
- 200G CASTER SUGAR
- AN ORANGE
- BAKING POWDER
- 50G SULTANAS
- 1/2 GLASS MILK

◆

PREPARATION TIME: 1 HOUR

WHISK THE EGG WHITES until stiff, add the yolks, milk, sugar and grated orange zest and beat for a few minutes. With a spoon, beat in the flour, the melted butter and the baking powder, lastly adding the sultanas, which have previously been softened in hot water, then pressed dry and floured. Work it all together for 5 minutes.

Grease a ring-mould, pour in the mixture and bake at 200°C for 20 minutes.

FOR MANY FLORENTINES over various epochs, this cake (which keeps very well), has been the answer to the problem of what to eat at tea-time. Only a few bakeries now continue to make it. There is another recipe for *Ciambellone* which is also known as "Easter cake": whole beaten eggs, all the ingredients worked together, the addition of a liqueur and the lot baked in a medium oven for 40 minutes. With all due respect, I still prefer my version, which, though more elaborate in the making, with perhaps a somewhat "poorer" outcome, pays a little more attention to detail.

Ciambellone bicolore
BICOLOUR RING CAKE

◆

- 4 EGGS (TOTAL WEIGHT SHOULD BE ABOUT 300G)
- 300G FLOUR
- 300G BUTTER
- 2 TABLESPOONS BITTER COCOA
- 300G ICING SUGAR
- PINCH OF SALT

◆

PREPARATION TIME: 1 HOUR

TO PREPARE THE BASE, proceed as for the *Tortina 4/4* (p. 188). When the mixture is ready, divide it between two bowls; in one you will also mix 2 tablespoons of bitter cocoa. Butter and flour a ring mould and pour in the two mixtures in alternation, separating them with greasproof paper (to be removed once the cake is cooked). Bake at 180°C for a quarter-hour.

IF THE TWO MIXTURES (the one with cocoa and the other without) are spooned in alternatively, the result will be a nice, decorative effect. This cake, not to be confused with the Ciambellone given above, keeps well for several days if kept in a cool, dry place.

Cotognata
QUINCE JELLY

- 3KG QUINCES
- 2KG CASTER SUGAR
- 1/2 GLASS OIL, AROMA-TISED WITH CLOVES

PREPARATION TIME: 1 1/2 HOURS

DRY THE PEELED quinces in a slow oven for 40 minutes. Core and sieve them. Weigh the resultant amount (reduced to about 2kg) and add the equivalent weight in caster sugar.

Cook for half-an-hour in a saucepan over very gentle heat, stirring frequently with a wooden spoon.

Grease a shallow, rectangular baking tin with the aromatised oil, pour in the quince mixture and level out the surface with the wooden spoon.

Leave to stand in a cool place for at least three days. Then cut it into large cubes and coat with sugar. Keep well wrapped in foil.

QUINCES ARE excellent to eat, even though they may appear like those stupendous creatures who, as soon as they open their mouths… Indeed, they are wonderful for making table compositions (together with various varieties of yellow vegetable squash and finished off with bunches of black grapes; the effect is picturesque). But try and taste them raw and you are in for a disappointment, because they are inedible. They are, however, delicious once cooked and eaten with sugar.

Crema fritta
FRIED CUSTARD

- 100G FLOUR
- 150G CASTER SUGAR
- 3 EGGS
- 1/2 L MILK
- LEMON ZEST
- 50G DRIED BREAD-CRUMBS
- OLIVE OIL

PREPARATION TIME: 2 HOURS

WHISK TWO EGG yolks with the sugar. Add the grated lemon zest and the milk, a little at a time. Place over gentle heat, stirring carefully. When the custard begins to thicken, keep on stirring with a wooden spoon for a further 5 minutes.

Pour into a shallow, square cake tin. Leave to cool, then cut into fingers. Dip these in the beaten egg, then in the dried breadcrumbs and deep fry in oil, draining them when they are evenly golden all over. Serve with a liberal sprinkling of caster sugar.

THIS IS EXCELLENT WHETHER served hot in winter or else cold in summer.

Mix a little powdered vanilla into the sugar (or keep a pod in your air-tight sugar jar) to lend grace and a very pleasant flavour to this age-old dish.

Crostini dolci della nonna

GRANNY'S SWEET CROUTONS

◆

- $^1/_2$ KG STALE BREAD
- $^1/_2$ L MILK
- 50G VANILLA SUGAR
- 100G FLOUR
- 1 EGG
- 100G DRIED BREAD-
  CRUMBS
- MIXED POACHED FRUIT
  (APPLES, PLUMS,
  PEARS, ETC.)
- OLIVE OIL

THE COMPOTE:

- 1 EATING PEAR
- 1 EATING APPLE
- 200G PITTED PRUNES
- 50G CASTER SUGAR
- A LITTLE WATER, $^1/_2$
  LEMON

THE APRICOT SYRUP:

- $^1/_2$ L WATER
- 200G CASTER SUGAR
- 400G VERY RIPE APRI-
  COTS
- 1 LEMON

◆

PREPARATION TIME: 1 $^1/_2$
HOURS

CUT SOME SLICES of bread and dunk them in a bowl of milk, previously warmed over a flame and in which you will have dissolved the vanilla sugar. The croutons should be steeped in the milk, drained, floured, egg-and-crumbed and deep fried in oil.

Still hot, arrange them on a platter around the fruit compote in the centre. Serve the apricot sauce separately, to dunk your crisp bread in.

To make the compote, peel the fruit (which must be

nice and ripe), cut into pieces and place in a saucepan where you will have put the sugar and the zest of half a lemon (the prunes can be added when the rest is half-cooked). Poach over moderate heat for a quarter-hour. Leave to cool and serve the compote drained of its syrup.

The apricot syrup is prepared by washing and pitting the apricots and heating them in a saucepan with the water, sugar and a piece of lemon peel. Simmer gently for 20 minutes. Then filter the resultant syrup several times and serve cold.

To accompany biscuits or to use a s a filling for cakes.

A SWEET INTERVAL while studying or labouring away which my children highly appreciate (and they are not alone). It was (and still is) a clever, thrifty way of using up simple ingredients such as bread and fruit which are a considerable source of energy.

Dolce Firenze

FLORENCE PUDDING

- 4 SLICES OF BREAD
- 100G SUGAR
- KNOB OF BUTTER
- 3 EGGS
- 1/2 L MILK
- 40G SULTANAS MOISTENED IN A SWEET LIQUEUR
- LEMON ZEST

PREPARATION TIME: 1 1/4 HOURS

THIS PUDDING WAS GIVEN its name by the great Italian scholar Pellegrino Artusi, who teamed it with the "Turin Pudding" (the only one with an authentic "title") and the "Rome Pudding" (also baptised by the same), joining them together in a post-*Risorgimento* triptych to the glory of the three capitals of Italy. I translate from his manual *La scienza in cucina e l'arte di mangiar bene*: "I came across it in the ancient, beautiful city of flowers and as no-one has bothered giving it a name, I venture to suggest calling it "Dolce Firenze". If it is of too modest a nature to do honour to this illustrious city, the excuse it offers could be, "Welcome me as a family pudding so that I may sweeten the mouth with little expenditure". Wise words. The pudding could be found on Florentine tables long before Pellegrino discovered it and baptised it. I shall suggest a variation. Sometimes I substitute the slices of Tuscan-style bread with toasted slices of stale baker's loaves of softer bread (not the industrial product, though!). The outcome is a more delicate pudding which is not so heavy, more in line with our unsettled times.

TOAST THE THIN SLICES of bread, butter them and arrange in a deep ovenproof dish. Sprinkle with sultanas and grated lemon zest. Whisk the eggs with the sugar and add the milk. Pour the mixture over the bread and bake at 180°C for an hour.

Donzelline

FRIED PASTRY RINGS

- 250G FLOUR
- 10 FENNEL SEEDS
- 30G SUGAR
- 30G BUTTER
- 2 EGGS
- 3-4 TABLESPOONS OF MARSALA
- 200G VANILLA SUGAR
- OLIVE OIL

PREPARATION TIME: 1 1/2 HOURS

MIX THE FLOUR, sugar, flakes of softened butter, the whole eggs and a little salt in a bowl. While you are working the mixture, add the Marsala and the fennel seeds. The result will be quite a thick dough, form it into a ball and cover, leaving it to "rest" in a dry place for an hour. Roll it out quite thinly on a floured pastry board. Cut into inch-wide strips that you will form into rings with your fingers. Fry them in hot oil until the surface is nicely golden. Drain and dry them and dredge with vanilla sugar.

AT FIRST SIGHT YOU will think that the recipe is the same as for *cenci*, but the fennel seeds and the circular shape make this a dish of Florentine cuisine in its own right. How about this idea; make them to accompany ordinary *cenci*, so that you can alternate flavours, shapes and aromas on one platter.

Ficattole

SWEET FRIED BREAD

- ◆
- ■ 500G BREAD DOUGH
- ■ 200G CASTER SUGAR
- ■ OLIVE OIL

◆

PREPARATION TIME: 1 ¹/4
HOURS

L EAVE THE DOUGH to rise (please see the relative recipe on page 180 for the preparation).

Then, with your hands, form fingers about 2ins in length that you will deep fry in boiling oil until they are of a delicate golden colour.

Dredge the *ficattole* with sugar and serve them very hot, otherwise they become rubbery and hard, thus losing all their fragrance which, given the simplicity of the ingredients, is an essential component of their success.

IN TIMES GONE by they were called "fried bread" or "fritters", rather unimaginative names compared to the name which the passage of time gave to them (the reference in Italian to a fig shape has a clear anatomical allusion). If you wish to add an unusual flavour, then make little pellets of dough instead of fingers, into which you will place a piece of apple (preferably an eating apple), sealing the pellet up well in your fingertips, so that the apple does not spill out during cooking. Fry in the same way as before and serve very hot, still dredged with sugar.

In other recipes, the *ficattole* are described as lozenges of dough with a longitudinal split (this would explain the name). All well and good, but I prefer to do it my way and have something to get my teeth into.

Frittelle

FRITTERS

- ◆
- ■ 120G SEMOLINA
- ■ ¹/2 L MILK
- ■ 100G CASTER SUGAR
- ■ 1 ORANGE
- ■ 50G SULTANAS
- ■ BICARBONATE OF SODA
- ■ 3 EGGS
- ■ OLIVE OIL

◆

PREPARATION TIME: ³/4
HOUR

S OAK THE SULTANAS. Bring the milk almost to the boil, dissolving the sugar in it. Toss in the semolina and stir with a whisk. Simmer gently for 10 minutes, continuously stirring. Press the moisture out of the sultanas and add, together with the grated orange zest, to the semolina. Turn off the heat and leave to cool. Add a pinch of bicarbonate of soda and the beaten eggs. Mix it all well and leave to stand for half an hour. Fry the fritters (use about half a tablespoon of the batter for each one), taking care that they do not sink but float (if they do sink, raise the heat). Drain and dry. Dredge with caster sugar and preferably eat hot.

TO TELL YOU the truth, they will look more like little, sweet "balls" than like the flatter fritters. Indeed, in the Tuscan countryside they are referred to as "Muscat balls".

Frittelle di riso

RICE FRITTERS

- 500G RICE
- 1/2 L MILK
- 200G MUSCATEL RAISINS
- 1 ORANGE AND 1 LEMON
- 500G CASTER SUGAR
- 1 LIQUEUR GLASS OF MARSALA
- 1 TABLESPOON WHITE FLOUR
- 3 WHOLE EGGS AND 2 EGG YOLKS
- PINCH OF BAKING POWDER
- OLIVE OIL

PREPARATION TIME: 1 HOUR

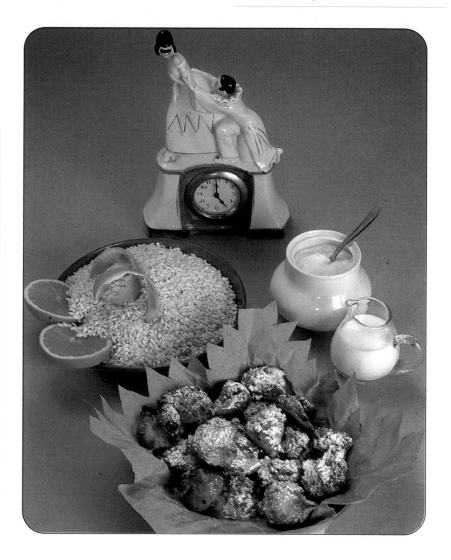

ACCORDING TO TRADITION, rice fritters are prepared for St Joseph's Day on 19 March which used to be a holiday, but is now a day like any other. A pity! Even if we have been robbed of a holiday in the interests of productivity, we will certainly not give up the habit of these delicious little fritters, typical of Florentine cookery. I warn you that they seem easy to make, but that, on the contrary, a lot of care is needed to make them nice and golden and not soggy with oil as are so many of those you find in the shops.

PUT THE RICE in a saucepan with half a litre of cold water, the cold milk, the orange and the lemon, sliced. Cook for 20 minutes over low heat, stirring with a wooden spoon. Add 300g of sugar and continue cooking over gentle heat for another 20 minutes, still stirring.

Before drawing off the heat, add the muscatel raisins and the Marsala. Allow to cool and remove the orange and lemon slices.

Add the flour, whole eggs, yolks and the baking powder. Stir with a wooden spoon and deep fry, dropping spoonfuls of the mixture into the oil. The fritters must float on top (if they sink, raise the heat because the oil is obviously at too low a temperature). Allow to brown evenly all over, drain well and roll in plenty of caster sugar. Serve them hot.

Frittelline tonde
ROUND FRITTERS

◆

- 400G FLOUR
- 100G CORNMEAL
- MARSALA
- 2 PINCHES BAKING POWDER
- 1 ORANGE
- 1 GLASS MILK
- 300G CASTER SUGAR
- OLIVE OIL

◆

PREPARATION TIME: 1 ¹/₂ HOURS

MIX THE TWO FLOURS and heap into a mound with a hollow in the middle. Add the baking powder dissolved in the warm milk, the grated orange zest, a glass of Marsala and 200g of sugar.

Knead the mixture in your fingers until you get a soft, but firm, dough (if necessary, flour your hands during the kneading operation). Allow to stand for an hour, covered with a tea towel, until double in size. Then pull off a little dough in your fingers, roll it in the palms of your hands to make a little ball and continue until all the dough has been used up.

Deep fry the balls in oil. Allow to brown for a few minutes, drain them and toss in the remaining sugar.

THEY ARE EXCELLENT served boiling hot, covered in sugar. Use a very sweet Marsala with a well-defined flavour which will linger after cooking and use very finely-ground cornmeal, so that the dough of the fritters does not "unwind".

Gialletti
CORNMEAL BISCUITS

◆

- 200G FLOUR
- 300G CORNMEAL
- 100G BUTTER
- 100G CASTER SUGAR
- 2 WHOLE EGGS
- ¹/₂ GLASS MILK

◆

PREPARATION TIME: 1 ¹/₄ HOURS

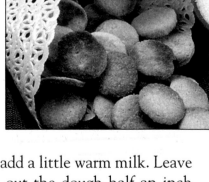

HEAP BOTH TYPES OF flour into a "volcano" and pour the eggs, sugar and butter into the crater, working them in to make a firm dough. If the cornmeal does not absorb the butter properly, add a little warm milk. Leave covered for half an hour. Roll out the dough half an inch thick and cut out some round biscuits with the aid of biscuit moulds or glasses. Place on a buttered baking tray and cook in a moderate oven for 15 minutes. Crisp and yellow, these biscuits are excellent served with home-made liqueurs such as walnut-flavoured *nocino*. They keep well in air-tight jars.

Lattaiolo

BAKED CUSTARD

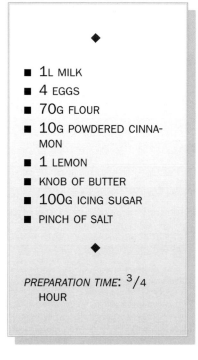

- ◆
- ■ 1L MILK
- ■ 4 EGGS
- ■ 70G FLOUR
- ■ 10G POWDERED CINNA-MON
- ■ 1 LEMON
- ■ KNOB OF BUTTER
- ■ 100G ICING SUGAR
- ■ PINCH OF SALT
- ◆

PREPARATION TIME: 3/4 HOUR

IN A BOWL, beat the eggs and add the flour, milk, cinnamon, grated lemon zest and a pinch of salt, stirring constantly. Butter a rectangular cake tin, pour in the custard and bake at 180°C for half an hour.

Cool the *lattaiolo* well and turn it out onto a big platter. Only when it is completely cold (absolutely not before!), dust liberally with icing sugar.

A SIMPLE, DELICIOUS sweet, it is often cooked with fresh cream instead of milk (then it becomes the so-called *Panna cotta* or "Cooked Cream"). Perhaps this is because now-a-days a lot of flavour is lost in the processes of pasteurisation and sterilisation to which the milk is subjected and so a stronger flavour is desired. For those of us who have had the good fortune to grow up with the taste of a good glass of milk as it comes straight from the cow, nothing can compare to the flavour of this sweet cooked with "real" milk. Luckily, the recent launch onto the market of high-quality types of milk with a more pronounced flavour can assist us, at least in part, in getting round the problem.

Mele fritte

FRIED APPLES

- ◆
- ■ 300G CHESTNUT FLOUR
- ■ 1 GLASS WATER
- ■ 4 EATING APPLES
- ■ 200G CASTER SUGAR
- ■ OLIVE OIL
- ◆

PREPARATION TIME: 1 HOUR

BEAT THE FLOUR into the water, without allowing lumps to form. When the batter is smooth and of a coating consistency, leave to stand for half an hour. Peel and core the apples, cut them crosswise to get rings about 1/2 in thick, dunk these in the batter and fry them. Turn them over so that they can brown completely. Drain and toss in the sugar. Serve at once, hot and tempting.

INSTEAD of water, add a glass of *vin nuovo* to the flour (the light, sharp wine bottled in November of the same year of harvest). The batter will have with an unusual, appetising taste.

Mostarda toscana
TUSCAN FRUIT MUSTARD

◆

- 2KG WHITE GRAPES
- 1KG COOKING APPLES
- 2 DESSERT PEARS
- 50G MUSTARD POWDER
- 1 GLASS VINSANTO
- 120G CANDIED CITRON-PEEL
- PINCH POWDERED CINNA-MON

◆

PREPARATION TIME: 1 HOUR

WASH THE GRAPES and strip them off the stem. Put in a bowl, pressing them down, and leave for two or three days to macerate, before crushing them. Over a slow flame, cook the peeled apples and pears with a glass of vinsanto for half-an-hour. When the wine has evaporated, add the "grape-must". Allow to thicken over gentle heat, stirring frequently and continue cooking for another 10 minutes before adding the mustard (dissolved in a little warmed vinsanto) and the candied citron-peel cut into small pieces. Keep stirring over low heat for some minutes, then leave to cool.

THIS IS EXCELLENT served with boiled or roast meat and game. If you wish to keep for some time, pour into little jars and dust with the powdered cinnamon before screwing on the airtight tops and storing in a cool, dry, preferably dark place.

Pan dolce alla cannella
CINNAMON FRUIT CAKE

◆

- 125G CANE SUGAR
- 1 EGG
- MILK AND CINNAMON
- 400G FLOUR
- BAKING POWDER
- 2 HANDFULS SULTANAS
- 20 WALNUTS
- KNOB OF BUTTER

◆

PREPARATION TIME: 1 HOUR

AS CUSTOM HAS IT, the sultanas are first of all put to soak in warm water.

Whisk the sugar into the egg and add the flour together with a pinch of baking powder, the cinnamon and a glass-and-a-half of milk.

The result should be a rather dense mixture.

Now add the drained sultanas, thoroughly dried in a clean cloth and lightly floured and two generous handfuls of walnuts, which have been previously broken into rough pieces.

Pour the mixture into a rectangular oven mould, evenly buttered, and have your cake baking at 180°C for at least an hour.

Pandiramerino

ROSEMARY BUNS

- 1KG WHITE FLOUR
- 50G FRESH YEAST
- 50G SUGAR
- 2 GLASSES OLIVE OIL
- 300G MUSCATEL RAISINS
- HANDFUL ROSEMARY NEEDLES
- 1 EGG

PREPARATION TIME: 1 HOUR

MAKE A SOFT dough with the flour, yeast and sugar, binding with warm water. Cover and leave to rise in a dry place until doubled in volume. Put on a pastry board and add the raisins, oil and rosemary. Knead the dough for a few minutes and form a quantity of dome-shaped buns, brushing the surface with beaten egg. With a sharp knife, slash a cross on top of each one and bake in the oven at 220°C for half-an-hour until the buns have a nice, even, brown crust.

Pane al limone

LEMON CAKE

- 125G BUTTER
- 200G SUGAR, 100G ICING SUGAR
- 1 LEMON AND 6 WAL-NUTS
- 4 EGGS
- 370G FLOUR
- 20G BAKING POWDER
- MILK

PREPARATION TIME: 2 HOURS

BEAT THE BUTTER (softened at room temperature) with the sugar until creamy. Add the salt and a couple of spoonfuls of lemon juice and then the eggs, one by one, beating energetically. Gradually incorporate the flour (sieved with the baking powder) and the milk, both in small quantities, in alternation. Add the chopped nuts and the grated lemon peel. Pour the mixture into a buttered rectangular cake tin. Bake in the oven at 180°C for an hour-and-a-half. Dissolve the icing sugar in the remaining lemon juice to make a delicious, stringy syrup and spread it over the top of the cake immediately on removing from the oven. If possible, use lemons which have not been treated with pesticides or other weird concoctions.

Panettone
SPICED BRIOCHE

◆

- 800G FLOUR
- 15G BAKING POWDER
- 15G BUTTER
- 6 EGGS
- 400G SUGAR
- 80G CANDIED PEEL
- 15G ANISEED
- 50G PINE-NUTS
- 40G SULTANAS
- 25G VANILLA SUGAR
- A LITTLE MILK

◆

PREPARATION TIME: 1 HOUR (PLUS LEAVENING PERIOD)

MIX THE BAKING POWDER into 200g of flour, adding the warm milk. Shape into a ball and leave in a dry place to rise overnight, covered with a cloth. Add the remaining flour with 2 beaten eggs. Shape into a ball and leave for 4 hours to prove again, well-covered in a warm place. When it has doubled in size, knead it with your floured hands, adding the remaining ingredients. Butter and flour a large, deep cake tin (there are special *panettone* tins available on the market). Transfer the dough to it and bake in a pre-heated medium oven for three quarters-of-an-hour. The brioche is cooked when the top has become nice and brown and has split open. Remove from the oven, allow to "rest" for 5 minutes, then, banging the tin lightly on the table, dislodge the cake from the tin without overturning it completely, supporting the "head" of the brioche (the part rising above the level of the tin) in your hand.

Serve it only when it has thoroughly cooled, otherwise it tends to crumble.

Pasta di pane
BREAD DOUGH

◆

- 400G FLOUR
- 20G FRESH YEAST
- 4 TABLESPOONS OLIVE OIL

◆

PREPARATION TIME: 1 ¼ HOURS

DISSOLVE THE YEAST in a little warm water and add it to the flour and oil in a bowl. Knead the dough, then set aside in a dry place for an hour, covered with a tea towel. The dough is now ready for use in other recipes.

I RECOMMEND THIS simple dough because, if your oven is suitable, you could make your own bread (with what a great satisfaction!), but principally because it is an ideal, simple base both for savoury dishes and (with the addition of 4 tablespoons of sugar) for unpretentious desserts such as the *schiacciata con l'uva* (dough cake with grapes). Here is the opportunity for you all to give your fantasy a free rein!

With a little dough, a touch of creativity and an oven, you can make pizzas and delicious first and second courses and *en croute* side-dishes, as well as quiches which would even go down well in the Lorraine!

Quaresimali
LENTEN BISCUITS

◆

- 100G WHITE FLOUR
- 20G BITTER COCOA
- 2 EGG WHITES
- 1 ORANGE
- 150G ICING SUGAR

◆

PREPARATION TIME: $^1/2$ HOUR

GRATE THE ORANGE PEEL (it should not be too thick) and place all the ingredients in a bowl where you will blend them thoroughly, by giving a good, lengthy beating with the wooden spoon.

A thick cream will be the end result. Spoon a portion into a pastry bag with a smooth nozzle and squeeze the mixture onto a lightly-buttered baking tray, forming the letters of the alphabet.

Do not write them too big (1 $^1/2$ in - 2in high at the most) and space them out well, because they need room to spread in the cooking. Bake in a slow oven for at least 10 minutes.

IF YOUR EFFORTS with a pastry bag are not entirely satisfactory, you can easily get hold of little letter-shaped moulds which will provide you with more aesthetically acceptable *quaresimali*.

All things considered, the originality of the recipe, which is exceedingly simple, resides in the shape of the biscuits, so they might as well be done properly.

The name of this biscuit tells us when they were traditionally made. At one time, there was not a pastry-shop or baker's here in Florence which, during Lent, did not exhibit conspicuous heaps of the biscuits, which sold like … hotcakes! Understandably so, because the abstemious period following the Carnival festival offers the palate scarce gratification. Now that they have rather gone out of fashion, make them yourselves, for the children's birthdays, perhaps. They will have great fun - like I do, too - making up words from the brown letters, only to crunch them up happily!

Salame di cioccolata

CHOCOLATE SAUSAGE

◆

- 300G BISCUITS (NOT ONES CONTAINING EGGS)
- 150G CASTER SUGAR
- 150G BUTTER
- 50G PINE-NUTS
- 2 TABLESPOONS BITTER COCOA
- 1 LIQUEUR GLASS OF SWEET MARSALA

◆

PREPARATION TIME: 20 MINUTES

FINELY CRUMBLE the biscuits into a bowl and add the butter (melted, but not hot), sugar and cocoa. Blend the mixture with a spoon and gradually add the Marsala. Continue working with your hands and add the coarsely-chopped pine-nuts. Form the mixture into an elongated sausage shape and place in the refrigerator, well-wrapped in aluminium foil. When it is time to serve it, cut into slices half-an-inch thick and offer them on a round plate.

IF YOU LIKE, you could complement this with a light custard for spreading on top.

To make it, you need 2 egg yolks, beaten in a bowl with 50g of caster sugar. Add 20g flour and half a litre of milk at room temperature. First whisk well to blend off the heat, then put over very low heat, drawing it off as soon as it shows signs of bubbling at the sides.

Schiacciata alla fiorentina

FLORENTINE FLAT CAKE

◆

- 500G WHITE FLOUR
- 150G LARD
- 20G YEAST
- 150G SUGAR
- 4 EGG YOLKS
- 1 ORANGE
- SALT
- VANILLA SUGAR

◆

PREPARATION TIME: 3 1/2 HOURS

DISSOLVE THE YEAST in water which is barely warm and add to the flour in a bowl, working it in until you get a firm dough (that comes away easily from the sides of the bowl). Cover and leave in a dry place to prove for an hour. When doubled in size, mix in the egg yolks, sugar, 100g lard, a pinch of salt and the finely-grated orange peel, working it all in your fingers to blend the ingredients thoroughly. With the lard left over, grease a deep, rectangular cake tin and press the dough in, making sure that it is of even thickness all over (about an inch). Be careful here, because herein lies the secret of success. Leave it to rise again for 2 hours. Bake in a hot oven for half-an-hour. Turn out and dust with vanilla sugar.

THIS IS TYPICALLY eaten on Carnival Thursday (just before Lent) and, as for the *cenci*, there are several variations. The main one consists in replacing the lard with butter (there are those who fill the cake with whipped cream or confectioner's custard).

— 182 —

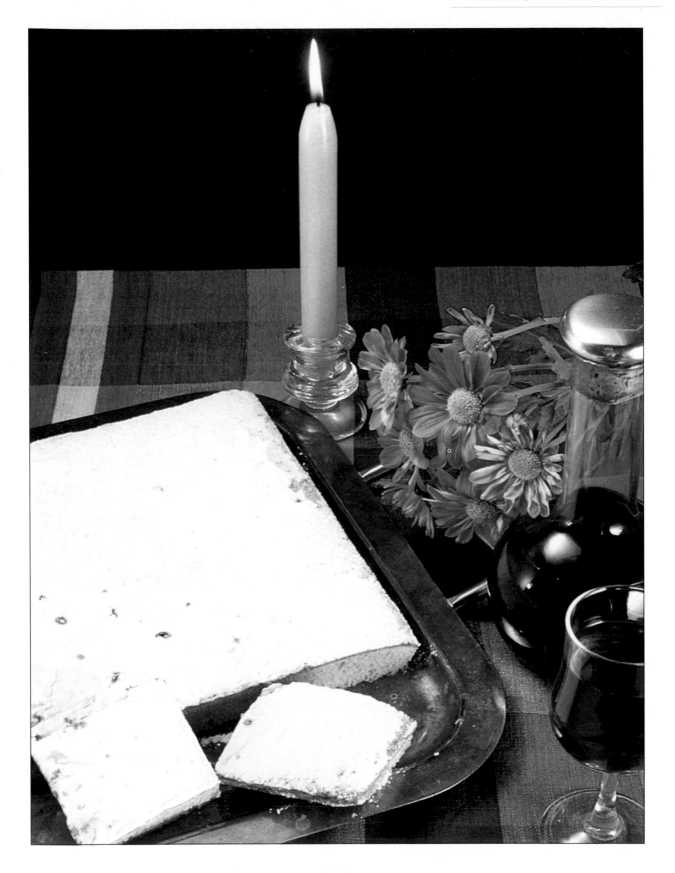

Schiacciata con l'uva

GRAPE DOUGH CAKE

◆

- 500G BREAD DOUGH
- 1KG WINE GRAPES
- 8 TABLESPOONS CASTER SUGAR
- ROSEMARY
- 2 TABLESPOONS OLIVE OIL

◆

PREPARATION TIME: 1 ¹/₂ HOURS

KNEAD THE DOUGH (see the relative recipe), rendered more pliable with the addition of a tablespoon of oil, for five minutes. Grease a deep, rectangular cake tin and spread half of the dough on the bottom. Scatter over two thirds of the grapes, pressing them down and dusting with 3 tablespoons of sugar. Cover with the remaining dough, knocking it up well against the sides of the tin. Strew the remaining grapes on top, pushing down, and dredge with the remaining sugar. Sprinkle over a few rosemary needles and a little olive oil. Leave for 40 minutes and bake in a hot oven for half-an-hour. until a nice, golden crust has formed.

SPRINKLE OVER a glass of red wine before baking. Besides imparting flavour, it will lend an attractive dark red colour.

I advise using small, juicy black wine grapes for this cake, typically baked in the period between the end of summer and the beginning of autumn.

Schiacciata "povera"

"POOR MAN'S" DOUGH CAKE WITH GRAPES

◆

- 400G FLOUR
- 5 TABLESPOONS CASTER SUGAR
- BAKING POWDER
- ROSEMARY
- 2 TABLESPOONS OLIVE OIL
- 200G BLACK GRAPES

◆

PREPARATION TIME: 1 ¹/₄ HOURS

MIX THE FLOUR and sugar in a bowl. Wash the grapes (preferably wine and not table grapes), pull them off their stalks, dry them and add to the flour mixture. Separately, heat the rosemary in the oil in a saucepan, leave to cool, then toss into the mixture. Last of all, add the baking powder and bake in an oil-greased cake tin at 180°C for three quarters-of-an-hour. Once cool, dust with caster sugar.

THIS IS A SIMPLER, more meagre version of the *schiacciata con l'uva*. At the outbreak of autumn, my grandmother used to knock it up speedily any time we children clamoured for a snack. This goes to show (as if there were any need) the great importance of grandmothers and their huge utility in inducing snack manufacturers to turn their skills to other, more deserving trades.

Torta dei certosini

CARTHUSIAN CAKE

- 300G FLOUR
- 120G SUGAR
- 150G ALMONDS
- 150G HAZEL NUTS
- 150G HONEY
- 50G EACH SULTANAS AND DRIED FIGS
- 30G CANDIED CITRON-PEEL
- 2 EGGS
- 50G BUTTER
- A LITTLE CINNAMON
- 10G VANILLA
- 10G BAKING POWDER
- MILK, A LITTLE *GRAPPA*

PREPARATION TIME: 1 1/2 HOURS

SOAK THE SULTANAS in warm water. Cream the sugar and eggs, then sprinkle in the flour, with the skinned hazel nuts and the toasted, shredded almonds. Add the honey, the figs cut up small, the sultanas squeezed dry, the cubed candied citron-peel and the softened butter. Combine the ingredients with a wooden spoon. Bind with the milk and half a glass of the liqueur. Spice the mixture with a pinch of cinnamon and the vanilla. Leave to stand for 20 minutes, then add the baking powder. Butter and flour a shallow, square cake tin and pour in the mixture. Bake for three quarters-of-an-hour at 180°C. After half-an-hour, place a sheet of foil over the cake so that the surface does not harden. Leave until almost completely cool, loosen the cake from the sides of the tin and, with a firm tap on the table, turn the cake out.

THIS CAKE IS for great occasions. It was concocted by the Carthusian monks of Florence for the pastoral visit of a pope (I know not which). It is delicious if cut into inch-thick slices and served with a strong, sweet liqueur e.g. Chartreuse (just like the one that the Carthusians, well-known for their distilled liquors and infusions as well as for their proverbial patience, prepare with great skill).

Torta di mele

TUSCAN APPLE CAKE

- 1.2KG EATING APPLES
- 100G BUTTER
- 2 EGGS
- 200G SUGAR
- 200G FLOUR
- BAKING POWDER
- A LITTLE DRY LIQUEUR

PREPARATION TIME: 1 1/4 HOURS

WHISK THE EGGS with the sugar. Add the softened butter and the dry liqueur. Blend the ingredients well with a spoon. Add the flour, sieved together with the baking powder, and the peeled apples, sliced paper thin. Butter a deep, square cake tin and bake the cake for 50 minutes at 180°C. It will be perfect if served with a chocolate sauce: mix 50g of sweet powdered cocoa, 50g of sugar and 20g of white flour in a small saucepan. Bind with 2 glasses of milk and cook over gentle heat for a quarter- hour. Allow to cool and spread a little on each slice of cake.

Garnish the dish by sprinkling liberally with vanilla sugar (if a little comes to rest on the plate, the effect will be even more decorative).

Torta di ricotta

RICOTTA CHEESE PIE

- 200G FLOUR
- 50G CORNFLOUR
- 300G SUGAR
- 100G BUTTER
- 1 WHOLE EGG AND 3 YOLKS
- ICING SUGAR
- 300G RICOTTA (COTTAGE) CHEESE
- LEMON ZEST
- $1/2$ L MILK

PREPARATION TIME: 1 $1/2$ HOURS

MAKE THE CONFECTIONER'S custard (see page 190) and leave to cool, stirring from time to time so that a skin does not form on the surface. If the ricotta is fresh and wet, dry it in a cloth. When the custard has cooled, pour into a bowl and add the ricotta, sugar, an egg yolk and the lemon zest (I would prefer orange, but tradition has it differently). Mix well and leave to stand.

Now prepare the pastry. Mix the flour and cornflour, heap into a mound and hollow out the centre, into which you will place the whole egg, sugar and softened butter. Work everything in together and form into a ball. Lightly butter and flour the bottom of a cake tin. Line the bottom and sides of the tin with the pastry. Pour in the cheese filling and fold a little of the pastry over the top. Bake for half-an-hour in a hot, pre-heated oven. Leave to cool.

This ricotta cheese pie is tasty and fragrant eaten at any hour during the day. Garnish with lemon (or orange) slices and leaves and dredge with icing sugar.

Torta di riso

SWEET RICE PUDDING

- 1 EGG, SEPARATED
- 1L MILK
- 300G RICE
- 1 ORANGE
- 50G SUGAR
- 3 LARGE APPLES
- KNOB OF BUTTER
- 100G SULTANAS

PREPARATION TIME: 1 $1/2$ HOURS

HEAT THE MILK over a moderate flame, adding a pinch of salt and the sugar. Bring to the boil and sprinkle in the rice and the grated orange peel. Boil for 20 minutes over low heat, stirring with a wooden spoon. Draw off the flame and allow to cool. Whisk the egg white until stiff and add to the mixture, together with the beaten egg yolk and the sultanas (softened in warm water and then dried). Butter a cake tin, pour in half of the mixture. Peel the apples, cut them up and distribute them over the surface. Sprinkle with sugar and then cover with the remaining rice. Bake for three quarters-of-an-hour at 180°C until a nice crust has formed. Serve the pudding cold (but not straight out of the refrigerator), or else barely warm.

Torta "ai 7 cucchiai"

"7-SPOON" CAKE

- 400g WHITE FLOUR
- 7 TABLESPOONS OLIVE OIL
- 7 TABLESPOONS CASTER SUGAR
- 7 TABLESPOONS MILK
- 3 EGGS
- PINCH OF BAKING POWDER
- 1 ORANGE
- KNOB OF BUTTER

PREPARATION TIME: 1 HOUR

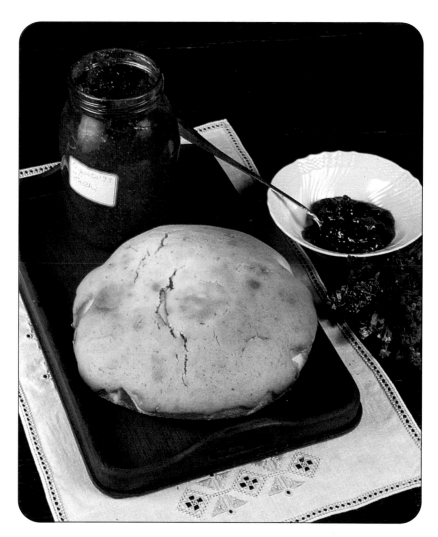

THIS MAKES AN ideal cake base for fillings (e.g. with confectioner's custard, or with a sumptuous fig jam, as in the illustration).

Or, if sliced, it provides an ideal base for the preparation of Florentine Trifle.

If you wish to obtain a still softer cake, increase the quantity of olive oil by 1 or 2 tablespoons - *ça va sans dire* – that it will of course be *extravergine*.

IN A BOWL, WHISK together the oil, sugar and milk, gradually adding the eggs and the grated orange zest. Then, still whisking, sprinkle in the flour and finally the baking powder. Lightly butter and flour a deep, round cake tin. Bake the cake for three quarters-of-an-hour in a moderate oven and test it is cooked by inserting a toothpick or skewer into the cake, which should come out dry. Only at that point will the cake be ready.

Remove from the oven and leave to stand for a few minutes before turning it out onto a plate.

Tortelli alla vaniglia

TUSCAN VANILLA FRITTERS

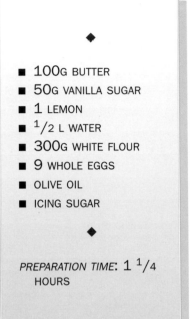

◆

- 100G BUTTER
- 50G VANILLA SUGAR
- 1 LEMON
- 1/2 L WATER
- 300G WHITE FLOUR
- 9 WHOLE EGGS
- OLIVE OIL
- ICING SUGAR

◆

PREPARATION TIME: 1 1/4 HOURS

I N A SAUCEPAN OVER gentle heat, melt the butter and dissolve the vanilla sugar in the water. When everything is blended in together, add the grated lemon zest. Raise the heat, drawing the pan off as soon as boiling point is reached. Sprinkle in the flour, beating with a wooden spoon so that lumps do not form. Return to a low flame and continue stirring until the mixture comes away from the pan easily, which means that it is cooked.

Allow to cool. Add the 9 whole eggs and work them in with your fingers on a floured worktop or pastry board. Prepare a frying pan with hot oil and deep fry the fritters one at a time (shape them as you please or simply toss a spoonful into the oil). Allow to float on the surface of the oil and turn golden all over.

Then remove with the aid of a skimmer, drain on kitchen or brown paper and serve boiling hot, dusted with sugar.

Tortina 4/4

FOUR-BY-FOUR CAKE

◆

- 4 EGGS (ABOUT 300G IN TOTAL WEIGHT), SEPARATED
- 300G FLOUR
- 300G ICING SUGAR
- 300G BUTTER
- PINCH OF SALT

◆

PREPARATION TIME: 1 HOUR

C REAM THE BUTTER with the sugar, add the egg yolks, the flour and the stiffly-whisked egg whites (use the electrical attachment for whipping cream on a medium speed for 20 minutes).

Finally add a pinch of salt. Butter and flour a cake (or loaf) tin, pour in the mixture and bake at 190°C for a quarter-hour.

This light cake is suitable for eating on its own at teatime, accompanied by tea or milk.

If you like, you may complete the delicate flavour of this simple cake by adding 50g sultanas, previously softened up in Marsala for 20 minutes and then dried and floured (this to prevent the fruit from sinking while cooking).

Zuccotto

FLORENTINE CREAM GATEAU

- ■ 4 EGGS
- ■ 150G SUGAR
- ■ 150G FLOUR
- ■ LEMON ZEST
- ■ $^1/_2$L CREAM
- ■ 100G PLAIN CHOCOLATE
- ■ 100G MIXED CANDIED PEEL
- ■ 50G ICING SUGAR
- ■ COCOA
- ■ 20G BUTTER
- ■ SWEET VINSANTO (OR SHERRY)

PREPARATION TIME: 2 HOURS

TO MAKE THE SPONGE BASE, whisk the eggs and sugar at length until the mixture is light and fluffy and can "write", i.e. a thread of the egg falling back into the bowl from the whisk will float for a moment. Should it immediately sink in, then the eggs are not sufficiently whisked. You will need about a quarter-hour, but do not rush the operation or the cake will come out barely risen and rubbery. Add the flour, grated lemon zest and a pinch of salt. Pour into the buttered and floured cake tin and bake for half-an-hour in a pre-heated, hot oven. Allow to cool before turning out, or the sponge will crumble. Whip the cream with the icing sugar and chill. Prepare a dense chocolate sauce: put the butter, cocoa, sugar and about 4 tablespoons of water in a small saucepan, simmering for 5 minutes. Allow to cool, frequently stirring so that a skin does not form on the surface. When it is cold, add a third to the whipped cream and replace in the refrigerator. Mix the cubed candied peel and the roughly-grated chocolate with the rest of the whipped cream and allow this, too, to cool in the refrigerator. Cut the sponge cake into rectangular slices, brush them well with vinsanto (or sherry) and use to line the calotte-shaped mould (which looks precisely like a cardinal's *zucchetto*). Pour the chocolate cream into the mould and fill up with the cream containing the candied peel. Cover with a disc of sponge cake steeped in vinsanto, pressing it down with your hands. Chill the gateau in the refrigerator (not in the freezer) for 4-5 hours.

Zuppa dolce

TRIFLE

◆

- 1 "7-SPOON CAKE" (PLEASE SEE THE RELATIVE RECIPE)

THE CONFECTIONER'S CUSTARD:

- 2 EGGS, SEPARATED
- 1/2 L MILK
- 50G WHITE FLOUR
- LEMON ZEST, GRATED
- 50G CASTER SUGAR

THE CHOCOLATE SAUCE:

- 50G BITTER COCOA
- 30G FLOUR
- 1/2 L MILK
- 80G CASTER SUGAR
- KNOB OF BUTTER
- A GLASS SWEET MARSALA

◆

PREPARATION TIME: 1 1/2 HOURS

SOME SUBSTITUTE coffee for Marsala, but I find the flavour too definite to blend well with the confectioner's custard and the chocolate sauce and at the same time "respect" their virtues.

The outcome may indeed be a trifle, but the flavour which prevails (overbearingly) is of coffee!

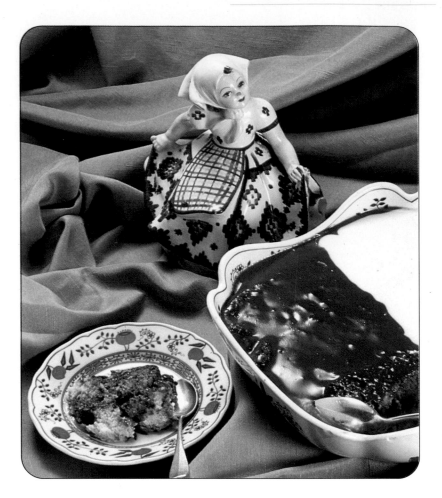

MAKE THE CONFECTIONER'S custard by whisking the egg yolks with the sugar and sprinkling in the flour and the milk. Bring to simmering point over a low flame, stirring continuously. Draw off the heat and dust with caster sugar so that a skin does not form on the surface. The chocolate sauce is made by putting the cocoa, sugar and flour in another saucepan, all thinned down with the milk. Work everything in together well before placing over the heat. Cook very, very gently for about a quarter-hour. Lastly, add the butter and leave to cool.

Take a deep (preferably glass) dish and line it with inch-thick slices of the "7-Spoon" cake. Brush with Marsala. Pour a little custard into the bottom, cover with one or two slices of cake steeped in Marsala, then some chocolate sauce and so on until the dish is filled up. Place in the refrigerator and serve in ice-cream bowls (because it looks and tastes like an ice-cream cake) after two hours.

Zuppa "della nonna"

GRANDMOTHER'S REFRIGERATOR CAKE

- 300G RICOTTA (COTTAGE) CHEESE
- 200G FINGER BISCUITS
- GLASS OF MARSALA
- 100G ICING SUGAR
- 150G CHERRY JAM
- $^1/_2$ GLASS FRESH MILK

PREPARATION TIME: 2 $^1/_2$ HOURS

WORK THE ICING SUGAR into the ricotta with a fork and leave aside for 10 minutes. Mix the Marsala in a bowl with the milk and steep the finger biscuits in this liquid. Be careful that the quality of biscuit is just right; they must soak up the liquid and become soft, not staying hard inside and crumbling on the outside. Arrange a layer of finger biscuits in a deep, rectangular mould, then spread over a couple of tablespoons of the sugared ricotta. Alternate these two layers with another layer of biscuits, covered with a generous spoonful of cherry jam, continuing like this until the dish has filled up. Press down each layer of biscuits into the ricotta and the jam to keep them in place. The trifle should stay in the refrigerator for 2 hours before serving. Tap it lightly on the table before turning out onto a serving dish.

SAVE A LITTLE *ricotta* (about 2 spoonfuls) for decorating all around the cake (pipe it from a pastry bag). Add a touch of red with a few glacé cherries to finish it off.

Finito di stampare
nel mese di Agosto 1995
presso il
Centro Stampa Editoriale Bonechi
Sesto Fiorentino - Firenze

More praise for

DEATHS OF DESPAIR AND
THE FUTURE OF CAPITALISM

"[A] highly important book."
—ARLIE RUSSELL HOCHSCHILD, *New York Times Book Review*

"Gripping. . . . [Case and Deaton] catalogue how an entire way of life
first frayed and then fell apart over the past half-century, and the
cruelty of an American meritocracy that heaps lavish rewards
on the winners while increasingly leaving others to rot."
—JOSHUA CHAFFIN, *Financial Times*

"This is a terrific book. . . . The opioid crisis Case and Deaton analyze
is a microcosm of the anguish the world is experiencing today, and
we would be remiss not to pay attention to their insights."
—KENNETH ROGOFF, *Finance and Development*

"This is an essential portrait of America in crisis."
—*Publishers Weekly*

"Remarkable and poignant."
—DANI RODRIK, *Project Syndicate*

"*Deaths of Despair* is designed to shine a light on a generational
catastrophe that could—perhaps will—become a multigenerational
disaster. It does this with chilling precision."
—MIKE JAKEMAN, *Strategy+Business*

"We Americans are reluctant to acknowledge that our economy serves
the educated classes and penalizes the rest. But that's exactly the situation,
and *Deaths of Despair* shows how the immiseration of the less educated
has resulted in the loss of hundreds of thousands of lives, even as
the economy has thrived and the stock market has soared."
—ATUL GAWANDE, *New Yorker*

"This book will be an instant classic, applying high quality social science
to an urgent national matter of life and death. In exploring the
recent epidemic of 'deaths of despair,' the distinguished authors uncover
an absorbing historical story that raises basic questions about the
future of capitalism. It is hard to imagine a timelier—or in the end,
more hopeful—book in this season of our national despair."
—ROBERT D. PUTNAM, author of *Bowling Alone and Our Kids*

"In the face of a government that failed to protect ordinary working-class Americans from the greed-fueled opioid epidemic and a media that was slow to notice the problem, Anne Case and Angus Deaton are true sentinels. *Deaths of Despair and the Future of Capitalism* is an urgent and clarion call to rethink pain, inequality, justice, and the business of being human in America. This book explains America to itself. I underlined damn near every sentence."
—BETH MACY, author of *Dopesick: Dealers, Doctors, and the Drug Company That Addicted America*

"In this superb book, Case and Deaton connect the dots to explain the dramatic rise of deaths of despair among working-class white Americans. Totally unexpectedly, they trace the root cause to an exorbitantly expensive health-care system that sucks—and wastes—billions of dollars and so much human talent away from improving lives."
—EZEKIEL J. EMANUEL, University of Pennsylvania

"With stunning data analysis, close observation, and smoldering urgency, Case and Deaton show why mounting deaths of despair are not only a public health disaster but also an indictment of the metastasizing stratification that is undermining working-class America."
—DAVID AUTOR, Massachusetts Institute of Technology

"This book explains so many of today's headlines with clear writing, sharp storytelling, and an almost symphonic use of research in economics, public health, and history. What it summons is a powerful analysis of who we are as Americans and what we have become as a country."
—SAM QUINONES, author of *Dreamland: The True Tale of America's Opiate Epidemic*

"America is experiencing a catastrophe. Those without a college degree are not just being left behind; they are dying from deaths of despair. Case and Deaton brilliantly describe and dissect the causes and explain how we can return to a path of rising prosperity and health. All citizens— voters as well as politicians aspiring to office—should read and discuss this book."
—MERVYN KING, former governor of the Bank of England

"Deaths of despair among US whites with low education cannot be attributed to lack of access to health care or ignorance of healthy lifestyles. When two leading economists turn their attention to the social determinants of this modern epidemic, the result is brilliant."
—SIR MICHAEL G. MARMOT, author of *The Health Gap*

DEATHS OF DESPAIR AND THE
FUTURE OF CAPITALISM

Deaths of Despair and the Future of Capitalism

ANNE CASE

ANGUS DEATON

With a new preface by the authors

PRINCETON UNIVERSITY PRESS

PRINCETON & OXFORD

Published by Princeton University Press
41 William Street, Princeton, New Jersey 08540
6 Oxford Street, Woodstock, Oxfordshire OX20 1TR

press.princeton.edu

First paperback edition, 2021
Paperback ISBN 978-0-691-21707-9

Library of Congress Control Number: 2020949713

The Library of Congress has cataloged the cloth edition as follows:

Names: Case, Anne, 1958– author. | Deaton, Angus, author.
Title: Deaths of despair and the future of capitalism / Anne Case, Angus Deaton.
Description: Princeton : Princeton University Press, [2020] | Includes bibliographical references and index.
Identifiers: LCCN 2019040360 (print) | LCCN 2019040361 (ebook) |
    ISBN 9780691190785 (hardback ; alk. paper) | ISBN 9780691199955 (ebook)
Subjects: MESH: Suicide—economics | Socioeconomic Factors | Drug Overdose—economics | Capitalism | Educational Status | Politics | United States
Classification: LCC HV6548.U6 (print) | LCC HV6548.U6 (ebook) |
    NLM HV 6548.U6 | DDC 362.28—dc23
LC record available at https://lccn.loc.gov/2019040360
LC ebook record available at https://lccn.loc.gov/2019040361

British Library Cataloging-in-Publication Data is available

Editorial: Joe Jackson, Jacqueline Delaney
Production Editorial: Terri O'Prey
Jacket/Cover Design: Karl Spurzem
Production: Erin Suydam
Publicity: James Schneider, Caroline Priday

This book has been composed in Arno Pro

Printed in the United States of America

For Julian, Celestine, Lark, Andrew, Ryan,
James, John, Marie, and Will
May they enjoy a world with more fairness and less despair.

CONTENTS

The hardcover edition of *Deaths of Despair* was published on March 17, 2020, four days after President Trump declared the COVID-19 outbreak a national emergency, in a week that saw states and municipalities begin to issue stay-at-home orders to protect citizens from the spread of the coronavirus. When researching and writing *Deaths of Despair*, we did not anticipate that the planet would be overtaken by a deadly virus, much less that the US would lead the world in deaths from it. But long before the arrival of COVID-19, the lives of Americans without a college degree had been disintegrating, with deaths from suicide, drug overdose, and alcoholic liver disease rising year on year. This book is about that other epidemic, one that began to take lives in the early 1990s, killing 158,000 Americans a year by 2018. As we write this preface, in September 2020, there have been 200,000 deaths officially attributed to COVID, though this is almost certainly an underestimate and will certainly rise by the end of the year.

Although far from identical, the patterns of death in the two epidemics have much in common. Death from drugs, suicide, and alcohol pose the greatest risk to less-educated Americans, and almost all of the increase in these deaths since the mid-1990s is among people without a four-year college degree. We will not know for some time, perhaps not until the end of 2021, about the educational status of those who have died from the virus, but it is already clear that less-educated people face higher risk of infection. In June 2020, the Bureau of Labor Statistics calculated that more than a third of those with a high school degree but no college were "highly exposed" by their occupation, as opposed to a fifth of those with a bachelor's degree.[1] Many highly educated people are working from home and face little risk of losing their jobs. In

June 2020, 75 percent of those using computers to work remotely because of the pandemic have a bachelor's or more advanced degree, greater than twice their share in the population.[2] At the same time, less-educated Americans are more likely to use public transportation and to live in crowded quarters.

It is already clear that the pandemic is having a much larger negative effect on the earnings and employment of less-educated Americans, further accentuating the gap between those with and without a college degree. Many less-educated Americans work in retail, food preparation, cleaning and security services, and transportation—many of which are small businesses that have closed and may not reopen.[3] High-tech businesses have prospered relative to the rest of the economy, and these firms employ few workers relative to their size. Meanwhile, professionals have lost little in the way of earnings and have seen their stock and retirement portfolios rise to record levels. The gap between those with and without a four-year degree, which is a constant theme in the book, is widening still further in the pandemic.

There are also major differences between the epidemics. Deaths of despair have been concentrated among young and midlife adults, with later-born birth cohorts at ever-higher risk than those born earlier in the twentieth century. COVID deaths have disproportionately hit the elderly. Deaths of despair are more concentrated in white non-Hispanics, although, after 2013, drug mortality in the black community began to rise with the arrival of street fentanyl, an opioid many times more powerful than heroin. COVID deaths have disproportionately hit African Americans. COVID is a worldwide pandemic, affecting rich and poor countries, while deaths of despair, although not exclusively American, are much more serious in the US than in other rich countries.

There has been some speculation that the COVID epidemic, or the lockdowns that have accompanied it, will lead to further deaths of despair. There are media reports of increased use of suicide hotlines, some local reports of increases in suicides, as well as an increase in mental health problems, including suicidal ideation.[4] People are reportedly having difficulty accessing routine addiction treatment during the pandemic, and most twelve-step meetings have been closed or moved online. Again, we will not have a full accounting for some time. In 2018, there were 158,000 deaths of despair, the same number as in 2017, the latest year covered in the book. Overdose deaths were down somewhat from 2017, but suicide and alcohol-related deaths were up. Preliminary data for 2019 suggest that drug deaths have resumed their upward trend,[5] and information on drug overdoses treated in emergency rooms suggest that this trend continued into 2020 before the epidemic.[6] As a result, there will likely be more drug deaths in 2020 than in 2019, even if the pandemic itself has no direct effect.

There have also been suggestions that the economic recession induced to deal with the pandemic will spur suicides, as has been the case in some recessions in the past. That is certainly possible, and social isolation also brings a risk of suicide. But evidence from the most recent recession, the Great Recession after the financial crisis of 2008, provides no support for any automatic link. As we document in chapter 10, deaths of despair were rising before the recession, they rose during the recession, and they rose after the recession; there is no sign of the recession in the mortality numbers. Even so, the current recession is different. No previous downturns brought social distancing nor fear of infection, so they may be a poor guide to what is happening today.

The US health-care system is deeply involved in both epidemics, albeit in different ways. In what follows, we argue that this structure, because it is so expensive, and because so much of it is funded through employment, has effectively taken a wrecking ball to the job market for less-educated Americans. Pharmaceutical companies and distributors made immense profits by manufacturing and distributing highly addictive drugs, essentially legalized heroin. In the COVID pandemic, the fact that we tie health insurance to employers has left us with a different kind of disaster: tens of millions of people lost their insurance when they lost their jobs, without any guarantee of alternative coverage. Even those who have health insurance can find themselves at risk for financial ruin if they become ill from COVID or from any other cause.

In the first six months of the COVID epidemic, health-care lobbyists succeeded in weakening price restrictions should a vaccine be found.[7] Both epidemics highlight the inadequacies of the public health system and Americans' distrust of their government. Many less-skilled workers believe the system is rigged against them and have lost hope of a better life, leading them to find comfort in drugs and alcohol. In the COVID epidemic, pronouncements on the importance of wearing a mask and social distancing were met with skepticism by many, because they were seen as decrees coming down from a government they do not trust. In early August, Gallup reported that more than a third of Americans said that they would refuse to accept an FDA-approved free vaccination.[8]

We can hope that, within a few years at the outside, COVID deaths may be contained by treatments and vaccines. But there will be no vaccine for those at risk of losing their lives to drugs, alcohol, or suicide. The development of vaccines and treatments is difficult enough, but harder still is the implementation of reforms in the way that American capitalism works, reforms that will make it work for everyone, not just an educated elite.

Anne Case
Angus Deaton
Princeton, August 2020

Notes

1. Bureau of Labor Statistics, 2020, "Demographics, earnings, and family characteristics of workers in sectors initially affected by COVID-19 shutdowns," Monthly Labor Review, June, https://www.bls.gov/opub/mlr/2020/article/demographics-earnings-and-family-characteristics -of-workers-in-sectors-initially-affected-by-covid-19-shutdowns.htm.

2. Bureau of Labor Statistics, 2020, "Supplemental data measuring the effects of the coronavirus (COVID-19) pandemic on the labor market," Labor Force Statistics from the Current Population Survey, May, https://www.bls.gov/cps/effects-of-the-coronavirus-covid-19-pandemic.htm.

3. David Autor and Elisabeth Reynolds, 2020, *The nature of work after the COVID crisis: Too few low-wage jobs*, The Hamilton Project, July, https://www.brookings.edu/wp-content /uploads/2020/08/AutorReynolds_LO_FINAL.pdf.

4. Centers for Disease Control and Prevention, 2020, "Mental health, substance use, and suicidal ideation during the COVID-19 pandemic—United States, June 24–30, 2020," Morbidity and Mortality Weekly Report, August 14, https://www.cdc.gov/mmwr/volumes/69/wr /mm6932a1.htm?s_cid=mm6932a1_e&deliveryName=USCDC_921-DM35222.

5. Centers for Disease Control and Prevention, 2020, "Provisional Drug Overdose Death Counts," National Center for Health Statistics, https://www.cdc.gov/nchs/nvss/vsrr/drug -overdose-data.htm.

6. Aliese Alter and Christopher Yeager, 2020, "COVID-19 impact on US national overdose crisis," Overdose Detection Mapping Application Program, http://www.odmap.org/Content/docs/news/2020/ODMAP-Report-June-2020.pdf.

7. https://www.politico.com/news/2020/03/05/coronavirus-drug-industry-prices-122412

8. Shannon Mullen O'Keefe, 2020, "One in three Americans would not get COVID-19 vaccine," Gallup, August 7, https://news.gallup.com/poll/317018/one-three-americans-not-covid-vaccine.aspx.

In *The Great Escape*, published in 2013, one of us told a positive story about human progress over the last two hundred and fifty years. The story there was one of previously unimaginable material progress, a decline in poverty and deprivation, and extensions in the length of human life. The generation and application of useful knowledge made this progress possible. A star of the show was capitalism, which freed millions from dire poverty, supported by the positive forces of globalization. Democracy spread around the planet, allowing more and more people to participate in shaping their communities and societies.

This book is much less upbeat. It documents despair and death, it critiques aspects of capitalism, and it questions how globalization and technical change are working in America today. Yet we remain optimistic. We believe in capitalism, and we continue to believe that globalization and technical change can be managed to the general benefit. Capitalism does not have to work as it does in America today. It does not need to be abolished, but it should be redirected to work in the public interest. Free market competition can do many things, but there are also many areas where it cannot work well, including in the provision of healthcare, the exorbitant cost of which is doing immense harm to the health and wellbeing of America. If governments are unwilling to exercise compulsion over health insurance and to take the power to control costs—as other rich countries have done—tragedies are inevitable. Deaths of despair have much to do with the failure—the unique failure—of America to learn this lesson.

There have been previous periods when capitalism failed most people, as the Industrial Revolution got under way at the beginning of the nineteenth century, and again after the Great Depression. But the beast was tamed, not slain, and it brought the great benefits laid out in *The Great Escape*. If we can get the policies right, we can ensure that what is happening today is not a prelude to another great disaster but rather a temporary setback from which we can return to rising prosperity and better health. We hope this book, while not as heartening as *The Great Escape*, will help put us back on track to make the progress in this century that we have generally made in the past. The future of capitalism should be a future of hope and not of despair.

We have written the book so that it can be read without consulting the notes at the end or, for our audio listeners, without looking at the figures. The text is self-contained and the figures are described in sufficient detail to make the argument comprehensible without them. We use endnotes for two purposes. The vast majority are citations that provide data for or document the point we are making. In a few cases, endnotes are used to expand on more technical material that academic readers might wish to check. They are not necessary to our story.

Our account of despair was often distressing to write, and it will be distressing to some readers. For people who are suffering from the depression or addictions that we describe, there is help available. If you are having thoughts of suicide, call the National Suicide Prevention Lifeline at 1-800-273-8255 (TALK). You can find a list of additional resources at SpeakingOfSuicide.com/resources. If you, someone in your family, or someone you know is suffering from addiction to drugs or alcohol, talking to a trusted family doctor or spiritual adviser is a good first step. We also recommend Alcoholics Anonymous (aa.org) and Al-Anon (al-anon.org), the latter of which works with family members of those affected. These organizations have meetings in most places in the US and around the world, providing help for many as well as an effective support community that is welcoming and that presents no risk. Their websites are set up to help find local groups.

Anne Case and Angus Deaton
Princeton, NJ, October 2019

DEATHS OF DESPAIR AND THE
FUTURE OF CAPITALISM

Introduction

THIS BOOK WAS BORN in a cabin in Montana in the summer of 2014. We spend August each year in the hamlet of Varney Bridge on the Madison River, overlooking the mountains of the Madison Range. We had promised to investigate the link between happiness and suicide, whether it was true that unhappy places—counties, cities, or countries where people report that their lives are going really badly—are also places where suicide is more common. Over the past ten years, Madison County, Montana, has had a suicide rate that is four times that of Mercer County, New Jersey, where we spend the rest of the year. We were curious, especially because we were generally happy in Montana, and others there seemed happy too.

Along the way, we had discovered that suicide rates among middle-aged white Americans were rising rapidly. We found something else that puzzled us. Middle-aged white Americans were hurting in other ways. They were reporting more pain and poorer overall health, not as much as older Americans—health worsens with age, after all—but the gap was closing. Health among the elderly was improving while health among the middle-aged was worsening. We knew that pain could drive people to suicide, so perhaps the two findings were linked?

That was the beginning. As we thought about how to write up our results, we wanted to put the suicides in context. How big a deal was suicide relative to all other deaths, and compared with the big causes like cancer or heart disease? We went back to the Centers for Disease Control, downloaded the numbers, and made the calculations. To our astonishment, it was not only suicide that was rising among middle-aged whites; it was *all* deaths. Not by much, but death rates are supposed to fall year on year, so even a pause was news, let alone an increase.

We thought we must have hit a wrong key. Constantly falling death rates were one of the best and best-established features of the twentieth century. All-cause mortality is not supposed to increase for *any* large group. There are exceptions, such as the great influenza epidemic at the tail end of the First World War, or mortality from HIV/AIDS among young men thirty years ago. But the steady decrease in death rates, especially in middle age, had been one of the greatest (and most reliable) achievements of the twentieth century, driving up life expectancy at birth not only in the United States but also in other wealthy countries around the world.

What was happening? There were not enough suicides to account for the turnaround in total deaths. We looked at what other causes might be responsible. To our surprise, "accidental poisonings" were a big part of the story. How could this be? Were people somehow accidentally drinking Drano or weed killer? In our (then) innocence, we did not know that "accidental poisonings" was the category that contained drug overdoses, or that there was an epidemic of deaths from opioids, already well established and still rapidly spreading. Deaths from alcoholic liver disease were rising rapidly too, so that the fastest-rising death rates were from three causes: suicides, drug overdoses, and alcoholic liver disease. These kinds of deaths are all self-inflicted, quickly with a gun, more slowly and less certainly with drug addiction, and more slowly still through alcohol. We came to call them "deaths of despair," mostly as a convenient label for the three causes taken together. Exactly what kind of despair, whether economic, social, or psychological, we did not know, and did not presume. But the label stuck, and this book is an in-depth exploration of that despair.

The book is about these deaths and about the people who are dying. We document what we found then, and what we and others have found since. Other writers, in the press and in a series of fine books, have put names and faces to the deaths and told the stories behind them. We shall draw on these accounts too. Our own previous work was primarily focused on documenting what was happening, but here we go further and try to follow trails back to the underlying economic and social roots.

Who is dying? When a person dies, a death certificate is filled out, and one of the boxes asks about the deceased's education. Here was another surprise. The increase in deaths of despair was almost all among those without a bachelor's degree. Those with a four-year degree are mostly exempt; it is those without the degree who are at risk. This was particularly surprising for suicide; for more than a century, suicides were generally more common among the educated,[1] but that is not true in the current epidemic of deaths of despair.

The four-year college degree is increasingly dividing America, and the extraordinarily beneficial effects of the degree are a constant theme running through the book. The widening gap between those with and without a bachelor's degree is not only in death but also in quality of life; those without a degree are seeing increases in their levels of pain, ill health, and serious mental distress, and declines in their ability to work and to socialize. The gap is also widening in earnings, in family stability, and in community.[2] A four-year degree has become *the* key marker of social status, as if there were a requirement for nongraduates to wear a circular scarlet badge bearing the letters *BA* crossed through by a diagonal red line.

In the last half century, America (like Britain and other rich countries) has built a meritocracy that we rightly see as a great achievement. But there is a dark side that was long ago predicted by Michael Young, the British economist and social scientist who invented the term in 1958 and who saw meritocracy as leading to social calamity.[3] Those who do not pass the exams and graduate to the cosmopolitan elite do not get to live in the fast-growing, high-tech, and flourishing cities and are assigned jobs threatened by globalization and by robots. The elite can sometimes be smug about their accomplishments, attributing them to their own merit, and dismissive of those without degrees, who had their chance but blew it. The less educated are devalued or even disrespected, are encouraged to think of themselves as losers, and may feel that the system is rigged against them.[4] When the fruits of success are as large as they are today, so are the penalties for failing the tests of meritocracy. Young presciently referred to the left-behind group as "the populists" and the elite as "the hypocrisy."

We tell the story not only of death but of pain and addiction and of lives that have come apart and have lost their structure and significance. For Americans without a bachelor's degree, marriage rates are in decline, though cohabitation and the fraction of children born out of wedlock continue to rise. Many middle-aged men do not know their own children. They have parted from the woman with whom they once cohabited, and the children of that relationship are now living with a man who is not their father. The comfort that used to come from organized religion, especially from the traditional churches, is now absent from many lives. People have less attachment to work; many are out of the labor force altogether, and fewer have a long-term commitment to an employer who, in turn, was once committed to them, a relationship that, for many, conferred status and was one of the foundations of a meaningful life.

More workers used to belong to a union. Unions help keep wages up and help give workers some control over their workplace and working conditions. In many towns and cities, the union hall was a center of social life. The good wages that once supported the blue-collar aristocracy have largely vanished, and manufacturing has been replaced by service jobs—for example, in healthcare, in food preparation and service, in janitorial and cleaning services, and in maintenance and repair.

Our story of deaths of despair; of pain; of addiction, alcoholism, and suicide; of worse jobs with lower wages; of declining marriage; and of declining religion is mostly a story of non-Hispanic white Americans without a four-year degree. In 2018, the Census Bureau estimated that there were 171 million Americans between the ages of twenty-five and sixty-four. Of those, 62 percent were white non-Hispanics, and 62 percent of those did not have a four-year college degree; the less educated white Americans who are the group at risk are 38 percent of the working-age population. The economic forces that are harming labor are common to all working-class Americans, regardless of race or ethnicity, but the stories of blacks and whites are markedly different.

In the 1970s and 1980s, African Americans working in inner cities experienced events that, in retrospect, share some features with what happened to working-class whites thirty years later. The first wave of globalization hit blacks particularly hard, and jobs in the central city became scarce for this long-disadvantaged group. Better-educated and more talented blacks deserted the inner cities for safer city neighborhoods or the suburbs. Marriage rates fell as once-marriageable men no longer had work.[5] Crime rates rose, as did mortality from violence, from drug overdoses in the crack cocaine epidemic, and from HIV/AIDS, which disproportionately affected blacks. Blacks, always the least favored group, had that status reinforced by being the first to experience the downside of a changing national and global economy that was increasingly shedding less skilled workers.

African Americans have long had harder lives than whites. Blacks die younger, today as in the past. Blacks are also less likely to go to college, or to find employment. Those who work earn less than whites on average. Blacks have less wealth, are less likely to own their own home, are more likely to be incarcerated, and more likely to live in poverty. In many but not all of these areas, black lives have improved; since 1970, black education, wages, income, and wealth have risen. From 1970 to 2000, black mortality rates declined by more than those of whites, and they fell in the first fifteen years of the twenty-first century while those of working-class whites were rising.

There is less overt discrimination than in 1970. There has been a black president. The large majority who used to think intermarriage was wrong has now become a large majority who thinks it is just fine. Some whites undoubtedly resent the loss of their long-standing white privilege in a way that hurts them but not blacks.[6] Poor whites, it has long been said, suffered from a racist system that was primarily directed against blacks. Poor whites were co-opted by the rich, who told them that they might not have much, but at least they were white. As Martin Luther King Jr. summarized, "The southern aristocracy took the world and gave the poor white man Jim Crow," so that when he had no money for food, "he ate Jim Crow, a psychological bird that told him that no matter how bad off he was, at least he was a white man, better than a black man."[7] As Jim Crow weakened, along with other forms of discrimination, working-class whites lost whatever benefits they got from it. More than half of white working-class Americans believe that discrimination against whites has become as big a problem as discrimination against blacks and other minorities, while only 30 percent of white, college-educated Americans agree.[8] The historian Carol Anderson states that to someone who has "always been privileged, equality begins to look like oppression."[9]

Black mortality rates remain above those for whites but, in the past three decades, the gap in mortality rates between blacks and whites with less than a bachelor's degree fell markedly. Black rates, which were more than twice those of whites as late as the early 1990s, fell as white rates rose, closing the distance between them to 20 percent. Since 2013 the opioid epidemic has spread to black communities, but until then, the epidemic of deaths of despair was white.

In the chapters that follow, we document the decline of white working-class lives over the last half century. White non-Hispanics are 62 percent of the working-age population, so understanding their mortality is important in and of itself. The story of what happened to African Americans in the seventies and eighties has been extensively researched and debated,[10] and we have nothing to add to that literature except to note that there are some parallels with whites today. Hispanics are a widely heterogeneous group, defined only by their common language. US mortality trends for Hispanics change with changes in the composition of people who have immigrated—for example, from Mexico, Cuba, or El Salvador; we do not try to tell a coherent story for them.

We describe the social and economic forces that have slowly made working-class lives so much more difficult. One line of argument focuses on a decline in values or on an increasingly dysfunctional culture within the white working class itself.[11] There is little doubt that the collapse of social norms about not having children out of wedlock, which seemed so liberating to so many at first, has brought a heavy price in the long term. Young men who thought they could live a life free of commitment found themselves alone and adrift in middle age. The turning away from religion is perhaps a similar force, but it is also possible to think of it as a failure of organized religion to adapt to political and economic change and to continue to provide meaning and comfort in a changing world. These arguments about social norms are clearly right, but our story is primarily about the external forces that have eaten away the foundations that characterized working-class life as it was half a century ago. There is strong factual evidence against the view that workers brought the calamity on themselves by losing interest in work.

After correction for inflation, the median wages of American men have been stagnant for half a century; for white men without a four-year degree, median earnings lost 13 percent of their purchasing power between 1979 and 2017. Over the same period, national income per head grew by 85 percent. Although there was a welcome turnaround in earnings for the less educated between 2013 and 2017, it is very small compared with the long-term decline. Since the end of the Great Recession, between January 2010 and January 2019 nearly sixteen million new jobs were created, but fewer than three million were for those without a four-year degree. Only fifty-five thousand were for those with only a high school degree.[12]

The prolonged decline in wages is one of the fundamental forces working against less educated Americans. But a simple link to despair from falling material living standards cannot by itself account for what has happened. For a start, the wage decline has come with job decline—from better jobs to worse jobs—with many leaving the labor force altogether because the worse jobs are unattractive, because there are few jobs at all, or because they cannot easily move, or some combination of these reasons. Deterioration in job quality, and detachment from the labor force, bring miseries over and above the loss of earnings.

Many of the jobs that have come with the lower wages do not bring the sense of pride that can come with being part of a successful enterprise, even in a low-ranked position. Cleaners, janitors, drivers, and customer service representatives "belonged" when they were directly employed by a large company, but they do not "belong" when the large company outsources to a business-service firm that offers low wages and little prospect of promotion. Even when workers are doing the same jobs that they did before they were outsourced, they are no longer part of a marquee corporation. As economist Nicholas Bloom memorably puts it, they are no longer invited to the holiday party.[13] The days are gone when a janitor for Eastman Kodak could rise through the ranks to become the CEO of a related firm.[14] In some of these jobs, working conditions are closely monitored by software that deprives workers of control or initiative, even compared with the old, and once much hated, assembly lines.[15] Workers, even in dangerous, dirty occupations, such as coal mining, or in low-level employment for famous corporations, could be proud of their roles.

Men without prospects do not make good marriage partners. Marriage rates among less educated whites fell, and more people lost out on the benefits of marriage, of seeing their children grow, and of knowing their grandchildren. A majority of less educated white mothers have currently had at least one child outside marriage. Poorer prospects make it harder for people to build the life that their parents had, to own a home, or to save to send kids to college. The lack of well-paying jobs threatens communities and the services they provide, such as schools, parks, and libraries.

Jobs are not just the source of money; they are the basis for the rituals, customs, and routines of working-class life. Destroy work and, in the end, working-class life cannot survive. It is the loss of meaning, of dignity, of pride, and of self-respect that comes with the loss of marriage and of community that brings on despair, not just or even primarily the loss of money.

Our account echoes the account of suicide by Emile Durkheim, the founder of sociology, of how suicide happens when society fails to provide some of its members with the framework within which they can live dignified and meaningful lives.[16]

We do not focus on economic hardship, though hardship undoubtedly exists. Whites without a college degree are not the poorest group in the US; they are much less likely to be poor than African Americans. Instead, we see the decline in wages as slowly undermining all aspects of people's lives.

Why has the economy been failing the working class? If we are to come up with ideas for change, then we need to know what happened, where to begin, and what sort of policies might make a difference.

Again, we could turn to the failings of the people themselves and argue that, in the modern economy, it is impossible to prosper without a bachelor's degree, and that people should simply get more education. We have nothing against education, and it has certainly become more valuable over time. We would like to see a world in which everyone who can benefit from going to college, and wants to go to college, is able to do so. But we do not accept the basic premise that people are useless to the economy unless they have a bachelor's degree. And we certainly do not think that those who do not get one should be somehow disrespected or treated as second-class citizens.

Globalization and technological change are often held up as the main villains because they have reduced the value of uneducated labor, replacing it with cheaper, foreign labor or cheaper machines. Yet other rich countries, in Europe and elsewhere, face globalization and technological change but have not seen long-term stagnation of wages, nor an epidemic of deaths of despair. There is something going on in America that is different, and that is particularly toxic for the working class. Much of this book is concerned with trying to find out just what that something might be.

We believe that the healthcare system is a uniquely American calamity that is undermining American lives. We shall also argue that in America, more than elsewhere, market and political power have moved away from labor toward capital. Globalization has aided the shift, both weakening unions and empowering employers,[17] and American institutions have helped push this further than elsewhere. Corporations have become more powerful as unions have weakened, and as politics has become more favorable to them. In part, this comes from the phenomenal growth of high-tech firms, such as Apple and Google, that employ few workers for their size and have high profits per worker. This is good for productivity and for national income, but little of the gain is shared by labor, especially by less educated labor. Less positively, consolidation in some American industries—hospitals and airlines are just two of many examples—has brought an increase in market power in some product markets so that it is possible for firms to raise prices above what they would be in a freely competitive market. The rising economic and political power of corporations, and the declining economic and political power of workers, allows corporations to gain at the expense of ordinary people, consumers, and particularly workers. At its worst, this power has allowed some pharmaceutical companies, protected by government licensing, to make billions of dollars from sales of addictive opioids that were falsely peddled as safe, profiting by destroying lives. More generally, the American healthcare system is a leading example of an institution that, under political protection, redistributes income upward to hospitals, physicians, device makers, and pharmaceutical companies while delivering among the worst health outcomes of any rich country.

As we write, in August 2019, the opioid manufacturers are being held to account in the courts; a judge ordered Johnson & Johnson to pay more than half a billion dollars to the state of Oklahoma. A subsidiary of Johnson & Johnson grew the poppies in Tasmania that were the raw material for almost all the opioids produced in the US. Early reports of a settlement with the worst offender, Purdue, the maker of OxyContin, suggest that the Sackler family, who own the company, may lose it, as well as several billion dollars of their past profit. Yet the aggressive marketing of pharmaceuticals to doctors and patients is still in place, as are the rules whereby the Food and Drug Administration approved the use of what is essentially legalized heroin. Many of those who have followed the opioid scandal see little difference between the behavior of the legalized drug dealers and the illegal suppliers of heroin and cocaine who are so widely despised and condemned.[18]

The problems with the healthcare industry go far beyond the opioid scandal. The US spends huge sums of money for some of the worst health outcomes in the Western world. We will argue that the industry is a cancer at the heart of the economy, one that has widely metastasized, bringing down wages, destroying good jobs, and making it harder and harder for state and federal governments to afford what their constituents need. Public purpose and the wellbeing of ordinary people are being subordinated to the private gain of the already well-off. None of this would be possible without the acquiescence—and sometimes enthusiastic participation—of the politicians who are supposed to act in the interest of the public.

Robin Hood was said to have robbed the rich to benefit the poor. What is happening today in America is the reverse of Robin Hood, from poor to rich, what might be called a Sheriff of Nottingham redistribution. Political protection is being used for personal enrichment, by stealing from the poor on behalf of the rich, a process known to economists and political scientists as rent-seeking. It is, in a sense, the opposite of free-market capitalism, and it is opposed by the Left, because of its distributional consequences, and the Right, because it undermines freedom and a truly free market. It is as old as capitalism itself, as Adam Smith knew very well even in 1776. In his *Wealth of Nations,* often seen as the bible of capitalism, Smith noted that while tax laws could be cruel, they were "mild and gentle" in comparison with the laws that the pressure of "our merchants and manufacturers has extorted from the legislature, for the support of their own absurd and oppressive monopolies." He suggested that "these laws may be said to be all written in blood."[19] Rent-seeking is a major cause of wage stagnation among working-class Americans and has had much to do with deaths of despair. We shall have much to say about it.

The most common explanations for the decline in living standards of less educated Americans are that globalization has caused factories to close and move to Mexico or China and that automation has displaced workers. These forces are real enough, and they underlie much of our discussion. But, as the experience of other rich countries shows, globalization and automation, which are faced by all, need not reduce wages as has happened in the US, let alone bring an epidemic of death. American healthcare bears much of the blame, as does policy, particularly the failure to use antitrust to combat market power, in labor markets perhaps even more than goods markets, and to rein in the rent-seeking by pharma, by healthcare more generally, and by banks and many small- or medium-size business entrepreneurs, such as doctors, hedge fund managers, the owners of sports franchises, real estate businesspeople, and car dealers. All of these get rich from the "oppressive monopolies" and special deals, tax breaks, and regulations that they have "extorted from the legislature." The very top ranks of the American income distribution, the top 1 percenters and top tenth of 1 percenters, are less likely to be corporate heads than they are to be entrepreneurs who run their own businesses,[20] many of whom are protected by rent-seeking.

Inequality is much cited for its baleful impacts. In this book, we see inequality as a consequence as much as a cause; if the rich are allowed to enrich themselves through unfair processes that hold down wages, and raise prices, then inequality will certainly rise. But not everyone gets rich that way. Some people invent new tools, drugs, or gadgets, or new ways of doing things, and benefit many, not just themselves. They profit from improving and extending other people's lives. It is good for great innovators to get rich. Making is not the same as taking. It is not inequality itself that is unfair but rather the process that generates it.

The people who are being left behind care about their own falling living standards and loss of community, not about Jeff Bezos (of Amazon) or Tim Cook (of Apple) being rich. Yet when they think the inequality comes from cheating or from special favors, the situation becomes intolerable. The financial crisis has much to answer for. Before it, many believed that the bankers knew what they were doing and that their salaries were being earned in the public interest. Afterward, when so many people lost their jobs and their homes, and the bankers continued to be rewarded and were not held to account, American capitalism began to look more like a racket for redistributing upward than an engine of general prosperity.

We do not think that taxation is the solution to rent-seeking; the right way to stop thieves is to stop them stealing, not to raise their taxes.[21] We need to stop the abuse and overprescription of opioids, not tax the profits. We need to correct the process, not try to fix the outcomes. We need to make it easier for foreign doctors to qualify to practice in the US. We need to stop bankers and real estate dealers writing regulations and tax laws in their own interests. The problem for less educated people is stagnant and declining wages, not inequality in and of itself, and indeed much inequality is the consequence of forcing down wages in order to enrich a minority. Reducing rent-seeking would do much to reduce inequality. When the owners of a pharmaceutical company get fabulously rich from the high prices, extended patents, approvals, and convenient regulations that their lobbyists have persuaded the government to grant, they greatly contribute to inequality, both by pushing down the real incomes of those who have to pay for the drugs and by pushing up the highest incomes at the top of the distribution. The same is true of the bankers who rewrote bankruptcy law in their favor and against borrowers; as one commentator noted, "Never before in our history has such a well-organized, well-orchestrated, and well-financed campaign been run to change the balance of power between creditors and debtors."[22]

As is often noted, even confiscatory taxes on the rich do not provide much relief for the poor, because there are so many poor people and so few rich people. In today's world, however, we need to think about the process working in the other direction—that squeezing even small amounts out of each of a large number of working people can provide enormous fortunes for the rich who are doing the squeezing. That is what is happening today, and we should stop it.

What might be done to make lives better, not just for the elite but also for working people? It is easy to be pessimistic. Once political and financial power are increasingly concentrated, the dynamic does not appear to be self-correcting. The election of Donald Trump is understandable in the circumstances, but it is a gesture of frustration and rage that will make things worse, not better. Working-class whites do not believe that democracy can help them; in 2016, more than two-thirds of white working-class Americans believed that elections are controlled by the rich and by big corporations, so that it does not matter if they vote. Analysis by political scientists of voting patterns in Congress supports their skepticism; both Democratic and Republican lawmakers consistently vote for the interests of their more prosperous constituents with little attention to the interests of others.[23]

Justice Louis Brandeis campaigned against the misbehavior of giant trusts at the end of the nineteenth century and was later nominated to the Supreme Court by Woodrow Wilson, becoming its first Jewish member. He thought that extreme inequality was incompatible with the preservation of democracy. This applies both to "good" and "bad" inequality; it doesn't matter how people got rich if even those who earned their wealth legitimately use it to undermine the rights and interests of the non-rich. For us, the best way to deal with this is to stop the rent-seeking, lobbying, and misuse of market power that is behind the extreme inequality, to stop the unfair process. If that is impossible, high marginal income taxes or, better—but practically much more difficult—a wealth tax would lessen the influence of fortunes in politics. But it is sometimes difficult to be optimistic. One historian has argued that inequality, once it is established, is only overcome by violent ruptures and that this has been true since the Stone Age.[24] We think that is too pessimistic, but it is hard to see today's levels of inequality lessening without reforms of the processes and institutions that produced them.

Yet there are some reasons for optimism, and there are policies that, even in our current flawed democracy, might be feasible and might make things better. Institutions can change. There is much intellectual ferment around these issues, and many good new ideas that we will discuss later in the book. But we end this introduction with another, but more optimistic, historical parallel.

In Britain at the beginning of the nineteenth century, inequality was greater than anything we see today. The hereditary landowners not only were rich but also controlled Parliament through a severely limited franchise. After 1815, the notorious Corn Laws kept out imports of wheat until the local price was so high that people were at risk of starving; high prices of wheat, even if they hurt ordinary people, were very much in the interests of the land-owning aristocracy, who lived off the rents supported by the restriction on imports—rent-seeking of the classic and here literal kind, and rent-seeking that did not stop at killing people; laws that were "written in blood." The Industrial Revolution had begun, there was a ferment of innovation and invention, and national income was rising. Yet working people were not benefiting. Mortality rates rose as people moved from the relatively healthy countryside to stinking, unsanitary cities. Each generation of military recruits was shorter than the last, speaking to their ever-worsening undernutrition in childhood, from not getting enough to eat and from the nutritional insults of unsanitary conditions. Religious observance fell, if only because churches were in the countryside, not in the new industrial cities. Wages were stagnant and would remain so for half a century. Profits were rising, and the share of profits in national income rose at the expense of labor. It would have been hard to predict a positive outcome of this process.

Yet by century's end, the Corn Laws were gone and the rents and fortunes of the aristocrats had fallen along with the world price of wheat, especially after 1870 when wheat from the American prairie flooded the market. A series of reform acts had extended the franchise, from one in ten males at the beginning of the century to more than half by its end, though the enfranchisement of women would wait until 1918.[25] Wages had begun to rise in 1850, and the more than century-long decline in mortality had begun.[26] All of this happened without a collapse of the state, without a war or a pandemic, through gradual change in institutions that slowly gave way to the demands of those who had been left behind. Even if we do not know just why, or whether the logic applies to our own times, the facts themselves surely justify at least a limited optimism.

Past as Prologue

1

The Calm before the Storm

Our nation has gained about one year of longevity every six years since 1990. A child born today can look forward to an average lifespan of about 78 years—nearly three decades longer than a baby born in 1900. Deaths from heart disease have been reduced by more than 70 percent since I was born. HIV/AIDS treatment and prevention may now enable us to envision the first AIDS-free generation since the virus emerged more than 30 years ago. Cancer death rates have been dropping about 1 percent annually for the past 15 years.

—FRANCIS COLLINS, DIRECTOR OF
NATIONAL INSTITUTES OF HEALTH,
SENATE TESTIMONY, APRIL 28, 2014

THE TWENTIETH CENTURY saw an improvement in health that was unprecedented in history. By 2000, continuously improving human health was the expected, normal state of events. Children lived longer than their parents, who, in turn, lived longer than *their* parents. Decade by decade, the risk of dying fell. Better health was supported by better living standards, by advances in medicines and treatments, and by changes in behavior based on a better understanding of how behavior—especially cigarette smoking—affected health. Other rich countries saw similar improvements for similar reasons. In poor countries, especially in the second half of the twentieth century, improvements were even more spectacular. In 2000, all of this progress seemed set to continue, presumably indefinitely.

Economic progress was remarkable, too. Almost everyone in the world was richer in 2000 than their grandparents, or great- or great-great-grandparents, had been when Queen Victoria died and Louis Armstrong was born in 1901, adding to another century of progress before that, from 1800 to 1900. In the rich countries of western Europe and North America, the rate of income growth reached its all-time high in the period known in France as Les trente glorieuses, the thirty years after the Second World War. During those years in the United States, not only was the growth of national income per head faster than ever before, it was also widely shared by rich, poor, and middle class alike.

Education is a similar story. In 1900, only a quarter of people graduated from high school; by midcentury more than three-quarters did. Those with a college degree rose from one in twenty to one in five. And while better-educated people generally earned more than those with less education, the midcentury postwar labor market provided good jobs for those with only a high school diploma. Factory jobs, in steel works or auto plants, provided a good living, especially as people moved up the ladder. Men followed their fathers into unionized jobs, often with a lifetime commitment from both workers and the firm. Wages were high enough for a man to get married, to start a family and buy a house, and to enjoy the prospect of a life that was better in many ways than the life of his parents at the same age. Parents could think about sending their children to college to give them an even better life. Those were the days of what has been called the blue-collar aristocracy.

The last thing we want to argue is that the twentieth century was a paradise that was lost in the twenty-first. Nothing could be further from the truth.

The twentieth century also saw many of the worst catastrophes in history, in which tens or even hundreds of millions of people lost their lives. Two world wars and the murderous regimes of Hitler, Stalin, and Mao are the worst events in terms of the raw counts of people killed, but there were also deadly epidemics, including the influenza at the end of the First World War and HIV/AIDS at century's end. Millions of the world's children died from common childhood diseases long after it was understood how to prevent those deaths. Wars, mass murders, epidemics, and the unnecessary deaths of children brought down life expectancy, sometimes very sharply. There were economic catastrophes too, and wellbeing was far from universally shared. The Great Depression brought poverty and misery to millions. Jim Crow was alive and well, institutionalizing educational, economic, and social deprivation for black Americans.

Nor is our claim that there was constant, steady progress, only that, over a long period, such as from 1900 to 2000, people were less likely to die and more likely to prosper. Some outcomes showed steadier progress than others, and some countries did better than others. But progress in health and in living standards in the twentieth century was prolonged enough that, by century's end, people could reasonably expect it to continue and to bless their children's lives just as it had blessed their own. For most of the world's population, the end of the twentieth century saw greater prosperity and greater longevity than at any time in history. Not only that, but the rate of improvement since the end of the Second World War had been so steady and so prolonged that it seemed obvious that future generations would do better still.

To understand these past changes, as well as the much less beneficent changes that we will describe in this book, we need to clarify how progress is measured.

Life and Death: Keeping Score

We shall frequently talk about mortality and life expectancy. They are, in a sense, opposites; mortality measures dying, and life expectancy measures the length of life. The mortality rate is the risk of dying; life expectancy is how many years a newborn can be expected to live. When and where mortality rates are high, life expectancy is low, and vice versa. Mortality rates are different at different ages—high among babies and young children, then low among older children, teenagers, and young adults. In middle age, the threat of death begins to be real, and after age thirty, the risk of dying increases every year. In the US in 2017, the probability of dying between thirty and thirty-one was 1.3 in 1,000, by age forty it was 2.0 in 1,000, by fifty it was 4.1 per 1,000, and by sixty it was 9.2 per 1,000. Through midlife, the probability of dying doubles for every decade of life. In other rich countries, these risks are a little lower, but in the absence of epidemics or wars, patterns like these appear in all places and all times.

For a newborn, we think of life as a hurdle race, with a hurdle at each birthday. Mortality rates are the probabilities of falling at each hurdle, high at the beginning until the newborn hits his or her stride, then low for a while as the more experienced runner deals easily with each hurdle, and then getting higher and higher in midlife and old age as the runner tires. Throughout the book we will talk about life expectancy, which is how many hurdles an average newborn can be expected to clear, as well as about mortality rates, which are the probabilities of falling at each of the hurdles. We need both concepts, because the events that we are going to describe affect different hurdles differently, so that risks can rise in middle age even when they are falling among the elderly, something that may not show up in life expectancy at all if these changes happen to cancel each other out.

When the hurdles are high at the beginning, not many runners are going to get far down the track. In the US, at the beginning of the twentieth century, children faced high risks of dying. Not all children got enough or good enough food, childhood diseases like measles were often fatal, vaccinations were far from universal, and many places in the US had yet to make their water safe to drink, failing to properly separate the disposal of sewage from the provision of drinking water, among other things. It is not only unpleasant but extremely dangerous to drink out of a river that someone else, living upstream, is using as a toilet. It is expensive to supply safe water and good sanitation, and it took public health officials a long time to make these arrangements everywhere, even once the basic science—the germ theory of disease—was understood and accepted.

The chance of dying increases with age, except at the very beginning of life. Life is most dangerous for babies and for the elderly. In rich countries, infancy is safe; only six out of one thousand American babies do not live to their first birthday, and other countries do even better. In Sweden and Singapore, for example, only two out of one thousand die.

The risks are much higher in some poor countries, but even here, progress has been rapid, and there is not a single country in the world whose infant mortality rate is higher now than it was fifty years ago.

Over the twentieth century, overall life expectancy at birth in the United States increased from 49 to 77 years. By the end of the century, from 1970 to 2000, life expectancy increased from 70.8 to 76.8, 2 additional years of life for every decade of actual time. From 1933, when the comprehensive US data begin, the trend has been almost continuously positive, with declines in life expectancy lasting no more than one or two years. While the data before 1933 are not complete, because not all states kept records, there appears to have been a three-year decline from 1915 to 1918 at the end of the First World War and during the influenza epidemic.

Had this rate of increase continued, life expectancy by 2100 could have been expected to be more than ninety, with substantial fractions of people living to be one hundred. Similar statements can be made for the countries of Western Europe and for Japan, Australia, New Zealand, and Canada.

The Changing Face of Mortality

In 1900, the three leading causes of death were infectious diseases—pneumonia, tuberculosis, and gastrointestinal infections. By midcentury, with the public health and vaccination programs largely complete, and with antibiotics invented and about to be widely used, infectious disease had become less important as a cause of death. The early-life hurdles had been lowered and mortality moved into middle and old age. Death itself aged, moving out of the bowels of children and into the lungs and arteries of the middle-aged and elderly. Once this happens, it is much harder to increase life expectancy. Lowering the hurdles at the beginning makes a big difference to how far people run, but once almost everyone makes it into middle and old age, saving lives among the elderly stretches life spans by much less.

By the end of the twentieth century, the leading causes of death were heart disease and cancer. Heart disease and lung cancer become less common when people stop smoking, and the substantial reductions in the

portion of the population who smoked made a large contribution to falling mortality. Preventive treatments for heart   disease also helped.
Antihypertensives are cheap and easy-to-take drugs that help control
blood pressure and make heart attacks less likely; statins are cholesterol-
lowering drugs that help to reduce heart attacks and strokes. The reduction in heart disease mortality was one of the great success stories of the
last quarter of the twentieth century. There were also drug-based and
screening successes against some cancers, including breast cancer.

New drugs are perhaps not as important for reducing death rates as
are people's behaviors, but they are nevertheless often life saving, and
when, later in the book, we talk about excesses in the pharmaceutical industry, it should always be kept in mind that drugs have saved many
lives. The world would be a much worse place without antibiotics, with-
out insulin for diabetes, without aspirin or ibuprofen, without anesthet-
ics, without antihypertensives, without antiretrovirals, or without the
birth control pill. The key puzzle for public policy is to find a way of getting the benefits of longer and better lives without socially unacceptable
consequences, including, but going beyond, financial costs.

As some diseases are eliminated and others reduced, other causes step
up to take their place as leaders. Most of these causes are not new. They
have always been there but were previously dwarfed by the scale of the
earlier mass killers. Some causes of death, such as Alzheimer's or late-life
cancers, were uncommon simply because people rarely reached the ages
where they matter. But other causes, such as accidents, suicides, or diabetes, were always present but were minor killers in the age of smallpox
or cholera or even, in more recent times, tuberculosis or childhood diarrhea. As we move away from infectious disease, the nature of causes also
changes. Infections are spread by an agent, such as a bacterium or a virus,
so that discovering the biological mechanisms in the body or in the means
of transmission—dirty water, mosquitoes, fleas, or rats—offers not only
an understanding of the cause but also a potential route to its cure or even
elimination.

But biology is never everything—where and how people live always
plays a part. When it comes to smoking-related disease or to suicide, poisoning, or accidents, biology, as we shall see throughout the book, is

often less important than behavior or the economic and social conditions under which people live.

Biology and Behavior

The root cause of an epidemic of typhus in 1848, as the great pathologist Rudolf Virchow saw it, was poverty and lack of political representation. Robert Koch, the founder of microbiology, who identified the bacteria responsible for cholera, tuberculosis, and anthrax, triumphantly wrote, "One has been accustomed until now to regard tuberculosis as the outcome of social misery and to hope by relief of distress to diminish the disease. But in the final struggle against this dreadful plague of the human race one will no longer have to contend with an indefinite something but with an actual parasite."[1] The dichotomy between biology and behavior is an old one that has often been fought over. In the deaths we will discuss, behavior will usually be the key, and we will not focus on an actual parasite. We do not need much biology to understand how a gun kills, or how a traffic accident can maim, yet biology controls how eating and exercise affect obesity, how stress causes pain, how alcohol destroys the liver, or how smoking causes heart disease. We need always to bring social science and medicine together.

Figure 1.1 illustrates these ideas. It shows mortality rates in midlife for white Americans from 1900 to 2000. The line shows the death rate for men and women aged forty-five to fifty-four in each year. In later chapters, we explore death rates at other ages, but we shall often highlight this midlife age-group. It is in midlife that death rates pick up, and it is often a good place to see evolving trends in mortality. Death in midlife is rare and is usually shown as the number out of every 100,000 who die in a year. The numbers in the figure start out at around 1,500 (1.5 percent a year) in 1900 and fall to around 400 (0.4 percent a year) in 2000. This reduction, of more than two-thirds, is the main takeaway from the graph. We will see that there were similar reductions in death rates for other age and ethnic and racial groups.

Other notable events can be seen. The spike in mortality in 1918 is the influenza epidemic that swept the United States and the world at the end

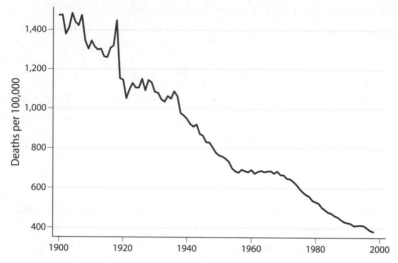

FIGURE 1.1. Mortality rates for white American men and women ages 45–54 in the twentieth century (deaths per 100,000). Authors' calculations using Centers for Disease Control and Prevention data.

of the First World War. There was some slowdown in progress during the 1930s and the Great Depression, but progress was also slow in the booming 1920s; there is no obvious relationship between mortality rates and the state of the economy. Indeed, research going back into the 1920s has documented the somewhat surprising results that deaths are often *higher* when the economy is doing well.[2] Mortality decline stagnated for several years around 1960 when many of those who had smoked heavily in their twenties and thirties died of lung cancer and heart disease. After 1970, mortality decline resumed in force, largely driven by the decline in mortality from heart disease. The post-1970 pattern also appears in other rich countries with the spread of knowledge about the harmful effects of smoking and as doctors prescribed pills to control hypertension and cholesterol.

Figure 1.1 shows all the main drivers of death. Epidemic disease is represented by influenza, itself conditioned by the economic, social, and human devastation of the Great War. Behavior shows in smoking, medical knowledge in the understanding of the effects of smoking, and the medical care system in the control of high blood pressure.

Figure 1.1 looks only at whites aged forty-five to fifty-four. But other groups also benefited from declining mortality in the twentieth century. African Americans are more likely to die than white Americans and have shorter life expectancy; this has long been true, and it is true today. But black men and women have also seen progress, at faster rates than whites, and the gap between black and white mortality rates has been narrowing. Death rates have also fallen among the elderly. In 1900, a sixty-year-old American woman could expect to live fifteen more years, and a man of the same age could expect to live another fourteen years; by the end of the century, those numbers had risen to twenty-three for women and twenty for men.

We know rather less about trends in morbidity—sickness other than death—than about trends in mortality. Yet we can be sure not just that people were living longer but also that their lives were better and healthier. For the last quarter century, we have direct measures from surveys that ask people about disability, pain, and their ability to undertake routine tasks. It was once feared that, as people lived to older ages, their old age would be one of pain and disability, not dead but sick, but this did not happen. Medical advances have not just reduced mortality but also helped people live better when they are alive. Joint replacements reduce pain and allow people to function in ways that would have been impossible without them. Cataract surgery restores the sight of those who would otherwise lose it. And drugs are sometimes effective at reducing pain and relieving depression and other mental distress.

Americans also became taller, which is a good reflection of improvements in nutrition and public health in their childhood. Men born in 1980 were about an inch and a half taller as adults than those born a century before. Other rich countries did even better. Americans used to be the tallest people in the world, but they have now been overtaken by Germans, Norwegians, and especially the Dutch—a sign, perhaps, that not all is well.[3]

2

Things Come Apart

BY ITS END, much of the optimism of the twentieth century had faded. Towns and cities in the heartland of America that used to produce steel, glass, furniture, or shoes, and that are fondly remembered by people in their seventies as having been great places to grow up, had been gutted, their factories closed and shops boarded up. In the wreckage, the temptations of alcohol and drugs lured many to their deaths. Most of these stories are never told. Stigma often removes the cause of death from obituaries when suicide, overdose, or alcoholism is involved. Addiction is seen as a moral weakness, not a disease, and it is believed that its effects are best covered up.

Exceptions are made when a famous chef kills himself or a music icon overdoses on fentanyl, or when the death is shocking to the community—for example, as reported by Congresswoman Ann McLane Kuster, "in a little town called Keene New Hampshire. There's not a quieter place on this earth, and a beloved high school teacher, mother of three children, died of a heroin overdose."[1] Each story is real and tragic, but it needs to be considered in perspective. When we look at the numbers, all the numbers, we see an even bigger, more frightening, and tragic story. The events that reach the media are selected for their news value, celebrities get attention, and the firsthand accounts of addiction or attempted suicide often come from those who are accustomed to writing about their experiences. Spectacular and unusual deaths—upper-class suicides and drug deaths—are exhaustively reported; those of ordinary people rarely make headlines, although they too leave behind devastated families and friends. Today's events are news; long-term trends are yesterday's news, which usually means not news at all. Deaths from lung cancer, heart disease, or diabetes are not news in and of themselves—lung cancer is not like Ebola or AIDS, though it takes many more lives—and we find out about them only incidentally when we read obituaries. Without the numbers to make comparisons, we don't know whether we are looking at an event, like a plane crash or a terrorist attack, where the deaths are few but shocking and newsworthy, or an epidemic, like Ebola or SARS, which terrified many but killed few, or whether we are dealing with something much larger, something that actually threatens the public health and upends a century of progress in human health.

All deaths in the US are reported to the authorities, and the information is assembled by the Centers for Disease Control and Prevention (CDC) in Atlanta. When someone dies, a great deal of information is collected on the death certificate, including, for the last thirty years, the highest level of education attained. The CDC has a website, charmingly called CDC Wonder, where much of this information is readily available. The death certificates themselves, with confidential information (such as name and social security number) removed, can also be downloaded and examined. It is with these data that we begin.

They are every bit as distressing as the stories.

American Exceptionalism, Breaking with the Past, and Leaving the Herd: The Facts

We saw in the previous chapter that the mortality rate for midlife whites in the US was 1,500 per 100,000 in 1900, and that by 2000 it had fallen to 400 per 100,000. We now follow this group into the twenty-first century.

We can also look at other countries around the world that, like the United States, are rich in terms of income per head and that share and implement the scientific and medical knowledge that is common across such countries. Those countries showed rapid declines in midlife mortality after 1945, and as in the US, the decline was particularly rapid after

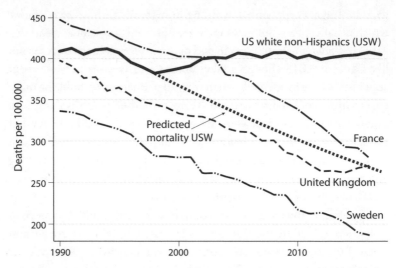

FIGURE 2.1. Age-adjusted mortality rates, ages 45–54, for US white non-Hispanics (USW), France, the United Kingdom, and Sweden, and a predicted mortality rate for USW, a counterfactual that assumes the mortality rate for USW would continue falling at 2 percent per year after 1998. Authors' calculations using CDC data and the Human Mortality Database.

1970. In almost all wealthy countries, mortality rates for those aged forty-five to fifty-four declined at an average rate of 2 percent per year from the late 1970s to 2000.

Figure 2.1 shows what happened. We call this the "things come apart" picture. Midlife mortality continued to decline in France, Britain, and Sweden; other rich countries, not shown, display similar progress. An entirely different pattern emerged for US white non-Hispanic Americans. Not only did whites not keep pace with mortality declines in other countries, but mortality for them stopped falling altogether and began to rise.

The future that we might have predicted for white Americans in midlife,[2] based on what had happened in the twentieth century, is shown here by the thick dotted line. Over time, white mortality pulled markedly away from what was seen in other wealthy countries, and what we might have predicted its path to be.

Something important, awful, and unexpected is happening. But is it just white men and women in middle age, or are other age-groups affected too? Is it men more than women, or women more than men? And what about other groups? Is it focused in one part of the country, or much the same everywhere? And, above all, why is it happening? As we shall see, the alcohol, suicide, and opioid epidemics are an essential part of the story, but we need to discuss a few other issues before we get there.

In chapter 1, when we showed falling midlife mortality through the twentieth century, we noted that other age-groups also benefited. But the reversal in figure 2.1 is not universally shared. As we shall see, while there have been similar changes in mortality trends for younger age-groups, mortality among the elderly continued to fall as it had done at the end of the twentieth century. We shall explore this a good deal further as we go, and we shall see that the reversal has begun to affect the youngest elderly too.

In figure 2.1 we switched from all whites to non-Hispanic whites, a narrower category for which data did not exist for most of the twentieth century. Hispanics, who are much poorer on average than non-Hispanics, have *lower* mortality rates than non-Hispanics, and their progress kept pace with that in other countries; their mortality rates look like those for Britain over this period. African Americans have *higher* mortality rates than any of the groups or countries shown in the picture, but their rate of mortality *decline* has been faster than for any of the groups or countries shown here. The midlife gap between US black and white mortality fell dramatically between 1990 and 2015, after which point the decline in midlife black mortality also came to an end, likely linked to opioids, as we shall see. The story of racial differences in mortality is an important one, and we shall later argue that the differences between black and white mortality rates can be reconciled once we look carefully at the history. The differences have less to do with *what* than with *when*.

These differences in mortality by race and ethnicity are far from fully understood, but they have existed for many years. For African Americans, there is widespread agreement that the worse outcomes, like so many other important outcomes, are tied to long-standing discrimination, as well as to poorer access to high-quality medical care.[3] The superior longevity of Hispanics over non-Hispanic whites has been much researched but not fully explained. It is worth noting that other groups, such as Asian

Americans, do better still, better than either Hispanics or whites. As to the recent trends, which have been so different across the three main groups, we will return to them repeatedly throughout the book, though we should confess from the start that we shall find much that is not easy to explain.

Figure 2.1 is drawn for men and women together, which is always potentially misleading. Women have lower mortality rates than men throughout life, and so they live longer, about five years longer in the US. Men and women suffer from different diseases, and to different extents from the same diseases and behaviors: men, for example, are three to four times more likely than women to kill themselves. But the turnaround—from continual progress in the twentieth century to stalled progress, or even regression, in the twenty-first—has happened to both men and women in midlife, though the reversal is somewhat larger for women than men. Even so, the gaps between whites in the US and other countries and between US whites and what we might have expected are large for both men and women, so that the figure does not mislead by taking men and women together.[4]

One measure of the importance of the white mortality reversal is to compare what actually happened with the trend shown by the dotted line. The gap between the two lines shows the difference in mortality rates in each year, from which we can calculate for each year how many people aged forty-five to fifty-four died who would have been alive had late twentieth-century progress continued. When we add up those numbers from 1999, the critical point where the turnaround began, to 2017, we get a very large total: 600,000 deaths of midlife Americans who would be alive if progress had gone on as expected. One immediate point of reference is the approximately 675,000 Americans who have died from HIV/AIDS since the beginning of the epidemic in the early 1980s. We shall refine our estimate as we go, extend it to other age-groups, and attribute it to specific causes, but it will serve for now as a ballpark estimate of what is involved, and to establish that what we are dealing with is indeed a major catastrophe.

Another measure of importance is to look at what has been happening to life expectancy at birth. Because life expectancy is more sensitive to deaths at younger ages, only large changes in midlife mortality can affect it. For whites, life expectancy at birth fell by one-tenth of a year between 2013 and 2014. In the next three years, between 2014 and 2015, 2015 and 2016, and again between 2016 and 2017, life expectancy fell for the US population as a whole. These declines reflect mortality at all ages, not just in midlife, but are, in fact, heavily influenced by what has been happening to whites in midlife. Any decline in life expectancy is extremely uncommon. With a three-year decline, we are in unfamiliar territory; American life expectancy has *never* fallen for three years in a row since states' vital registration coverage was completed in 1933.[5] For the subset of states that had registration of deaths before then, the only precedent is a century ago, from 1915 through 1918, during the First World War and the influenza epidemic that followed it. Catastrophes indeed.

The Geography of Mortality

If we are to begin to understand why these deaths are happening, we can first look for clues on *where* the deaths are happening. If we look across states at the changes in mortality rates for whites aged forty-five to fifty-four from 1999 to 2017, we find the increases in all but six states, with the largest increases in death rates in West Virginia, Kentucky, Arkansas, and Mississippi, all states with education levels lower than the national average. The only states where midlife white mortality fell by a noticeable amount were California, New York, New Jersey, and Illinois, all states with high levels of education.

A more detailed geography is shown in figure 2.2, where mortality rates for midlife whites are presented for about a thousand small areas across the United States in 2000 on the left and in 2016 on the right. These small areas are counties or, if the population of a county is small, a collection of adjacent counties. Darker areas indicate higher mortality, so the maps show high mortality in the West (except California), Appalachia, and the South in 2000, intensifying and spreading by 2016 into new areas, such as Maine, upper Michigan, and parts of Texas.

We will refer back to the patterns in these maps throughout the book.

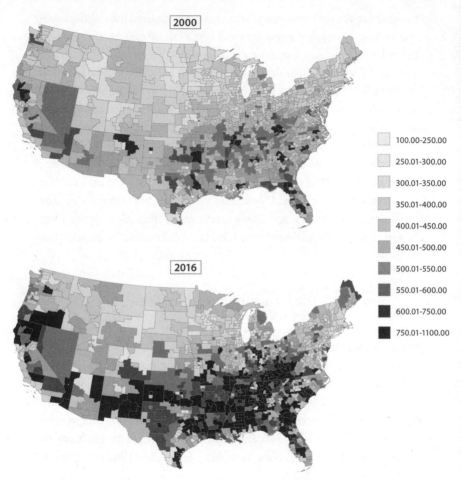

FIGURE 2.2. All-cause mortality rates, white non-Hispanics ages 45–54, by small area.
Authors' calculations using CDC data.

Carrying Their Troubles with Them:
Age versus Cohort Effects

Figure 2.1 compares death rates across countries for one specific age-group, those aged forty-five to fifty-four, but our concerns do not end there. White mortality progress has reversed throughout adulthood, in contrast to what is happening in the rest of the rich world. We highlight the midlife group, those aged forty-five to fifty-four. But, as we will see, rising mortality is not simply a baby-boomer phenomenon. For US whites, the hurdles at younger ages have also been raised.

The future of today's midlife adults is also in question. Will those in midlife "age out" of the mortality crisis if they survive? Or will they carry their troubles with them as they age, so that tomorrow's elderly will suffer like today's middle aged? Elderly Americans receive benefits, such as healthcare from Medicare and pensions from Social Security, that are not available to those in middle age so that, if these benefits are good for health, there is an argument for the positive alternative. But if the midlife deaths are happening to people born around 1950 because of the conditions under which they have lived their lives, or because of the way they have chosen to live their lives, there can be no expectation that they will do better as they age. Unfortunately, recent data are more consistent with the second, more negative outcome. The midlife increase in mortality has now begun to affect the elderly, as the birth cohorts born after the Second World War begin to move into old age. The all-cause mortality rate for whites ages sixty-five to seventy-four fell on average 2 percent per year between the early 1990s and 2012; since 2012, their mortality has stopped falling.

Social scientists often try to isolate two different phenomena. On the one hand, there may be "age" effects, when an outcome is tied to age, and on the other hand, "cohort" effects, when outcomes are attached to people born around the same time and are carried with them as they age. Cohort and age effects are not, of course, mutually exclusive, nor do they exhaust all of the possibilities. We will argue for (a version of) the cohort interpretation, which is, unfortunately, the more pessimistic of the two accounts. There is something about these people that makes them susceptible and that they carry with them through life. Discovering the nature of that something is our task in the rest of this book.

There are two stories, often seen as competing, though they need not be. One, the "external" or circumstantial account, emphasizes what happened to people, the opportunities that they had, the kind of education, occupation, or social environment that was available to them. The alternative, "internal" account emphasizes what people did to themselves, not their opportunities but their choices among those opportunities, or their own preferences. It is a debate between worsening opportunities, on the one hand, and worsening preferences, or declining values or even virtues, on the other.

Before we can take the story further, we have to return to our midlife Americans in the early twenty-first century and find out more about the causes of their deaths. Not surprisingly, suicide, opioids, and alcoholism feature in the story, but they are by no means the only players.

3

Deaths of Despair

BECKY MANNING: He just carried this tremendous guilt for
everything, for our son doing drugs. Then he started getting
depressed, and then my husband took his own life.

PAUL SOLMAN: How did he do it?

BECKY MANNING: He blew his head off. I came home to that.

PAUL SOLMAN: Best friend Marcy Conner's husband also killed
himself.

MARCY CONNER: He developed alcoholism very young in life.

PAUL SOLMAN: An addiction he shared with lifelong friends.

MARCY CONNER: One died with a heart attack, but drug use and
alcohol use played all the way through his life. Another one died
of cancer, drank up to the very end. And my husband actually
had a G-tube in, a feeding tube in, and poured alcohol down his
feeding tube until he died.[1]

What are middle-aged white Americans dying from? The foregoing extract, from an interview in Kentucky that aired on PBS, manages, in only
a few words, to capture the three different causes of death that we have
come to call deaths of despair: suicide, drugs, and alcohol. It also shows
how they are often closely related. Becky Manning's husband killed himself because of depression over his son's drug use. Manning's husband
and his friends abused alcohol and drugs throughout their adult lives, and
Marcy Conner's husband died by pouring alcohol directly into his stomach. One of the friends died of a heart attack in which alcohol could

have been indirectly involved, if it promoted a heart attack in someone who already had long-standing heart disease.

When we first saw an early version of the "coming apart" graph, we asked ourselves what people were dying of, which sent us back to the Centers for Disease Control and Prevention data to see what kinds of deaths had been rising most rapidly since 1999, the year white mortality rates began to rise. There were three immediate culprits. In order of importance, they were accidental or intent-undetermined poisonings (which are almost entirely drug overdoses), suicides, and alcoholic liver diseases and cirrhosis. While there are more deaths from drug overdoses than from either suicides or alcohol-related diseases, suicides and alcohol together kill more whites than do drugs. All three kinds of death are important. Death continues its journey. Having moved from the bowels of children into the lungs and arteries of the elderly, it is now backtracking into the minds, livers, and veins of the middle-aged.

The rapid rise in these deaths is affecting Americans, particularly whites, but not people in other rich countries. There have been increases in drug overdoses in other English-speaking countries—Canada, Ireland, Britain (especially Scotland), and Australia—and an increase in alcohol-related deaths in Britain and Ireland. (The data do not allow us to separate out deaths by ethnic or racial groups in these or in other rich countries.) These rising deaths elsewhere are serious threats to public health and may become more serious in the future. But, apart from drug deaths in Scotland, the numbers are very small compared with those in the United States. In the US, at least until 2013, when a deadly opioid, fentanyl, hit the streets, neither blacks nor Hispanics saw a rise in deaths of despair.

Although the surge in deaths in America is what we might see during the ravages of an infectious disease, like the Great Influenza Pandemic of 1918, this is an epidemic that is not carried by a virus or a bacterium, nor is it caused by an external agent, such as poisoning of the air or the fallout from a nuclear accident. Instead, people are doing this to themselves. They are drinking themselves to death, or poisoning themselves with drugs, or shooting or hanging themselves. Indeed, as we shall repeatedly see, the three causes of death are deeply related, and it is often hard for the coroner or medical examiner to classify a death; it is not always easy to tell a suicide from an accidental overdose. All the deaths show great unhappiness with life, either momentary or prolonged. It is tempting to classify them all as suicides, done either quickly, with a gun or by standing on and kicking away a chair with a rope around the neck, or slowly, with drugs or alcohol. Even so, many addicts do not want to die, even when they see death as the almost inevitable outcome of their addiction.

The vast majority of drug deaths are classified as "accidental poisonings," but these are not accidents in the same sense as falling off a ladder or being electrocuted by mistakenly touching a live wire. Certainly, some people get the dose wrong and accidentally inject themselves with more heroin than their systems can tolerate, or miscalculate the risk of combining drugs and alcohol. But what about the addicts who, when hearing of an "accidental death" nearby, seek out the dealer to make sure that they too can obtain high-strength drugs? Or those who seek out fentanyl, a drug that is many times stronger and more dangerous than heroin? The *Washington Post* reported the story of Amanda Bennett of Baltimore, aged twenty-six, who became addicted to opioids after a C-section, progressed to heroin, and then to fentanyl-laced heroin, and who noted, "If there is no fentanyl in it, I don't want it at all."[2]

People who seek out such drugs are not seeking death, just a powerful high or temporary relief from their cravings, but the high risk of death is no deterrent. There are addicts who, having overdosed, are miraculously brought back to life with a dose of naloxone (Narcan), only to overdose again within hours. Alcohol addiction is less immediately dangerous than addiction to opioids, and there are high-functioning alcoholics just as there are some high-functioning drug addicts. But there are also those who have lost their families, their jobs, and their lives to their addiction—addiction is a prison that separates its victims from a life worth living.

Robert DuPont, the first director of the National Institute on Drug Abuse, argues that the two essential characteristics of addiction are continued use of a substance despite serious consequences caused by that use, and dishonesty.[3] What he has called the "selfish brain" takes control and leaves no room for anything but the craving.[4] People who put themselves at risk of dying from the side effects of alcohol or drugs have already lost much of what makes life worth living, paralleling the loss experienced by many of those who decide to kill themselves.

We call the three kinds of death "deaths of despair." It is a convenient label, indicating the link with unhappiness, the link with mental or behavioral health, and the lack of any infectious agent, but it is not intended to identify the specific causes of despair. We shall have a great deal to say about those background causes, or "causes of causes," in what follows. For now, it is simply a good label. Deaths of despair among white men and women aged forty-five to fifty-four rose from thirty per one hundred thousand in 1990 to ninety-two per one hundred thousand in 2017. In every US state, suicide mortality rates for whites aged forty-five to fifty-four increased between 1999–2000 and 2016–17. In all but two states, mortality rates from alcoholic liver disease rose.[5] And in every state, drug overdose mortality rates increased.

We were far from the first to see the rise of drug overdoses. The current epidemic began in the early 1990s and gained momentum in 1996 with the Food and Drug Administration's approval and the subsequent marketing of the addictive prescription painkiller OxyContin, essentially legalized heroin, manufactured by Purdue Pharmaceutical. Scholars who worked on alcohol-related liver deaths and suicide had also seen increases, especially in middle-aged whites, though this had not received the same public attention as the deaths from drug overdoses. Our contribution was to link drug overdoses, suicides, and alcohol-related deaths, to note that all were rising together, that together they were afflicting mostly whites, and that, among that group, the long fall in total mortality had stopped or reversed. We also chose the collective label "deaths of despair," which helped publicize the combined epidemic and emphasize that it included more than just drug overdose.

But Something Else Must Be Going On

In an early comment on our work, the health economists Ellen Meara and Jonathan Skinner noted that, while it was true that deaths of despair were rising rapidly, their combined numbers were not enough, by themselves, to account for the flattening or reversal in total mortality.[6] Something else must be going on to account for the turnaround in white mortality, in comparison both with twentieth-century progress and with other groups in the US and other rich countries in the twenty-first century. We needed to find that "something else."

The remarkable decline in mortality after 1970, and the associated increase in life expectancy at birth, was in large part driven by rapid decreases in deaths from heart disease and cancer, the two largest killers in the US. Before age seventy-five, the risk of dying of cancer outpaces that of heart disease; after seventy-five, heart disease takes more victims. Because mortality rates are highest at the oldest ages, heart disease is America's number one killer. Progress against cancer, the number one killer in midlife, continued apace into the new century. The "something else" that, together with deaths of despair, halted midlife mortality decline turns out to be a marked slowdown in progress against mortality from heart disease, long an engine of better health and rising life expectancy. That previous progress is usually attributed to people quitting smoking—especially men, who quit earlier than women, and who are more likely than women to die from heart disease—and to more people taking preventive drugs for lower blood pressure and cholesterol (antihypertensives and statins). The risk of dying of heart disease for US whites ages forty-five to fifty-four fell at a brisk pace of 4 percent per year on average in the 1980s but decelerated to 2 percent per year in the 1990s, 1 percent per year in the 2000s, and began to rise after 2010.[7]

Figure 3.1 shows deaths from heart disease for whites ages forty-five to fifty-four in the United States, together with Britain and other English-speaking countries—Canada, Australia, and Ireland. After 1990, and as we would expect from continuing progress in reducing smoking and the spread of preventive medicine—whose treatments are readily available in all rich countries—mortality rates declined and became much more similar across countries. The exception is America, which once again has parted company with its neighbors. Indeed, the slowdown in progress against heart disease accounts for a substantial part of the "coming apart" in figure 2.1. Fifteen percent of the six hundred thousand extra deaths we

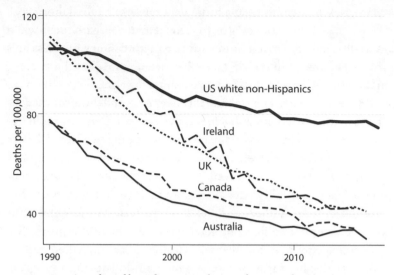

FIGURE 3.1. Age-adjusted heart disease mortality rates for men and women ages 45–54.
Authors' calculations using Centers for Disease Control and Prevention
and World Health Organization data.

estimated for forty-five-to-fifty-four-year-old whites in chapter 2 come from this source, and not just deaths of despair.

Progress against heart disease was robust until 2010 in the rest of the English-speaking world. However, that progress ended abruptly after 2011. This pattern, of steady progress through 2010 followed by mortality rates flatlining, is also true for blacks and Hispanics in the US. This puts the English-speaking world at odds with the rest of the rich world, where the risk of dying from heart disease in midlife continues to fall. Perhaps in the English-speaking world the improvements from prevention are running out, or perhaps as many people have quit smoking as are ever going to. But this cannot explain the poor performance of heart disease mortality in the United States, which was high by international standards in 1990, so that there ought to have been *more* room for improvement, not less.

When we look at drug overdoses or suicides, the classification of cause of death points to the immediate cause. But heart disease comes in many forms and has many underlying causes, so it is much harder to pin down the *why* of figure 3.1. One possibility is that the drugs and alcohol associated with deaths of despair may make people more likely to die of heart disease. While moderate drinking (one drink per day for women, two for men) is thought to increase "good" cholesterol (HDL) and reduce the effects of "bad" cholesterol (LDL), heavy drinking over the long term can lead to heart disease by increasing the risk of high blood pressure and by weakening the heart muscle. Binge drinking (three or more drinks in a one-to-two-hour period) can make the heart beat irregularly. The relationship between drug abuse and heart disease is more complicated, given that different drugs have different effects on the central nervous system. Methamphetamines and cocaine (dubbed "the perfect heart attack drug") are stimulants that increase blood pressure and heart rate, increasing the risk of both heart attack and sudden cardiac death. Less is known about the heart risks associated with opioid abuse. Recent research suggests links between long-acting opioids and cardiovascular death, but much work here remains to be done.[8] To the extent that heart failure or a fatal heart attack was the result of long-term alcohol or drug abuse, these deaths could also be classified as deaths of despair.

More general threats to heart health in midlife appear to lie in smoking, hypertension, and obesity. While American smoking rates have fallen overall in the past twenty years, in some areas of the country rates remain stubbornly high (this is particularly true of the East South-Central census division—Mississippi, Kentucky, Alabama, and Tennessee), and within some demographic groups, smoking rates have continued to increase (true of middle-aged white women without a bachelor's degree). There has also been some recent reduction in adherence to antihypertensive medicines.

By far the most popular story for heart disease deaths is obesity, that Americans weigh too much, that they are among the heaviest in the world, and that the prolonged increase in obesity, which many scholars have long predicted will undermine health progress, is now actually doing so. Many studies have documented the risks of obesity, which include heart disease, high blood pressure, and diabetes. The link from obesity to diabetes is particularly strong, and deaths from diabetes may often be recorded as deaths from heart disease when it is also present.[9] Eating too much, like drinking too much, is for some people a reaction to stress and a way of self-soothing in the face of life's difficulties and disappointments, so deaths associated with obesity could perhaps also be included as deaths of despair.

We do not take that route here, in part because it is so difficult to calculate which of the deaths from heart disease are related to overeating. But the obesity explanation is far from complete. The obesity gloom-mongers have been crying wolf for a long time and were predicting that life expectancy would start falling long before there was any sign of it.[10] It is also possible that the risks associated with obesity were lower in recent years and are lower now than when the studies of risk were done; studies have to follow people for many years and, with the arrival of new procedures and drugs, they always run the risk of being out of date before they are completed. Since one of the ways that obesity increases the risk of heart disease is through high blood pressure, the increased availability and use of antihypertensives may have made it safer to be heavy than it used to be.

Comparisons across countries also leave many questions unanswered on the role of obesity. In England and Australia, the rise in obesity for adults aged forty-five to fifty-four was nearly identical to that seen for whites in the US between the mid-1990s and 2010,[11] during which time heart disease mortality in the UK and Australia fell on average at 4 percent per year. The synchronized halt to progress in heart disease for US blacks and Hispanics and middle-aged adults in other English-speaking countries after 2011 leaves open the question of whether some additional factor is now also at work.

Whatever its ultimate cause, the unique pattern of heart disease mortality for US whites combined with the unique pattern of deaths of despair to generate a rise in white midlife mortality after 1998. We can think of what happened to overall mortality as the result of a tug-of-war. On one side, we have progress against heart disease, pulling mortality rates down. On the other, we have deaths of despair tugging, weakly at first, to pull mortality rates up. In 1990, heart disease progress was "winning," and overall mortality fell. But, over time, heart disease progress lost its strength, while deaths of despair grew stronger and overall mortality stopped declining and in some midlife groups began to rise.

This account is important for our story here, because both the level of heart disease mortality and the slowdown in progress against it vary with age, so the tug-of-war for the direction of all-cause mortality is different in different age-groups. For whites in their late twenties or early thirties, heart disease is not a big killer, and the rapid increase in deaths of despair has been driving up all-cause mortality in this part of adulthood for the past twenty years. For whites in their late thirties and early forties, declines in heart disease and cancer and increases in deaths of despair came to a standstill until 2013, when access to an even more deadly opioid (fentanyl) began to accelerate deaths from drug overdose. For those in their fifties, the complete collapse in progress against heart disease, pitted against rising mortality from drugs, alcohol, and suicide, has been driving up all-cause mortality since the start of the new century.

Not Just in Midlife: Deaths of Despair among Younger Americans

We are telling the story in the way that we uncovered it, starting with midlife deaths of all kinds. We then focused on the immediate causes, which turned out to be deaths of despair among whites plus a slowdown and reversal in deaths from heart disease, which, until then, had been a main engine of mortality decline. Unfortunately, deaths of despair are not only afflicting middle-aged whites. While the elderly have been largely exempt, there have also been rapid increases in deaths of despair— particularly from overdoses and suicides—among younger whites. For whites between the ages of forty-five and fifty-four, deaths of despair tripled from 1990 to 2017. In 2017, this midlife age-group had the highest rate of mortality from deaths of despair. But whites in younger age-groups were also doing badly and their deaths rose even more rapidly, accelerating in the last few years.

As we write, the epidemic is worsening. In the next chapter, we shall suggest a story of the epidemic in which, with the passage of time, each age-group does progressively worse than the same age-group did in earlier years. All the while, the pattern we see in midlife deaths is moving into old age. In 2005, deaths of despair started to increase beyond middle age.

Parents should not have to watch their grown children die. It is a reversal of the normal order of things; children are supposed to bury their parents, not the reverse. The death of a child, even an adult child, can tear families apart, and the loss of people in their prime, people who should not be dying, upends communities and workplaces too. At the outset of this chapter, we saw how Mr. Manning killed himself in the face of his son "doing drugs," and there are millions of American mothers and fathers today who are living in dread that the phone call to their adult son or daughter will go unanswered, or that a phone call will come from the police or the emergency room.

PART II

The Anatomy of the Battlefield

4

The Lives and Deaths of the More (and Less) Educated

IN THE STATE OF KENTUCKY, where Becky Manning and Marcy Conner told the stories of their husbands' suicides, the risk of dying in midlife from suicide, accidental drug overdose, or alcoholic liver disease was a third higher than the national average in 2017. But not all Kentuckians were at equal risk. The risk of dying a death of despair had risen markedly, but only for those who did not hold a four-year college degree. Figure 4.1 shows mortality rates over time from deaths of despair for whites aged forty-five to fifty-four in Kentucky. Without a bachelor's degree, the risk rose from 37 to 137 per 100,000 people between 1995 and 2015, while that for those who hold a bachelor's degree changed little.

Kentucky is among the states with relatively low educational attainment, and only a quarter of whites ages forty-five to fifty-four hold a bachelor's degree. But this pattern, of rapidly increasing risk for those without a four-year degree, is repeated in all US states. Education is clearly one of the keys to understanding who is dying and why. The march of death from arteries and lungs to minds, livers, and veins is largely confined to those who have not been to college. If we are to understand the extra risk borne by those without a bachelor's degree, we need to understand the role education plays in people's lives.

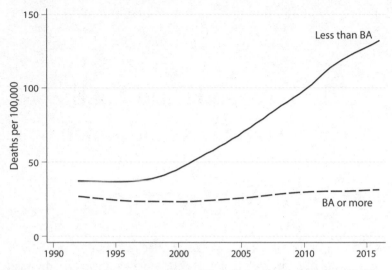

FIGURE 4.1. Suicide, drug overdose, and alcoholic liver disease mortality in Kentucky, by educational attainment, white non-Hispanics ages 45–54. Authors' calculations using Centers for Disease Control and Prevention data.

What Education Does to Life

In 2017, almost 40 percent of the American population aged twenty-five or older had no more than a high school diploma, 27 percent had some tertiary education but did not hold a bachelor's degree, and 33 percent held a four-year bachelor's degree or higher qualification. The proportions in each education category changed dramatically for Americans born between 1925 and 1945; 10 percent of adults ages twenty to twenty-four were enrolled in school in the late 1940s, doubling to 20 percent by the late 1960s.[1] Since then, tertiary education has nosed up slowly; the fraction holding a bachelor's degree increased from a quarter of people born in 1945 to a third of those born in 1970. For those born after 1970, and graduating after 1990, the fraction earning a bachelor's degree has changed little.

The most obvious advantage of having gone to college is that you earn more, and with more money, you can live a better life. In the late 1970s, those with a bachelor's degree or more earned on average 40 percent more than workers who left school with a high school diploma. But by 2000, that "earnings premium," as economists call it, had doubled, to an astronomical 80 percent.[2] In contrast, over that period, the earnings premium for Americans with some college education short of a bachelor's degree remained relatively flat, with earnings 15 to 20 percent higher than for those with a high school degree. Those who graduated from high school in the early 1970s and who decided *not* to go to college could not have known how much they would be giving up by the end of the century.

Many occupations that previously did not require a bachelor's degree now do, so that the opportunities for those who do not go to college are shrinking just as the opportunities for those who have been to college are expanding. In 2017, at a time when the unemployment rate was only 3.6 percent, a historical low, the unemployment rate was almost twice as high among those with a high school diploma as it was among those with a bachelor's degree. Eighty-four percent of Americans ages twenty-five to sixty-four with a bachelor's degree or higher were employed in 2017, while only 68 percent of those with a high school diploma but no additional education were employed.[3] American workers' earnings generally peak between the ages of forty-five and fifty-four. It is worrying that fully a quarter of Americans in that age-group who left school with a high school diploma were not in the labor force in 2017 compared with only 10 percent of those with at least a bachelor's degree.

As we shall see, there is much controversy about the *why* of the difference, whether less educated people simply do not want to work, at least at the wages that are available to them, or do want to but cannot because work is unavailable or because they are disabled. Whatever the answer, the fact remains that the labor market is delivering for those with more education in a way that it is not for those with less.

As business and government have adopted ever more sophisticated technologies and as their use of computers has increased significantly, the demand for higher skills and higher ability has expanded, which can explain part of the earnings and employment gap between those with less and more education. For the fortunate and talented few at the top, who become hedge fund traders, Silicon Valley entrepreneurs, CEOs, or top lawyers or doctors, the earnings possibilities are virtually unlimited, much more so than used to be the case. Among America's 350 largest firms, average CEO earnings in 2018 was $17.2 million, 278 times average earnings. In 1965 the ratio was only 20 to 1.[4] If we go back a hundred years, those who earned the very highest incomes derived them from capital; they were the inheritors of fortunes from the past. Among those who lived off interest and dividends, it was a badge of shame to have to work for a living. There was no greater disgrace than to have one's daughter marry a manufacturer. Today, the highest incomes are coming not from inherited wealth but rather from high earnings—for example, for CEOs—or from the profits of self-employed and highly skilled business proprietors such as consultants, doctors, and lawyers. Education is a required gateway for such jobs, not family or birth.[5]

People tend to marry people with similar interests and backgrounds. Women with college degrees are more likely to marry college-educated men. Where once college-educated women stayed at home, in the last part of the twentieth century they came out to work. As a result, during the period when the labor market returns to a college degree rose, and more high-paying professional positions opened to women, we began to see more couples in which both partners had high, professional earnings. A bachelor's degree or beyond was a ticket not just to a high-paying job but also to a marriage with two high salaries.

The worlds of the more and less educated have split apart, a divergence that we will see over and over in this book.[6] At work, companies are today more likely to be segregated by education, and as we shall see later, firms are outsourcing many low-skill jobs that used to be done in-house, where people with different levels of education worked together and were part of the same company. The more and less educated are now more segregated in where they live, the successful in places where house prices are high and to which the less successful do not have access. Greater geographical segregation has widened the gap in the quality of schools attended by the children of the more and less educated. The power couples have less time to participate in community activities, other than with their children's schools, so that the more and less educated are less likely to know each other, to understand each other's concerns, or to participate in common social activities. The tastes of the two groups are different; they eat in different kinds of restaurants, visit different websites, watch different television channels, get their news from different sources, worship in different kinds of churches, and read different books. And, as we shall see later, their attachment to the institution of marriage is different and increasingly so. More educated people marry later, they are more likely to stay married, they have children much later, and they are less likely to have children out of wedlock.

Gallup asks a large sample of Americans to rate their lives on a "ladder of life" from 0 ("the worst possible life you can imagine") to 10 ("the best possible life you can imagine"). From 2008 to 2017, more than 2.5 million people answered this question, and their average life evaluation was 6.9. For those with a bachelor's degree or above, the average was 7.3, compared with 6.6 for those with a high school diploma or less. About half of this ladder-of-life advantage comes from the higher incomes that the more educated enjoy, leaving a very substantial advantage attributable to education itself, or at least to the nonincome benefits that education brings. Gallup also asks people about whether they get to do something interesting or something they like every day; once again, the educated have a huge advantage.[7]

Education and Meritocracy

A more educated *society* is different in ways that go beyond the differences between individuals. At least to some extent, everyone benefits from the innovations and higher productivity of more educated people. Better equality of opportunity is a worthy goal, and everyone approves of opening educational opportunities to bright children who were previously excluded on grounds of their family, income, or birth. Meritocracy is a touchstone virtue of our age, and no one doubts the benefits of allowing everyone a chance to succeed and to rise to the level of their abilities. Indeed, it is clear that we need more of it in some areas. An excellent example is who becomes an inventor; inventions are key to economic growth and future prosperity. Children born in the top 1 percent of the income distribution are ten times more likely to become inventors than those in the bottom half of the income distribution. This failure of meritocracy is leaving "lost Einsteins" who might have changed the world for the better.[8]

Meritocracy has its downsides too, which were recognized by the British economist and sociologist Michael Young, who in 1958 invented the term *meritocracy* and who predicted a social disaster as a result of its rise.[9]

Indeed, we have already seen one problem, that some jobs that were once open to nongraduates are now reserved for those with a college degree. If the jobs—such as those in law enforcement, for example—are better done by those with a degree, that is a good thing, in and of itself. But if there are resources that are in fixed supply, such as nice places to live and work, they will be allocated away from those with less education. Most seriously, and this is what concerned Young, the loss of the smartest children from the less educated group deprives them of talent that is useful to the group itself. Young writes that "the bargaining over the distribution of national expenditure is a battle of wits, and that defeat was bound to go to those who lost their clever children to the enemy." He notes that the real reason the elites have been so relatively successful is that "the humble no longer have anyone—except themselves—to speak for them." When talented people lack a chance to move up, they miss the opportunity to shine and to benefit others in the wider world in which they become able to work, but the movement of talent also denudes the places and groups from where they came. Young refers to the less educated group as "the populists," and the elite as "the hypocrisy."[10]

Writing sixty years later, about our own times, the political philosopher Michael Sandel discusses the corrosive effects of meritocracy: "Winners are encouraged to consider their success their own doing, a measure of their virtue—and to look down upon those less fortunate than themselves. Those who lose out may complain that the system is rigged, that the winners have cheated and manipulated their way to the top. Or they may harbor the demoralizing thought that their failure is their own doing, that they simply lack the talent and drive to succeed."[11] According to a 2019 poll, only half of American adults think that colleges are having a positive effect on the country; 59 percent of Republicans—the party that has increasingly become the party of the less educated—think they are having a *negative* effect.[12]

Because they are selected on ability, not family wealth or position, meritocrats are more able than those they have replaced. Again, much of this will be personally and socially beneficial. But when a new group succeeds, it does what the previous group once tried to do, which is to entrench their own positions against the next generation of meritocrats. Being more able, they are more successful at the exclusionary and advantage-seeking strategies on behalf of themselves and their children that are privately enriching but socially destructive. The wealthy can pay for more, and higher-quality, coaching for college entrance exams and essays, as well as for diagnoses of disabilities that allow their children extra time for classwork and exams.[13]

When meritocracies are unequal, as is the case in the US today, with vast rewards for successfully identified merit—passing exams, promotions, making partner, speculating successfully, or getting elected—the rewards are paid not only for ability and virtue but also for cheating and for abandoning long-held ethical constraints that are seen as impediments to success. The saying "If you ain't cheating, you ain't trying" applies beyond sports. An unequal meritocracy is likely to be one in which standards of public behavior are low, and where some members of the elite are corrupt, or are seen as corrupt by those in the out-group. An extreme case is the college entrance scandal of 2019, when wealthy parents paid bribes to secure places for their children at elite colleges. Our guess is that the rise of the meritocracy in today's vastly unequal America has contributed to the "winner-take-all" and much harsher atmosphere in corporations today.[14] Perhaps meritocracies destroy themselves over time.[15]

Death and Education

That mortality rates are higher in the US for people with less education has long been known. One of the ways that education is protective against a preventable disease is when the way the disease works is understood but when that understanding is more accessible to those with more education. The demographers Samuel Preston and Michael Haines have shown that at the dawn of the twentieth century, before the germ theory of disease had been widely digested, "the children of physicians had mortality that was scarcely better than that for the average child, indicating fairly clearly that physicians had few weapons at their disposal to advance survival. By 1924, the mortality of physicians' children was 35 percent below the national average. Children of teachers advanced as rapidly, and all professionals made great strides during the period."[16] Moving closer to the present, smoking rates were very similar by education group before the release in 1964 of the surgeon general's report on the health risks associated with smoking. After that point, smoking rates began to diverge, with more educated people more likely to quit and less likely to start smoking. Of course, this does not explain why smoking rates for the less educated remain higher more than half a century after the health risks were understood. Knowledge is clearly not everything. Patterns of health-related behaviors by social status are frequently found, and status itself may be one of the keys to understanding them.[17]

Health behaviors continue to vary by education. In 2017, white American adults (twenty-five and over) with a high school degree or less were four times more likely to be current smokers than those with a bachelor's degree or more (29 versus 7 percent), while those with some college but no degree fell in between (19 percent). A third of whites with less than a bachelor's degree were obese in 2015, compared with less than a quarter of those with a bachelor's degree, and those without a bachelor's degree have lost ground in successfully controlling hypertension. Those with a bachelor's degree or more are also taller than those without, by about half an inch on average—a reflection of better childhood health and nutrition.[18]

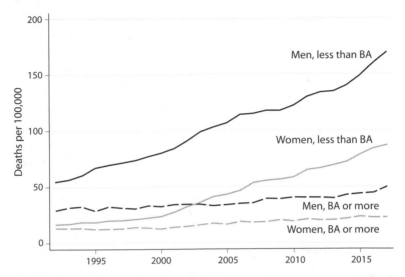

FIGURE 4.2. Drug, alcohol, and suicide mortality, white non-Hispanics ages 45–54. Authors' calculations using Centers for Disease Control and Prevention data. Data are adjusted for increases in average age within the age-group.

These factors contribute to the rapid widening of the mortality gap between whites with and without a bachelor's degree that we are witnessing today. Taken as a whole, white mortality in the age-group forty-five to fifty-four has held constant since the early 1990s. But this masks the fact that for those with less than a bachelor's degree, death rates rose by 25 percent, while for those with a bachelor's degree, mortality dropped by 40 percent.[19] In 2017, those with a bachelor's degree or more earned twice as much as those without, which speaks to the advantage of the more educated in life. That their risk of dying in midlife is only a quarter of that seen for those without a bachelor's degree speaks to their advantage in death.

While increases in mortality gaps for heart disease and cancer both contributed to the growing gap in mortality between education groups, it was the rise in deaths of despair among those with less than a bachelor's degree that largely accounts for the widening of the all-cause mortality gap. Figure 4.2 shows the numbers for the US as a whole, separately for men and for women.

Men and women in this age-group are much less likely to die deaths of despair if they have a bachelor's degree. A gap between the two groups is apparent for men in 1992. Men with less education were always more likely to die from alcohol, drugs, or suicide, but the gap widened rapidly as the epidemic progressed, so that by 2017, those in the less educated group were three times more likely to succumb to these deaths.

In the early 1990s, white women were at low risk of dying from alcohol, suicide, or drug overdose, regardless of their education. Early media coverage of our work often carried headlines about "angry" white *men* dying, which we think stemmed from an inability to imagine that women could kill themselves in these ways. Historically, they did not. But that has changed. Women are less likely to kill themselves—this appears to be true everywhere in the world where we have data, even in China, which used to be an exception—and they are less likely to die from alcoholic liver disease or from drug overdoses. Yet the graph shows that the epidemic is affecting men and women in almost equal numbers. This is true for each component— suicide, drug overdose, and alcoholic liver disease—examined separately. We argue against the view, espoused by some in the media, that this is an epidemic that is more serious for women. This plague has not discriminated by sex.[20]

The Destiny of Birth

Figure 4.3 plots deaths of despair among all adults, not just those in midlife. Here we look at people with and without a college degree according to their year of birth, tracking birth cohorts through time as they age. It is worth spending time on this figure, because it is important for understanding what has happened, and because we shall use similar figures in subsequent chapters. The fates of different Americans depend on when they were born, when they finished school, and when they started work, and these graphs help us to see all of this.

FIGURE 4.3. Alcohol, drug, and suicide mortality, white non-Hispanics, by birth cohort 1992–2017. Authors' calculations using Centers for Disease Control and Prevention data.

The left panel of the figure shows people without a bachelor's degree, while the right panel shows people with a bachelor's degree or more. The left panel is easier to see, though both panels are constructed in exactly the same way. Each line refers to a specific birth "cohort," or the group of people born in a given year, which is marked on the figure; farthest left is the cohort born in 1985, and farthest to the right is the cohort born in 1935. The horizontal axis shows age, and the people in each cohort age by twenty-six years as we follow each cohort through time from 1992 to 2017, which is all that our data allow. In order to make the figures legible, we show only every fifth birth cohort. Each line, or "track," in the figure shows how the rate of mortality from deaths of despair changed over time as each birth cohort aged.

As we look at younger and younger cohorts of those without a college degree, we find that their risk of dying a death of despair is higher than the risk for the cohorts that came before. At age forty-five, for those without a bachelor's degree, the birth cohort of 1960 faced a risk 50 percent higher than the cohort born in 1950, and the cohort of 1970 faced a risk more than twice as high. The later you were born, the higher your risk of dying a death of despair at any given age. The risk rises with age for all but the oldest cohorts (those born in 1935 and 1940). Each successive cohort faces a risk of death that is rising more rapidly with age than that faced by the cohorts that came before.

Remarkably, the right-hand panel, showing cohorts of those who have a bachelor's degree, is quite different. In contrast to the sharp differences by cohorts for those without a college degree, it is difficult to tell the birth cohorts apart. As with the less educated, the risk of a death of despair rises with age, at least until age sixty, but each cohort seems to be aging almost along the same trajectory. If we look closely, we can see that there are (much smaller) differences across cohorts and that here, too, later-born cohorts are doing slightly worse. But, in the language of the demographers, there are no or only very small "cohort effects"; each cohort is aging along the same profile.

The patterns for black non-Hispanics across birth cohorts, for both education groups, look very much like that for whites with a bachelor's degree—rising with age within an education group, but with very little difference between birth cohorts. For blacks, there is no progressive deterioration for younger cohorts.

For the cohort of non-Hispanic whites born in 1935, whom we see in their sixties and seventies in figure 4.3, the difference in the risk of a death of despair between those with and without a bachelor's degree is only three per one hundred thousand. But the difference between the less and more educated grew dramatically for later-born cohorts so that, in the cohort born in 1960, whom we see in their forties and fifties, the difference between those with and without a bachelor's degree is ten times larger than that for the cohort of 1935. The catastrophe that has come to less educated whites, and that is getting steadily worse the later they were born, is affecting the educated in a much less severe way.

Going back to the nineteenth century, and even before Emile Durkheim's foundational study of suicide in 1897, more educated people were *more* likely to kill themselves.[21] The epidemic has reversed that longstanding pattern. In the birth cohorts born between 1935 and 1945, suicide was equally common among those with and without a college degree. However, beginning with cohorts born in the early 1950s, those without a bachelor's degree were at higher risk. The divergence in the risk of suicide between the less and more educated has grown with each successive birth cohort. For those born in 1980, whites without a bachelor's degree are four times more likely to commit suicide than those with a four-year degree. These twenty-first-century suicides are different from past suicides; they are happening to different people and, we might reasonably presume, for different reasons.

5

Black and White Deaths

IN THE *DOONESBURY* CARTOON featuring B. D. and his friend Ray, Ray claims that blacks and Latinos are immune to deaths of despair because they are used to distress and deprivation. B. D. ironically refers to this immunity as "black privilege."[1] It is ironic because middle-aged blacks are far from privileged in their risk of dying, just as they are far from privileged in many other aspects of life.

Over the past quarter century, at least up to 2013, African Americans did not suffer the relentless increase in deaths of despair that we have documented among whites. However, earlier in the twentieth century, blacks faced a mortality crisis precipitated by the arrival of crack cocaine and HIV. This occurred after a period of large-scale job loss for lower-skilled black workers. Jobs in manufacturing and transportation left the inner city, which led to social upheaval, detachment from the labor force, and a disintegration of family and community life. As we shall see in later chapters, this story has many parallels with what has happened to less educated whites in the last twenty-five years. When the labor market turned against its least skilled workers, blacks were the first to lose out, in part because of their low skill levels, and in part because of long-standing patterns of discrimination. Decades later, less educated whites, long protected by white privilege, were next in line. The debates about causes, between lack of opportunity, on the one hand, and lack of virtue, on the other, are also remarkably similar in the two episodes. What happened to blacks and whites differs perhaps more in *when* than in *what*.

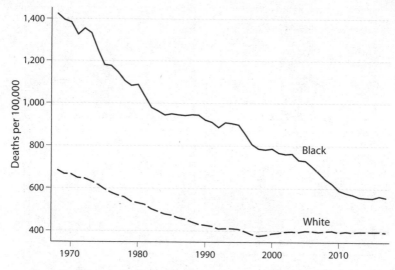

FIGURE 5.1. Mortality rates for blacks and whites ages 45–54, 1968–2017. Authors' calculations using Centers for Disease Control and Prevention data.

We will tell this story in more detail, but we start, as usual, with the numbers.

Black and White Mortality: Facts

Figure 5.1 shows mortality rates for blacks and whites since 1968 for the midlife group aged forty-five to fifty-four.[2] Black mortality rates have fallen more rapidly than those for whites but have been, and remain, consistently higher. This has been happening since the 1930s, when midlife death rates for blacks were an appalling two and a half times higher than for whites.

The black-white gap has closed, but at different rates in different periods. In the late 1960s, when white mortality rates stalled because of smoking in earlier years, the gap closed quickly. In the 1980s, it was black mortality's turn to stall; this was when the crack and HIV epidemics fell hard on the black community. We will come back to this episode.

From 1990, black mortality resumed its progress so that, when white mortality stopped falling in the late 1990s, the gap closed rapidly. Reducing the gap is most welcome, but it would have been much more so had it come more from increasingly rapid progress among blacks and less from the stalling of progress among whites. On the far right of the graph, black midlife mortality stops falling and starts rising; we will return to this too.

One point is obvious but important. Black mortality rates are higher than white mortality rates throughout the picture. Blacks are doing worse than whites. By contrast, black mortality rates have fallen faster than white mortality rates. From this one might say that blacks are "doing better" than whites even though they are more likely to die. We will always try to be very clear about whether we are talking about *levels* of mortality or *rates of change* (progress) in mortality. More fundamentally, it is the probability of dying that matters to people, not its rate of change, and in this, white privilege remains. Even with white death rates rising, the difference in *levels* between white and black mortality remains stark: black mortality rates in 2017 were only slightly lower than those experienced by whites forty years earlier.

It is understandable that B. D. would find it strange that there should be any health measurement—either change or level—that is not worse for blacks. A dispiriting fact is that deprivation in one aspect of life usually comes with deprivation in others. Health disparities between groups usually run parallel to social, economic, and educational disparities between those groups, and in the US, blacks are more likely to live in poverty, are less likely to hold a college degree, and continue to face discrimination. So it is indeed both unusual and surprising that all-cause death rates were falling for blacks while death rates for white rates were increasing.

Blacks and Whites in the Current Epidemic of Deaths of Despair

The main reason why death rates of blacks fell more rapidly than death rates of whites at the beginning of the twenty-first century is that blacks were not suffering the epidemic of overdoses, suicide, and alcoholism.

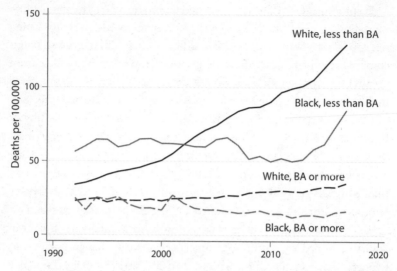

FIGURE 5.2. Drug, alcohol, and suicide mortality in midlife, 1992–2017, blacks and whites, with and without a college degree. Authors' calculations using Centers for Disease Control and Prevention data, ages 45–54 (age-adjusted).

Figure 5.2 shows deaths of despair—suicide, alcohol, and drug mortality—for ages forty-five to fifty-four, from 1992 to 2017, among whites (black lines) and blacks (gray lines). As we saw in chapter 4, a college degree makes a huge difference to the likelihood of dying, so we show separate lines for both groups.

For blacks, with or without a college degree, midlife mortality rates from deaths of despair were flat or falling for a quarter century, while white mortality rose, particularly for those without a college degree. For both blacks and whites, the contrast between those with and without a college degree is particularly notable.

The increase in black mortality in the most recent years comes from an interaction between the current opioid epidemic and the earlier drug epidemic in the black community. As we shall see in chapter 9, the epidemic has most recently been driven by fentanyl, an opioid that is much more powerful and dangerous than heroin. The earlier drug epidemic among blacks had left a substantial number of long-term but stably functioning addicts in the black community. But when dealers started mixing fentanyl with heroin and cocaine, those long-term addicts started dying; a customarily safe dose had, without the victim's knowledge, become a lethal cocktail. From the low point of black mortality from all causes (in 2014), increases in death rates involving synthetic narcotics (like fentanyl) can fully account for the increase in mortality observed for those aged forty-five to fifty-four. Half of the increase in deaths involved a mix of synthetic narcotics with heroin, and half with cocaine. In addition, as discussed in chapter 2, the fall in deaths from heart disease came to an end, possibly connected with the drug deaths. Until these events, the current epidemic was a white epidemic.

Drug overdoses and alcohol-related liver mortality caused many deaths among blacks in the earlier epidemic, and among whites in the current one. But in deaths from suicide, the parallel breaks down. African Americans are much less likely to kill themselves than are white Americans; their suicide rates in midlife have changed little in the past fifty years and are currently about a quarter of those for whites. The ratio is not fixed and differs by age, but the much lower rate for blacks has long been the case and was noted as early as 1897 by Emile Durkheim in his foundational book on suicide.[3] There is no widely accepted explanation for the difference. George Simpson, in his introduction to an English translation of Durkheim's book, summarizes Durkheim's view that perhaps "systematic oppression and underprivilege lead individuals to be adjusted to the misery and tragedy of human existence which is visited upon us all."[4] He also notes something else that remains relevant today: the lower suicide rate of blacks shows that underprivilege alone is not a cause of suicide.

African American Despair

What happened to inner-city African Americans after midcentury is, we shall argue, a foreshadowing of our account of whites in the twenty-first century. The earlier story is told by the eminent sociologist William Julius Wilson in his 1987 book *The Truly Disadvantaged*.

In the late 1960s and early 1970s, African Americans in inner cities were employed in old-economy industries in manufacturing and transportation. With the beginnings of postwar foreign competition, the switch from manufacturing to services, and the evolution of cities from centers of manufacturing to centers of administration and information processing, African Americans were hurt in the areas in which they had made the most progress. It is a tale of job loss and of social disintegration; according to Wilson, blacks who lived in the cities were predominantly employed where they were "vulnerable to structural economic changes, such as the shift from goods-producing to service-producing industries, the increasing polarization of the labor market into low-wage and high-wage sectors, technological innovations, and the relocation of manufacturing industries out of the central cities."[5] In the face of these transformations, and the passage of fair-housing legislation, the more educated and successful African Americans moved out of the inner cities, leaving behind neighborhoods that increasingly displayed a range of social pathologies, including deterioration of the black family, and ultimately crime and violence.

Women who conceived out of wedlock gave birth out of wedlock for lack of marriageable (i.e., employed) partners. As earlier predicted by Michael Young, the communities were denuded of the most talented and most successful, who moved out of the inner city. For blacks in the 1960s, the passage of civil rights legislation helped this to happen. Communities that had had a mix of professionals and manual workers, of more and less educated people, became increasingly deprived not only of successful and educated people but also of those in any kind of employment, with negative consequences for the community, and especially for young men. Wilson attributes the problems faced by the inner-city black community to "the large scale and harmful changes in the labor market, and its resulting spatial concentration as well as the isolation of such areas from the more affluent parts of the black community."[6] Writing about the parallel today, the economist Raghuram Rajan notes that talented and well-educated young people have headed to the growing, successful, high-tech towns and cities.[7]

African American inner-city communities faced a crisis of crack cocaine in the 1980s. The crack epidemic shows both contrasts and parallels with the current opioid epidemic. Crack was cheap and offered an immediate high that was highly addictive. Crime rates increased, as those addicted looked for money for their next fix. As crack dealers fought for a place on a street corner, homicide rates among young black men spiked. While crack is still available and remains a scourge, the epidemic largely burned itself out by the mid-1990s. The reasons for its subsidence are still debated, but the aging of the population that had turned to crack as well as disgust among a younger generation that saw crack ruin the lives of family members and friends both appear to have played a role. Recent research indicates that crack continues to cast a long shadow, having permanently increased the number of guns available in the inner city.[8] And as we have seen, the hangover of addiction from the epidemic has led to rising mortality from fentanyl.

Epidemics usually have causes that extend beyond the proximate causes, be it the availability of crack cocaine in inner cities in the 1980s or the increased availability of prescription opioids in predominantly white communities after the mid-1990s. A fundamental force in both cases was the long-term loss of working-class jobs, for blacks in northern cities in the 1970s and for less educated whites across much of the country more recently. With globalization, changing technology, rising healthcare costs of employees, and the shift from manufacturing to services, firms shed less educated labor, first blacks and then less educated whites.

In both epidemics, drugs that could ease psychological or physical pain were available at an (arguably) affordable price to populations that were hungry for the escape that they seemed to offer. During the crack epidemic, the inner city offered few legitimate avenues of progress. In the opioid crisis, it is less educated whites, many of whom do not see a promising economic future, or a promising future in any aspect of their lives, who are falling prey to drugs, alcohol, and suicide. We should also not exaggerate the similarities, especially when we are comparing blacks and whites today. Deaths of despair include suicides, and these differ markedly by race.

The misfortunes of African Americans in the 1970s and 1980s were widely attributed to a failure of black culture. Daniel Patrick Moynihan was a Harvard sociology professor, a longtime Democratic senator representing New York from 1977 to 2001, and an adviser to both the Johnson and Nixon administrations. In 1965 he wrote a famous report, *The Negro Family*,[9] in which he identified families without fathers as a central problem of African American communities and traced its roots back to slavery. The idea that the fundamental malady was not lack of opportunity was taken up by the political scientist Charles Murray in *Losing Ground*, which also argued that welfare benefits designed to combat poverty were undermining work and helping create the dysfunctional behavior. Murray's later book, *Coming Apart*, attributes many of the current problems of less educated whites to their own failures of virtue, particularly a failure of industriousness, meaning that they are no longer interested in working for a living or in supporting their families.[10]

In chapter 11, we look at the labor market and will show that Murray's thesis cannot explain what has happened recently for less educated whites. If people are withdrawing their labor, wages should rise; but in the late part of the twentieth century and into the twenty-first, wages fell along with employment, a clear indication that the problem lies with falling demand, not falling supply. As to the earlier episode, we endorse Wilson's view that "conservative assertions about underclass life and behavior were weakened because of a lack of direct evidence and because they seemed to be circular in the sense that cultural values were inferred from the behavior of the underclass to be explained, and then these values were used as the explanation of the behavior."[11]

6

The Health of the Living

IN *ANNA KARENINA*, Leo Tolstoy famously claims that for a family, there is only one way of being happy, but many different ways of being unhappy. We rather doubt the truth of this, but it certainly applies to death and sickness—you are either dead or alive, but there are many different ways of being sick. Sickness in its many forms compromises your ability to lead a life that is good for you; in the words of the economist and philosopher Amartya Sen, it reduces your capabilities.[1] We explore several measures of ill health in this chapter, and we will see that all of them show that ill health is increasing in midlife, just as deaths have risen. Not only are people dying, but their lives are becoming less worth living. Sickness is part of the despair in deaths of despair.

It is not inevitable that sickness and death should go up together. Although it is true that people at risk of death—for example, from alcoholism or from cancer—are in poor health before they die, there is no necessary connection between a population's health, what is sometimes called its nonfatal health, and its mortality rate. If it is the sickest people who die off, higher death rates can even lift the average health of those who are left. A new treatment may save many lives but leave many with a chronic but not fatal disease; antiretroviral therapy for HIV is an example.

This chapter looks at health among the living. The numbers are not pretty, especially for the less educated. As mortality rates have risen among midlife whites, indicators of health among those who are not dying are getting worse. Fewer people think that their health is very good or excellent. More people are experiencing pain, serious mental distress, and difficulty going about their day-to-day lives. People report that their health is making it harder for them to work. Not being able to work reduces income, which can lead to other deprivations and hardships, and work is itself a source of satisfaction and meaning for many people. Not being able to spend time with friends, go out for a meal, go to a ballgame, or just hang out all shrink and impoverish lives. As is the case for deaths, worsening health seems to be singling out those of working age with less education.

Measuring Health among the Living

The World Health Organization defines health as "a state of complete physical, mental, and social wellbeing, and not merely the absence of disease or infirmity."[2] Taking this broad view suggests many indicators to look at, both positive, such as aspects of flourishing, and negative, such as indicators of sickness. The technical term for ill health while alive is *morbidity*, in contrast to *mortality*, which refers to death. There are many ways of being sick, each with its own indicator. Some are measured at an annual physical examination. Samples of blood and urine give indicators of cholesterol, diabetes, and heart, kidney, and liver function. Your physician or another medical professional will also measure the four "vital signs": blood pressure, pulse rate, temperature, and rate of respiration. In recent years, it has become common for physicians to ask about pain, sometimes called the fifth vital sign, a topic to which we will return.

There are also indicators of health that you know without professional assistance: whether you are overweight; whether and how much you smoke and drink; how you are feeling in general, both physically and emotionally; which activities you can manage and which you cannot, including whether you are able to work; whether you sometimes or regularly experience pain and, if so, how severe it is. A good physician will also ask about mental health and about your social and emotional life. Losing a job, a friend, or a spouse can bring intense emotional pain. Good physicians also understand that pain can often exist without there being an injury, that pain without an injury cannot be dismissed as "all in your head," and that there is no bright line between emotional and physical pain.

It makes no sense to try to come up with a single comprehensive indicator of health—for example, to say that you are 73 percent healthy. Unlike being either alive or dead, a simple black-and-white distinction, health and morbidity have too many dimensions to allow any simple, uncontroversial measure. Some measures are inevitably "softer" than others; think of blood pressure or pulse rate, on the one hand, versus general feelings of health or of how life is going, on the other. Self-reports are often all that we have; life evaluation or pain is what people say it is, not what a medical professional says it is. There are no experts on how *your* life is going, or whether your world is circumscribed by pain. To neglect what people feel is a mistake, even if it is a mistake that the practice of medicine (and the economics profession) has made for much of its history.

When someone dies, the death and all of its details must be recorded on an official death certificate, and it is from those that we got the information on the mortality rates that we looked at in previous chapters. Such recording of vital statistics is standard in rich countries around the world. But when you go to the doctor for your physical, or with a medical issue, the results are not centrally recorded, so there is no national register of obesity, hypertension, or cholesterol, just to give some examples. For people treated under Medicare, medical records are centrally stored, but these records are short of information on the characteristics of the patients, so while they tell us a lot about conditions, treatments, and costs, they are much less informative about the personal attributes of those being treated. In some Scandinavian countries that have government-provided healthcare, all encounters are recorded, and those data can be linked, at least in principle, with other data about individuals— for example, about their education, marital history, income, and taxes.

In the US we rely on surveys that sample households or individuals, mostly run by the Centers for Disease Control and Prevention, though there are important private surveys too. The largest of these is the Behavioral Risk Factor Surveillance System (BRFSS),[3] a state-based telephone survey coordinated by the Centers for Disease Control and

Prevention in which people are asked to report health-related information. The BRFSS (affectionately pronounced "burr-fuss") obtains information from around four hundred thousand adults every year, asking them to rate their health, to report conditions such as pain, and to report behaviors that affect health—risk factors—such as smoking, drinking, height and weight, and exercise.

We also report numbers from the National Health Interview Survey (NHIS),[4] which visits around thirty-five thousand households annually, interviewing one adult in depth and collecting information on all other household members. These surveys also ask people about their contacts with the medical system—for example, whether a medical professional has ever told them that they have cancer, high blood pressure, or heart disease. Those reports are useful, but they depend not just on the prevalence of conditions but also on the extent to which people visit clinics and on how aggressive clinics are in diagnostic testing. For example, there has been a large increase in diagnoses of thyroid cancer in recent years but no change in the mortality rate from the disease, suggesting that actual prevalence has increased much less than has the extent of testing. Many diagnostic tests are quite profitable for providers, and overtesting (and subsequent overtreatment) is always a possibility. For our purposes here, if overtesting is different in different places, geographic or national patterns will be distorted.

Because the BRFSS and the NHIS are nationally representative and are run every year, we can use them to compare answers over time and look for signs that health and health behaviors are improving or deteriorating. Surveys on the scale of the BRFSS or the NHIS are expensive to run and rely on respondents' reports about their health, rather than on the results of physical examinations and lab tests, which are often conducted in surveys run on a much smaller scale, in specially designed mobile centers.[5] These smaller surveys collect blood, for example, as well as height, weight, and blood pressure measured by medical professionals, rather than self-reports. Perhaps not surprisingly, people systematically misreport their heights and weights; many people shrink after age fifty, but they remember and report their height as young adults, recollecting better days, though this is more often true for men than women.

Women, by contrast, tend to underreport their weights.[6] One can hardly begrudge people a little imaginary self-improvement, though it is good to know the truth for scientific purposes. Medical professionals often discount self-reports of height by elderly men—including one of us—and profess surprise when the claim is accurate. Examination surveys not only allow the collection of information about health that people cannot know themselves, but they also allow a cross-check on information from larger, less expensive, and less invasive interviews.

The Condition of the Living: What People Say about Their Health

The simplest of all health questions asks people to rate their own health in five categories: excellent, very good, good, fair, or poor. It is easy to pick holes in questions like this. Perhaps different people mean different things by "excellent" or "very good"—perhaps some are tough and feel wonderful in circumstances that would flatten the rest of us. The answers are undoubtedly affected by personal and social expectations about health—in poor countries, the poorest often say that they are in better health than the rich because they cannot afford to admit that their health is too poor to allow them to work.[7] Is my health "good"? Relative to what? In spite of all of this, the answers tend to match up with other measures, including objectively verifiable measures, and, perhaps surprisingly, they pick up health-relevant information over and above what a physician gleans from a full physical examination.[8] These reports contain real information, although it is good to verify it when possible, which gives us some confidence when verification is impossible.

Figure 6.1 shows, from the BRFSS, the fraction of the white, non-Hispanic population who report that their health is fair or poor (which we will refer to as "poor" health). Each line traces out that fraction, between ages twenty-five and seventy-five, for a particular year. Given the importance of education as a dividing line for deaths of despair, we present these self-reports of health separately for those without a four-year degree, in the left panel, and those with a bachelor's degree or more, in

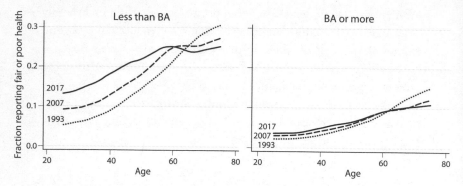

FIGURE 6.1. Fraction of white non-Hispanics reporting fair or poor health, 1993–2017.
Authors' calculations using the BRFSS.

the right panel, for the years 1993, 2007, and 2017. In each panel, the vertical axis is the fraction of respondents reporting that their health is fair or poor.

Reports of poor health rise with age, for both education groups; with age, life is more likely to deliver aches and pains and chronic conditions that interfere with good health. Indeed, if reports of poor health did not rise with age, we would reject self-reports as a useful measure of health. Even so, the rise tells us that people are not simply judging their health relative to other people their own age—if that were the case, the lines would be flat; on average, people are as healthy as the average of other people their own age.

The fractions reporting poor health are markedly different by education. In 1993, for example, at age forty, those without a bachelor's degree were almost three times more likely to report poor health than those with a four-year degree (8 percent versus 3 percent). But the big story in this figure is how the lines for those without a bachelor's degree have changed over time. (We have results for the other years in between, but we omit them to make the picture clear.) Younger people without a four-year degree—those from age twenty-five to around age fifty or fifty-five in the left panel—report worse health as time goes on. At age forty, the percentage reporting poor health doubled between 1993 and 2017 (from 8 to 16 percent). For those with a college degree, there was a small increase in reports of poor health, but as was true for deaths of despair, their changes are dwarfed by those for people with less education.

Over the same period, older whites, aged sixty or over, were reporting better health, with a smaller and smaller fraction saying that their health was fair or poor. By 2017, for those without a bachelor's degree, adults above age sixty were reporting better health than were those in their late fifties. This puzzling result comes from presenting different birth cohorts in the same figure. Among those without a bachelor's degree, later-born birth cohorts are reporting worse health at each age than did the cohorts that came before them, which gives rise to the anomalous-looking result.

That the increase in poor health between survey years holds only for those without a bachelor's degree speaks against there having been a simple change in how birth cohorts assess their health, with later-born cohorts being more sensitive, say, to pain or chronic conditions, leading them to report worse health. If that were true, we would expect to see the same change for those with a four-year college degree. Not at all co-incidentally, the changing age-health profile for those without a college degree matches the changing patterns of mortality discussed in chapter 2, with improvements among the elderly and deterioration in midlife. And as was true for deaths of despair, the reporting of poorer health started at least as far back as the early 1990s and gathered strength slowly, well before the financial crisis of 2008. What has happened to mortality is happening to morbidity; more midlife whites are dying, and those who are not dying are reporting worse health.[9]

The Condition of the Living: Other Measures

The increase in reports of poor health in midlife among less educated whites, presented in figure 6.1, can be seen in other health measures too; the graphs differ from measure to measure, but the fact that bad things are happening in midlife, especially to those without a bachelor's degree, applies to a lot of "things." One particularly important example is mental health, measured here using the Kessler Psychological Distress Scale. Since 1997, respondents in the NHIS have been asked a series of six

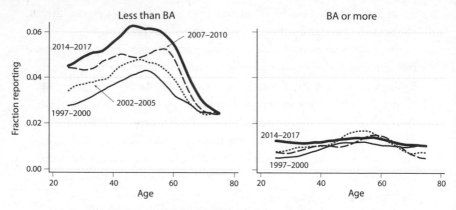

FIGURE 6.2. Serious mental distress, white non-Hispanics, by education. Authors'
calculations using the NHIS.

questions about their feelings over the last month, which are com-
pounded into a score based on how often they experienced each feeling.
When that score crosses a threshold, the respondent is classed as experiencing serious mental distress. The questions cover how often respondents felt sad, nervous, restless, hopeless, worthless, and that
"everything was an effort," all feelings that might contribute to despair.
Figure 6.2 shows the relationship of mental distress and age over the
period 1997 to 2017 for those without a bachelor's degree, in the left
panel, and for those with a bachelor's degree, in the right panel, for respondents ages twenty-five to seventy-five. In each panel, the vertical
axis is the fraction of respondents in serious mental distress according
to this scale.

For those without a degree, the risk of severe mental distress is highest in midlife, peaking between ages forty and sixty, the ages at which the
stresses of work, raising children, and caring for elderly parents may all
be pressing. In the late 1990s, severe mental distress was less common
among young adults and the elderly, although over the past twenty years
it has grown as much for young adults as it has for those in middle age.
Again, the upward trend has been slow and steady, and it does not appear to have accelerated during the Great Recession in response to economic difficulties. Around age fifty, the percentage of whites without a

bachelor's degree in severe mental distress rose from 4 to 6 percent from 1997–2000 to 2014–17.

As was true of deaths of despair, the picture looks very different for those with a four-year college degree, presented in the right panel of figure 6.2. The risk of severe mental distress in this group is also highest for adults in their middle years, but the risk is only a quarter of that faced by those without a bachelor's degree. Among young adults with a four-year degree, there has been an increase in severe mental distress, but it pales in comparison to that faced by those without a bachelor's degree.

Other measures also indicate that health is worsening for those with less education. In the next chapter, we shall show that the same is true for pain, which plays a particularly important role in this book. But there is more. Whites in midlife are having a harder time just going about their usual activities, which health surveys measure as difficulties with "instrumental activities of daily living." Since 1997, the NHIS has asked adults how difficult they would find it to walk a quarter of a mile (about three city blocks), climb ten steps, stand or sit for two hours, go out to do things like shop or go to the movies, relax at home, and socialize with friends. An ever-growing fraction of working-age whites without a four-year degree report "more than a little" difficulty in each of these activities— something that has not happened to whites with a bachelor's degree, and something that has not happened to older adults (ages sixty-five to seventy-four). The fraction of whites without a bachelor's degree who express difficulty in going out to do things like shop or go to the movies and the fraction finding it hard to relax at home have increased by 50 percent for those aged twenty-five to fifty-four, and the fraction finding it difficult to socialize with friends has nearly doubled in this twenty-year period. The inability to socialize with friends not only removes one of life's most pleasurable and important activities but also puts people at risk for suicide.

Rising obesity may play a part here. Carrying around extra weight can make it more difficult to enjoy activities of daily living, especially when people are not young. Obesity is often measured by the body mass index (BMI). BMI is defined as weight in kilos (1 kilo is 2.2 pounds) divided by the square of height measured in meters (1 meter is 39.4 inches). It is a "pounds per square inch" kind of measure, but done on a metric scale. You are officially "obese" if your BMI is above 30, and underweight if your BMI is less than 18.5. (One of us is beyond obese and one is on the cusp of being underweight, so we know what we are talking about.) Yet the increase in American obesity cannot explain the deterioration in these health indicators for the simple reason that we see similar deteriorations at all levels of BMI—among the underweight, normal weight, over-weight, and obese. Midlife Americans are not getting sicker just because they are getting fatter.

One measure that is not getting worse is the fraction of people who are smoking. For white non-Hispanics aged twenty-five to sixty-four, smoking rates have continued to fall, though they remain much higher for those without a bachelor's degree. The only group where smoking rates increased steadily from 1993 through 2017 is women aged forty-five to fifty-four without a university degree; even here the increase is small, 2 or 3 percentage points. We find it surprising that, overall, smoking rates have fallen for those without a four-year degree while mortality rates from drugs, alcohol, and suicide have been rising; one of us is an ex-smoker, and smoking used to soothe in much the same way that alcohol can, though perhaps not as much as the combination. It is also worth noting that the prevalence of tobacco use in the US is a good deal lower than in many other rich countries.

Ability to Work

Being sick makes life worse, in and of itself, but it also interferes with other activities that are either directly valuable, such as socializing with friends, or both directly and instrumentally valuable, such as being able to work. Note that not being able to work is different from reporting being out of work, which rises and falls with the state of the economy. In contrast, the share of whites of working age reporting that they are unable to work has risen steadily since at least the early 1990s. As is true for self-reports of physical and mental health, shown in figures 6.1 and 6.2, there are dramatic differences here by education. For those aged forty-five to fifty-four, historically the peak earning years, the percentage of whites reporting that they were unable to work rose from 4 percent in 1993 to 13 percent in 2017 for those without a bachelor's degree. The percentage for those with a four-year degree was initially low and remained so, between 1 and 2 percent.

Some of those who are unable to work are eligible for Social Security Disability Insurance benefits from the state. Eligibility depends on the number of years a worker has paid into the Social Security system, the nature of the worker's disability, and whether the worker is capable of performing a job in which his or her disability is not a barrier to work. For the discussion here, a concern is that the disability system may entice people to report being unable to work so as to escape work and live off the labor of everyone else.[10] It is certainly possible that some of the measures in this chapter are corrupted by such shading of the truth. If you are actually not disabled but have managed to claim disability, then it might be wise, when the survey statisticians ask, to remember that you are receiving disability payments because you are unable to work, and report so to the surveyors.

It is hard to be sure that the reports are not being distorted by the existence of the disability support system, but we suspect not by much.[11] The deterioration in health indicators is too uniform across too many different measures, as we have seen here and will see again in the next chapter, on pain. In addition, reports of being unable to work have grown for those who are not eligible for Social Security Disability Insurance benefits, those who do not have work histories to qualify. Most important of all is the concordance between the upsurge in morbidity of all kinds and the epidemic of death. Perhaps people feign illness to claim benefits, but the fact that they are dying is surely evidence that something real is going on.

In Summary

We have told a story in which death and sickness go together. Something is making life worse, especially for less educated whites. Crucial capabilities that make life worth living are being compromised, including the ability to work and the ability to enjoy life with others. Severe mental distress is on the rise. Of course, many more people are experiencing this deterioration in the quality of life than are dying, but the deterioration is surely the background to the deaths. In the next chapter, we turn to another kind of morbidity, pain, which turns out to be a link between social disintegration and deaths of despair.

7

The Misery and Mystery of Pain

In a time when kingdoms come
Joy is brief as summer's fun
Happiness, its race has run
Then pain stalks in to plunder.

—MAYA ANGELOU

PAIN HAS A SPECIAL place in our narrative. Social and community distress, the labor market, politics, and corporate interests all collide around pain, and pain is one of the channels through which each of them affects deaths of despair.

In our search for the story behind the deaths, pain kept coming up, in apparently different contexts. Pain is an important risk factor for suicide; the victim believes that the intolerable pain will never get better. The treatment of pain is a root of the opioid epidemic. The brain's natural opioid system controls both euphoria and pain relief. People use the language of pain and hurt to describe "social pain," from rejection, exclusion, or loss, and there is evidence that social pain uses some of the same neural processes that signal physical pain, from stubbing a toe or cutting a finger, or from arthritis. Tylenol can reduce social pain as well as physical pain. Americans are reporting more pain, especially less educated Americans.[1]

These connections are consistent with the account that we have come to favor, which is that the increase in pain among less educated Americans can be traced back to the slow disintegration of their social and economic lives, and that the pain is, in turn, one of the links through which disintegration leads to suicide and addiction. The story of a death of despair often passes through pain.

Pain in America

Every year, more Americans report that they are in pain. The largest increases are in midlife among those who do not have a college degree. Albert Schweitzer wrote that pain "is a more terrible lord of mankind than even death himself." The lives of many millions of Americans are compromised by pain; some cannot work, some cannot spend time with friends or loved ones in the way that they would like, some cannot sleep, and some cannot do the activities that make daily life possible and fulfilling. Pain can undermine appetite, induce fatigue, and inhibit healing; in extreme cases, it erodes the will to live.

Aging, even healthy aging, brings more aches and pains; arthritis is the most familiar but not the only cause. Even so, in America today, pain in midlife has grown so rapidly that we have the unusual situation that the middle-aged are actually reporting more pain than the elderly. People are experiencing pain from many causes and from no discernible cause at all. According to the National Academies of Sciences, Engineering, and Medicine, more than one hundred million Americans suffer from chronic pain, defined as pain that has lasted for at least three months.[2] Much of this chronic pain does not appear to be a response to an originating injury or cause that could be treated to eliminate the pain, and many health professionals now treat chronic pain as a disease in and of itself, even if it remains poorly understood and poorly treated. The long-held understanding of pain as a signal to the brain to deal with an injury has been discarded and replaced by the recognition that the mind is involved in *all* pain and that social distress or empathetic distress can engender pain in the same way as the distress from a physical injury.[3] One useful definition of pain is that it is "whatever the experiencing person says it is, existing whenever s/he says it does."[4] The patient is the only authority, not the physician or scientist.

The prevalence of pain varies by occupation, and people who work in manual occupations are more likely to be injured or to experience pain than those of us who work behind a desk or in front of a computer screen. They are also more likely to develop painful conditions as they age; their bodies wear down more rapidly.[5] For this and for other reasons, pain is more common and increases more rapidly with age among those with less education. Indeed, the very word *labor* is often synonymous with pain, as in labor pains or Adam's punishment and humankind's condemnation to painful toil in the book of Genesis. The words *pain* and *penalty* come from the same Latin root.

Causation runs from pain to work as well as from work to pain. People in pain may be unable to work and may make claims on disability insurance; some may doubt those claims, which has long generated legal, political, and academic battles over the reality of pain. We have devices to measure body temperature or blood pressure, but none that can assign a number to pain, perhaps with a cutoff that is generally accepted as disabling. It is often useful to imagine what would happen if there were such a device, an "afflictometer" perhaps, with implanted sensors and a dial on the forehead, that could provide an accurate assessment of overall pain. As it is, a definition that pain is "whatever the experiencing person says it is" poses obvious problems for disability policy.

Those who are in the business of treating pain—such as the pharmaceutical companies who manufacture painkillers—have goals of their own that do not always align with the best interests of those who are experiencing pain. Pharma companies have made many billions of dollars from selling drugs to combat pain even as reports of pain have risen with the number of prescriptions written. They are interested in selling their products, and in persuading governments to make it as easy as possible for them to do so. The behavior of corporations, and how they might be regulated to act in the public interest, is also part of the story of pain.

Pain Facts

Gallup regularly collects data from a large sample of Americans. One of the questions that it asks is whether the respondent experienced physical pain during a lot of the day "yesterday," meaning in the day before the survey. We look at the geography of pain in America using small

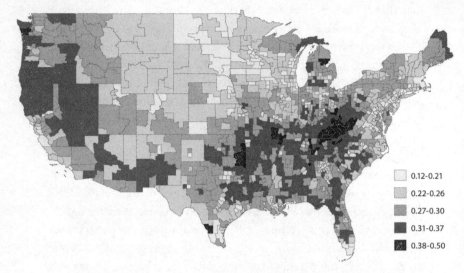

	0.12-0.21
	0.22-0.26
	0.27-0.30
	0.31-0.37
	0.38-0.50

FIGURE 7.1. The geography of pain, white non-Hispanics ages 25–64, 2008–17. Authors' calculations using Gallup tracking data.

areas—counties, when a county's population is large enough; otherwise, collections of adjacent counties. There are more than three thousand counties in the US, some of which are mostly mountains and trees. We aggregate these up to about one thousand small areas, each with at least one hundred thousand people. Figure 7.1 shows the pain map of the United States for white non-Hispanics ages twenty-five to sixty-four, averaged over 2008 to 2017, with darker colors showing areas where a larger fraction of people report such pain.[6]

Across the thousand areas, the fraction of people reporting pain yesterday (from the Gallup data) is strongly associated with suicides, and with deaths of despair more generally. One key takeaway is the distribution of pain across the country, with the West, Appalachia, the South, Maine, and northern Michigan doing badly, and with much less pain reported in the North Central Plains as well as along the I-95/Amtrak corridor in the Northeast and the Bay Area in California; again, pain tends to be lower in places where the population is more highly educated. The fraction of people reporting pain is higher in areas with higher

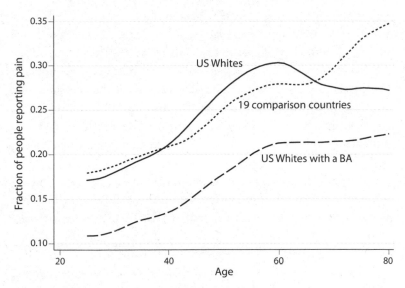

FIGURE 7.2. Fractions who experienced pain yesterday, US whites and comparison countries. Authors' calculations using Gallup tracking data and Gallup World Poll.

unemployment rates and more poverty.[7] The fraction of people in an area who voted for Donald Trump in 2016 is also strongly correlated with the fraction in pain.

Figure 7.2 uses the same data to plot the fraction who reported pain among the 1.8 million whites aged twenty-five to eighty who answered the question between 2008 and 2017. The solid line shows the fraction of all whites in pain; it rises from 17 percent at age twenty-five to a peak of 30 percent at age sixty, before falling and leveling out at 27 percent at age eighty. Note that the graph is not following the same people as they age; the people on the right (in their sixties and seventies) are different people from those on the left (in their twenties and thirties).

There is something very odd about this line. Age normally brings pain, and although some manage to stay perpetually young, average pain levels inevitably increase with age. For people in manual occupations, the onset of pain with age is often faster—think of the package-delivery worker whose back is eventually hurt by all the lifting, or the worker in mining or in agriculture who is constantly at risk of injury. When such people retire from work, there may be some temporary relief and reduction in pain, but then the inexorable effects of aging set in again. So we might expect the line of pain to rise with age, to flatten out around age sixty, and then to rise again. But the solid line in the figure does not look like this. Instead, people in their sixties are actually in *more* pain than people at age eighty. While it is likely true that those in the most pain die earlier, so that the survivors are in less pain, the death rate is never high enough for this to overcome the normal increase in pain with age among the living.

Gallup asks the same question about pain in most of the countries around the world.[8] The samples are not as large as for the US, but if we pool countries together, we can construct a reliable picture for each age-group. The dotted line in the figure is for a combination of nineteen other rich, industrialized countries.[9] Taken together, we have more than 243,000 observations from 2006 to 2017. The line starts out among young adults in the same way as the line for the US, but it diverges between ages forty and sixty-five. The other countries show an age profile closer to what we might expect, with pain rising with age, flattening around the usual retirement age, and resuming the upward trend thereafter. Whatever is happening to whites in the US is not happening in these other countries, just as the midlife increase in mortality in the US is not happening in these other countries.

A final clue comes from the bottom line, shown with dashes, which is for white Americans with a bachelor's degree. The top line is for all education levels taken together. More-educated people experience much less pain throughout life, with the fraction reporting pain about a third less than in the general population. But they too have the pattern that we would expect, rising with age, then slowing around retirement and rising, albeit more slowly, after retirement. Even a four-year degree cannot prevent arthritis.

The different patterns of pain by age can be reconciled once we realize that there has been a large recent upsurge of pain in midlife among whites without a bachelor's degree. The elderly in the figure did not experience this upsurge, and if we had tracked them through life, they would not have shown the midlife peak. Similarly, although we cannot

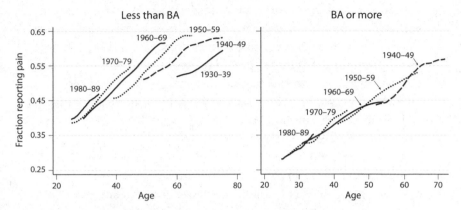

FIGURE 7.3. Fraction of white non-Hispanics experiencing neck, back, or joint pain, by birth cohort and education, 1997–2017. Authors' calculations using the NHIS.

do it until we get data from the future, we suspect that if we were to track today's midlife adults as they age, their pain will turn out to be much higher than the pain of today's elderly, a deeply depressing prediction. Midlife adults are suffering unusual amounts of pain today, but it is nothing compared with what they will feel when they are old.

We can see this clearly if we track the pain levels of the same people over time, or at least track people born in the same year, again using birth cohorts as we did in chapter 4. The Gallup data do not go far enough back in time to allow this, so we turn to the National Health Interview Survey (NHIS) and its questions to respondents about whether, in the last three months, they have experienced neck or back pain lasting for more than one day, or chronic joint pain. If we use these data to simply plot pain against age, we see a pattern similar to that in figure 7.2 using the Gallup data. But now we can also track successive birth cohorts over time and by educational attainment, just as we did for deaths of despair in chapter 4. Figure 7.3 shows the results, for ten-year birth cohorts, from those born in 1930–39 through to those born in 1980–89. Both panels show that, if we track the same group of people over time as they age, pain increases with age, as we would expect.

There is no sign in this picture of pain reversal at age sixty *within* any birth cohort, though the reversal seen in figure 7.2 would be seen here if we were to look *across* cohorts in any given year. For those without a bachelor's degree, pain increases with age, but those born later have more pain throughout their lives. Those born between 1930 and 1939, shown on the extreme right of the left panel, experience more pain as they age, observed at age sixty and above. The next line, for those born between 1940 and 1949, rises in much the same way, but the fraction reporting pain is higher at all ages. For those without a bachelor's degree, each successive birth cohort experiences more pain.

In the right panel, for those with a bachelor's degree, there is occasional upward drift in the fraction reporting pain, from one birth cohort to the next, but there is much overlap between the cohorts in the fraction reporting pain at any given age. The lines for those with a bachelor's degree show something like the natural progression of pain with age; whatever is driving up pain between birth cohorts among those without a bachelor's degree is nearly absent for those with a bachelor's degree. Which means that all of the midlife peak in pain and its decline in figure 7.2 are coming from those without a degree.[10]

One explanation for rising pain is what might be called the "snowflake" effect, that people are not as tough as they used to be. People used to sneer at those who accepted Novocain for dental work, and parents paid no attention to children's pain; it was just part of life. We cannot rule out the snowflake story, but it seems to us implausible that it is only those with less education who are snowflakes.

The cohort pictures in figure 7.3 look very much like the cohort pictures of deaths of despair in figure 4.3. Deaths of despair and pain both rise with age, but for those without a four-year degree, each birth cohort reports more pain with age and is at higher risk of a death than the cohorts that came before.

Over the past quarter century, the fraction of blacks reporting back, neck, and joint pain has been 20 percent lower than the fraction reported by whites throughout midlife, for both education groups. However, a larger fraction of both blacks and whites without a bachelor's degree report neck, back, and joint pain in each successive birth cohort. Blacks and whites have different recent mortality trends, but their shifting patterns of pain between birth cohorts are remarkably similar, which means that we must look elsewhere to explain differences in mortality from drugs, alcohol, and suicide, a topic to which we will return. If pain is a cause of deaths of despair, something else is stopping its effects among African Americans.

Causes and Consequences of the Increase in Pain

Because pain is one of these things that is both a cause and a consequence of other things, like work, it is difficult to figure out the story behind the increase in pain. But we can look at correlations and patterns, and use them to think about possible stories.

One story is that people are getting heavier, and that obesity brings pain. This is true, but it explains relatively little. Whites in prime age (twenty-five to sixty-four) were heavier in the 2010s than they had been in the late 1990s, with the average body mass index (BMI) for those with a four-year college degree moving from the "normal" weight range into the "overweight" range.[11] Those without a degree moved further up the "overweight" range, with the percentage tipping the scales in the obese range (BMI greater than thirty) increasing from 20 to 30 percent. Obesity can lead to higher pain levels; obviously more weight takes its toll on the back and joints. Comparing the period 1997–2000 with the period 2014–17, we find that the changes in BMI between these two periods can account for a quarter of the increase in reports of back, joint, and neck pain. This is not a trivial contribution, but it leaves three-quarters of the increased reports of pain without an explanation.

Another thought that occurs to most people is that losing a good job for a worse one brings more on-the-job pain. This is entirely plausible for social pain, but not for physical pain. Many jobs come with at least some risk of injury, or of pain without obvious injury. Certainly, it is true that people's pain (using the measure of neck, back, and joint pain in the NHIS) depends on what sort of job they have. Executives and professionals, as well as those who work in sales and administrative positions, report less pain than those in manual or blue-collar jobs such as farm work, construction, machine operation, or transportation and handling. The exception that proves the rule is police and fire services, where keeping your job depends on *not* being in pain; we suspect the same is true for professional athletes and those in the military.[12] But the changing balance of occupations cannot explain the recent increase in pain, because the shift has been *away* from occupations that come with pain and toward those that do not. If a worker loses his or her job on the assembly line for GM, or in a steelworks, and takes a minimum-wage job in retail, the worker's earnings will fall, and he or she may be extremely unhappy about the move, but the assembly-line job is not a job free of physical pain, and it involves more pain than working at McDonald's or Walmart.[13]

If we are to tell the story of pain, or deaths of despair, as coming from changes in the labor market, it thus cannot be told as a story of a shift from physically less demanding to physically more demanding jobs. Of course, there are other mechanisms. Lower earnings are associated with more pain, and it is entirely possible that the pain comes not from what happens at work but from the loss of status and meaning as a worker, or from the loss of the social structure that was supported by a well-paying job in a union town. There are experiments showing that the pain experienced by social exclusion works similarly in the brain to the pain experienced by an injury. If so, the slow destruction of the working class—the details of which we will document in subsequent chapters—may well be one of the causes of the increases in chronic pain.

The rise in pain has also come with a large increase in the number of people claiming disability payments, particularly from the Social Security Disability Insurance system. Depending on how you choose to think about it, the increase in the number of people on disability can be perceived as a good thing that recognizes the increased pain and morbidity in the population, or a bad thing that is driven by people who would rather not work but live off the labor of others, and who can claim that they suffer from pain and depression, neither of which is objectively measurable. *Chiselers, malingerers,* and *takers* (as opposed to *makers*) are among the unflattering terms that are sometimes used to describe the latter kind of people. We are sure that there are people who manipulate the system to their own benefit, but given what has been happening to pain for less educated people, and given how closely those patterns match deaths of despair, we suspect that the malingerers are relatively few.

The increase in pain, in spite of the huge increase in the use of opioid painkillers since the mid-1990s, is a real challenge to the effectiveness of these drugs, irrespective of their potential side effects, which include addiction and death. It is always possible that, in the absence of opioids, reported pain would have been even worse, with some so-far-unidentified cause pushing up pain levels more rapidly than opioids can hold them down.

Women report more pain than do men. This is true not only in the US but also in most of the other countries of the world, so it is unlikely to tell us much about the specifically American story of pain. In the US, the pattern of increasing pain across birth cohorts for those without a bachelor's degree, seen in figure 7.3, is the same for men and women, as is the absence of a shift in the age-pain pattern across birth cohorts for those with a bachelor's degree.

We can examine other individual characteristics that seem to come with more pain. One of these is unemployment or, more generally, being out of the labor force. This is hardly surprising given that disability is often a reason for not working. People who report pain also report that they are less able to go shopping, to relax at home, to socialize with friends, or to walk three blocks without difficulty. The degree of impediment is larger for those without a bachelor's degree; the same reported pain comes with more activity limitations for those who are less well educated. Pain is also highly correlated with the risk of serious mental distress—a correlation that is twice as large for those without a four-year degree.

As the summer fades, along with happiness and joy, "pain stalks in to plunder."

8

Suicide, Drugs, and Alcohol

IN 2017, 158,000 Americans died from what we call deaths of despair: suicide, overdoses, and alcoholic liver disease and cirrhosis. That is the equivalent of three full 737 MAXs falling out of the sky *every day*, with no survivors. In this chapter and the next, we look at the background of these deaths, at what is known about how and why they happen, and whether this can help us understand why they have risen so rapidly among less educated Americans in the last two decades.

All three kinds of deaths of despair involve the actions of those who die, most obviously in suicide—self-inflicted death—but also from taking drugs or drinking too much or for too long. Long ago, Emile Durkheim argued that to understand suicide—and the same could be argued for other deaths of despair—we must look beyond the individual to society, particularly to breakdown and turmoil in a society that can no longer provide its members an environment in which they can live a meaningful life.[1] Durkheim believed that more-educated people were more likely to kill themselves. Yet in the current American epidemic, and matching what has happened with pain and sickness, the increase in suicide has been mostly among the less educated, perhaps uniquely in history. Paradoxically, this is consonant with Durkheim, because it is the world of less educated whites that is currently in turmoil. As he would have predicted, the social and economic upheaval that has swept through their lives is causing increasing numbers of them to take their own lives.

People kill themselves when life no longer seems worth living, when it seems better to die than to stay alive. The feeling of desperation may have been at work for a long time, as for someone suffering from a terminal illness or from persistent depression, or it may have come on suddenly, the result of sudden feelings of depression, when "the balance of mind was disturbed," to use the British coroner's term. Most suicides involve depression or other mental illness. In 2017, forty-seven thousand people died from suicide in the US.

Suicides are deaths of despair. But the circumstances that can lead to suicide find less extreme forms when people turn to drugs or alcohol to seek refuge from pain, loneliness, and anxiety. Drugs and alcohol can induce a euphoria that, at least temporarily, may relieve physical and mental pain. Over time, the body can build up tolerance to these intoxicants, so that ever-larger amounts are needed to induce the same euphoric effect. Some become addicted. *Addiction* is not a technical medical term but rather describes behavior in which the need for the substance has become so absolute that it pushes everything else aside, making the person a slave to the addiction, willing to lie or steal to protect and feed it. Addiction, it is often said, is a prison where the locks are on the inside, but that makes escape no easier. The "selfish brain" cares only about ensuring that the habit gets fed,[2] and it makes people unable to care about how they behave, the havoc they create, or the lives they destroy.

In the words of a heroin user in recovery, addiction "tends to start (obviously) with liking the feelings that drugs produce (warmth, euphoria, belonging) or the erasure of other feelings (trauma, loneliness, anxiety)— usually both at once."[3] Warmth, euphoria, and belonging are the opposite of the feelings of a person contemplating suicide. One authority writes, "There are pleasure and pain centers in the brains of all animals, including human beings. These centers are governed by neurotransmitters that powerfully influence behavior. . . . By a wide variety of mechanisms, all abused drugs stimulate the pleasure centers of the brain and inhibit the brain's pain centers."[4]

Users of drugs and heavy users of alcohol are much more likely than others to kill themselves. When the euphoria fails to materialize or wears off, or when a person relapses in the struggle to remain sober and so experiences shame, worthlessness, and depression, death can seem better than another round of addiction. Many suicides involve both addiction and depression. The psychologist and writer Kay Redfield Jamison writes, "Drugs and mood disorders tend to bring out the worst in one another: alone they are dreadful, together they kill."[5] Addiction to alcohol can be just as destructive as addiction to drugs, both for those addicted and for their loved ones. Addiction to drugs or alcohol makes suicide seem more attractive; a person with an active addiction has often lost the parts of life that made it worth living. Yet many, even in the grip of their addiction, and even when they understand that they will die if they cannot break out, do not want to die.

It has long been understood that classifying a death as a suicide is extraordinarily difficult, and that the number of suicides is almost certainly underestimated in the statistics. Suicide carries stigma, and families resist the label; for much of history, felo-de-se was a crime, punishable by forfeiture of assets and prohibition of decent burial. People may choose to kill themselves by taking extreme risks, driving recklessly, or swimming alone in dangerous conditions. In the absence of the key person, who is dead, determining intent is always questionable. We therefore have a *measurement* issue, which is one reason to investigate suicides and alcohol- and drug-related deaths jointly; a collective count will often be more accurate than any piece taken alone. But there is also the *analytic* issue, that grouping deaths from suicide, alcohol, and drugs captures a common underlying cause—despair—that is not easily captured when they are treated separately.

Death from suicide often comes quickly, especially when firearms are used or when people jump from a great height or from a lesser height with a rope around their neck; in these cases, there is little chance of medical rescue. Suicide attempts involving drugs and alcohol are less certain. Death comes more slowly, so there is a greater chance that an attempt will fail or that rescuers will come.

With alcohol and substance abuse disorders, there is often a long progression from recreational use to tolerance and addiction. Many people consume alcohol pleasurably and safely throughout their adult lives, though it also can be a route to a death of despair. Heavy drinking is implicated in many deaths, including suicide, drug overdose (where the presence of alcohol is common), and death from cardiovascular disease, but especially in alcoholic liver disease and cirrhosis, which killed forty-one thousand Americans in 2017. But unlike suicides and drug overdoses, which are spread throughout midlife, deaths from alcohol-related liver diseases tend to happen in middle age or later because of the time it takes to destroy such a robust organ. Even so, binge drinking has grown rapidly among young people, and deaths related to alcohol are rising at much younger ages.

Deaths from drug overdoses are classified as "accidents," unless the overdose was deliberately intended to result in death. Yet, "although their deaths may have been unintended, there was nothing unintentional about their use of intoxicating substances. Therefore, the resulting fatal drug overdoses or interactions were not true accidents."[6] The death of a person found with a needle in his or her arm is recorded as an accident unless there is other evidence of intent to die. Such would even be the case if the person had overdosed repeatedly and been revived by medical responders. With drugs, relapse can bring immediate death; returning to the dose that was effective in producing euphoria safely before getting clean can be lethal when the body has lost its tolerance. In 2017, there were 70,237 "accidental deaths" from drug overdose in the US.

We focus on the common features of suicides, overdoses, and deaths from alcoholic liver disease, particularly the common background of social turmoil. All three kinds of death have been rising rapidly, with 158,000 deaths in 2017. By comparison, there were 40,100 traffic fatalities in 2017, lower than the number of suicides alone. There were 19,510 homicides.

In this chapter, we focus on suicide and on alcohol, though much of the discussion of alcohol applies to drugs too. In the next chapter, we turn to one particular facet of current drug overdoses, the opioid epidemic, in part because there is much to discuss, but also because the etiology of the drug epidemic provides a clue to the overall story of deaths of despair, especially the behavior of corporations and the federal government, which is our main theme in the last part of the book.

Suicide

Suicide, like the other deaths of despair, has been increasing among white non-Hispanics in the United States since the late 1990s. This is true at all ages from fifteen to seventy-four, and it has led to the US, whose suicide rate used to be unexceptional compared with those of other rich countries, now having one of the highest rates among them. Women are much less likely to kill themselves than men, in part because they choose less effective means—drugs versus guns—and in part because they are less susceptible to social isolation than men. Even so, the suicide rate among white women has been rising in parallel with the suicide rate among white men. Around the rest of the world, at least in countries that have credible data, suicide rates have been falling since 2000. The fall in rates, among young women (with more autonomy and more urbanization) in Asia, and especially in China, among middle-aged men (with more stability) in the former Soviet Union, and almost universally among the elderly (with more resources), has saved millions of lives. With its stubbornly upward trend, the suicide rate of US whites is a global outlier.

There is no simple theory of suicide, and no sure way of identifying who will kill themselves or why. For an individual, the best predictor of suicide is a previous attempt at suicide, which is useful for caregivers to know but does not help explain why suicides have been increasing. Yet there are potential contributing factors, such as pain, loneliness, depression, divorce, or being without a job, so if these factors are becoming more prevalent over time because of social changes, we have a possible account of why national rates are rising. There are also social causes that lie behind the individual behavior or that act directly. We have already referenced Durkheim's view; his text is a milestone of sociology with its insistence that to understand suicide, we must think about society, not just individuals. As is often noted, and only partially in jest, economists seek to explain why people choose to commit suicide, while sociologists explain why they have no such choice. On suicide, the sociologists have been rather more successful than the economists.

For their part, economists have proposed a "rational" theory of suicide that posits that people kill themselves in order to "maximize utility."[7]

We can think of this as the "Today is a good day to die" theory. The idea is that, although dying today is bad, it may be less bad than the suffering and pain that lie ahead. Such an account, although easily (and often rightly) made fun of, offers occasional insights, though, as we will see, it fails to explain much of what we know about suicide. Durkheim's story, by contrast, points to social turmoil, as in the economic, family, and community lives of working-class white Americans today.

Suicide is more likely when the means of death are easily available. Without doubt, someone who is determined to do away with himself or herself will find a way to do so; there is no shortage of high places to jump from, or ropes to hang oneself with. But the importance of means points to the fact that suicidal feelings are often transient, as well as to the potential for reducing suicides by controlling means.

In Britain, before gas from the North Sea became widely available, household gas for cooking and heating used to be coal gas, which contains carbon monoxide and can be used for suicide; there was a large increase in such suicides when coal gas was introduced at the end of the nineteenth century. One high-profile suicide was that of the poet and novelist Sylvia Plath, who died with her head in a gas oven in February 1963. (Plath may be a better example of the importance of previous attempts for predicting suicide than an example of means mattering; she had twice previously tried to kill herself using other means.) Between 1959 and 1971, coal gas was largely replaced by natural gas, which contains little or no carbon monoxide. The suicide rate then fell markedly in spite of some compensatory increase in suicides not involving gas.[8] Suicide by gassing from car-exhaust fumes increased, but then it fell again once cars were fitted with catalytic converters. This is what we would expect if some suicides are prompted by a fleeting depression that will not have deadly consequences if the means are not at hand.[9]

There are more guns in America than people, and although we do not know whether the availability of guns has increased, the annual number of gun deaths and the death rates involving firearms (including suicide) have increased since 2000.[10] The link between suicide and the availability of firearms in the US is both contentious and politicized. Most studies find a link, though there is also credible evidence to the contrary.[11]

We should certainly not discount the possibility that the rise in suicide is explained, in part, by increasing availability of guns. Good research has been hampered by the National Rifle Association, which has pressured Congress not to fund research or data collection on the topic.

Social isolation is a risk factor for suicide. In chapters 6 and 7 we documented an increase in social isolation, poor health, mental distress, and pain in midlife, especially among whites with less than a bachelor's degree. All of these could help explain the increase in suicide. Americans are less likely to trust others than used to be the case; declining trust is an indicator of falling social capital and a rising risk of death.[12] In chapters 11 and 12 we will document a parallel increase in the percentages of whites who are not in the labor force, who are unconnected with religious institutions, and who are not married. These detachments from protective institutions also increase the risk of suicide. Having a meaningful job, good family relationships with a spouse and children, and belonging to a church that helps address spiritual needs all help maintain a life that is worth living. Their increasing absence among white Americans without a university degree is a disaster.

We can also see the links between social isolation, pain, and suicide by looking across areas of the United States. There is a "suicide belt" in the US that runs along the Rocky Mountains, from Arizona in the south to Alaska in the north. The six highest suicide states are Montana, Alaska, Wyoming, New Mexico, Idaho, and Utah; all are among the ten states with the lowest population per square mile. The six lowest suicide states are New York, New Jersey, Massachusetts, Maryland, California, and Connecticut, five of which are among the ten states with the highest population per square mile; California is eleventh. Firearms are common in the least populated areas. Utah is one of the healthier states in the US, and life expectancy at birth there is two years longer than neighboring Nevada, which is one of the least healthy. Yet neither is exempt from a high suicide rate. Mercer County, New Jersey, which has a population density of 1,632 people per square mile, is where Princeton University is situated and is where we spend most of our year. It has a suicide rate that is a quarter of the suicide rate in the much more beautiful but mountainous and isolated Madison County, Montana, where we spend August each year.[13] Madison County has 2.1 people per square mile. Lack of population also means that medical help can be far away or slow to arrive, but likely more important is the fact that people are less likely to kill themselves when other people are around.

The high-suicide states in the US are also those where people report the most pain.[14] The same pattern shows up across the thousands of counties in the US; places where a higher fraction of the population reports that they experienced physical pain during "a lot of the day" yesterday are also places where suicide rates are higher.[15] Results like these, that rely on spatial evidence, are subject to what is known as the "ecological fallacy." If pain is a major risk factor for suicide—which we believe is true—we might expect that places with a lot of pain will also be places with a lot of suicide. Yet such a finding provides no proof that pain is the cause of higher suicide rates. People mending fences, working with animals, or moving irrigation pipes in the Rocky Mountains may develop sore shoulders or bad knees, and people living in the Rocky Mountains may be at higher risk of suicide because population density is low. In this example, we would find a positive correlation between pain levels and suicide rates across places, but in this case, the pain comes from the fact that agriculture is the main employment where there are few people, and has nothing to do with the higher suicide risk that comes from social isolation. Analyses based on aggregated geographic data can never rule out this kind of thing. Even so, the geographic evidence is a useful check on what we know from other sources. Durkheim relied heavily on geographic evidence, something that is hard to avoid when there is little information on the decedent, who, for obvious reasons, is not available for questioning.

What about education and suicide? Durkheim argued that educated people were *more* likely to kill themselves because education tended to weaken the traditional beliefs and values that prevented suicide. Whether this was true in the US in the past does not seem to be known. But since 1992, when educational attainment was recorded on death certificates in almost all states, there has been a remarkable change in the relationship. Figure 8.1 shows suicide rates by birth cohort and education (with and without a bachelor's degree) for whites, for those born in 1945 and for

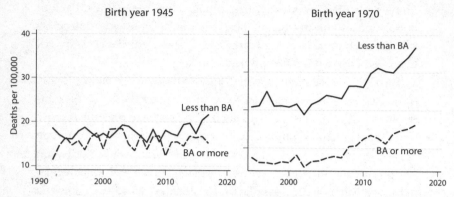

FIGURE 8.1. Suicide rates, white non-Hispanics, by year of birth and education. Authors' calculations using Centers for Disease Control and Prevention data.

those born twenty-five years later, in 1970; the first cohort entered the labor market before 1970, and the second in the mid-1990s.

The left panel, for those born in 1945, shows little daylight between the suicide rates for the less and more educated, while the right panel shows a large gap in suicide rates between education groups born in 1970. The gap first appears for the cohorts born in the late 1940s, and it grows wider and wider for later-born cohorts. The age profiles of suicide for those with a bachelor's degree overlap from one birth cohort to the next—the cohort born in 1950 follows the same age profile as that born in 1945, and the cohort born in 1955 follows that of the cohort born in 1950. In contrast, the age profiles for those without a bachelor's degree rise and steepen with each successive cohort.[16] Figure 8.1 is of course closely related to figure 4.3, albeit for suicide alone rather than deaths of despair as a whole. But if it was indeed once true that more education was a risk factor for suicide in the US, it is no longer so for whites. Or put another way that is more to our point, suicide is becoming steadily more common among whites who do not have a bachelor's degree.

Unemployment, including perhaps the fear of becoming unemployed, has been found to predict suicide. Detachment from the labor force is also a risk. Both fit the Durkheim story of social upheaval and suicide; indeed, Durkheim thought that "economic crises" caused suicide, though his definition of an economic crisis included not only slumps but also booms. It was the disruption that mattered, up or down, not the level of income itself, and this may be why the effects of income on suicide are less clear-cut.

Drugs and Alcohol

Praise of alcohol is easy to find. Benjamin Franklin said, "Wine makes daily living easier, less hurried, with fewer tensions and more tolerance." Ernest Hemingway wrote that wine "offers a greater range for enjoyment and appreciation than, possibly, any other purely sensory thing," though it did not prevent him from killing himself. Mark Twain said, "Too much of anything is bad. But too much good whiskey is barely enough." The web is full of reports (of varying quality) attesting to the health benefits of moderate drinking. A great deal of social life is dependent on, or at least oiled by, alcohol. Great wines command thousands of dollars a bottle, as do some of the rarest Scotch whiskies. Governments like alcohol too, as a source of revenue.

Yet the dangers of alcohol are also embedded in history and in policy. Alcohol is banned by Islam, by many evangelical Protestants, by the Church of Jesus Christ of Latter-day Saints, and by Seventh-day Adventists. It is discouraged by Baptists, by Methodists, and by many Hindus. Most rich countries have laws regulating when and where the sale and consumption of alcohol are allowed. In the US, there have been and are dry counties and dry towns. In the early twentieth century, the temperance movement, backed by many women—who saw alcohol as a women's and family issue—successfully argued for a total ban on alcohol in the US, implemented by a constitutional amendment in 1920 that was eventually repealed in 1933.

The anti-alcohol controls, although they have often been hijacked by special interests for their own purposes, reflect the fact that many people have difficulty regulating their own consumption of alcohol and so will do better if someone else does it for them. Ulysses had himself bound to the mast to prevent him from jumping into the sea when the sirens sang to him. People who drink too much can be a danger to others as well as themselves, by driving or operating machinery, or by neglecting their responsibilities to others. Before Prohibition, as today, many women believed that alcohol led men to fail to provide for their families and to unleash physical violence on their wives.

Alcoholism is an addiction to alcohol, and the chance of becoming an alcoholic varies from one person to another, and likely has a genetic component. Even among rats allowed to drink alcohol, only a minority cannot stop.[17] The eighteenth-century physician Benjamin Rush was one of the first to propose that alcoholism was a disease of the brain, not a failure of will, a view that is widely accepted today, though we are far from predicting just who is susceptible, let alone how to treat it. Abraham Lincoln thought that the disease tended to strike the "brilliant and the warm-blooded" and that the "demon of intemperance ever seems to have delighted in sucking the blood of genius and of generosity."[18] Lincoln was an abstainer himself, but with typical generosity and insight, he understood how "the demon" worked.

Many of those troubled by alcohol work with others to help maintain their sobriety; Alcoholics Anonymous (AA), founded in the 1930s, has around sixty thousand groups that meet regularly in communities all over the US. Before AA, there was an organization called the Washingtonians, to whom Lincoln addressed his remarks. There are also many thousands of family groups to support the families and friends of alcoholics, again attesting to the costs of addiction, not just to alcoholics but also to those who care for and about them. The evidence on the effectiveness of these groups is hard to be sure of, if only because anonymity precludes AA from keeping records, but upwards of a million people attend regularly, which suggests they get something from it, and the scientific evidence is more positive than not.[19]

Even governments are ambivalent toward alcohol, and some are dependent on it, perhaps even addicted to it. One of the reasons that alcohol taxes—like tobacco taxes—are accepted is that they are "sin" taxes, levied on substances that many people would prefer not to use yet, at the same time, have difficulty not using, so that their purchases are not very sensitive to increases in taxes. The state, in turn, can adopt a moralistic tone of helping people moderate their behavior, and do so all the way to the bank, or at least the state treasury. In its early history, the US government, like most poorer country governments today, was heavily reliant on taxes on goods, including taxes on alcohol. The introduction of the income tax, by another constitutional amendment in 1913, provided a revenue source that diminished the government's dependence on alcohol and helped make Prohibition possible. Indeed, the constitutional amendments that permitted the income tax and that enacted Prohibition were, along with female suffrage and the direct election of senators, among the achievements of the progressive movement in the early twentieth century.

While the merits of moderate drinking are still being debated, no one debates the debilitating effects on the body of long-term heavy drinking. Prolonged alcohol abuse eventually destroys the liver, primarily through cirrhosis, an ultimately irreversible scarring of the liver that makes it difficult for it to carry out its vital functions and that increases the risk of liver cancer. The National Institute on Alcohol Abuse and Alcoholism, one of the National Institutes of Health, states that research has found a link between alcohol and cancers beyond liver cancer—breast, esophageal, head and neck, and colorectal cancer. It also lists other organs at risk, including the heart, the brain, the pancreas, and the immune system.[20] If all of the various studies are taken together and treated as correct—a very big *if* for many of the studies—even a very small amount of alcohol increases the risk of death.[21] Of course, the risks are very small for moderate amounts, no bigger than everyday risks, and they must be set against the pleasures and easier living that alcohol brings to most drinkers.

Drinking rates in the US are *higher* among those who are *better* educated, though binge drinking, which is particularly harmful, is more common among the less educated. In 2015, Gallup found that 80 percent of college graduates sometimes drank alcohol, with 20 percent total abstainers. For those with no more than a high school degree, the percentages were more equally balanced, with 48 percent totally abstaining. Patterns by income were similar, with higher-income Americans less likely to abstain. In 2018, 63 percent of Americans drank beer, wine, or spirits, a proportion that has not changed much in three-quarters of a century. Gallup also asks, "Has drinking ever been a cause of trouble in your family?"

FIGURE 8.2. Average drinks per occasion when drinking, US whites by birth cohort.
Authors' calculations using the BRFSS.

The percentage saying yes was around 15 percent in 1948 and 12 percent
in the early 1970s, but it has risen markedly since then to more than
33 percent in 2018, the highest number recorded.[22] This is an important
finding for our story, in which 1970 is a key date when things started to
go wrong, and the upward trend in problem drinking is just one of many
pathologies in economic and social outcomes.

Figure 8.2 shows the average number of drinks reported, on occasions
when people drink, for whites with and without a four-year college degree. Members of each birth cohort report drinking fewer drinks as they
age. But the troubling finding in the figure is that among those without a
degree, younger birth cohorts report drinking more at a sitting at any
given age. Consuming many drinks in a short period of time ("binge-like"
drinking) with lower frequency is more dangerous to the liver than
moderate daily drinking, putting those with less education at higher risk
for alcoholic liver diseases. Echoing this, we are beginning to see deaths
from alcoholic liver diseases rising among whites in their late twenties and
early thirties.

Alcohol was implicated in another recent episode of mortality, not in
the US but in Russia, before and after the collapse of the Soviet Union.

Alcohol consumption was (and is) extraordinarily high in Russia. In the early 1980s, annual consumption of pure alcohol was more than fourteen liters per person per year, almost twice as much as in the United States. Life expectancy had been stagnant for women and falling for men for more than two decades, at a time when life expectancy had been improving in the US and Europe, especially after 1970. Starting in 1984, Mikhail Gorbachev introduced a drastic anti-alcohol policy that sharply reduced production, raised prices, and restricted opportunities for consumption. Over the next three years, life expectancy rose by 3.2 years for men and by 1.3 years for women, driven by rapid decreases in mortality from alcohol-related causes (suicides, accidents, and heart disease). The policy was enormously unpopular and reduced government revenues, and it was officially terminated in 1988, though it took some time to unwind. Of course, the policy then got swept up in larger historical events, particularly the dissolution of the Soviet Union at the end of 1991. The improvements in life expectancy rapidly reversed themselves, and life expectancy fell between 1987 and 1994 by 7.3 years for men and by 3.3 years for women, with some rebound thereafter.[23] By the early years of the twenty-first century, life expectancy for both men and women was close to where we might have expected it to be based on the (unfortunate) trends through the 1960s and 1970s, as if there never had been an alcohol campaign and as if the Soviet Union had never collapsed. Since about 2005, however, there has been rapid progress, perhaps because, after many years of delay, Russia is at last seeing the decline in cardiovascular disease that came to North America and Europe forty years earlier. As the US suffers from its epidemic of deaths, Russia appears to have overcome its own.[24]

What should we make of this Russian story? Many commentators have connected the Russian mortality crisis to the social upheaval that came with the dissolution of the old order, a perfect Durkheimian story. We suspect that this is true, but the role of alcohol, the Gorbachev campaign, and its subsequent collapse is widely accepted and needs to be taken into account. Some of the spike in mortality was the rebound of deaths that had been temporarily postponed by the campaign, and there was nothing to stop the rebound from being larger than the original effect. But many other bad things happened at the same time as the collapse of the state. Many elderly people lost their pensions and their access to health-care.[25] And while many young people relished the new opportunities for foreign travel and education, there was little but despair left for their grandparents, who had no opportunity left to start a new life; in all of the countries of the former Soviet Union and its satellites, there is a huge gap between the young and the elderly in how they evaluate their lives.[26]

It is perhaps too easy to dismiss the relevance of the dramatic events in Russia for events in the United States in the last twenty years. They are very different places, and Russians have suffered untold miseries for generations, including through the communist period. One indication of that misery was Russia's high suicide rate, shared by many of its Eastern European satellites, such as Hungary, Latvia, Estonia, Poland, and Slovenia. Although the suicides rates in Russia and other countries have declined, they still are among the highest in the world. What is both startling and deeply concerning is that, while those countries have seen their suicide rates fall, the rise in the American suicide rate has put US whites among them on this index of misery. Across these countries suicide rates are correlated with deaths from alcohol, just as is true across the states of the US. This group of countries might reasonably be called the group of shame. They are countries that are simply not delivering an acceptable life for a substantial fraction of their people. It is no exaggeration to compare the long-standing misery of these Eastern Europeans with the wave of despair that is driving suicides, alcohol, and drug abuse among less educated white Americans.

9

Opioids

IN HIS BOOK *Imperial Twilight*,[1] the historian Stephen Platt tells the story of the origins of the Opium War between Britain and China. Like the American South after the Civil War, and like working-class America today, the Chinese empire was in distress. The British East India Company was struggling to be profitable, and its most profitable line of business in the 1830s was opium, produced in India and sold to China. The physician William Jardine, born in Edinburgh, was one of the most important merchants in the business. His partner was fellow Scot James Matheson, and together they founded Jardine, Matheson & Company in 1832. Known today as Jardine Matheson Holdings, it has more than four hundred thousand employees and is in the top three hundred companies in the world. As Platt notes, Jardine, Matheson, and other drug dealers, "far from being stigmatized by their line of business, back home . . . would count among the most admired members of their respective societies."[2]

The Chinese authorities were not so impressed. They sought to exclude the British from all of the Chinese coast except for Canton (today's Guangzhou) and to suppress the opium trade. Yet enforcement was erratic and intermittent. The emperor had many troubles on his hands, trying to hold together a disintegrating empire and suppress rebellion, and the opium trade was not always his first priority. But in 1839, Lin Zexu was sent to Canton by the Daoguang Emperor with full authority to suppress the trade. Lin believed not only in interdiction but also in what today is called medication-assisted treatment for addiction. A statue of him now stands in Chinatown in Manhattan with the inscription

"Pioneer in the war against drugs"; in China, he is regarded as a national hero.

When in June 1839, under direct instructions from the emperor, Lin destroyed more than a thousand tons of British opium, a year's supply, the traders lobbied the British government for compensation, which was not feasible politically. But sending in the gunboats to make the Chinese pay was another matter, as was seizing the opportunity to open up the rest of the Chinese coast, not only to opium but also to other British trade. The opium trade was *not* legal; it is as if the Mexican government were asked to compensate Mexican drug dealers for a shipment seized by the US Drug Enforcement Agency (DEA) and the Mexican government, while declining to pay out of its own resources, invaded Texas to make Americans pay. Yet the British Parliament narrowly approved the war, in spite of serious criticism; slavery had not long been abolished in Britain, and many believed that the opium trade was Britain's other great crime. It was not as if the members of Parliament did not understand the ethics of what they were doing, but profit won out over principle, and Prime Minister Melbourne sent the navy to the East.

There is another part to the story that is less well known. The East India Company did not control the western part of India, where the opium poppy also flourished, and the company faced severe competition from drug dealers in Bombay, the best known of whom was a Parsi merchant called Jamsetjee Jejeebhoy. It was his supply that helped drive down the price of opium in China, enabling the drug to move from a luxury for the rich to a much wider population. Jejeebhoy used his drug profits for good works, a playbook that is still familiar today. He was knighted by the Queen of England for his philanthropy, the first Indian ever to be so honored. In 1858, he was elevated to become a lord, becoming Baronet Jejeebhoy of Bombay. The title was a hereditary one and was inherited by his son.

What of Jardine and Matheson? Jardine became a member of Parliament and was succeeded by Matheson on his death in 1843. Matheson became a fellow of the Royal Society and governor of the Bank of England, and he was one of the richest men and largest landholders in Britain. He purchased the Isle of Lewis in the Outer Hebrides in 1844, and in 1851

he became Sir James Matheson, first Baronet of Lewis. The Highland potato famine reached Lewis not long after his purchase, and he was a
generous landowner, who spent large sums on relief and on improvements; he also financed the (more or less voluntary) emigration of 2,337
islanders, about 13 percent of the population, to Quebec and Ontario, and
paid for their clergymen to travel with them. He too earned his baron-
etcy by his philanthropy.[3]

In the words of economic historian Tom Devine, writers have often
seen the Highland Clearances as "the brazen subordination of human
need to human profit."[4] Unlike some of his fellow landowners of the time,
Matheson seems not to have deserved this condemnation, but the same
can hardly be said of his earlier activities, nor of the government-
supported drug dealers of our own time, whom we shall meet in this
chapter.

Opioids

Accidental drug overdoses are the largest and fastest growing of the three
midlife deaths of despair, though suicide and alcohol-related mortality
together accounted for more deaths in 2017. In chapter 8, we explored
suicide and alcohol-related deaths, and how they were linked to the social and economic turmoil among white working-class Americans. We
now turn to the story of opioids and the deaths that they have wrought.

Opioids are either the natural derivatives of the opium poppy, such
as opium itself and morphine, which have been used for thousands of
years and are technically referred to as opiates, or synthetic or partially
synthetic compounds that have some or all of the same properties, technically known as opioids. The term *opioid* is now routinely used for
both. Opioids are implicated in 70 percent of drug deaths, either alone
or in combination with other drugs. Heroin is an opioid; it was synthesized in 1874 and cannot be legally used in the US, though it is used in
medicine in several other countries.

The strength of an opioid is measured by comparing it with morphine.
A milligram of heroin is equivalent to three milligrams of morphine (or
opium), so its morphine milligram equivalent (MME) is 3. One of the

most important opioids in the current epidemic is oxycodone (MME 1.5), which is sold in an extended-release form as OxyContin, manufactured by Purdue Pharmaceutical. OxyContin, known on the street by many names, including "hillbilly heroin," was approved by the Food and Drug Administration (FDA) in 1995. Another is hydrocodone (MME 1), which is in Vicodin. Yet another currently important opioid is fentanyl (MME 100), which was approved by the FDA in 1968. Unlike heroin (illegal only) or OxyContin (legally *manufactured*, but often sold illegally), fentanyl is available both legally and illegally; today, the illegal version is imported into the US from China via Mexico.

Opioids relieve pain. But they are more than painkillers and can produce a euphoria that people find enjoyable and want to repeat. We say "can" because not everyone gets the high or the pain relief. The body can build up tolerance to opioids, so that ever-higher doses may be required to keep pain under control, or to get to the same high. Users can find it difficult to stop using them, because they have become physically dependent and face fierce withdrawal symptoms when they try to stop. These can include vomiting, diarrhea, sweating, insomnia, cramps, and the experience known technically as *delusional parasitosis* or *formication* (alas, the *m* is not a typo), a feeling that ants or other insects are crawling underneath the skin.

Opioids can also lead to addiction, and to the destruction of self and of family that addiction brings. Even dependence can compromise lives; people become focused on maintaining their consumption of the drug, which can make it difficult to work, socialize, or tend to family.

The progression from prescription to tolerance to dependence to addiction is far from automatic. Heroin has been demonized in movies so often that many people think one injection is enough to destroy your life. That is not true in general, but opioids are dangerous, and long-term pain relief through opioids comes with terrible risks, and with questionable effectiveness. The secret, if there is one, is to get the relief without the horrors, to get rid of the pain without the formication.

In the late 1990s, thinking about pain management changed. As we have seen, there was (and still is) a great deal of pain in the US. Pain-relief advocates argued that the US was undertreating pain, and enormous quantities of very powerful opioids were unleashed on the American population. By 2012, enough opioid prescriptions were written for each American adult to have a month's supply. People began to die from prescription overdoses, small numbers at the start, but rising over time to 17,087 deaths from prescription opioids in 2016, then falling to 17,029 in 2017, perhaps the beginning of a downward trend.[5] The people who die are sometimes the people who were given the prescription, but these drugs are often diverted to others, through black-market sales or through theft.

Opioids prescribed by physicians accounted for fully a third of all opioid deaths in 2017, and a quarter of the 70,237 drug overdose deaths that year. This overall number is greater than the peak annual number of deaths from HIV, from guns, or from automobile crashes. It is greater than the total number of Americans who died in Vietnam. The cumulative total from 2000 to 2017 is greater than the total number of Americans who died in the two world wars. The overuse of prescription opioids triggered the secondary epidemic of illegal drugs when Purdue introduced an abuse-resistant form of OxyContin and as physicians became more aware of the dangers and held back, or at least reduced the growth of the legal supply.

Most people who use opioids do not die. And some of those who die may have intended to kill themselves; the distinction between an accidental overdose and a suicide is not always clear, even to the victim.[6] For every death, there are more than thirty visits to emergency rooms for misuse or abuse, ten of which lead to a hospital admission. Each death corresponds to more than a hundred people abusing the drugs; these numbers have been increasing in parallel with the numbers of deaths. In 2016, nearly 29 million Americans ages twelve and over self-reported using illicit drugs in the last month (including misused prescription drugs) and 948,000 reported using heroin in the preceding twelve months.[7] Given that these are self-reports, from people participating in the National Survey on Drug Use and Health, the number is likely to be an underestimate. More than a third of *all* adults, 98 million people, were prescribed opioids in 2015. Many employers will not hire new workers without a drug test, so it seems likely that drug use is keeping people out of the labor force, in addition to those who are unable to participate because of their dependence on drugs.[8]

Opioid deaths, like other deaths of despair, are not equal opportunity. Overdose deaths involving legal and illegal opioids are predominantly of Americans who do not have a bachelor's degree. For whites, since the early 1990s, the percentage of accidental drug overdose deaths accounted for by those with a bachelor's degree has held constant at 9 percent. Two-thirds of victims have no more than a high school education. Blacks and Hispanics were largely exempt until the arrival of illegal fentanyl in 2013, after which they, too, have seen a large increase in overdose deaths. With a few exceptions, mostly English-speaking countries—Canada, the UK (especially Scotland), Australia, Ireland—and Sweden, there are no similar epidemics elsewhere, and apart from Scotland, the numbers dying are very small compared with the US. Yet opioids are used in other rich countries too, usually in hospitals for cancer or for postsurgical pain. But they are much less commonly used by doctors or dentists working in the community, or for the long-term treatment of chronic pain.

Producers made huge sums of money from legal opioids. According to various reports, including investigative work by the *Los Angeles Times*, Purdue Pharmaceutical, which is privately owned by the Sackler family, has sold somewhere between $30 and $50 *billion* worth of OxyContin. Recently released court documents show that the family itself received $12 billion or $13 billion.[9] Illegal drug dealers, many from Mexico, have also prospered,[10] but legal producers have the advantage of not having arrest or violence as a routine business risk.

Physicians are also implicated in the epidemic and, at the least, have been guilty of careless overprescribing, especially in the early days of the epidemic. A substantial fraction of opioid deaths was *caused* by the American healthcare system; the standard term for such deaths is *iatrogenic*, meaning "brought forth by the healer." It is one of the ironies of the epidemic that the US healthcare system, by far the most expensive in the world, not only is failing to prevent the decline in life expectancy but is actually contributing to its fall. And as we shall see in chapter 13, this is not only a result of its mishandling of opioids.

How Did It Happen?

Throughout history, people have used the products of the opium poppy to relieve pain and to get high. The suppliers of those products have often been motivated to help others, and often to enrich themselves, aims that are not necessarily contradictory. The genius of free markets is that people can prosper by helping others. But free markets do not work well for healthcare in general or, in particular, for addictive drugs, whose users often do things that are manifestly against their own interests. Suppliers have an interest in addicting consumers, and mutual gain is likely to be replaced by conflict. At the beginning of this chapter, we saw how this was resolved in favor of British drug dealers in China.

In the American Civil War, upwards of ten million opium pills and nearly three million ounces of opium in tinctures and powders were given to Union soldiers, according to historian David Courtwright, who has written extensively on the history of drugs.[11] The then recently invented hypodermic needle (initially thought to reduce the chances of addiction by bypassing the digestive system) was widely used after the war to bring opium-based pain relief to veterans. Courtwright notes that "for the first time in the entire history of medicine, near-instantaneous, symptomatic relief for a wide range of diseases was possible. A syringe of morphine was, in a very real sense, a magic wand."[12] Around one hundred thousand veterans eventually became addicted. By the late nineteenth century, morphine and opium were widely available in the US and were widely used, including by children. Addiction was especially prevalent among white Southerners, whose postwar world was in disarray. By the end of the century, heroin had been synthesized and marketed by Bayer as, once again, a nonaddictive substitute for morphine. Many more Americans became addicted. And heroin helped many a difficult child go to sleep.[13]

Eventually, the medical profession pushed back, working to restrict the use of opioids both by the public and by physicians, and the Harrison Narcotics Act of 1914 marked the end of the first great American opioid epidemic. The act severely restricted the use and sale of opioids, and heroin was entirely banned ten years later. The sale and possession of opioids became criminal activities, and their use vanished from the vast majority of the population. Respectable people no longer used opium or heroin for minor aches and pains, nor did they feed them to babies with colic.

How, then, could a new epidemic spring up less than a century later? People forget the past, and even those who remember it may think that circumstances have changed, that this time is different, and that the risks of the past are safely locked up in the past. That drugs can be so enormously profitable will always bring a supply of people who say the risks have been exaggerated. Pain certainly had not been abolished and, as we have already seen, chronic pain was rising, and treating (or not treating) it posed an enormous challenge to physicians. Ronald Melzack, whose gate-control theory of pain had revolutionized the understanding of pain twenty-five years earlier, wrote a paper in 1990 entitled "The Tragedy of Needless Pain," which eloquently documented the horrors of pain and argued that "the fact is that when patients take morphine to combat pain, it is rare to see addiction."[14] For terminal cancer patients, the risk of addiction is irrelevant. But many cancer patients survive, many more patients face acute postsurgical pain, and beyond that, there is an ocean of patients with chronic pain. By 2017, 54.4 million American adults had been diagnosed with arthritis, and arthritis is only one of many painful conditions that become more prevalent as the population ages.[15]

Starting around 1990, pain experts increasingly called for pain to be better recognized, and for physicians to ask their patients about their pain level. In his 1995 Presidential Address to the American Pain Society, physician James Campbell argued that "we should consider pain the *fifth vital sign*" (italics in the original), meaning that physicians should assess pain routinely, just as they assess respiration, blood pressure, pulse, and body temperature. Campbell also called into question the usefulness of the distinction between cancer and noncancer pain and between acute and chronic pain.[16] The American Pain Society was shuttered in June 2019, a casualty of the twenty-first-century Opioid Wars, bankrupted by legal fees in its defense against charges (that it denies) that it had acted as a pawn of the pharmaceutical companies.[17]

Debate continues to this day on whether, as Melzack argued, those who take opioids for pain relief need not fear addiction. The Mayo

Clinic's website, often a reliable source, offers contradictory advice. In its discussion of hydrocodone, it states that "when hydrocodone is used for a long time, it may become habit-forming, causing mental or physical dependence. However, people who have continuing pain should not let the fear of dependence keep them from using narcotics to relieve their pain. Mental dependence (addiction) is not likely to occur when narcotics are used for this purpose."[18] But in a different area of the Mayo Clinic's website, more caution is offered: "Anyone who takes opioids is at risk of developing addiction. . . . The odds you'll still be on opioids a year after starting a short course increase after only five days on opioids."[19] Doctors want to help patients and are reluctant to give up their magic wand.

In this changed atmosphere, doctors and dentists increasingly prescribed opioids for all kinds of pain, especially after the introduction of OxyContin in 1996. Its twelve-hour slow-release mechanism, it was claimed, allowed pain sufferers to sleep through the night. Unfortunately, in a large share of users, pain returned and opioid withdrawal began well short of the twelve-hour mark, and many physicians responded by shortening the interval to eight hours or increasing dosages. The cycle of relief followed by pain and withdrawal increased the risks of abuse and addiction.

The introduction of OxyContin was met by a seemingly unlimited demand by patients in pain. Most doctors practiced under extreme time and financial constraints that made the prescription of a pill attractive compared with approaches that were expensive and time consuming. The interdisciplinary treatment of pain, which was the earlier standard, used some combination of medication—for example, the much less dangerous nonsteroidal anti-inflammatory drugs (NSAIDs), like (nonprescription) aspirin, acetaminophen (Tylenol), ibuprofen (Advil), or naproxen (Aleve) or (prescription) celecoxib (Celebrex)—together with counseling, exercise, yoga, acupuncture, and meditation, all of which are difficult to fit into a standard doctor's appointment. Patient satisfaction surveys also became common, and opioids did well on such metrics. Satisfaction was doubtless also high a century before among colicky babies and their heroin-dispensing parents. Arthritis patients were prescribed opioids by primary care doctors, people were sent home from their dentists with many days' supply, and all manner of injuries treated in emergency departments were sent home with opioids.

It is arguably possible for a doctor to assess which patients are at risk for addiction, but not in a few minutes, nor in a system in which many people do not have regular doctors and there are no unified medical records. Doctors may not even know that their patients have died from drugs that they have prescribed; when they are sent a letter informing them, many reduce their prescribing of opioids.[20]

A century after the last epidemic, the conditions were once again in place for another iatrogenic wave of opioid abuse, addiction, and death. David Courtwright told the journalist and author Beth Macy, "What surprised me in my lifetime were things like the internet, or seeing tattoos on respectable women. But I've got to add this to the list of real shockers. I'm sixty-four years old, and I have to admit, I didn't think I would ever see another massive wave of iatrogenic opiate addiction in my lifetime."[21]

As religion faltered, opioids became the opium of the masses.

Overdose deaths began to rise in the early 1990s, gathering real momentum after 2000, a year in which more than fourteen thousand people died of accidental overdoses. Assigning overdoses to the drug responsible is complicated. In a large minority of overdose deaths, more than one drug is present. Benzodiazepines taken alone are unlikely to kill you, but mixed with opioids or alcohol, they can become deadly. In addition, details on the drugs responsible are often not written on death certificates and are instead recorded as "unspecified." In 2000, between a third and a half of all accidental overdoses involved (mostly prescription) opioids, with the exact count dependent on how we attribute deaths from "unspecified" narcotics. Heroin, a long-standing scourge, was recorded as present in 1,999 deaths that year. Before 2011, the increases in deaths were powered by prescription opioids, particularly those based on hydrocodone (Vicodin) and oxycodone (Percocet, OxyContin). In 2011, Purdue Pharmaceutical reformulated OxyContin to make it resistant to abuse. The original formulation had warnings against taking it other than as directed, but those warnings, by telling you exactly what *not* to do, were easily reversed to give accurate instructions for how to convert the extended-release pill into one giving an immediate high, or to prepare it for injection.[22] Deaths from prescription opioids stopped rising in 2011, almost certainly in response to the reformulation, though the increasing awareness of physicians of their part in the epidemic was by then playing a role in limiting unmindful prescription. It is possible that the reformulation actually *cost* lives, if users switched to relatively unsafe street drugs. At the same time, the reformulation allowed Purdue's about-to-expire patent to be renewed, which was possibly of more concern to the company than saving lives.

In any case, by 2011 it was too late to put the genie back in the bottle. Illegal heroin, an almost perfect substitute for oxycodone, quickly picked up the slack; deaths from prescription drugs were replaced by deaths from heroin, and the total of overdose deaths continued its climb. Drug dealers waited outside pain clinics for patients whose doctors had denied them refills. Some bought (diverted) OxyContin on the street until discovering that heroin was both cheaper and more potent. It was also more dangerous, because the quality of street drugs is never guaranteed. At the same time, there was an explosion of high-quality black-tar heroin from new suppliers in Mexico, so for many, the switch was an easy one. Misappropriated OxyContin prescriptions could be sold for morphine-equivalent doses of heroin, maintaining a habit and producing a profit on the deal.[23]

Heroin deaths continued to increase but were soon overtaken by deaths from fentanyl, which rose to 28,400 in 2017. The rise of fentanyl reflects its potency, the ease of its importation given that it is effective in much smaller quantities than heroin, and the fact that it can be mixed with heroin, cocaine ("speedballs"), and methamphetamine ("goofballs") to deliver a more effective high.[24] Heroin and illegal fentanyl became widely available in part to meet the demand of those addicted to prescription opioids who were finding it harder to feed their habits. But their presence appears to have led to an epidemic of its own, in which users start out not on prescription opioids but rather on these illegal substitutes. Cutting cocaine and heroin with fentanyl has been one of the causes of rising overdose mortality among African Americans; death certificates listing fentanyl can account for three-quarters of the increase in midlife African American mortality after 2012.[25]

The fire had jumped its boundaries.

One might think that overdose deaths would drive customers away from dealers whose customers die, but anecdotal evidence suggests that the opposite is true. Those addicted to opioids are so desperate to be numb that they see a death as an indicator that the source of supply is desirable, the "real thing." Indeed, this is not the only hint of suicide in these deaths. The drug naloxone (Narcan) has the almost magical property of bringing back to life people who are about to die from an overdose. Yet there are multiple reports from police and fire departments of their administering naloxone to the same person on multiple occasions, sometimes within a single day. Either people want to die, or they do not care about anything other than feeding their addiction, even if it kills them. The addiction is in control.

The Epidemic and Deaths of Despair

The term *epidemic* invites comparison with an epidemic of smallpox or the influenza epidemic that killed millions in the US and around the world in 1918–19. In the opioid epidemic, the agents were not viruses or bacteria but rather the pharmaceutical companies that manufactured the drugs and aggressively pushed their sales; the members of Congress who prevented the DEA from prosecuting mindful overprescription; the DEA, which acceded to lobbyists' requests not to close the legal loophole that was allowing importation of raw material from poppy farms in Tasmania that had been planted to feed the epidemic; the FDA, which approved the drugs without considering the broad social consequences of doing so and which acceded to producer requests to approve label changes that greatly widened use and profits; the medical professionals who carelessly overprescribed them; and the drug dealers from Mexico and China who took over when the medical profession began to pull back. This is a story of supply, where immense profits were made by addicting and killing people, and where political power protected the perpetrators. Once you have started using opioids, it is as if you have caught the virus, and while you will probably survive, there is some chance that you will die. No one should doubt the importance of supply in the epidemic—which is why we have told the story as we have—but it does not offer anything like a complete account.

Why is it that the epidemic is so much worse in America and almost absent in most other rich countries? Even in America, some opioids, such as Vicodin and even fentanyl, have long been available. Other countries use opioids for postsurgical and cancer-related pain, and some, including Britain, have long used heroin, even when it was banned in the US. What is it that has prevented those drugs leaking out from intended uses into the population at large?

Why, too, is it that Americans with a bachelor's degree rarely die of overdoses, and why are 90 percent of the deaths among those without a four-year degree? Certainly, those with less education are more likely to be injured at work, or to work at jobs that bring a high risk of acute or chronic pain, and so to be prescribed opioids, but this cannot be the whole story. Arthritis, which is one of the leading conditions for opioid prescriptions, is largely a consequence of age, and if access to opioids is more common among the elderly, it is not killing them. In chapter 7, we saw that about half of sixty-year-old whites with a bachelor's degree reported back, neck, or joint pain, as opposed to 60 percent of those without the degree. This is not nearly enough of a difference to explain the sevenfold-higher overdose mortality rate if it is those with pain who get opioids, if a constant fraction of those prescribed become addicted, and if a constant fraction of those people die. It is possible that the pain of the less educated is more suitable for opioid treatment, but we see no evidence of it. Something else is going on.

Here is our own account and interpretation of what happened.

While there was plenty of misbehavior and greed by all of the players in the drama, we think it is a mistake to think of doctors as little better than drug dealers. Certainly, there were some doctors who took the opportunity to operate "pill mills," selling prescriptions for cash (or for sex) without examining or even interviewing the "patient."[26] Many of those doctors are now (or have been) in jail. But few physicians are corrupt and, given the state of medical knowledge in the mid-1990s, they had good reason to prescribe opioids to patients in pain, and little reason not to. Our guess is that it is true that the appropriate dose of opioids for acute pain relief is not, in and of itself, very likely to lead to addiction. Nor will it do so for those who are terminally ill. The appropriateness of the drugs for the long-term treatment of chronic pain is another matter. Clearly, there are exceptions where appropriate short-term prescription led to addiction. One was the case of Travis Rieder, a philosopher and bioethicist at Johns Hopkins in Baltimore, whose left foot was crushed in a motorcycle accident, who was prescribed ever-increasing doses to control his pain after multiple surgeries, and who escaped his addiction only with terrible difficulty and with no help at all from the doctors who had prescribed the painkillers.[27] His story is worth keeping in mind as a cautionary tale of what can happen. Addiction is extraordinarily hard to overcome under even the best of circumstances.

However, it is simply *false* that a single injection of heroin will immediately and inevitably addict anyone and everyone. It is estimated that around a million people in America today use heroin daily or near daily; most of them not only do not die but in fact live functional lives. Many "mature out" of their addiction, and many others quit by themselves, with medical treatment or with social support.

During the Nixon administration, there were reports from Congressmen Robert Steele and Morgan Murphy, who on an official visit to Vietnam in 1971 found that servicemen were using heroin. Nixon immediately declared that heroin addiction was the nation's number one public health problem. Servicemen could be compelled to take urine tests, and the results—in line with the soldiers' own reports—showed that 34 percent had tried heroin and as many as 20 percent were addicted. Much to the surprise of the investigators, 38 percent were using opium. (More than 90 percent used alcohol, and three-quarters used marijuana.) Those who tested positive were detoxed and urine-tested before being allowed to go home, a powerful incentive to get clean. The program became known as Operation Golden Flow, and its veterans were followed up once they got home. Only 12 percent returned to opioid addiction in the US within three years; in most of those cases, the readdiction was brief. Perhaps the detox was successful; it was not expected to be, so if it was, it was much more successful than detox usually is. Perhaps it was because, under the stress of combat, opium and heroin offered some relief. But most servicemen who used opioids started very soon after arriving in Vietnam, and those who had seen more combat were no more likely to use.

The most plausible story, and that of Lee Robins, one of the investigators, on whose description of events this account is based, is that these men used opioids because "they said it was enjoyable and made life in the service bearable."[28] They used opioids not to make combat risks tolerable—and they knew very well the risks of being high in combat—but because they were bored out of their minds. When they returned home and were no longer in the army, there were other means of enjoyment, and life made sense and was bearable without drugs. The environment matters. The drugs were also extraordinarily cheap in Vietnam. The daily triggers for use in Vietnam were absent at home, and because the men were detoxed in Vietnam rather than at home, the detox-readdiction cycle was broken by geography.[29] Robins argues that the widespread perception of heroin addiction comes from the fact that so many studies have been done on special populations that are more likely to be addicted in the first place, and not on more general populations such as those who served in Vietnam.

It is something in people's lives that drives them to seek euphoria or numbness through drugs, not some inherent property of the drugs themselves that will addict anyone who touches them. It is impossible to understand drug use without understanding the environments in which users live, and how those environments are treating them and have treated them in the past. As one physician put it to us, biographies matter.[30] We give our own account of the disintegration of working-class lives in chapters 11 and 12.

Few doctors were or are directly addicting their patients. But they were perhaps too ready to believe the claims that opioids provided more successful long-term relief than the earlier, interdisciplinary approaches. Indeed, there has been little such evidence, and we note again that national levels of pain have been rising, not falling, though the latter would be expected if these drugs were usually effective, given the enormous amounts being prescribed. Physicians are rightly responsive to the pain of their patients and may not consider the wider social costs of prescriptions. They were also exposed to great pressure by the manufacturers, through direct marketing and well-funded "educational" campaigns, and through advocacy organizations for pain sufferers, some of which accepted large donations from pharma. (These fake or infiltrated grassroots associations are sometimes referred to as "Astroturf" groups.) Physicians prescribed strong opioids in numbers beyond those needed, at times to patients who did not need them at all, leaving unused pills that could find their way onto the black market, itself evidence against inevitable addiction. They also prescribed to patients who intended to resell the drugs rather than use them, and who shopped for doctors until they found one who would write a prescription. Doctors try not to prescribe to such people, but it is unclear how they are supposed to know, particularly given the time pressure that they face, and even people who are at risk and have a previous history of abuse can be in real pain. Doctors were being asked to police and prevent abuse in a way that was beyond their ability under the circumstances in which they work.

Some commentators have argued that the rollout of Obamacare was in part responsible for the epidemic, that the expansion of Medicaid made opioids more widely available. But the timing on this is wrong, because the epidemic was in full swing before any Medicaid expansion. By contrast, Medicaid has played an important role in making available affordable treatment for people with opioid abuse disorder, with levels of therapy much higher in states that expanded Medicaid after 2014.[31]

The producers, directly and through prescription benefit managers, did everything possible to increase sales and profits, even when it was clear that the drugs were being abused. In one two-year period, nine million pills were shipped to a pharmacy in Kermit, West Virginia, population 406. Between 2007 and 2012, according to a report by the Energy and Commerce Committee, "drug distributors shipped more than 780 million hydrocodone and oxycodone pills to West Virginia."[32] According to an investigation by the CBS program *60 Minutes* and the *Washington Post*, when the DEA, which is charged with stopping such abuse, tried to do so, Congress passed the 2016 Ensuring Patient Access and Effective Drug Enforcement Act, whose language effectively prevented the DEA from stopping the flood.[33] President Donald Trump then nominated one of the moving forces for the bill, Representative Tom Marino of Pennsylvania, to be his drug czar. Marino withdrew in the face of public outrage after the exposés on *60 Minutes* and in the *Washington Post* revealed his multiyear effort to pass such a bill on behalf of the industry. The investigative journalism also revealed the role of an important "revolver," D. Linden Barber, previously a senior lawyer in the DEA, who switched sides to advise the industry and help write the bill.

Johnson & Johnson, one of the best-known American pharmaceutical companies, supplied most of the raw material for opioid painkillers in the US from a subsidiary, Tasmanian Alkaloids, which grew poppies on farms in Tasmania. According to journalist Peter Audrey Smith, the DEA was aware of what was going on but backed off from closing the legal loophole at the request of pharmaceutical lobbyists.[34] At a time when the American military was bombing the opium supply in Helmand province in Afghanistan, Johnson & Johnson was legally growing the raw material for the nation's opioid supply in Tasmania. In August 2019, Johnson & Johnson was ordered to pay $572 million to the State of Oklahoma for its role in fueling the epidemic. The company is expected to appeal, but other suits are pending.[35]

We tell these stories because they illustrate the failure of democratic politics to address the opioid epidemic. Marino's district was heavily affected by opioids, as was that of one of the bill's sponsors in the House, Representative Marsha Blackburn of Tennessee. Yet they fought against effective regulation, not for it; money and pro-business ideology subordinated the voices of those who had been addicted or were dying. The scandal did not prevent Marino being reelected to Congress in 2018, but he resigned in January 2019 in the face of ill health. Blackburn was also reelected and is now the junior senator for Tennessee. Senator Orrin Hatch, a lifelong friend to a pharmaceutical industry that long supported him, smoothed the bill's way with the DEA. For forty-two years, Hatch represented Utah—a state whose drug-induced mortality rate increased sevenfold between 1999 and the signing of the bill into law in 2016.

The epidemic would not have happened without the carelessness of doctors, without a flawed approval process at the FDA, or without the pursuit of profits by the industry at whatever human cost. The story of that industry, unrestrained and running amok, is being told in American courtrooms today as pharmaceutical executives are being pursued for accountability and compensation by nearly two thousand municipalities. One case, settled in May 2019, saw the conviction on federal racketeering charges of five top executives of Insys Therapeutics, whose salespeople bribed doctors to prescribe fentanyl to patients who did not need it.[36]

Our story is that the misbehavior poured fuel on the fire, making the epidemic worse, rather than creating the conditions under which such an epidemic could take place in the first place. The people who used the opioids, the many millions who became opioid abusers or became addicted, who became zombies walking the streets of once-prosperous towns, were those whose lives had already come apart, whose economic and social lives were no longer supporting them. The *supply* side of the epidemic was important—the pharma companies and their enablers in Congress, the doctors who were imprudent with their prescriptions— but so was the *demand* side—the white working class, less educated people, whose already distressed lives were fertile ground for corporate greed, a dysfunctional regulatory system, and a flawed medical system. The opioid epidemic did not happen in other countries both because they had not destroyed their working class and because their pharmaceutical companies are better controlled and their governments are less easily influenced by corporations seeking profits.

Corporate Power and Individual Wellbeing

One of the themes of this book, which we address at length in later chapters, is how the American economy has shifted away from serving ordinary people and toward serving businesses, their managers, and their owners. Government and the law have been complicit. This chapter, on opioids, provides a dramatic example of this general process. Later, we focus largely on the mechanisms that redistribute money upward, away from working people, and toward firms and their shareholders. The American healthcare industry is the prime example, even beyond the opioid manufacturers and distributors. Their behavior, for which, as we write, they are being called to account in the courts, is not typical, but the use of market power to bring about upward redistribution, from a large number of people with little, to a smaller number with a great deal, is symptomatic of the industry and, more arguably, of American capitalism more generally. The beneficiaries are not only the rich people who are large shareholders but also the many members of the educated elite who hold stock indirectly in their retirement funds, and who benefit from anything that increases corporate profits, including lower wages. We shall argue that this process, run out over half a century, has slowly eaten away at the foundations of working-class life, high wages and good jobs, and has been central in causing deaths of despair. The opioid story fits with this more general theme but is much more flagrant, because it is rare that corporations can so directly benefit from death.

We do not believe that the FDA has been captured by the industry. Even so, much went wrong with its approval of opioids, especially Oxy-Contin. The FDA (and the general public) greatly reveres the randomized controlled trials that are required to demonstrate that drugs work, but even here there were problems with opioids. Those who were in the control group for OxyContin—the randomly selected group that did not receive the drug—had previously been taking OxyContin in an earlier phase of the trial, called the open-label phase; this is done to exclude from the trial those who cannot tolerate the drug.[37] In this type of trial there is a "washout" period between the two phases, in which the drug is supposed to wash out of the patients' systems. The danger in the case of OxyContin (or any addictive drug) is that if the washout period is not long enough, some of those in the control group, no longer receiving the drug, may suffer withdrawal symptoms, which would make them look bad relative to those who go into the treatment group and receive it again. Moreover, the exclusion of those who, in the earlier, open-label phase, could not tolerate the drug means that the trial understates the rate of problems in the wider population for which the drug will be prescribed. Manufacturers are allowed to discuss these and other aspects of trial design with the FDA before the trials are run.

More generally, and as has been correctly argued by a panel of the National Academies of Sciences, Engineering, and Medicine, a testing and approval process that looks only at what these drugs do for individuals ignores the broader effects of releasing a powerful and highly addictive drug into society.[38] It is a lot to ask the FDA to anticipate everything that happened after its approval of OxyContin, but the failure of a system that does not consider the public health consequences of approving the drug is surely inexcusable. After all, the FDA was essentially putting a government stamp of approval on legalized heroin.

The opioid story shows the power of money to prevent politics from protecting ordinary citizens, even against death. Until 2019, at least, when rising public outrage eventually changed perceptions, those who got rich were neither ostracized nor condemned but rather recognized and lauded as successful businesspeople and philanthropists. Purdue Pharmaceutical is the leading example. The Sackler family name appears on museums, universities, and institutions, not only in the US but also in Britain and in France. Arthur M. Sackler, who died before OxyContin was developed, was the donor to many of the institutions, including the Metropolitan Museum in New York (the Temple of Dendur), Princeton University, the Smithsonian, and the National Academy of Sciences. Sackler's fortune came from developing the system of pharmaceutical advertising and sales that is in place in the US today. In the words of one commentator, "Most of the questionable practices that propelled the pharmaceutical industry into the scourge it is today can be attributed to Arthur Sackler."[39]

Arthur Sackler's brothers Raymond and Mortimer, together with Raymond's son Richard, controlled the company during the launch and marketing of OxyContin. Both Raymond and Mortimer were knighted by Queen Elizabeth in 1995, an uncanny echo of Jamsetjee Jejeebhoy a century and a half before.[40] Like an eighteenth-century wig, the perfume disguises, but does not eliminate, the stench of moral decay.[41]

The Queen would be unlikely to convey these honors today. Most of the organizations just listed have stopped using the Sackler name—sometimes after resisting the step for years—and others have said that they will accept no more money.

The pharmaceutical companies, having made so much money from creating the crisis, now stand ready to profit from its treatment. There are no easy or surefire cures for addiction, but the best available—albeit on relatively weak evidence—is known as medication-assisted treatment (MAT), whereby those with addictions use different opioids (methadone or buprenorphine) to control their craving while quitting. While we suspect that MAT is likely being oversold, because the demonstrations of effectiveness come only from patients who admit to their addiction and seek treatment—which many do not—and because a substantial fraction drop out along the way, it has an advantage over abstinence-only treatment because relapsing from the latter is often how overdose deaths happen. Those who have been clean for a while will lose their tolerance to the drug and can die after relapse from the same dose that they used when they first quit. Even so, it takes a strong stomach to watch pharma and their allies push MAT so that they can profit both by causing the epidemic and by curing it. Indeed, in the summer of 2018, Purdue Pharmaceutical was granted a patent for a variant of MAT, setting itself up to repeat its earlier success with OxyContin. It is as if the poisoner of the water supply, having killed and sickened tens of thousands, were to demand a huge ransom for the antidote to save the survivors.

What of the lawsuits against the pharmaceutical companies that are raging as we write? These will permanently reduce the supply of prescription opioids, a reduction that is already under way. They will do little to reduce the use of illegal drugs, and may even increase it, as demand switches from legal to illegal sources. The settlements will probably bankrupt some companies, including Purdue, though others have easily paid large fines in the past out of their even larger resources, or by raising the prices of their drugs. Purdue is trying to retain control over its European subsidiary, Mundipharma, in order to continue the business elsewhere in the world, just as the tobacco companies have done. Whether the states and localities that receive the payments will use them well is not clear. A not reassuring parallel is the Master Tobacco Settlement of 1998 between states and tobacco companies. Since then, the states have received hundreds of billions of dollars from the companies—paid for by the predominantly poorer and less educated Americans who smoke—but have used nearly all of it for general revenue and thus to reduce property and income taxes. In the case of opioids, the surviving companies have the ability to raise prices, making healthcare even more expensive, so that, once again, it is ordinary people, those who pay for healthcare or health insurance, who will be paying for the transfers to the states who win the verdicts. Nor will the payments do much to incentivize the companies to change their behavior. Only admissions of wrongdoing and criminal verdicts against executives are likely to do that, and such verdicts, although not unknown, are rare.

The benefits of free-market capitalism are often rightly noted, including its ability to give people what they want, its incentives for innovation, and its ability to promote economic growth. We agree. But the American medical system, including the pharmaceutical industry, is nothing like a free market. The existence of moneymaking corporations does not imply competitive free markets. Instead, these highly regulated corporations are largely concerned with seeking protective regulations from government and government agencies to protect their profits and limit competition in a way that would be impossible in a free market. We are certainly not arguing for a free-market solution to the American healthcare system, only that what we have now cannot be defended as a free-market system. It is outrageous when an industry that makes so much from *corrupting* free-market competition should be able to dismiss its critics as opponents of free markets. There is nothing antimarket about condemning theft. Other countries have a range of other ways of organizing healthcare, all have their strengths and weaknesses, but none are killing people. None are supporting "the brazen subordination of human need to human profit."[42]

It would be a tragedy if the profits of the drug trade were allowed to corrupt America and were later seen, as was the case in China a century and a half ago, as the beginning of a hundred years of humiliation and decline.

PART III

What's the Economy Got to Do with It?

10

False Trails: Poverty, Income, and the Great Recession

DEATHS OF DESPAIR are concentrated among those with less education, and the epidemic is widening the gap in years lived between those with and without a bachelor's degree. But we have said little about money, or about its absence, and just how income or poverty fits into the story. Even for those who are not poor, people with higher incomes live longer,[1] and there is evidence that education matters too, even among people with the same incomes.[2] In America, money buys access to better healthcare, and beyond that, life is easier when you do not have to worry about how you are going to pay for a car repair, or childcare, or an unexpectedly large heating bill after an especially cold winter month. Financial worry can suck the joy out of life and bring on stress, often a trigger for pain and ill health. It would be surprising if money did not have its own beneficial effect on health even if much of the link between wealth and health is explained in other ways, through the impact of poor health on earnings, through education's effects on both health and wealth, or through childhood circumstances setting the stage for adult health and wealth.

The United States has a much less comprehensive safety net than other rich countries, in Europe and elsewhere. The absence of benefits gives people sharp incentives to work and earn, which is good for those who can, but can be disastrous for those who, for one reason or another, cannot. The United States is also different from other rich countries in having several million extremely poor people, who arguably live in conditions as bad as poor people in Africa and Asia.[3] Poverty is an obvious place to look when trying to explain an epidemic of death that is unique to the US.

Income inequality often features in popular discussion of deaths of despair and of American ill health more generally. Inequalities in income and wealth are higher in the US than in other rich countries, so inequality is a popular candidate to explain other outcomes where the US is exceptional. Poverty and inequality are seen as twin curses that are routinely, if usually not very precisely, blamed for all manner of evils, not just for contributing to poor and declining health but also for undermining democratic governance, for slowing economic growth, for inducing economic instability, for eroding trust and happiness, and even for spurring the rise in obesity.[4] Poverty may be harder to bear in more unequal societies; poor people not only have to suffer their own poverty but can also see that there are others who have vastly more than they need. We have much to say about inequality in this book, especially in the chapters to come. We will argue that deaths of despair and income inequality are indeed closely linked, but not, as is often argued, with a simple causal arrow running from inequality to death. Instead, it is the deeper forces of power, politics, and social change that are causing both the epidemic and the extreme inequality. Inequality and death are joint consequences of the forces that are destroying the white working class.

We resist the notion that income inequality is like pollution in the air, or deadly radiation, so that living in a more unequal society is something that sickens everyone, rich and poor alike. For one thing, the huge expansion of income inequality in the US came after 1970, precisely during the period when mortality was falling rapidly and life expectancy rising rapidly (see figure 1.1). Beyond that, although some states in America are much less equal than others, the epidemic of deaths of despair is no worse in less equal states. New Hampshire and Utah, two states with the lowest levels of income inequality, have been much harder hit than New York and California, two states with the highest.

The Great Recession began in 2008 with the collapse of Lehman Brothers and quickly led to large-scale unemployment and distress, not only in the United States but also in other rich countries. The US unemployment rate, which had been less than 5 percent in February 2008, was nearly 10 percent by the end of 2009, and it did not regain the 5 percent level until September 2016. The recovery is still incomplete in some aspects, especially for the less educated. Throughout the period from January 2010 to January 2019, the number of college graduates aged twenty-five and over in employment increased in total by 13 million (about a quarter). Employment for those without a degree rose by 2.7 million, but by only 55 *thousand* for those with a high school degree or less. Job growth for those with a college degree was barely affected by the Great Recession.[5] The recovery—although it has seen some growth in wages for the least skilled—has not provided them with jobs. From 2008 to 2016, when deaths of despair were rising rapidly and progress against heart disease mortality was reversing, income and employment were much lower for less educated Americans than they would (or should) have been had the bubble not burst.

The policy response to the financial crisis in the US was less than it should have been, but it was relatively successful compared with Europe. Different countries in Europe experienced the recession in different ways; some remained untouched while others, either because of their own choices or because they had no choice given their debt position and their membership in the euro area, experienced more or less severe austerity, with cuts in state spending and benefits. The cross-country variation in Europe gives us a laboratory in which we can compare health outcomes with different degrees of economic distress.

As the title of the chapter suggests, we do not believe that poverty or the Great Recession is central to our story of a rapid increase in deaths of despair. We do not deny the depth of poverty, nor the misery and ill health that comes with it, and we acknowledge and deplore the disgraceful living conditions and low life expectancy in parts of America. That these are worse than in Europe is a direct testament to the inadequacies of the American safety net and its healthcare system. But it is not possible to explain deaths of despair in terms of America's exceptional poverty or the Great Recession.

We pick up the story of what *did* happen in chapter 11, but the detour we take here is important because when people are asked what might be causing deaths of despair, the common response is poverty, or inequality, or the financial crisis, or all three. All are important, but none is the main cause of deaths of despair. Yet the contrary view is so widespread that we need to explain why it is wrong while, at the same time, fitting poverty, inequality, and the crisis into our story.

Poverty

We know a lot about the people who have died from the information on their death certificates, including, as we have seen, their educational attainment. But there is a great deal more that we do *not* know but would like to, including their occupation, income, wealth, and whether they were poor. Without that, we cannot immediately see whether deaths of despair are tied to poverty. We have to work indirectly.

There was no increase in the national poverty rate to match the timing of the epidemic. Official poverty counts, which tally the number of people living in households with incomes below the poverty line, were falling throughout the 1990s, when the epidemic was getting under way, down to a low of 11 percent of the population in 2000. There was then a slow rise to 13 percent on the eve of the Great Recession, followed by a rapid rise through the recession and slow decline thereafter; 2017 marked the third consecutive year of decline in the poverty rate. This looks nothing like the pattern of deaths of despair, which rose uninterruptedly and increasingly rapidly from the early 1990s. The official poverty counts have a number of serious flaws; in particular, they take no account of taxes or benefits, such as the Earned Income Tax Credit, or food stamps, now called the Supplemental Nutrition Assistance Program. While it is important to adjust for these, especially when assessing how the welfare system helped people during the Great Recession, none of the adjustments would make the poverty counts better match the steady rise in deaths of despair. There is simply no increase over time in poverty that can explain the surging epidemic.

The racial patterns of the epidemic are also difficult to reconcile with a poverty story. Among adults without a bachelor's degree, the fraction of white non-Hispanics living in poverty was less than half that among blacks over the period from 1990 to 2017.[6] Yet, at least up to 2013, African Americans were almost exempt from the epidemic. From the early 1980s through the start of the Great Recession, midlife white poverty rates were roughly constant at 7 percent (9 percent for those with less than a bachelor's degree), while deaths of despair among whites increased year by year. More generally, a wide range of measures of living standards are worse for blacks than for whites,[7] but it was almost exclusively whites who were dying from deaths of despair from the 1990s through to 2013. Whatever was differentially affecting white non-Hispanics, it was not that they were poorer than other groups.

Long-established deep poverty in the United States exists, especially among African Americans. Indeed, it is the long and disgraceful history of race in America that has done much to prevent poverty relief in the South—where governments have long been white and the actual or potential recipients of relief are black. Deep financial poverty maintained over many years brings health poverty too, worsened by racism and the low levels of healthcare, education, and sometimes even sanitation.

Yet poverty is not the source of the surge in deaths of despair. The timing is wrong, and the deaths are too white. The geography is wrong too. Figure 10.1 shows age-adjusted mortality rates for accidental (or intent-undetermined) drug overdoses for whites ages twenty-five to sixty-four, by state, mapped against state poverty rates for whites, in 2017.

Certainly, Appalachia and especially West Virginia and Kentucky are centers of drug overdoses and have high rates of poverty, but poverty does a poor job of matching deaths across the country. Drug overdoses are also prevalent in less economically deprived states along the Eastern Seaboard from Florida up the coast to Maryland, Delaware, New Jersey, Connecticut, Rhode Island, Massachusetts, New Hampshire, and Maine. There are also states with high levels of poverty, such as Arkansas and Mississippi, that are much less affected by overdose deaths.[8] At the same time, suicide is much more prevalent in the Rocky Mountain

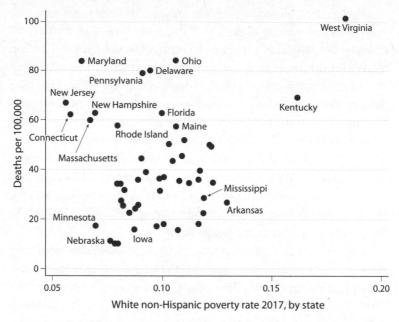

FIGURE 10.1. Drug overdose death rates for white non-Hispanics ages 25–64 and state poverty rates for white non-Hispanics in 2017. Authors' calculations using Centers for Disease Control and Prevention data and the March Current Population Survey.

States, where poverty is not particularly high. Suicide-rate increases from 1999 to 2017 were also larger in the Mountain States, where they were already taking the highest toll. There is no part of the country that has been left untouched by suicide; two-thirds of all states saw midlife suicide rates for whites increase by at least 50 percent between 2000 and 2017. There is a positive correlation between alcohol-related liver mortality and state poverty. But the states with the highest poverty rates (West Virginia, Kentucky, and Arkansas) do not have the highest death rates from alcoholism, in part because a large fraction of their residents are nondrinkers. Alcohol-related death rates are highest in Nevada, New Mexico, and Florida, and they are rising most rapidly in western states (Wyoming, New Mexico, Oregon, and Washington) and in the South.

Whatever is the nature of the despair driving the epidemic, it is widespread, and it is not captured by income poverty at the state level.

Inequality

Deaths of despair are prevalent among those who have been left behind, whose lives have not worked out as they expected. Income is a part of this story, though we shall argue in chapter 12 that declines in income work alongside negative social and political factors. But the fact that working-class people have been left behind economically is important, especially when there has been real growth in the economy. That growth has accrued to a more educated elite, leaving others behind. Widening income gaps are a consequence of this process, as are deaths of despair.

There is another line of thought that blames inequality itself for social disruptions, including mortality. In this account, inequality hurts people by undermining the social solidarity and relationships that are essential to a good life. The British epidemiologist Richard Wilkinson has argued that healthy societies have relationships that "are structured by low-stress affiliative strategies which foster social solidarity," while unhealthy societies are characterized by "much more stressful strategies of dominance, conflict and submission." Which kind of society we live in is "mainly determined by how equal and unequal a society is."[9] This is different from arguing that poverty is the root of ill health. In that story, the poor are unhealthy because of their poverty. By contrast, if inequality makes a society unhealthy, everyone's health suffers, rich as well as poor.

Wilkinson's theory has a lot to recommend it, especially its focus on social as opposed to individual circumstance. But here we are interested in whether it can help account for mortality in America today, and whether income inequality is linked to the epidemic of deaths of despair. We agree that the increase in American inequality since 1970 is indeed linked to increases in deaths of despair, not directly—as in "inequality makes us all sick"—but because in the US the rich got richer at the expense of the rest of America—"reverse Robin Hood" in action. For twenty to thirty years, while income inequality rose, mortality declined, but eventually, after 1990, we began to see an increase in deaths of despair among the less educated. We will argue that this is the result not of the increasing prosperity of those in the top 1 percent but instead of what has been happening to the white working class itself. Of course, the increasing prosperity at the top may have a good deal to do with the distress at the bottom, and it will be central when we come to think about what should be done. But those in despair are in despair because of what is happening to their own lives and to the communities in which they live, not because the top 1 percent got richer.

Income inequality is different in different places—cities and states— across the country. At times in the past, mortality rates were higher and life expectancy lower in states with higher income inequality. But the relationship is much weaker today. Historically, the states in the South with high mortality—West Virginia, Alabama, Kentucky, Mississippi, Arkansas, Oklahoma, Louisiana, and Tennessee—had higher levels of income inequality than the majority of states, in most cases because they had large African American populations, who were relatively poor, which drove up overall income inequality, and who had relatively high mortality, which drove up overall mortality. States in the central plains and in most of the West had more homogeneous populations and lower mortality rates. Today, however, New York and California are two of the most unequal states; they have a high degree of heterogeneity, with large Hispanic and Asian populations, but have among the lowest mortality rates.

To search for a simple and direct relationship from income inequality to mortality is to follow another false trail.

Many people feel that income inequality is less of a problem if it is easy for people to move from poverty to riches, or at least for children to do better than their parents. To check this, we need a measure of intergenerational mobility—for example, the fraction of children whose parents were in the bottom fifth of the income distribution and who managed to move to the top fifth. We might suppose that when intergenerational mobility is high, everyone has a chance of succeeding (or failing!), and when it is low, people are trapped by the accident of their birth. The economist Raj Chetty and his coauthors have calculated measures of intergenerational mobility for children born between 1980 and 1991 for different places across the United States.[10] Children born in the Southeast of the US have had the least chance of moving up, at least for this particular cohort. While there is a good deal of overlap between low mobility and deaths of despair, the relationship is no closer than for inequality itself. Indeed, inequality is itself strongly related to low mobility.

Incomes and the Great Recession

The stock market crash of October 1929 was followed by a decade of misery and economic failure that remains the worst-ever crisis of Western capitalism. Millions lost everything—their jobs, their savings, and their homes or their farms. More than 20 percent of the population was unemployed, depriving not only themselves but also their families of economic support. Personal income per head fell by a quarter from 1929 to 1933, and it did not recover its pre-Depression level until 1937. Suicide rates reached peaks that they have never subsequently attained; this is true in both the US[11] and Britain.[12] In Europe, the Depression and its aftermath saw the rise of fascism.

Nothing as bad as this has happened since, but the events after 2008 are the next worst—not the Great Depression, just the Great Recession. Unemployment doubled, from 5 percent to 10 percent, not as bad as 20 percent, but no better for the millions affected. (For those with a college degree, unemployment peaked at only 5.3 percent.) Because the crisis was rooted in a housing bubble, with bankers making huge sums from mortgages that should never have been lent, millions of people lost their homes. People who had worked hard to hold on to a middle-class life were suddenly without a job, without a place to live, and without the means to continue their own or their children's education. Banks stopped lending, and millions of small businesses went bankrupt.

There have been many studies of how mortality varies over the business cycle, whether more people die in bad times—as we might at first expect—or during economic booms, when times are good. Perhaps the first study to look at the question was published as long ago as 1922, by the sociologist and statistician William Ogburn and sociologist and demographer Dorothy Thomas;[13] Thomas was the first woman to be a professor at the Wharton School of the University of Pennsylvania. Ogburn and Thomas discovered, to their surprise, that the good economic times were bad times for mortality. Their conclusion has been replicated many times since, including in work for the United States on national and state-level business cycles before the Great Recession.[14] Much the same happens in other rich countries, with slumps better for mortality than booms, though not every study confirms the pattern. While it is true that suicides are higher in bad times, as was true in the Great Depression— remember the famous images of bankrupt ex-millionaires jumping out of skyscrapers in 1929—there are other mechanisms at work. During slumps, people have less money to spend on hurting themselves by driving fast cars or drinking too much, working less can reduce stress and heart attacks, and when wages are low and labor available, it can be cheaper to find good people to take care of the elderly.[15]

Yet each boom and each slump is different and has its own history. In the Great Recession, quite apart from the economic disaster, there was also the epidemic of deaths that is the topic of this book. So what happened this time?

An essential starting point is to look back to chapter 4 and to figure 4.2, which shows the trajectory of deaths of despair after 1990. The upward trajectory rises inexorably, and there is no sign of an effect of the 2008 crash or of its long aftermath. Suicides were certainly high after the crash, but they had been rising for many years before. Whatever the other consequences of the crash, there is no evidence of a jump in deaths of despair after Lehman Brothers failed or as unemployment doubled from the fall of 2008 through 2009. The idea that the crashed economy caused deaths of despair is another false trail.

Even so, the Great Recession may be implicated in other types of deaths, or in deaths for some groups but not others. For example, whites ages forty-five to fifty-four saw their median household incomes per member rise through the 1990s, then fall after 2000.[16] Their all-cause mortality rate—not just from deaths of despair but including them—fell from 1990 to 1999, then rose until 2016, matching income trends in reverse, as one might expect. But if we look more closely, the match is coincidental. The down and up in all-cause mortality happened because deaths of despair, although rising in the 1990s, were small at first and were more than offset by improvements in death rates from heart disease.

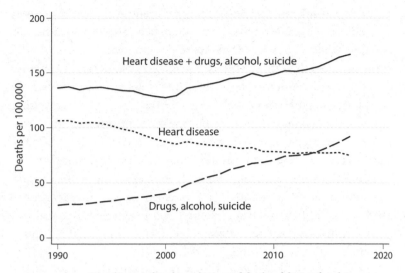

FIGURE 10.2. Mortality rates from heart disease and deaths of despair for white non-Hispanics ages 45–54 (age-adjusted). Authors' calculations using Centers for Disease Control and Prevention data.

Figure 10.2 presents the mortality rates from deaths of despair (drugs, alcohol, and suicide) and those from heart disease for forty-five-to-fifty-four-year-old whites over this period, as well as the sum of these two types of mortality.

As the decline in deaths from heart disease slowed and as the rate of deaths of despair became high enough, the all-cause mortality decline turned into a mortality increase. Yet the underlying components, deaths of despair and heart disease mortality, are both unrelated to the pattern of incomes, and the fact that their sum mirrors incomes is simply coincidental.

Older whites saw their mortality rates fall throughout the period as their median incomes rose. The incomes of older Americans were better protected than those of people in middle age—social security benefits for retirees have done better than have median wages for people who are working. But all we have here is one trend up (incomes) and one trend down (mortality), and it would be a real leap to attribute the falling mortality rates of the elderly to their rising incomes.

When we look more widely, it becomes even clearer that patterns of incomes from 1990 through 2017 do not match patterns of deaths. For example, while whites ages forty-five to fifty-four with a bachelor's degree earn more than those with some college, who, in turn, earn more than those with no more than a high school degree, median household incomes per member for the three groups tracked one another, rising until 2000 and falling thereafter. But the mortality rates for the three groups diverged, rising for the least educated, staying almost flat for the middle group, and falling for the most educated. The link also fails when we compare blacks and whites, both of whom experienced the rise and fall of median income, but with sharply divergent mortality experiences— blacks good, whites bad. Just as poverty fails to explain the spatial pattern of deaths, so does the pattern of incomes after 1990 fail to explain the pattern of deaths over the same period.

We are *not* arguing here that incomes (or wages) do not matter; in the rest of the book, we put much of the blame for deaths of despair on the long-term deterioration in opportunities for less educated Americans. The operative expression here is "long-term." Our skepticism about the effects of the Great Recession is to do with the lack of a relationship between movements in mortality and movements in income in the past two decades, a much shorter period.

Recession, Austerity, and Mortality in Europe

The Great Recession was different in the US and Europe, and for many European countries it was much worse, in terms of both increases in unemployment rates and declines in income. For countries that implemented austerity policies, voluntarily or involuntarily, there were cuts in unemployment benefits in spite of rising levels of unemployment, as well as cuts in health spending, especially on preventive services such as vaccinations and breast cancer screening, and on pharmaceuticals. Government spending toward the elderly, such as pensions and long-term care, was largely protected. Greece, which suffered the most, cut public expenditure on health by 30 percent, though, even there, spending on long-term care for the elderly was protected.[17]

In spite of the austerity in some countries, or lack of it in others, there was (and is) no epidemic of deaths of despair in Europe; the slowdown and reversals in mortality rates in the United States have no general counterpart in Europe. Indeed, between 2007 and 2013, while unemployment rates in Greece and Spain more than tripled—to the point where more than a quarter of the population was unemployed—life expectancy was rising more rapidly than in most other European countries. In Europe over this period, there was some *convergence* in life expectancy. Countries that started out at the low end, such as Estonia, Poland, or the Czech Republic, had faster growth in life expectancy than those, such as Norway, France, or Switzerland, that already had relatively high life expectancy. But the data for Greece and Spain are not explained this way; both had high life expectancy to start, and both had substantial mortality improvement over the austerity years.[18] Looking to Europe does nothing to help us develop any general story of unemployment, declining incomes, and mortality.

Is there another wealthy, industrialized country at risk of following the US down the path to poorer long-run outcomes for working-class families and deaths of despair? Storm clouds appear to be gathering in the UK. Low-earning working British households have seen little rise in household earnings since the mid-1990s. Life expectancy, which rose at more than a fifth of a year per year from 1980 to 2011, has flatlined since then. As in the US, progress on midlife heart disease mortality has faltered, and deaths of despair in England and (especially) Scotland have risen. (The numbers here are small relative to what we currently see in the US, but the US also started from a small base in the early 1990s.) Britain is currently experiencing an extended period of austerity and of rising geographic inequality—London is flourishing while most of the rest of the UK is not. Like the US, the country is politically divided, with half having voted for Brexit and half for remaining in the European Union. While the long-term effects on mortality remain unclear as of mid-2019, it is possible that the long-term decline in working-class lives witnessed among US whites from 1970 may be on its way to the UK, with deaths of despair beginning to stir.[19] But there is, as yet, no clear and accepted understanding of recent changes in mortality in Britain.[20]

Deaths and Deindustrialization

We are not quite done with income and unemployment. Some of the writing about the epidemic, such as Sam Quinones's outstanding book *Dreamland*, highlights opioid abuse and deaths in once-prosperous towns or cities where jobs have disappeared, where factories have been lost to automation or have moved abroad, and where at least some of the people who remain are abusing opioids.

Correlating deaths of despair with employment rates at a fine level, using our one thousand small areas across the US, confirms what Quinones saw. Places with a low fraction of the prime-age population in work are also places with high rates of deaths of despair; this holds for suicides, drug overdoses, and alcoholic liver disease taken separately. Several studies have looked at a more specific episode, the accession of China to the World Trade Organization in 2000 and the sharp local increases in unemployment that resulted from the sudden competition from much cheaper Chinese goods. Again, those increases in unemployment are associated with increases in mortality.[21]

Our main argument in this book is that the deaths of despair reflect a long-term and slowly unfolding loss of a way of life for the white, less educated, working class. Unemployment is part of that story, but only a part. People who have given up on finding a job and are not looking are not counted as unemployed, but they still reduce the fraction of people in work. Unemployment rates rise and fall, certainly for the country as a whole, but also in specific places as one kind of job is replaced by another—often a worse job replacing a better job. In some places where manufacturing has disappeared and people have lost jobs with a high-paying employer, they find other jobs, in services, or order fulfillment, or call centers, or driving for Uber. These jobs may pay less, and working conditions may be more stressful, but they keep people in the labor force. The journalist Amy Goldstein tells such a story about Janesville, Wisconsin, Paul Ryan's hometown, after General Motors—known as "Generous" Motors because of its high hourly wages—closed its plant in 2008 after making Chevrolets there for eighty-five years. By the end of the story, the unemployment rate is only 4 percent, yet that hardly means that all is well.[22]

Lower unemployment rates are associated with lower rates of deaths of despair. Yet there may be others who lost their jobs and remain out of the labor force, and out of the unemployment statistics. They too contribute to distress and to despair, so that deaths are high even when unemployment is low but when there are many people doing nothing and with nothing to do.

In summary, unemployment is not always good at identifying the places where social and economic structures have been destroyed. Worse jobs are still counted as jobs, and when people give up altogether and stop looking for work, they are no longer counted as unemployed. But these changes, prolonged for long enough, undermine social life and the structure of society, and it is that destruction that brings deaths of despair. The link between mortality and unemployment is part of this process, as is the "China shock." It is important for our story that these results point in the same direction, but they are simply the latest installment in a longer-running movie.

The Great Recession Redux

We have emphasized that the Great Recession did not bring deaths of despair in the way that the Great Depression brought epidemics of suicide in the US and Britain, but that does not mean that it did not matter. We suspect that the upsurge of populism on the right and of rage against inequality on the left have much to do with the financial crisis. Until the crash, it was possible to believe that the elites knew what they were doing, that the salaries of the CEOs and the bankers were being earned in the public interest, and that economic growth and prosperity would make up for the ugliness of the system. After the crash, when so many ordinary people lost so much, including their jobs and their homes, the bankers continued to be rewarded and went unpunished, and politicians continued to protect them. Capitalism began to look more like a racket for redistributing upward than an engine of general prosperity.

11

Growing Apart at Work

EDUCATION, PARTICULARLY THE DIVIDE between those with and without a bachelor's degree, has increasingly split the population into those who are doing well and those who are doing badly. As we have seen, the unprecedented increases in deaths—from drugs, suicide, and alcohol—are largely confined to the less educated. The same is true for the increases in ill health, including physical and mental health and pain, that we documented in chapters 6 and 7.

These health outcomes are only the lead items in the catalog of misfortune for those with less education. The divide is growing in economic outcomes, in wages, in participation in work, in the kinds of jobs that are available, and in the chances to get ahead. Geography is increasingly patterned by education, with the well educated moving to successful and innovative cities that have good jobs, good schools, and good entertainment, while the less educated are left behind in the countryside, in small towns, or in stagnant or decaying communities, places whose most talented children have moved elsewhere. Sixty years ago, Michael Young predicted that a meritocracy would bring this separation, and in chapter 5, we saw how it happened in African American communities in the 1970s and 1980s.

Earnings from work provide the material support for a good life through the goods and services that earnings buy, but work matters as much or more for other aspects of life. Work gives structure and meaning to lives; it confers status, which is not the same as earnings. It supports marriage and child rearing. Here too there is a widening split, with less educated people becoming increasingly less likely to marry, more likely to divorce, more likely to have children outside marriage, and more likely to be separated from their children. We will have more to say on these aspects of life in chapter 12.

It is a mistake to think of wellbeing as money, or what money can buy. Many of the things that people have reason to care about are not reducible to money or measurable in monetary terms. It is true that those other things are more difficult when money is scarce, so the decline in material wellbeing is a cause of distress in other aspects of life. Being left behind financially is a key part of the story, but it is only the beginning. When we use the term *deaths of despair*, the despair is much broader, and much worse, than just material deprivation.

In this chapter, we focus on the bases for material wellbeing, wages and jobs, and the growing divide by education. In the next, we chart the divides in other outcomes.

One Escalator Becomes Two Escalators, One of Which Stopped

There is another division in America that is not between people but rather between eras. The eras are before and after 1970, although somewhat different dates work for different events. From the end of the Second World War to 1970, economic growth was relatively rapid and its fruits were relatively equally distributed. Growth was an escalator that lifted people of all education levels and all incomes. After 1970, the escalator became two escalators—one, for the well educated and already well-off, that was faster than before, while the other, for those without a college degree and the already less well-off, was stalled or hardly moving at all. Before 1970, there was growth and no increase in inequality. Afterward, there was lower growth and growing inequality. We shall discuss some of the causes as we go, but the consequence was a slowly unfolding calamity for the working class.

In chapter 10, we showed that the Great Recession that began in 2008, disastrous though it was, cannot be blamed for the epidemic of deaths of despair, which began much earlier and continued unabated through the slump. By contrast, the longer-term evolution of living standards, going back to 1970, had much to do with the epidemic. The deterioration in living standards, together with the social disintegration of the white working class, is a slow process that the political scientist Robert Putnam has aptly compared to climate change, working inexorably but slowly and largely out of sight. Neither climate change nor its consequences are revealed in year-to-year fluctuations in temperature, but its long-term (and sometimes contested) consequences threaten civilization. As economic growth declined, working-class people were left further and further behind by an economy that increasingly reserved its rewards for those with higher education.

Growth, Income Inequality, and Wages

The state of the economy at large sets the limits of what is possible for the individuals and families within it. Growth in per capita gross domestic product can be used for many purposes, to support government expenditure, spending by people, or spending on equipment by firms, and the fraction that goes to people can go to the rich, to the poor, or to everyone; overall economic growth is a starting point that needs to be taken apart to see who gets what. In the 1950s, per capita economic growth averaged 2.5 percent a year, and a decade later, in the 1960s, it was 3.1 percent, the highest ten-year average in the period since the Second World War. By 1960, the gross domestic product per person was 28 percent higher than in 1950; by 1970, it was 36 percent higher than in 1960 and 75 percent higher than in 1950. In the 1970s and 1980s, growth slipped to 2.2 percent a year, and in the 1990s, today seen as a *good* decade, annual growth averaged just under 2.0 percent.

The first decade of the twenty-first century was host to the Great Recession, and overall growth was less than 1.0 percent, but even in the second decade, at least up to 2018, in a period when the economy was recovering, growth was just below 1.5 percent a year. Importantly, America is not the only rich economy in which growth rates fell. The Organisation for Economic Co-operation and Development is an organization of advanced countries, today containing thirty-four mostly rich members, and the group as a whole has shown the same general decline in growth since the Second World War.

The division of resources, who gets what, becomes more difficult when growth slows.[1] What may seem like small differences in growth rates have huge effects over long periods of time. In an economy growing at 2.5 percent, living standards double in twenty-eight years, little more than a generation. At 1.5 percent, it takes forty-seven years. When there is lots of growth, distribution is less pressing because even if one group gets more than its fair share, there is still something left for others. With lower growth, there is more pressure to shut out less successful groups altogether. Lower growth sharpens the fight over resources, it gives each group incentives to lobby to get more than its share, and it poisons politics, much of which is concerned with the division of resources. Since 1970, growth has predominantly gone to those who are already better off, who are much better equipped to defend their share. When people feel they must protect their economic position in a tougher world, they divert their time and their resources to the zero-sum game of distribution and away from the positive-sum game of innovation and growth. Rent-seeking replaces creation, and we can get into a vicious circle that impoverishes everyone.

Today, the facts about income inequality are widely known, that those in the middle and bottom of the distribution have gained very little while those above the middle, and especially those at the very top—the famous 1 percent—have done very well indeed. The combination of low growth and less equal distribution is a double calamity for the living standards of those who are not at the top.

The divergence between the elite and the rest has happened not only in the United States but in many other advanced countries too. But while the decline in growth was similar in the US and other rich countries, the increase in inequality was not. Several advanced countries—Germany, France, and Japan, for example—managed to have little increase in income inequality until quite recently. On top of this, the level of inequality was much higher in the US to start with. The US has long been one of the most unequal among the rich countries, and the recent increase, whose direction is indeed common to many rich countries, started earlier in the US and has been larger than elsewhere.

Another way to think about growth and distribution is to look at how much of national income goes to labor (wages) and how much to capital (profits). Economists long thought that the ratio of wages to profits was an immutable constant, about two to one. But this too has changed since 1970, and the percentage of wages has fallen from 67 to around 60 percent. Similar declines have happened in other rich countries, as well as in several developing countries, including India and China.[2] Not all profits go to rich people—think of pensioners holding stocks to finance their retirement—but they predominantly do, and the shift toward profits in national income has been one reason for the increase in income inequality across households. The declining labor share means that productivity growth in the economy no longer feeds one for one into growth in wages. Not only has productivity grown more slowly since the early 1970s, but wages have not kept up with the slower growth. Until 1979, productivity growth and worker compensation grew together, but from 1979 to 2018, productivity grew by 70 percent and hourly pay by only 12 percent.[3]

Earnings and Wages

National income is an important general indicator of the state of the economy, but it does not tell us who gets what. For that we need to look at individuals or families. A central element of our story is how earnings differ across people with different amounts of education, especially between those who do or do not have a four-year college degree. Given the differences in health and other outcomes by education, we are here more interested in how earnings differ by education than in earnings inequality in general.

Once again, we emphasize that earnings are likely less important than social changes, including the nature of work, of status, of marriage, and of social life. All these social and economic changes are happening at once, and all shape people's lives. But they also affect one another in ways that we shall try to pick apart. Earnings from the labor market have a claim to being one of the prime causes of these other outcomes, so it is useful to look at them first.

People with a college degree earn more than those without. As we saw in chapter 4, the additional earnings for those with a bachelor's degree or more, above what is earned with a high school diploma, *doubled* between 1980 and 2000—what had been a 40 percent pay difference skyrocketed to an 80 percent difference.[4] Education is rewarded in the market, because of what is learned in college, because those who get educated have more drive or higher cognitive skills in the first place, because of better family connections, or some combination of all three. The leading explanation for the doubling of the college premium is that education and cognitive ability have become more valued in the labor market as production has come to depend more on complex technologies, moving toward computers and away from agriculture, toward brains and away from brawn. This process is known as skill-biased technical change.

The increase in the college premium is, once again, not peculiar to the US, though, as is the case for overall inequality, both the premium and its rate of increase are larger in the US than in other advanced countries. The forces of skill-biased technical change are at work in all advanced countries, but the US is the most extreme case, followed—at some distance—by other English-speaking countries. The US is not unique, just different, and more exaggerated, something we see many times in this book.

The earnings premium of a bachelor's degree is a reward for getting educated and is an incentive to go to college, a signal to young people interested in material rewards that going to college is a good idea, and increasingly so over time. Interpreted thus, it seems innocuous, simply an indicator that capitalism is working, drawing resources to where they are most needed, and creating the human capital that the economy needs. However, those incentives do not seem to be working very well: the fraction of young adults who completed a bachelor's degree did not change between 1996 and 2007, and it has increased only slowly since that time, rising from 27 percent of twenty-five-year-olds in 2008 to 33 percent in 2017.[5]

FIGURE 11.1. Median earnings, white non-Hispanic men by birth cohort, with and without a bachelor's degree. Authors' calculations using the Current Population Survey.

Worse still, the widening gap has come not just through an increase in the earnings of the college educated but also through a *reduction* in the earnings of those without a four-year degree. Not only are the college-educated rewarded with higher earnings, but those who do not heed the incentive are punished with lower earnings. The winners get the prizes, and the losers get worse than nothing.

Figure 11.1 shows how this has happened for white men, tracking hourly earnings (or wages, for short), by birth cohort. Each line shows median wages, adjusted for inflation, for a specific birth cohort over its working life; the horizontal axis shows age, which allows us to follow the progress of each birth cohort as it ages. To keep the figure readable, we show re-sults for four cohorts, those born in 1940–44, 1955–59, 1975–79, and 1990–94, and we divide each cohort into those with a four-year degree and those without. The lines have been smoothed to make the figure easier to read.

What immediately jumps out from the figure is the gap in wages be-tween those with and without a bachelor's degree; all of the lines for the more educated (at the top) are always above all of the lines for the less educated (at the bottom). Within the bachelor's degree group, the lines are moving *up* as we move from the cohort born in the 1940s, to that born in the 1950s, to that born in the 1970s. It is less clear how the picture will evolve for the cohort born in 1990s, who are still young. Within the group lacking a bachelor's degree, the lines are moving *down* as we move from earlier- to later-born cohorts. The arrows are there to point to these opposite trends for the two sets of lifetime earnings profiles.

The gap between the two sets of lines widens with age; just after graduation, college-educated men earn somewhat more than those who did not go to college, but the gap widens as they grow older. For men born in 1955, at age twenty-two (when those with a degree were just entering the labor force as full-time workers), men with a degree earned 7 percent more than men without. That premium grew to 77 percent by age fifty-four. The increase in wages with age for each birth cohort is much steeper for those with a bachelor's degree than for those without, for whom there is little prospect of substantial wage growth as they age. In the 1955 cohort, for those without a degree, their highest median wage (at age forty-five) was 50 percent greater than that at age twenty-two. For those with a degree, their highest median wage (at age fifty) was two and a half times higher. Professional earnings keep rising throughout most of working life, while earnings in more manual jobs peak in midlife and fall thereafter.

As a consequence of the earnings profiles for the more educated shifting up, and those for the less educated shifting down, the gaps between those with and without a bachelor's degree in the same cohort are larger for later-born cohorts; each generation has a higher college premium throughout life than the last.

There is a lot of information in figure 11.1, but the key difference between the two groups is the almost continuous *decrease* in wages from one birth cohort to the next for the less educated at the bottom of the graph, especially at younger working ages, and the almost continuous *increase* from one birth cohort to the next for those who hold a bachelor's degree at the top of the graph. The rewards to a life of work are turning against those without a bachelor's degree.

Women with a college degree saw the same cohort-to-cohort increase in hourly earnings observed for men in figure 11.1. For women without a degree, wages rose between the cohort of 1940 and 1950, but cohorts born after midcentury saw no additional progress. In cohorts born after 1965, median wages for women without a degree have also fallen.

For all white workers ages twenty-five to sixty-four, taken together and adjusted for inflation, median hourly earnings grew by 11 percent from 1979 to 2017. This works out to an average growth rate of 0.4 percent per year, in an economy that grew at an average rate of 2.5 percent per year. Median wages for men in the US have been flat for fifty years, and for white men without a bachelor's degree, the average growth in median wages from 1979 to 2017 was *minus* 0.2 percent a year.

The long-term stagnation in median wages appears to be unique to the United States, at least among advanced countries. In Europe, the Great Recession and its aftermath also hurt wages. Many countries suffered more than the US, and several European countries took a second, double-dip, downturn. Median wages in Greece, Spain, Portugal, Ireland, and Britain fell in the decade after 2007. But in none of those countries has there been the long-term stagnation of wages that workers saw in the United States. Britain is an instructive comparison. In the twenty years before wages started falling, real median wages in Britain had increased by almost a half, compared with stagnation in the US, so that even once wages started falling, the typical British worker was being paid more than two decades before, while the typical American worker without a bachelor's degree was being paid less.[6]

Are We Exaggerating Decline and Stagnation?

Perhaps the government data are incorrect, or are being misinterpreted, and wages are doing better than figure 11.1 shows.[7] If working wages are doing better than stagnation, then perhaps American capitalism is really delivering for workers in a way that the statistics do not capture. The argument of this book is that working-class Americans have *not* done well, and although wages are only part of the story, they are an important part.

The first point to note is a familiar one, that wages are not the same thing as material wellbeing, which itself is a much narrower concept than wellbeing. Even if wage rates are doing badly, people might still be seeing increases in the money they have to spend. Women are now more likely to work than was true in 1970—see figure 11.2, later in this chapter—so family incomes can go up even when individual earnings do not, and indeed, median family incomes have done better than median earnings. If women are working by preference, and not just to make ends meet in an increasingly difficult environment, then the increase in their participation is a good thing, even beyond the money they earn. But to the extent that one member of a couple would prefer not to work, in order to raise children, but takes a job to hold the family together financially, the welfare of all family members may suffer. According to one survey, "Virtually all the increase in full-time employment of American women over the last twenty years (1978–1999) is attributable to financial pressures, not personal fulfillment."[8] Although both parents work full time in half of two-parent households, 59 percent of Americans (and half of all working mothers) think that it would be better if one parent stayed home with the children.[9] Children and commuting costs often take a large bite out of an additional paycheck, which is not taken into account when we look at family incomes.

Wages take no account of taxes or benefits, and some benefits, such as the Earned Income Tax Credit, raise the after-tax incomes of working people with low earnings. Workers also receive benefits through their employers, especially healthcare, as well as benefits from the government, especially Medicaid (Medicare is generally for people sixty-five or over, who are not our main concern here), and through the safety net, including food stamps and disability benefits. Accounting for these items is difficult, especially those, such as healthcare, that do not come as cash. What they cost employers or the state to provide is not the same as what they are worth to those who receive them—and we must be careful not to count the exorbitant costs of American healthcare as if they were a cash *benefit* to working people. If the healthcare industry, by lobbying or mergers or lack of competition, raises prices, depriving some people of health insurance and holding down wages for those who are covered by their employers, this is a transfer of income from workers to the industry, and it would be outrageous to count it as making people *better* off; precisely the opposite is true. Since most of the increase in the costs of healthcare insurance benefits are attributable to rising prices, adding the price of health benefits to household incomes would almost certainly overestimate income growth more than omitting them underestimates income growth. The rising cost of employer-provided health insurance also contributes to the gap between growth in earnings and growth in productivity.

Even if the benefits were valued at what people would pay for them, they are not cash benefits and, unless they free up income that would otherwise be used to buy the benefits, they do not give people the same freedoms that they get from cash. Medicaid cannot be used for food or for rent, and cash gives the ability to do things that in-kind benefits do not. After-tax cash income, and underlying that, the after-tax wage, remains a key measure of the ability of people to live their lives as they wish.

Wages and income are spent on food, housing, entertainment, and healthcare, among other things, and if prices go up, wages are worth less. We deal with this by correcting money wages for changes in the prices of what people buy, using the consumer price index (CPI), a widely used summary of prices published by the Bureau of Labor Statistics. If the CPI overstates increases in prices, from year to year, then earnings over time are doing better than we think, and better—for both education groups—than what is shown in figure 11.1.

One way in which the CPI could overstate prices is if it fails to make a big enough allowance for the fact that many goods and services are *better* than they used to be; *quality* is rising. Perhaps healthcare *costs* more than it did, but healthcare also *does* more than it did, with routine hip replacements, cataract surgery, drugs to control high blood pressure, and a myriad of other miracles that were not available half a century ago. It is true that there are certainly technological improvements that make our lives better without showing up either in earnings or in lower prices. But making corrections is even more controversial than making none.

The crucial question is whether the higher quality allows people to do as well while spending less, in which case the quality change makes them better off. In some cases, this is the way it works. Think of a higher-quality gasoline that gives twice as much mileage as the original; this is *exactly* the same as if the price of gasoline had been cut by half. But most quality changes are not like this. The older, lower-quality good is often unavailable, so there is no choice but to pay for the improved version. Your car now has an airbag and is thus a higher-quality vehicle, but you cannot buy a car without one. You may love a new good, such as your cellphone, but it generally does not make life cheaper. An extreme example is the rising life expectancy that the US used to enjoy. If the number of years lived beyond sixty-five is rising, that surely increases the wellbeing of the elderly, but do we really want to argue that, because the elderly are better off—as indeed they are—the cost of living has fallen, and their pensions are now too generous? To do so, or to say that the typical worker is doing better than his or her earnings show, is correct only if the improvements—in healthcare, or in better entertainment through the internet, or in more convenience from ATMs—can be turned into hard cash by buying less of the good affected, or less of something else, a possibility that, however desirable, is usually not available. People may be happier as a result of the innovations, but while it is often disputed whether money buys happiness, we have yet to discover a way of using happiness to buy money.

In and Out of the Labor Force

Not only have wages for those with less education done badly in recent decades, but there has also been a decline in working at all, as measured by the fraction of the population who report being employed. For men of prime working age, from twenty-five to fifty-four, there has been a long decline in the employment-to-population ratio. In the late 1960s, all but 5 percent of the group was working; by 2010, at the end of the Great Recession, 20 percent were not employed. In 2018, long into the recovery, 14 percent were still not at work. Of that 14 percent, only a fifth reported being unemployed and looking for work. The rest were not in the labor force.

This trend also shows a marked divide by education. Figure 11.2 presents the employment-to-population ratios from 1980 to 2018 for white men and women aged twenty-five to fifty-four, separately for those with a college degree (in gray) and without (in black). The vertical lines mark

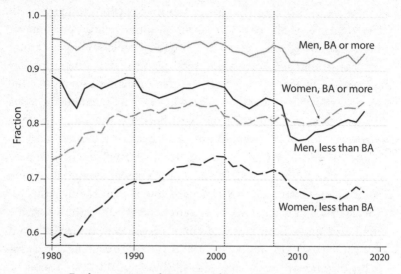

FIGURE 11.2. Employment-to-population ratios, white non-Hispanic men and women, ages 25–54. Recessions noted by vertical lines in the year the recession started. Authors' calculations using the Current Population Survey.

recession years, when we would expect to see employment drop as jobs are lost. When good times return, many of the displaced workers go back to work. However, not all of the prime-age men returned to work after each successive recession, so while the employment-to-population ratio rose following each downturn, it never returned to its level prior to the recession. Over time, the employment-to-population ratio ratcheted down.

After 2000, this downward ratchet was more severe for men with less education; good jobs for less educated men were disappearing, and some of them left the labor force altogether, widening the gap in employment between those with and without a college degree. In the second half of the twentieth century (in part as a result of the arrival of the pill and a lessening of discrimination), women entered the labor force in ever-larger numbers. Their employment proved to be more recession proof than that of men. However, after 2000, women's employment rates fell too—slightly for those with a bachelor's degree, more dramatically for those without. These differing patterns have led to a period in which a larger fraction of women with a degree are working than are men without a degree.

Much of the decline, perhaps half, can be explained by the fall in wages[10]—people are less likely to be in the labor market when wages are lower; some can be explained by the increase in disability that we have already documented, including dependence on opioids; and some by the declining attractiveness of the jobs that are available.

In the American economy since 1970, many jobs have ceased to exist, many of them well paid, such as jobs working in factories for General Motors (recall "Generous Motors") or for Bethlehem Steel. Men followed their fathers, and sometimes even their grandfathers, into well-paid union jobs in manufacturing and earned enough to build a middle-class life, with home ownership, children who attended good schools, and regular vacations. Those men have evocatively been called blue-collar aristocrats. Many of those jobs have gone. Although production by American manufacturing plants continues to grow, jobs in manufacturing have declined rapidly; more than 5 million jobs were eliminated between 1979, which had the all-time peak of 19.5 million, and the eve of the Great Recession in 2007, when they had fallen to 13.8 million. Manufacturing jobs took a large hit during the financial crisis, with another 2 million jobs disappearing, and while employment in manufacturing has rebounded somewhat, the sector is unlikely to regain all of the jobs lost during the Great Recession. These jobs have been replaced by imports from abroad or by automation in factories, globalization, or robots.

None of this is good for the workers who have been displaced. Some withdraw from the search. Most find other jobs, but those other jobs will typically have lower wages or be less attractive in other ways. They may have less autonomy, less opportunity for initiative or for interaction with other people, fewer benefits, and less protection. Workers who are classed as temps, for example, are not covered by compensation for accidents. They may be in jobs where workers are replaceable, turnover is high, and there is little commitment by the employer. People rarely if ever have their wages reduced in a particular job, so it is the movement from good jobs to not-so-good jobs that is largely responsible for the decline in wages for less educated Americans. As we write this (in 2019), the unemployment rate among men aged twenty-five to fifty-four is around 3 percent, so there are plenty of jobs for those who are looking, just not the jobs that once were there, especially high-paying manufacturing jobs for less educated men. This is also why so many people are not looking for work.

If people are not working, it is because they *choose* not to work given their options. Of course, choosing does not imply that people are happy with their choices. Joan of Arc *chose* to burn at the stake, but only because the alternatives were much worse, at least to her. Workers who choose not to work today do not have the alternatives that were once available, though this does not rule out the possibility that they have simply become lazier or less inclined to work, or that they have been induced to be idle through their ability to live off someone else or off the state.

The debate between loss of industriousness, on the one hand, and worsening circumstance, on the other, is an old one, as we saw in chapter 5 on the experience of African Americans in the 1970s and 1980s. But the data in this chapter point clearly toward circumstance. Figure 11.2 shows that workers leave the labor force during recessions, causing the clear ratcheting in the picture. It would be very strange if sudden bursts of laziness were somehow to coincide with recessions; rather, we would expect the increase in laziness to be smooth.[11] Instead, people are leaving the labor force because their jobs have gone, after which most search for and, in time, find other work. The other evidence for circumstance is the combination of figures 11.1 and 11.2. For less educated Americans, participation is falling at the same time that wages are falling. If people were becoming less industrious and pulling out of the labor force to enjoy themselves, wages would go *up*, not *down*; there would be the same number of jobs but fewer people willing to do them. That wages *and* workers fall together is clear evidence that employers want fewer employees.

Some people may choose not to work because the social safety net makes it possible for them to live without work, particularly (although not only) through the disability system, which is increasingly financing people who are not working. Yet recall the large increases in pain and the deterioration in physical and mental health that we documented in chapters 6 and 7; much of the increase in disability can be attributed to the higher prevalence of ill health, rather than to people gaming the system.[12] Europe has a much more extensive safety net than does the United States, including long-term payments for those without work and generous disability systems, especially for older workers. In spite of this, a *larger* fraction of people participates in the labor force in most other rich countries, including in Denmark, Norway, and Sweden, with their famously generous benefit systems. One story notes the range of subsidies those countries provide to services, such as childcare, that make it easier for people to work.[13] The other story is just that Americans are different, and uniquely sensitive to even small benefits, but the evidence suggests not.[14]

When people choose not to work, the supply of workers is lower and wages do not fall as much as they would have to if everyone had to find alternative work. The argument against the safety net, or in favor of work requirements to use it, is an argument for lower wages. If more people had been made to work, the decline in wages for less educated Americans in figure 11.1 would have been larger. The same goes for proposals to make work a condition of receiving health or other benefits, or for schemes such as the Earned Income Tax Credit, which can only be received by those who work; they all push people into the labor market and, by increasing the supply of labor, decrease its price, which is the wage.

If it is indeed true that work is good in and of itself, then the lower wage is offset by the benefits of being at work. People want a job, the job gives their life meaning and social standing, they learn on the job, they meet others, and they have better lives. The contrary argument is that many jobs are pure drudgery, that leisure is itself pleasurable and freedom enhancing, so even if the cost of supporting that leisure is paid by others, it might be a good thing to do. We are often happy to subsidize food or shelter for those who cannot provide it for themselves, the argument goes, so why not leisure? As Bertrand Russell once noted, among the strongest advocates that the poor should work more are the idle rich, who have never done any.[15] Such arguments are important when we come to think about what to do, in chapter 16, and particularly about the much-discussed universal basic income.

The Changing Nature of Work for Those
with Less Education

The American working class has not always existed. The manufacturing
jobs that supported and defined it began to take workers out of agriculture into factories in the nineteenth century, more rapidly so after the
Civil War, and reached a peak around 1950. The rise of the stay-at-home
housewife was relatively new even in 1950; before that, husbands and
wives had cooperated in earning a living. Now the man went to the factory, where he had no more need of advanced education than in agriculture, and found meaning in the dignity of his difficult and productive
labor rather than in the size of his paycheck.[16] He left the home and the
children in the care of his spouse, working *for* his family, not *in* his family.
This life came with strictly enforced social norms about having settled
prospects before getting married and about not having sex outside marriage, let alone having children out of wedlock. Manufacturing and the
working-class life that came with it defined the roles of men and women
and what their family life should look like.[17]

The rise of manufacturing brought a new way of living, and new ways
of finding meaning in work and life. Membership in unions peaked at
about the same time. While not everything that unions did was good, and
while some of the benefits that they long argued for are now provided
by employers as a matter of law, no one else in the workplace argues for
the interests of workers as unions once did. Unions had a seat at the table
when profits were being divided. They raised members' wages (and, to
a lesser extent, the wages of those not in unions), and they policed health
and safety in the workplace. Unionized workers were less likely to quit
and were often more productive.[18] Unions brought some democratic control to workers, at work and more broadly, and were often a key part of
local social life. When unions in America reached their peak in the early
1950s, roughly 33 percent of those in the labor force were members.[19] The
number in 2018 was 10.5 percent, with only 6.4 percent of private-sector
workers members of unions.[20]

As manufacturing jobs have evaporated, workers have had to move
into less desirable, more casual work, more in services—healthcare, food

services, cleaning, and security—and less in manufacturing. The decline in commitment by employers is only matched by the decline in commitment by employees; the war between union and employer has been replaced by mutual disengagement.[21] Many of the less desirable service jobs are jobs where there is little potential for personal or productivity growth, or where people must do exactly what they are told and exactly when they are told, leaving no room for personal initiative. Workers in these jobs are effectively temporary stand-ins for robots, holding their slots until the programmers can teach the robots to replace them.[22]

In James Bloodworth's account of an Amazon warehouse in Britain, located in an ex-mining area north of Birmingham, he meets a man called Alex who reports, "People actually say, 'I'm only at Amazon,' and in the past they would've never said, 'I'm only at the pit.' You'd have said 'I'm a collier,' because that's what you were, and you were proud of it."[23]

In the United States and in other rich countries, there are large corporations that supply labor—cleaners, security, food service workers, or drivers—workers who once would have worked for the firms they are now supplied to and who would have earned relatively high wages there but are today not employed in the place where they work. They earn relatively low wages, often without benefits or full worker protections. This enables high-tech firms—think Google, for example—to employ only people with bachelor's or more advanced degrees, while the support staff around them are outsourced from another firm. According to Bloodworth's account from Britain, as well as an almost identical account from the US,[24] few of the workers in Amazon warehouses ("fulfillment centers") actually work for Amazon. In the American case, the only visible difference between the few employees of Amazon and the many "temps" who work for Integrity Staffing Solutions is the color of their badges, blue versus white. Everything looks the same, similar people are doing similar jobs, but the working conditions of those who are outsourced—sometimes ex-employees—are often worse, with lower wages, fewer benefits, and limited or no possibilities of promotion.

The talented kid who, for one reason or another, did not get educated to his or her ability can no longer work his or her way up from being a janitor to being a CEO, because the janitors and CEOs work for different companies and live in different worlds.[25] There is a world of the more educated, and a world of the less educated; no one in the latter has hope of joining the former. Perhaps most crucially, the outsourced workers are no longer a part of the main company, they do not identify with it, and, in the evocative words of the economist Nicholas Bloom,[26] they are no longer invited to the holiday party. They cannot find pride, meaning, and hope in being a part—however humble—of a great enterprise.

There is yet another side to the collapse of the white working class in America. In many places, and many firms, it was a *white* working class. African Americans were excluded. Whites had a special privilege over blacks, a privilege that lasted for many years. That privilege has diminished or vanished, and, in the words of sociologist Andrew Cherlin, "in an environment in which overall opportunities for blue-collar labor are constricting, white workers perceive black progress as an unfair usurpation of opportunities rather than as a weakening of the privileged racial position they held."[27] According to a Pew survey, more than 50 percent of white working-class Americans believe discrimination against whites has become as big a problem as discrimination against blacks and other minorities, while 70 percent of white college-educated Americans disagree.[28]

The simultaneous loss of a world of work, of the family life that it created and supported, and at least the perception of a loss of racial privilege or even reverse discrimination is a toxic combination that is more powerful than a real but manageable decline in incomes.

12

Widening Gaps at Home

AS THE MARKET has supplied fewer and fewer good jobs for less educated workers, and as people have had to move to worse jobs or to no jobs
at all, there have been consequences not just for their lives at work but
also for their lives at home. The gulf between the less and the more educated has widened, not only in the labor market but also in marriage, in
child rearing, in religion, in social activities, and in participation in the
community. Economists often focus on real income as a measure of how
well people are doing and, indeed, income is important, but it is far from
the only thing that matters. If we want to understand how disruption in
people's lives might drive them to suicide, or to other deaths of despair,
it is to these other aspects of life that we need to look. Not surprisingly,
much of the work on this, which we summarize in this chapter, has been
done by sociologists, who often take a broader approach to life than do
economists.

Marriage

Throughout Western history, a man who wanted to live with a woman
and have children had to be "marriageable." This meant, among other
things, that he could support his bride and had good future "prospects."
Once upon a time, grooms asked permission from the prospective bride's
father before asking for her hand, and the father's obligation was to check
that the groom was likely to be able to provide for his daughter. Such
customs persist today, though the couple is now typically left to check

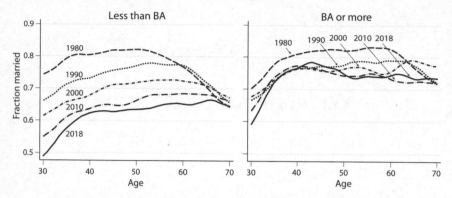

FIGURE 12.1. Fraction of white non-Hispanics who are currently married, by age, year, and education. Authors' calculations using the Current Population Survey.

on their financial situation themselves. As good jobs have become scarcer for less educated men and wages have fallen, so has the supply of marriageable men, and marriage has fallen with it.[1] The working-class family, which had its heyday in the 1950s, had a single male earner, whose wage was enough to support a family, but this ideal has become less attainable for less educated men. Working-class marriage is being undermined by changes in the labor market.

We can see the dramatic change in marriage rates for less educated white non-Hispanics in figure 12.1, which shows the fraction of adults ages thirty to seventy reporting that they are currently married, in decadal years between 1980 and 2018.[2] The left panel reports for those without a four-year degree, and the right panel for those with a degree. In 1980 (the long-dashed lines at the top of each panel), the fraction of whites who were married at any given age was virtually identical for those with and without a bachelor's degree. By 1990, fewer adults reported being married at any given age in both education groups, with the decline generally larger for those without a bachelor's degree. From 1990 to 2018, and in contrast to those with a bachelor's degree, those without a four-year degree continued to see marriage rates fall, decade by decade. In 1980, 82 percent of whites with and without a bachelor's degree were married at age forty-five. By 1990, the rate had dropped to 75 percent for both education groups. Beyond 1990, those with a bachelor's degree maintained that rate, while that for forty-five-year-olds without a bachelor's degree kept declining, to a low of 62 percent in 2018.

There are many benefits of marriage. Not everybody wants to be married, but for those who do, marriage brings intimacy, companionship, fulfillment, and, for many, the joys of children and grandchildren. Married people live longer, are healthier, and are more satisfied with their lives, especially married men, and while it is true that healthier people are more likely to get married in the first place, that is unlikely to explain the difference. To the extent that couples are not marrying because less educated men are less marriageable, the problems in the labor market are not only making them worse off materially but also depriving them of all the benefits that marriage brings, both to themselves and to society more broadly.

For some who do not want to marry, and who might have felt required to do so in the past, the decline in marriage is a positive. Others may choose to postpone marriage to an older age than once was the norm in order to get more education, to develop a career, or simply to play the market and find, or at least search for, the ideal partner. Marriage delay explains the steep increase in marriage rates in their thirties for those with a bachelor's degree. The widespread availability of the contraceptive pill after the late 1960s, and the radical change in attitudes to sex that came with the sexual revolution from 1965 to 1975, made it socially acceptable for couples to have sex outside marriage, and to do so without the fear of unintended pregnancies. The availability of legal abortion after *Roe v. Wade* in 1973 may have also made people less concerned about the consequences of sex. For many women, especially, these changes brought greater freedom—or in economists' jargon, reduced the price—to become better educated or to follow careers in the labor market. Women, equipped with the pill, increasingly enrolled in professional schools.[3] Rapidly spreading feminism in the 1960s and 1970s encouraged women to take advantage of these newfound freedoms. Those who choose the route to later marriage, or even to no marriage at all, are taking advantage of opportunities that previously did not exist, and they are better off. That said, the college educated appear to have simply postponed marriage by a few years; beyond age thirty-five, 75 percent of those in midlife are married.

There is thus a split between those, on the one hand, who miss out on a marriage that they would have liked to have, because their options have become more limited, and those, on the other hand, who opt out, permanently or temporarily, because there are now more options available to them. As is often the case with new possibilities—whether technological or social—some gain and some lose, and those who are better off or better educated are usually more likely to be informed about and in a position to take advantage of the new opportunities and to finish up among the gainers. The divergence, as so often in this book, in large part follows the educational split.

This change in marriage patterns for less educated whites follows parallel changes seen in the black community that began thirty years earlier,[4] and largely for the same reasons.[5] Without a job that can provide for a family, men become less marriageable, and one of the pillars of a stable life moves out of reach.

Childbearing

Once upon a time, when marriage and childbearing were closely related, a decline in marriage would have meant a decline in childbearing. Indeed, for much of Western history, men's wage rates were part of the mechanism that regulated fertility.[6] Over the last half century, the link between marriage and having children has been broken, or is at least breakable at will. There are many socially permissible routes to sexual intimacy, and safe, convenient, and reliable contraception means that sexual intimacy need not risk pregnancy. Marriage can be postponed without giving up intimate partnerships, and childbearing can be postponed until a career is well established or there is a (relatively) convenient window to take time off for parenting. At the same time, the availability of contraception and on-demand abortion has absolved men from their erstwhile responsibility to marry their pregnant partner, with or without her family holding the traditional shotgun. Out-of-wedlock sex and out-of-wedlock childbearing are no longer socially stigmatized.[7]

Yet all of this liberation has a dark side, at least for some. For the women who get pregnant but who do not get married when they have a child, many do not stay with or even remain in contact with the father of their child but move on to another man, with whom they may also have children. Cohabitation has increased in other wealthy countries and has also increased in the US among more educated couples. But unstable and fragile serial cohabitations *with* children are rare elsewhere and rare in America among well-educated women, who generally postpone child-bearing until they complete their education and are married.[8] To paraphrase sociologist Andrew Cherlin,[9] there are now two different modes of transitioning to adulthood. One, among the more educated, involves finishing college, taking a job, and developing a career before marrying and having children. The other, among the less educated, involves serial cohabitation and childbearing out of wedlock. Americans who have had children with multiple partners are most likely to be found among those without a bachelor's degree.

The sociology literature rightly focuses on the consequences of these patterns for children, who tend to do much worse in fractured, fragile relationships than they would do in intact families where both parents are present. But there are also consequences of serial cohabitation and out-of-wedlock childbearing for the adults; such dysfunctional family arrangements are a prime suspect in the spread of despair.

For the women, one might wonder why they make the choices they do; it is no secret that men are no longer bound by the old rules, and that, if the woman has a child, she is likely to face a cycle of economic hardship, emotional instability, and lack of support from which some will find it hard to escape. Yet they may have limited choices. When so many women are prepared to engage in sexual relationships outside marriage, it undercuts the bargaining power of those who would prefer to wait. Once pregnant, many women do not want to have an abortion, although many do; while the number of abortions is falling rapidly, abortion is not rare. At 2014 rates, one in four women in the US will have an abortion by age forty-five, and in the same year there were 14.6 abortions per 1,000 women aged fifteen to forty-four[10] (compared with 62.9 live births). For many women, having a child is seen as a blessing, an affirmation of the value of life, a redemption and a hope for the future. It is a success that is within the grasp of women who cannot imagine themselves going to college. The joy of announcing a pregnancy is just as real and full of hope as the joy of announcing admission to a good college or an important promotion at work. The future is bright and full of blessings, if only for the moment.[11]

For single mothers, once the child or children exist, the welfare support provided by the Aid to Families with Dependent Children program penalized marriage. This may have had some effect on preventing mothers from marrying postpregnancy, and it was one of the reasons that Aid to Families with Dependent Children was replaced in 1996 after sixty years in place.

That the fathers are victims too may seem unlikely. They get the pleasure without the commitment and are liberated from some of their financial and emotional responsibilities. But they have struck a Faustian bargain, splendid and promising at first, but with a high price to be paid in the end. By the time they reach middle age, not only have many of their careers and earnings failed to match those of their parents, or what they expected of themselves, but they have no stable family with which they have shared lives and memories. They may have children from a series of relationships, some or none of whom they know and some of whom are living with other men. Such fractured and fragile relationships bring little daily joy or comfort and do little to assure middle-aged men that they are living a good life.

For both men and women, the old social rules—restrictive and unforgiving although they might have been—encapsulated long-accreted social wisdom that prevented people from making lifetime decisions that they might well live to regret.

We are here writing about less educated whites, but the same descriptions have long been used to describe family arrangements among African Americans. Once again, we are seeing a convergence across races. The rate of nonmarital childbearing among black women without a college degree has been high, but stable, since 1990 and has been declining since 2010. In contrast, the rate among white women without a college degree more than doubled between 1990 and 2017, rising from 20 percent to more than 40 percent of births. As nonmarital births fall among blacks and rise among less educated whites, class is becoming a more important divide than race. Cherlin notes, "If you want a mental image of the typical woman who has several intimate partners while raising children, picture a white woman with a high school education."[12]

Community

In his famous book *Bowling Alone*, political scientist Robert Putnam describes a marked decline in social capital in the last third of the twentieth century;[13] Americans participated less and less in a wide range of social activities involving other people—family dinners, evenings at home with friends, and activities in institutions, like churches, unions and clubs. Since Putnam wrote in 2000, most of these downward trends have continued and, in some cases, have accelerated. As with family arrangements, there are divides by the level of education, some of which are widening.

Material living standards, health, family, and children are foundations of wellbeing, and so is community and, for most Americans, religious faith. In Gallup data from 2008 to 2012, two-thirds of Americans said that religion was very important in their daily lives.[14] Once again, we need not follow the economists' practice of trying to value these other aspects of life or reduce them to a monetary equivalent. There is no need to force health, family, community, and religion into the straitjacket that the metric of wealth requires; their importance cannot be measured by how much they cost or how much people would pay to have them.

One way in which people get involved in their local and national communities is by participating in politics, most obviously by voting for their preferred candidates or policies. Community participation brings its own direct rewards, even if you do not always get what you want. But those who participate are indeed more likely to get what they want. People aged sixty-five and over are 50 percent more likely to vote in presidential elections than those aged eighteen to twenty-nine—78 percent of the elderly voted in the elections from 1996 to 2016, while 53 percent of young adults did so—which has much to do with the relative

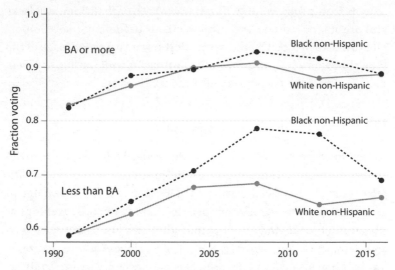

FIGURE 12.2. Presidential election turnout, by race and education, ages 25–64. Authors' calculations using the Current Population Survey.

generosity of public policy toward the elderly. Income is correlated with voting, as is education, and legislators are more likely to favor the richer and better-educated voters among their constituents.[15]

Figure 12.2 presents voter turnout by race and education in the six most recent presidential elections (1996 to 2016). Each point represents the fraction of twenty-five-to-sixty-four-year-olds who reported voting in that election year. Participation rose from 1996 to the first Obama election in 2008 and fell thereafter. The largest divide, evident in the figure, is by education: those with a four-year degree are consistently 20 percentage points more likely to vote than those without. Aside from the Obama elections, when turnout among African American voters was higher, there was little daylight in participation between whites and blacks within an education group. The divide is one of class, not race.

Union membership has rapidly declined since midcentury; it is a form of social capital that is obviously most important for working-class people. More than a third of nonagricultural employees belonged to unions in the mid-1950s; since then, membership has fallen, to less than 10 percent in 2017, with close to equal numbers of union members in the public and private sectors. But the private sector employs many more workers than does the public sector, and workers in the latter are more than five times more likely to belong to a union than workers in the former. The rapid decline in private-sector unionization has been a major factor in enhancing the power of capital relative to labor (and may have been caused in part by the change in the relative power of capital), an issue that we will come back to in chapter 15. But as with political participation, belonging to a union does more than help represent a worker's economic interests. Union meetings and union-based clubs are, or once were, part of social life in many places.

When I join a union, that is good not only for me but also for others; my joining strengthens the union, and thus brings benefits to other members. The same is true when I join a club or a church, and it applies generally to social capital. My joining brings what is called a network externality; the behavior of one person affects the costs and benefits of others. This happens for social media, such as Facebook, and church, where the benefits of belonging expand with the number of members. As with Facebook, network externalities can lead to very rapid growth in membership because the rate of growth goes up with the number of members; the more members, the faster the growth, at least until there are no more people who have an interest in joining. The process also works in reverse. As people drop out, the union or the church is less attractive to the remaining members, and organizations with network externalities can collapse as rapidly as they expand. For private-sector unions, this is surely part of the story. Once people start leaving, not only does the union hall or the union sports team close, but the union loses some of its power to deliver benefits to its members, so there is less and less point in belonging.

Religion is an important part of life for most Americans, much more so than in other rich countries, at least with the exception of Italy and, to a lesser extent, Ireland. Religious people do better in many ways: they are happier, more generous, and less likely to smoke, drink, or use drugs. Friends make a good life better, and friends from church do so by more than other friends.[16]

Church membership in the US has been declining in recent decades, especially among the less educated, who were less likely to go to church in the first place. Not everyone who says that religion is important to them belongs to a church or goes to one regularly; today about a third of Americans report that they have been to a place of worship in the last week.[17] The number was closer to a half in the late 1950s; there was a slow decline until 1980, after which attendance held steady at around 40 percent until 2000, after which there was a steep plunge.

We often think of religion as something that you inherit from your parents and that is constant through life, at least if you do not lapse. And indeed, the large number of Catholics in the Northeast is a legacy of Irish and Italian immigration, just as the expanding number of Catholics in the South and West today is a consequence of Hispanic immigration. But religious affiliation is not just the fossilized history of immigration. It also reflects the fact that people change their affiliations, sometimes by drifting away from the church in which they grew up, and sometimes by a move to a different church when the teaching of the old church no longer seems relevant or no longer matches people's political and social beliefs. In the 1960s and 1970s, a period of great social upheaval in sexual norms and civil rights, and of increasing distrust in government, many people stopped going to church altogether, while others, disturbed by the changes and unimpressed by the lack of a vigorous response by mainline churches, moved to evangelical and socially conservative churches.[18] After 2000, the decline in membership in the mainline churches was complemented by a decline in membership in evangelical churches, especially among young people who were not as attracted as their parents had been by the socially conservative political beliefs those churches espoused. Large numbers of Americans seem to choose their religion to suit their politics.

There has been a rapid rise in those who report themselves to be unaffiliated with any religion. From the mid-1970s until 1990, only 7 or 8 percent were "nones." In 2016, almost 25 percent of the population was unaffiliated, and among young working-class whites (ages eighteen to twenty-nine), the percentage rises to nearly 50.[19] Parenthetically, these are a part of wider changes in American religion, and in America more generally. Only 43 percent of Americans identify as white Christians, compared with 65 percent in 1996, and 54 percent as late as 2006. The white Christian majority in America no longer exists, and this may be seen as yet another unwelcome change to some among the white working class.

Evangelical and mainline churches are different beyond their political beliefs. Many mainline churches provide what sociologist Robert Wuthnow calls "spirituality of dwelling."[20] These churches are spiritual homes that have been refuges and places of worship for generations, often reaching back to the country of the original immigrants; examples are Catholics from Italy, Ireland, or Mexico and Lutherans from Scandinavia or Germany. These churches provide a spiritual sanctuary when economic or family life is challenging. They can also be seen as stultifying and oppressive. Wuthnow's contrast with dwelling is "seeking," where people try to satisfy their spirituality on their own terms—for example, by turning to evangelical churches that suit their social conservatism, or by creating their own unique blend of beliefs outside an organized church. This is one aspect of the increase in individualism, something that sociologist Andrew Cherlin calls one of the "master trends in the development of Western society over the last few centuries."[21] These alternatives can provide freedom to explore spirituality more freely, outside what some see as abusive church organizations, but they may not provide the reassurance or unquestioning acceptance that comes in mainline churches whose rituals and traditions have been familiar since childhood, have provided succor in time of trouble, and have done the same for previous generations. Many Americans are currently unconnected to any organized religion but explore their spirituality through self-constructed beliefs that are sometimes isolating: the social ethnographers Kathryn Edin and her collaborators report on a man whose spirituality centers on ancient-astronaut theories and who complains of the difficulty of finding people to talk to about it.[22] This isolation is an example of what Edin and her coauthors call the tenuous attachment of working-class men.

The General Social Survey asks people how often they go to church, and figure 12.3 shows the fraction of the middle-aged white population

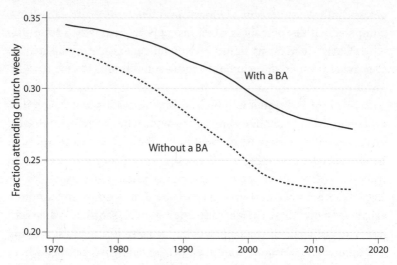

FIGURE 12.3. Weekly church attendance, whites ages 40–59. Authors' calculations using the
General Social Survey.

(aged forty to fifty-nine) who report that they attend church weekly; the
samples are small here, so we have used a twenty-year age range and
smoothed out year-to-year fluctuations.

Those with a bachelor's degree are more likely to attend church
weekly, and the gap between the education groups has been widening
over time. Even among these older adults, who have been less ready to
opt out of church than the young, attendance is falling, and more rapidly
so among the less educated. The white working class is losing the community support that can come from both unions and church.

If we draw the same figure for African Americans, with due warnings
about small sample size, there is no evidence of a decrease in weekly attendance for those without a bachelor's degree. About a third of midlife
blacks without a bachelor's degree attend church weekly, about the same
rate as that for less educated midlife whites in the early 1970s, but for
blacks, unlike whites, attendance has held steady.

Why is lack of religiosity and the decline in churchgoing a problem?
West Virginia, the state worst affected by deaths of despair, is among the
most religious in America; 70 percent of white working-age people say

that religion is very important in their lives. In both New York and California, much less severely affected, only 51 percent say that religion is very important to them. Perhaps it would be no bad thing if West Virginians were *less* religious?

One answer is that, over long enough periods of time, religiosity responds to the social and economic environment. In poor countries around the world, especially in Asia and Africa, almost everyone identifies as very religious, but religiosity is lower in richer industrialized countries, particularly in Western Europe. The argument—the secularization hypothesis—is that as education spreads, as incomes rise, and as the state takes over many functions of the church, people turn away from religion. Put crudely, people need religion more in more hostile environments. This would fit the American states, where those with lower incomes and less supportive state governments have a higher fraction of religious people. It would also explain why it is true that, while more religious *people* do better than less religious people on many outcomes—they are happier, less likely to commit crimes, less likely to abuse drugs and alcohol, and less likely to smoke—more religious *places*—including US states—do worse on the same outcomes.[23] Religion helps people do better, and they espouse religion in part *because* their local environment is difficult. When religiosity falls over time, it is the *people* side of this story that applies, and people lose the benefits that religion brings.

How Do People Evaluate Their Own Lives?

It is tempting to look for an overall measure of people's lives, one that somehow combines all of the things that matter to people, including material wellbeing, health, family, community, and religion. We do not think that this is either possible or desirable; too much is lost by forcing the different aspects of life into a single measure, and very little is gained beyond what we get by thinking about each aspect one at a time. In recent years, some writers have taken a different view and argued that if we ask people how happy they are, or how their lives are going, we will get the magic number that can stand in for everything else.[24] There are good philosophical and empirical arguments for rejecting this claim. Even

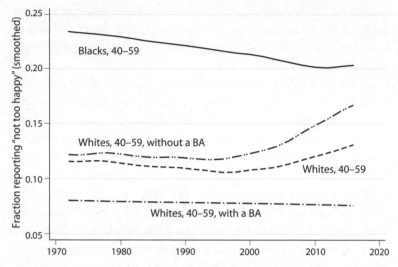

FIGURE 12.4. The fraction of adults ages 40–59 reporting they are "not too happy." Authors' calculations using the General Social Survey.

so, people's evaluations of their own lives are valuable, provided we do not expect too much of them. They capture what people themselves think, not "expert" measures like income, life expectancy, or church attendance, each of which is at best a proxy and which may not seem relevant to those who experience them. Beyond that, the evidence shows that self-reported life evaluation measures vary as we would expect with life circumstances, including income, health, religion, and education. For people to think that their lives are going well is a good thing in and of itself, even if it does not capture all the things they care about. Similarly, when we are trying to get an idea of the quality of people's lives, we can use self-reports of how life is going as a supplement to the other measures.

The General Social Survey, which we used in the previous section to look at religion, asks respondents how happy they are "with things these days," with three possible answers: very happy, pretty happy, and not too happy. Figure 12.4 presents the fractions of different groups, ages forty to fifty-nine, reporting that they were "not too happy," over the period from 1972 to 2016. For all whites in midlife taken together (presented in the dashed line), this measure showed little change until the late 1990s, after which the fraction of midlife whites who are "not too happy" began to rise. That this change is being driven by those without a bachelor's degree can be seen by comparing the responses by education. Throughout this period, a larger fraction of whites without a bachelor's degree reported being dissatisfied, but that dissatisfaction appears to have been stable until the mid-1990s. Beyond that point, dissatisfaction among those with less than a bachelor's degree began to grow, and the gap between whites with and without a bachelor's degree steadily increased.

More midlife African Americans are unhappy than midlife whites, but the fraction who report being "not too happy" fell steadily until 2010, after which it leveled off at 20 percent. (The samples in the survey are too small to split blacks by college degree.) If this is real—and we repeat the caveats about self-reported happiness measures—the happiness responses are showing something that does not show up in the material wellbeing data: that African American lives, though unhappier than whites, are getting better in a way that is not true for whites, especially less educated whites.

A more precise evaluation of how life is going comes from a different question. The Cantril ladder asks people to place themselves on a ladder with rungs, labeled from zero to ten, in which zero is the worst possible life that you can imagine for yourself, and ten is the best possible. This measure is sometimes referred to as the "ladder of life." Note that this question does not mention happiness; it is simply a way of asking people to evaluate their own lives. Gallup has asked this question to several million Americans since 2008, so, although we cannot go back in time, we have enough data to look in detail, particularly by race, age, and education.

The most remarkable feature of figure 12.5 is that the big differences are between those with and without a bachelor's degree, not between blacks (shown as solid lines) and whites (shown as broken lines). Indeed, after age forty, blacks without a bachelor's degree have better self-reports than whites, though the reverse is true for younger blacks

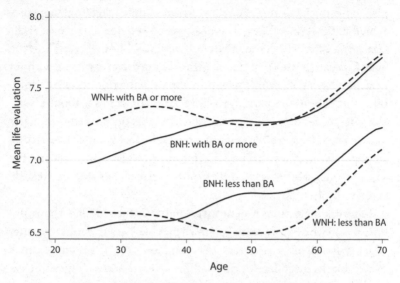

FIGURE 12.5. Self-reports of life evaluation by age, race, and education.
WNH = white non-Hispanics; BNH = black non-Hispanics. Authors'
calculations using Gallup tracking data, US, 2010–17.

with a bachelor's degree. Blacks do not experience the midlife dip in
wellbeing that whites do, whether or not they have a bachelor's degree.
Lest we are misunderstood, we say again that self-evaluation is not a
measure of everything that is important to people, and the rough equiv-
alence of life evaluation for blacks and whites within education groups
provides no warrant for ignoring measures on which blacks do worse,
or for ignoring the fact that many fewer blacks have college degrees.

Gallup also asks questions about whether people are experiencing
stress or physical pain, and whether they are happy or sad. For most of
these measures, as for the ladder of life, the biggest divisions are by education, not by race. This is true for a summary measure of daily positive
mood—that averages how much people smile, enjoy themselves, and are
happy—as well as for pain;[25] the divisions in experience are entirely by
education, with no difference by race given education. Stress, by contrast,
shows little difference by education, but a large difference by race. Remarkably, this difference is in *favor* of blacks, many fewer of whom

report that they experienced a lot of stress on the day before the survey. Taken as a whole, for these measures of experience, it is education that matters, not race, except for stress, where blacks do better than whites.

In Summary

Life is about much more than money, and in this chapter, we have looked at several nonmonetary outcomes—family, child rearing, religion, and political participation—as well as self-reported assessments of life. Less educated whites, whose wage rates have fallen for half a century, do worse than better-educated whites, and in several aspects, especially marriage and childbearing, the gap between the two groups is widening in an alarming way. The decline of unions has worsened working and social life for less educated whites, who have also become increasingly detached from the support and community that religion can bring. We find it hard to believe that the spread of the internet and of social media has made up for the loss of these institutions.

Ultimately, of course, we are trying to find an explanation for the dreadful mortality trends with which we began, the deaths of despair. Declining wages are part of the story, but we believe that it is impossible to explain despair through declining material advantage. We believe that much more important for despair is the decline of family, community, and religion. These declines may not have happened without the decline in wages and in the quality of jobs that made traditional working-class life possible. But it was the destruction of a way of life that we see as central, not the decrease in material wellbeing; wages work through these factors, not directly.

The contrasting outcomes for African Americans are informative. Even though blacks have made at best modest wage gains in recent years, and little or none since the 1970s, and although blacks do worse than whites on most indicators, even than less educated whites, black lives are improving on many dimensions while the lives of less educated whites are worsening. When we look more broadly, the mortality trends between blacks and whites make much more sense.

PART IV

Why Is Capitalism
Failing So Many?

WE HAVE DOCUMENTED DESPAIR AND DISTRESS, death by suicide, drug overdose, and alcoholism, as well as pain, decreasing attachment to work, falling wages, and failing family life. The plague that has visited less educated whites over the last three decades descended on African Americans fifty years ago. While racial divisions are diminishing in many outcomes, class divisions are widening, at least if we think of class in terms of education.

In this final part of the book, we tell a story about why it happened and what might be done. What has eaten away at the foundations of working-class life?

This part of the book is the only one with an introduction. The other three parts are largely about *what* happened, while this part is about *why* it happened, and why is always more complicated than what. The first three chapters that follow all tell stories about what is happening in the labor market for less educated Americans, why the real value of their earnings has fallen, through either lower wages or higher prices or both, and why working conditions have deteriorated. There are many different forces that are undermining working life for people with less education, but they all lead to the consequences for marriage and for community that we have documented and, ultimately, set the conditions for the rise in deaths of despair.

Our first story is peculiarly American: that it is some feature of *American* capitalism that is failing so many. There have been increases in deaths of despair in a few other rich countries, but where they do exist, the numbers are dwarfed by those in the United States. Perhaps our title should be *Deaths of Despair and the Future of* American *Capitalism*?

There is a second story: that the faults of contemporary capitalism are widespread and America is simply the leader of a more general disaster that is already taking root elsewhere and will spread further in the future.

We suspect that the truth has elements of both stories, that specific American arrangements exaggerate and catalyze the catastrophe, so that while the US is indeed in the vanguard, with others following, other countries are unlikely to be ever as severely affected.

There are many features of the United States that are relevant, and that differ from other countries. The history of race is different in America; the shadow of slavery and racism still haunts American life today. As we have seen in chapter 11, the improvements in the lives of African Americans have not been perceived as an unmixed blessing by many whites. Another leading explanation centers on social protection. Other rich countries have more extensive safety nets than does the United States, and they are differently organized, depending more on government and less on the private sector. American politics is different too, with its dependence on large sums of campaign finance and on lobbying.

Yet our candidate for leading villain is none of these but rather the American healthcare system. This is the topic of chapter 13.

There is a paradox here. America spends more on healthcare than does any other nation, and it boasts some of the finest hospitals and doctors in the world; patients come from all over the globe to be treated in American hospitals. How is it then possible that life expectancy at birth has fallen for three years in a row—something that has not happened in other countries and that has not happened in America since the Great Influenza Pandemic of a century ago? The truth is that these horrors are happening not *in spite of* the American healthcare system but *because of* it. The next chapter makes the argument. It is *not* an argument about poor healthcare or lack of coverage, though there is much that could be said about both; the deaths from prescription opioids were caused by the healthcare system, and even after Obamacare twenty-seven million Americans have no health insurance.[1] But a far worse problem is the enormous *cost*. The vast sums that are being spent on healthcare are an unsustainable drag on the economy, pushing down wages, reducing the number of good jobs, and undermining financing for education, infrastructure, and the provision of public goods and services that are (or might be) provided by federal and state governments. Working-class life is certainly under threat from automation and from globalization, but healthcare costs are both precipitating and accelerating the decline.

The cost of healthcare is like a tribute that Americans have to pay to a foreign power.[2] An analogy comes from the reparations that Germany had to pay after the First World War. John Maynard Keynes wrote a famous book predicting that the payments would be a disaster.[3] While historians today argue about how much was actually paid, and about the effects on the destruction of the Weimar Republic and the rise of Hitler, it is clear that reparations dominated European international relations for many years.[4] Yet the fraction of national income that Germany paid in the 1920s was substantially smaller than the fraction of American income that is *unnecessarily* spent on healthcare today.[5] Even if the healthcare system were delivering in terms of health—which it is not—the cost would still debilitate the economy, especially the part of the economy that serves less educated Americans. Warren Buffett likened the effects of healthcare costs on American business to those of a tapeworm; we think of them as a cancer that has metastasized throughout the economy, strangling its ability to deliver what Americans need.

We believe that the healthcare debacle is a cause of decline and despair, but it is not the only one. Other stories point to the way that modern capitalism works, arguing that it has turned increasingly against less-educated labor and more in favor of an educated minority. One key argument is that corporations have accumulated market power that is increasingly used against both workers and consumers. Many of these practices are prohibited by antitrust law, and many believe that these laws are not being as vigorously enforced as they should be. In addition, unions were once a countervailing power that could resist the power of capital and protect the wages and working conditions of workers, but unions have greatly declined in importance, especially in the private sector. There has also been much consolidation of firms, so that, if American business is less competitive than it used to be, firms have power to artificially lower the wages of their workers and artificially raise the prices of their goods; these actions redistribute real income from workers and consumers to managers and the owners of capital. This upward redistribution would not happen under free-market capitalism with well-enforced antitrust laws, without government granting favors to special interests and cronies.

The arguments about harm are controversial among professional economists and among politicians and policy makers. On one side are claims that modern large corporations are monopolies that have brought a new gilded age in which consumers and workers are immiserated. On the other side are claims that large corporations are enormously beneficial to us all because they bring low prices and marvelous innovations. Critiques of capitalism are not peculiar to the United States, though the policies that regulate it are different in Europe. It is also possible that both the good and the bad are more developed in the US than elsewhere, which would play into the argument that what we document for the US is a simply a precursor of events that will unfold elsewhere.

We cannot resolve these issues here because the research is far from complete. Instead, we attempt to provide a balanced account in chapter 15, if only to identify those aspects of modern capitalism that are arguably undermining the lives of less educated Americans.

The arguments in the next three chapters apply to all Americans, not only to white non-Hispanics. Yet, as we saw in chapter 5, the deaths of despair have been primarily among whites, at least until fentanyl hit black communities after 2012.

Our argument is that the deaths of despair among whites would not have happened, or would not have been so severe, without the destruction of the white working class, which, in turn, would not have happened without the failure of the healthcare system and other problems of the capitalism we have today—particularly persistent upward redistribution through manipulation of markets. We argued in chapter 5 that African Americans have not escaped the crisis but rather experienced their own version first, thirty years earlier. During that earlier episode of black despair, job loss, and family and community destruction, much of the dysfunction was attributed to peculiarities of black culture. Now this episode looks like something different, that if any group is treated badly enough for long enough, it is susceptible to suffering social breakdown of one kind or another. African Americans, long the least-favored group, were the first to suffer, but less educated whites were next in line. It is not absurd to imagine the distress moving up to more highly educated groups next.

The reduction in racial animus toward blacks and their gradually increasing opportunities have provided offsetting forces that, for blacks, have counteracted the negative pressures faced by all workers. We have seen that African Americans have, in the last two decades, seen some absolute improvements, not just relative to whites. Black mortality rates fell rapidly, at least until 2014. The percentage of blacks with a bachelor's degree rose from 16 percent in the birth cohort of 1945 to 25 percent in the birth cohort of 1985.[6] Once we take education into account, blacks do as well as or better than whites on a range of measures of life satisfaction and affect. Yet there is nothing in the economic record in recent decades to suggest any systematic improvement in material outcomes for blacks relative to whites. The relative improvement for African Americans must have come from somewhere else. Perhaps the most obvious source of improvement is that black lives are better in nonmaterial ways. Discrimination is far from gone, but it is less severe and pervasive than it used to be; it is no longer socially sanctioned. One excellent indicator of respect is the acceptability of intermarriage; it was once taboo and is now considered normal. According to Gallup, 87 percent of Americans surveyed in 2013 approved of black-white marriage; in 1958, the percentage was only 4. It was only 29 percent in 1973, and still less than two-thirds in 2000. The Gallup pollster Frank Newport refers to this as "one of the largest shifts of public opinion in Gallup history."[7] There have been many successful black politicians and, most importantly, there has been a black president of the United States. The differences between blacks and whites, once predominantly about skin color and racism, now have more to do with education and skills.

For whites, it might be argued that the same process works in reverse, as the privileges of Jim Crow have been withdrawn. Sociologist Andrew Cherlin writes that whites "did not consider their status until their whiteness premium was lessened by legislation in the last few decades of the twentieth century. At that late date, the old, whiteness-based system had been in place so long as to be invisible to them, and the new equal opportunity laws seemed to white workers less like the removal of racial privilege and more like the imposition of reverse discrimination."[8] The economist Ilyana Kuziemko and her coauthors have found evidence from the laboratory that people greatly dislike being in last place, irrespective of their material conditions, and will resist changes that improve the lot of those below them if, in consequence, that bottom group threatens to overtake them.[9]

A final note on how we think about "why." We think about causes more in the spirit of historians and sociologists, which is very different from the way many economists think about causality today. Some economists now endorse the idea that a controlled experiment is required to demonstrate causality, or at least some historical circumstance that separates otherwise-identical people into groups that are differentially exposed to an event. Such techniques have their uses, but they are of little use to us here in describing a slowly evolving and large-scale disintegration that involves a historically contingent set of forces, many of which interact. Some hard-nosed social scientists argue that anything learned in such circumstances is illusory.[10] We fundamentally disagree. Our readers will have to decide whether our account is persuasive without the benefit of controlled trials or anything of the sort.

13

How American Healthcare Is Undermining Lives

AMERICANS SPEND VAST sums on healthcare, and that spending affects almost every part of the economy. Healthcare is expensive everywhere, and it makes good sense for rich countries to spend a large share of what they have to extend their citizens' lives and to reduce pain and suffering. But America does this about as badly as it is possible to imagine.

Our argument is less about the *direct* harm that healthcare can sometimes do, through medical mistakes, through poor treatment, through the overprescription of opioids, or through not providing treatment when it is needed. It is more about the *indirect* harm to people's lives and work that comes from its extraordinary and extraordinarily inappropriate costs. The US healthcare system, which absorbs 18 percent of the American gross domestic product (GDP)—$10,739 per person in 2017,[1] about four times what the country spends on defense and about three times what it spends on education—is needlessly eating away at workers' wages. Paying for it reduces take-home pay as well as the value of what that pay will buy. It inflates the earnings of those in the healthcare industry and makes the industry larger than it ought to be. The cost of employer-provided health insurance, largely invisible to employees, not only holds down wages but also destroys jobs, especially for less skilled workers, and replaces good jobs with worse jobs. As people take worse jobs, their wages fall. Healthcare costs also strike directly those individuals who are without insurance or have inadequate insurance, and they affect those who *are* insured through copayments, deductibles, and employee contributions. They also affect the federal government as well as state governments, which pay for Medicare and Medicaid. Governments must collect more taxes; provide less of something else, such as infrastructure or public education, on which poorer Americans particularly depend; or run deficits that can compromise future economic growth, shifting the burden to our children and to future taxpayers.

To use Adam Smith's words about monopolies, the American healthcare system is both "absurd and oppressive."[2]

Healthcare is necessarily expensive, and there is no doubt that we *should* be spending a lot on it; it makes good sense to give up some of our wealth for better and longer lives, and to do so by more the richer we get.[3] New treatments that prolong life or make it better are continually being produced; they can be expensive to invent or to use, and it will often be a good idea to pay those costs. That said, we spend too much and needlessly so. We will argue that we could cut back costs by at least a third without compromising our health.

As we saw in chapter 9 on opioids, one part of the healthcare industry— manufacturers and distributors of pharmaceuticals—became enormously wealthy by triggering an epidemic that has killed tens of thousands of people. This is an extreme example of direct harm to health, as well as of the process of upward redistribution in which those at the top got rich at the expense of everyone else, many of whom were put at risk of addiction and death. This direct harm to health must be charged to the healthcare industry along with the indirect harm from the economic tribute that it is exacting from the economy as a whole. Death by accidental overdose is the most prevalent of the three kinds of deaths of despair; many of these can be attributed to the opioid epidemic spurred by the industry, though we need also to look at the deterioration in lives that predisposed some people to addiction. Deaths by suicide and alcohol are rising among those who are finding work and family life increasingly difficult. Those deaths are being hastened by the costs of healthcare.

In the next chapter, we discuss other industries and how they too may have contributed to deaths of despair. Yet healthcare is different, not only because it can kill directly but also because the economics of healthcare are fundamentally different from the economics of other industries. While free-market competition is a good benchmark for much of the economy, where we can rely on the market to produce good outcomes, that is not true for healthcare. Free-market competition does not and cannot deliver socially acceptable healthcare.[4]

Healthcare Expenditures and Health Outcomes

American healthcare is the most expensive in the world, and yet American health is among the worst among rich countries, something that has been true for a long time, well before the recent epidemic of deaths and the decrease in life expectancy. The costs of providing healthcare are a heavy drag on the economy, contribute to the long-term stagnation in wages, and are a good example of reverse Robin Hood redistribution, what we have called Sheriff of Nottingham redistribution. The industry is not very good at promoting health, but it excels at promoting wealth among healthcare providers, including some successful private physicians who operate extremely profitable practices. It also delivers vast sums to the owners and executives of pharmaceutical companies, of medical device manufacturers, of insurers—including "nonprofit" insurers—and of large, ever more monopolistic hospitals.

Figure 13.1 shows how other countries differ from the United States, and how the difference is widening over time. Britain, Australia, France, Canada, and Switzerland are used as comparison countries, and they are representative of what is found in the rest of the rich world.[5] The vertical and horizontal axes show life expectancy and health expenditure per capita, respectively, and each line shows the trajectory of the two magnitudes from 1970 through to 2017, one year at a time. (Expenditures are in real international dollars, so the US figure for 2017 differs from the $10,739 quoted earlier.)

The United States is the outlier in the picture; it has lower life expectancy than the other countries, but vastly higher expenditures per person on health. In 1970, which is the first year in the figure, the countries were not very far apart, with American life expectancy not much worse

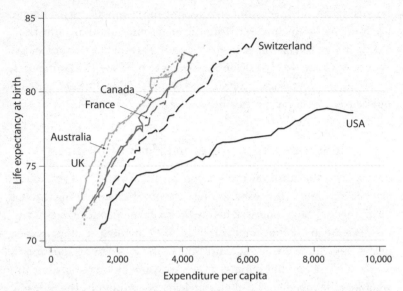

FIGURE 13.1. Life expectancy at birth and health expenditure per capita, US, Switzerland, and other select countries. Life expectancy in years; expenditures in 2010 international dollars. Updated by the authors from Roser (2017).

and expenditures not much higher, but other countries have done much better since, in terms of both faster improvements in health and slower cost increases. Switzerland is the nearest to the United States, with other countries close to one another; if other wealthy countries were added, they would look more like the lower-spending countries than either Switzerland or the United States.

In 2017, the Swiss lived 5.1 years longer than Americans but spent 30 percent less per person; other countries achieve a similar length of life for still fewer health dollars. Expenditure on healthcare in 2017 was 17.9 percent of GDP in the United States; the next highest in the world was Switzerland at 12.3 percent. If a fairy godmother were somehow to reduce the share of healthcare in American GDP not to the average of rich countries but, less ambitiously, only to the second highest, Switzerland, 5.6 percent of GDP would be available for other things, freeing up more than a *trillion* dollars.[6] That is more than $3,000 a year for each man, woman, and child in the US, or about $8,300 for each household. Median household income in 2017 was $61,000, and the poverty line for a family of two adults and two children was $25,000. If each household were given an additional $8,300 in 2017, median income growth over the past thirty years would have been double what it actually was. And at the risk of pushing our fairy godmother too far: If Switzerland, why not Canada? That would save $1.4 trillion, $4,250 for each person, or $11,000 per household.

Another way to count the waste is to identify directly the parts of spending that are not contributing to Americans' health. The most recent calculation[7] is that waste is about a quarter of total spending, which is about the same as we get by the comparison with Switzerland.

These very large numbers are the *waste*, not the total costs. This waste has been eating away at living standards gradually but cumulatively for nearly half a century. American workers would have much better lives today if they had not had to pay this enormous tribute.

What Do Americans Get for What They Spend?

Given the great costs, we might hope that Americans have superior health outcomes. Not so. As we have seen, the United States does not do well in life expectancy, which is one important measure of health. While many factors influence life expectancy other than healthcare, healthcare is important and increasingly so in recent years. Life expectancy in the United States was 78.6 years in 2017, with Hispanics notably higher than the national average (81.8) and non-Hispanic blacks notably lower (74.9).[8] These numbers are lower than the life expectancies of twenty-five other member countries in the Organisation for Economic Co-operation and Development. Among these others, the *lowest* life expectancy was 81.1, in Germany, two and a half years longer than in the United States, and the highest was 84.2, in Japan.[9] Whatever Americans are getting from their healthcare system, it is not more years of life.

Perhaps they are getting something else? America is a very rich country, and it makes sense for Americans to ask and pay for more and better healthcare. Yet Americans do not use more of most medical services than other countries, though there has been a large expansion of jobs in healthcare—2.8 million between 2007 and 2017, a third of all new jobs in the country—mostly funded by the "profits" from nonprofits.[10] Indeed, the US has fewer doctors per head—the American Medical Association has been effective in holding salaries up by holding down the number of places in medical schools—and has about as many nurses per head. Medical schools are expensive, which is often cited to justify doctors' salaries, but if the schools were opened up to competition with no caps on places, they would cost less. If qualified foreign doctors were not so systematically excluded, both salaries and medical school fees would fall. For some procedures, the numbers performed are similar in the US and the rest of the rich world, though there are more of the more profitable procedures in the US.[11] Americans do seem to have a more luxurious system—business rather than coach, as it were—but like business and coach passengers, they usually get to their destination at the same time (or in this case, perhaps earlier if their destination is the afterlife). Compared with patients in some other countries, Americans wait for a shorter period for procedures (such as hip or knee replacements) or for tests, such as mammograms; short waits are possible because there is a lot of expensive machinery that is not used very intensively. Hospital rooms are private or semiprivate compared with the multibed wards that are common in other countries.

Morbidity is much harder to measure than mortality or the number of procedures, but one study used identical health surveys in Britain and the US and found that, on a range of health outcomes, some self-reported and some "hard" biological measures from blood tests, Britons in late middle age were in *better* health than Americans.[12] The British spend less than 10 percent of their GDP on healthcare, and about one-third as much for each person.

Americans are not happy with their healthcare system. In the Gallup World Poll surveys between 2005 and 2010, only 19 percent of Americans answered affirmatively to the question, "Do you have confidence in the health care or medical system?" putting America eighty-ninth out of the 130 countries that were surveyed.[13] Gallup also asked whether people were satisfied with the "availability of quality healthcare in the city or area" in which they lived. America does better on this more specific and local question, with 77 percent of people reporting positively, about the same percentage as in Canada or Japan, but worse than in other rich countries and worse than in a number of much poorer Asian countries, such as Cambodia, Taiwan, the Philippines, Malaysia, and Thailand. In Switzerland, 94 percent of people report themselves satisfied with the local availability of quality healthcare, and 58 percent of the population thinks that the national healthcare or medical system works well. Much of the dissatisfaction in the US is about *access* to healthcare in an inequitable system; according to a 2007 report from the Commonwealth Fund, the US ranked last among seven rich countries on "dimensions of access, patient safety, coordination, efficiency, and equity."[14]

Where Does the Money Go?

How is it possible that Americans pay so much and get so little? The money is certainly going somewhere. What is waste to a patient is income to a provider. Once again, it is helpful to compare with other rich countries. Much of the difference in costs comes from higher prices and from higher salaries for healthcare providers. American doctors get paid almost twice as much as the average doctor in other Organisation for Economic Co-operation and Development member countries,[15] though their smaller numbers in relation to population limits their share of the higher cost.[16] Doctors numbers are held down by limiting the number of places in medical schools, at the behest of doctors' groups and Congress, and by making it difficult for foreign doctors to practice in the US.[17] Sixteen percent of those in the top 1 percent of incomes in 2005 were physicians; 6 percent among the top tenth of 1 percent.[18] Nurses get paid more in the US too, but the gap with other countries is smaller. Pharmaceuticals are about three times more expensive in the US.[19] The anticholesterol drug Crestor costs eighty-six dollars a month (after discounts) in the US, but forty-one dollars in Germany and only nine dollars in Australia. If you have rheumatoid arthritis, your Humira is $2,505 a month in the US, $1,749 in Germany, and $1,243 in Australia. And procedures cost more. A hip replacement costs more than $40,000 on average in the US, but $11,000 in France; the devices that replace hips and knees are more than three times as expensive in the US as elsewhere, even when they are identical devices from the same manufacturer. An MRI examination costs $1,100 in the US, but about $300 in Britain. American physicians pay more for malpractice insurance, although the total cost of around 2.4 percent of total healthcare expenditures is small compared with the expenditures on hospitals (33 percent), physicians (20 percent), and prescription drugs (10 percent).[20] Compared with those in other rich countries, American hospitals and doctors make more intensive use of "high margin, high volume" procedures, such as imaging, joint replacements, coronary artery bypass graft surgery, angioplasty, and cesarean deliveries.[21] When one of us had his hip replaced in 2006, a famous New York hospital charged $10,000 a day for the (shared) room; it had a good view of ships passing on the East River, but television was extra, as of course were medicines and treatments.

Defenders of American pharmaceutical companies argue that much of the development of drugs is done in the United States (although not always by American companies), so other countries are freeloading on American innovation and discovery. Critics note that drug companies spend more on marketing than on research, that much of the basic research is done by or financed by government (for example, by the National Institutes of Health), and suggest that shortening or even eliminating patent protection might not be as disastrous as we are led to believe.[22] The current system is often indefensible. For example, insulin, without which diabetics would die, was sold to the University of Toronto by its three discoverers for one dollar each, in order to guarantee that it would be freely available in perpetuity. Some patients are now paying as much as $1,000 a month, sometimes forgoing their medication, while the producers tweak the drugs to maintain their patents.[23] At the same time, according to reporting by the *Economist*, pharmaceutical companies have spun off large charitable foundations that, by covering patients' copayments, make it easier for the companies to keep up their prices. Moreover, for every dollar of copayment, the pharma company can take a tax deduction of two dollars.[24] Reducing the cost of drugs could pay for a substantial expansion of research by the National Institutes of Health.

It would also save a great deal of money and relieve some of the pressures on everything else we need.

There are other factors beyond price. New medicines, new scanners, and new procedures are constantly appearing. Some of these save lives and reduce suffering, but many do not, yet they are used—and paid for—anyway. This is "flat of the curve medicine," more inputs and more money, but little increase in health. Britain, unlike the United States, has a regulatory agency (the National Institute for Health and Care Excellence, or NICE) that evaluates new medicines and procedures, estimates how much additional health they bring for each additional pound, and recommends against their use (effectively excluding them, given the British system) if they do not meet a minimum cutoff. Such an agency in America would be a direct threat to profits and would be fought to the death by the industry, meaning the death of the agency, not the industry.

Sir Michael Rawlins, first chair of NICE, relates that its first drug tested was Relenza, an antiviral for influenza made by Glaxo Wellcome. NICE recommended against it, not because it was ineffective but because of its "external" effects, that the flu patients in doctors' offices waiting for prescriptions would spread the disease. The chair of the company "stormed into Downing Street and threatened to take his research out of the country." But Prime Minister Tony Blair and Health Secretary Frank Dobson backed NICE, saving it from stillbirth.[25] We suspect that the resolution might have been different in Washington. Note also that the Food and Drug Administration is not permitted to consider wider social effects in its drug approval process—for example, the likelihood that opioids would be diverted.

Health insurance companies are often pilloried in the media, especially when they refuse to cover a treatment, or send incomprehensible bills to patients who thought they were fully covered. The big problem here is that, in a private system, insurance companies, doctors' offices, and hospitals spend huge sums on administration, negotiating rates, and trying to limit expenses. In single-payer systems—which have other advantages and disadvantages, depending on the design—more than half of these costs would be eliminated. It is not just the *profits* of the insurers that are problematic; much of what they do would not be needed at all if the system were organized differently.[26]

Last but not least, hospitals are raising prices not because of their costs but because they are consolidating in order to reduce or eliminate competition and using their market power to raise prices; they are steadily winning the war against the insurance companies (and the public). Hospitals that are local monopolies charge 12 percent higher prices than do hospitals that face competition. Moreover, when a hospital merges with another hospital within five miles, competition between hospitals goes down, and prices go up by 6 percent on average.[27]

Patients are at their most vulnerable during medical emergencies, which are increasingly being seen and used as profit opportunities. Ambulance services and emergency rooms have been outsourced to physician and ambulance service companies, and their doctors and ambulances are sending "surprise" medical bills. Many of these services are not covered by insurance, so that patients are billed even when they are taken to a hospital that is part of their network and covered by their insurance. In 2016, a large fraction of emergency room visits incurred "surprise" ambulance bills. Air ambulances are becoming more common as rural hospitals close, and they can bring surprise charges in the tens of thousands of dollars. When someone is in distress, or perhaps even unconscious, there is no bargaining over rates, and no competition to restrain prices. In such conditions, you pay what you are asked, even supposing you are conscious. The companies, many of which are owned by private equity firms, well understand that these are ideal situations to ramp up prices.[28] Ambulance chasers have become ambulance owners, and traffic accident victims wake up in the hospital with a $2,000 bill attached to their gurney.

This sort of predation is a prime example of a system that transfers money upward, in this case from people in distress to private equity firms and their investors. It also illustrates why capitalism, with its many virtues in many contexts, cannot provide healthcare in a socially tolerable way. During medical emergencies, people are not well positioned to make the informed choices on which competition depends, just as people cannot make informed choices when they are dependent on opioids.

Hospitals that used to be run by doctors are now run by corporate executives—some are doctors who have turned in their white coats for business suits—who are paid CEO salaries to build empires and to raise prices. A good example is New York Presbyterian Hospital, an octopus of once-independent hospitals. The hospital is a nonprofit whose CEO, Dr. Steven Corwin, was paid $4.5 million in 2014[29] (the CEO of North Shore University Hospital was paid twice as much).[30] New York Presbyterian ran a beautifully produced series of video stories, which were aired on public television immediately before the immensely popular *Downton Abbey* series, each documenting an extraordinary recovery that could only have happened at New York Presbyterian.[31] These advertisements were aimed at inducing employees to demand that the hospital be included in their insurance plan, giving the hospital increased negotiating power with the insurance companies, which helped to raise their prices and earn Corwin his salary. Other hospitals soon followed suit with similar advertisements of their own. In 2017, hospitals spent $450 million on advertising in the US.[32] It is hard to see how these tactics do anything to improve patient health.

Doctors, hospitals, pharma, and device manufacturers work together in a way that raises prices. Makers of high-tech scanners offer attractive leases and pricing schedules to doctors, dentists, and hospitals that can generate cash flows without demonstrated improvement in results. Scanners and scammers are sometimes hard to tell apart. Pharma works with hospitals and doctors to help develop new products and raise the demand for them. In 2018, José Baselga, a distinguished breast cancer researcher, was forced to step down as chief medical officer of Memorial Sloan Kettering in New York,[33] which describes itself as the world's oldest and largest private cancer center. He was ousted for failing to disclose potential conflicts of interest in his published papers, conflicts stemming from his financial ties to biotech startups and pharmaceutical companies, one of which, AstraZeneca, immediately appointed him as head of research and development. As the management of the hospital (correctly) argued,[34] there is a potentially beneficial symbiosis when hospitals provide patients for trials of new drugs and when doctors try out and help spread the word about effective new products. Indeed, new cancer drugs have recently had a good record in reducing cancer mortality. Yet patients' best interests are not always aligned with those of drug companies, so they might reasonably want to know just who their doctors are working for, and to be reassured that their hospital is not just a wing of a pharma company.

The CEOs of pharma companies are well paid. According to a 2018 report in the *Wall Street Journal*, the top ten CEO salaries in 2017 ranged from $38 million for Ari Bousbib of Iqvia (a data company that analyzes patient information for drug companies, insurance companies, and governments) to $18 million for Kenneth Frazier at Merck.[35] In 2014, the very top incomes in America, exceeding those of the CEOs of large companies, came from profits from small, privately held businesses, among which doctors in private practice are well represented.[36]

The excess cost of American healthcare goes to hospitals, to doctors, to device manufacturers, and to drug manufacturers. The trillion dollars that, from a health perspective, is waste and abuse is, from the providers' perspective, well-earned income. Which still leaves us with two questions: What effects do these costs have on Americans' lives, and how does the industry manage to get away with it?

Who Pays? The Consequences of High Healthcare Spending

Understanding just who pays is straightforward enough in a mechanical sense, but figuring out the effects on people's lives is harder. In the end, and no matter who gets the bills, everything is paid for by individuals, so a good figure to keep in mind is the $10,739 that is the total cost per person. Many Americans find it incredible that they are paying such a sum, or even that people do so on average. The bills are typically paid by insurers, by employers, or by government, and most of us are fortunate enough never to receive or even to see a crippling medical bill. Yet the lack of transparency and the sense that someone else is usually paying

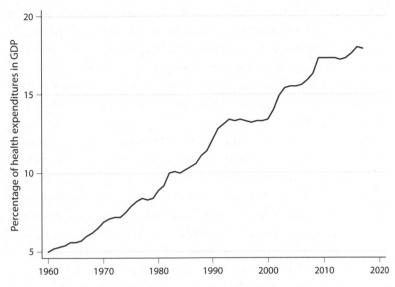

FIGURE 13.2. Healthcare expenditures as a percentage of GDP, 1960–2017. Data from Centers for Medicare and Medicaid Services.

help prop up a system that would be challenged more vigorously if its effects were better known.[37]

Figure 13.2 shows how the percentage of national income that is absorbed by healthcare has grown over the last half century, from 5 percent in 1960 to 18 percent in 2017. The converse of this figure may be as or more useful—that the percentage of income that is available for things other than healthcare has *fallen* from 95 percent in 1960 to 82 percent today. The graph also identifies periods when the burden of healthcare rose most rapidly, particularly from the early 1980s to the early 1990s and from 2000 to 2008. As noted by Ezekiel Emanuel and Victor Fuchs,[38] these were also periods when average hourly earnings did badly, especially compared with the mid-1990s, when earnings did well while the percentage spent on healthcare fell. If we look at white men aged forty-five to fifty-four without a college degree, whose median wages were 15 percent *lower* in 2017 than in 1979, we see the same pattern, with rapid declines in the 1980s, followed by some wage recovery in the mid-1990s and again in the last few years. Of course, wages are affected by much else, particularly the state of the labor market more generally, and the burden of healthcare is ongoing and slowly acting, so these broad patterns over decades are probably the most we can expect to see.

If we start with who pays the bills, individuals and the federal government each pay 28 percent, another 20 percent is paid by businesses on behalf of their employees, and 17 percent is paid by state and local governments; other private payers cover the remaining 7 percent.[39] Individuals who do not have insurance—in 2017, 9 percent of the population, or 29.7 million people—must pay directly, often at much higher prices than are charged to government or to insurance companies. Those who cannot pay may receive charity care or have their care cross-subsidized by someone else, or they may be pursued by debt collectors for many years. It has often been noted that health insurance is less about protecting your health than about protecting your wallet against the healthcare system. Individuals without insurance will often forgo nonurgent treatment. Without contact with a physician, they are less likely to use life-saving preventive measures like antihypertensives or statins. Healthcare paid for by individuals reduces their ability to buy other things, or to save for the future, contributing to the decline in the household saving rate in the US.[40]

About half of working-age Americans (about 158 million people) have health insurance through their employers,[41] and those aged sixty-five or over are covered by Medicare, an entitlement paid for by the federal government. Medicaid is the national health program for people with low incomes and is paid for in part by the federal government and in part by state governments.

Employer-provided insurance is typically well liked by those who are covered, although it is not without costs for the employee. On average, employees in 2017 paid about $1,200 (18 percent) of the cost of an individual policy, or $5,700 (29 percent) of a family policy.[42] They also pay health-related taxes, and they have to meet copayments at the time of treatment, as well as a deductible before any reimbursement. It is often very difficult for patients to know in advance what a treatment will cost, or to understand the subsequent bills. For example, insurers may cover

90 percent of the cost of a procedure, which turns out to be 90 percent of the insurer's internal price, which can be much less than is billed. Surprise medical bills are common even among those who have insurance, and even for nonemergency care. At the same time, in the face of the rising costs of healthcare, employer plans are deteriorating in both quality and comprehensiveness.[43]

One study looked at the decade up to 2009, during which time median income for a family of four with employer-based health insurance rose from $76,000 to $99,000. All but $95 of this was wiped out by increases in the employee premium, out-of-pocket expenditures for healthcare, taxes devoted to healthcare, and the prices of other goods.[44]

Employer-provided insurance has serious problems that are not always apparent to those who receive it. Many employees think that the employer contribution—the other 71 percent of the (average) $20,000 family policy—is free to them. Yet it is not free to the firm, and it affects how much firms are prepared to pay in wages and how many workers they employ. For an employer deciding about a hire, it is not the wage that matters but rather what the firm has to pay to hire the worker, including the costs of health insurance and other benefits. Employers' contributions are wage costs, as are wages themselves, so the rising costs of insurance premiums—for example, from $2,000 in 1999 to $6,896 in 2017 for the average single-person plan—have played a large part in holding down wages. Employees may think they are being given a gift, little realizing that what the employer cares about is the total that they pay for the employee, not to whom they pay it. The employee may be unaware that the "gift" is being deducted, partially or fully, from wages.[45] In the foregoing example, the family of four would likely have had more than $99,000 in 2009 if employer premiums had not risen too.

There is more. Employers faced with large increases in health premiums may decide that some positions will no longer come with health insurance or, more drastically, that they can do with fewer workers, or at least outsource the work to be done. One executive explained to us that, when his firm was presented with a very large increase in its health insurance premiums one year, they called in management consultants who helped them cut their "head count," identifying workers who were dispensable altogether, or whose positions in food service, security, janitorial, or transport activities could be outsourced. The outsourcing firms would then be responsible—or not—for wages and healthcare premiums, when indeed they offered them at all. Working for an outsourcing company is often a less attractive and less meaningful option than working for a large corporation. Healthcare costs are a larger share of the total wage cost of employing a less well-paid worker. For a well-paid employee earning a salary of $150,000, the average family policy adds less than 10 percent to the cost of employing the worker; for a low-wage worker on half the median wage, it is 60 percent. This is one of the ways in which rising health costs turn good jobs into worse jobs and eliminate jobs altogether.

Employer-provided healthcare contributes to the rising cost of healthcare, as well as to the size of the healthcare industry. More highly skilled and better-paid workers are more likely to have insurance, so policies are designed to fit their needs and tastes. The employer's contribution to the premiums is not treated as income for tax purposes, so employers have incentives to provide more and more luxurious healthcare through benefits—which are not taxed—rather than letting employees pay out of their after-tax income. This not only costs the federal government some $150 billion in lost taxes[46] but also encourages employers and employees to negotiate salaries with a higher healthcare content. As Victor Fuchs has noted, it is as if the government were encouraging "Whole Foods" healthcare and discouraging "Walmart" healthcare, even though many, perhaps most, people, given their budgets, would prefer the latter. The employer-based system is biased toward higher-earning workers, in terms of both access and the kind of healthcare offered.[47]

Federal and state governments are also responsible for paying for healthcare. For the federal government, the cost of the health entitlements has to compete against all of the other things that it does or could do. The failure to maintain and replace infrastructure is a leading example; because of the state of roads in the US, FedEx trucks need their tires changed twice as often as twenty years ago.[48] Perhaps less obvious is the burden of Medicaid on *state* budgets. Because Medicaid is an entitlement, states have no option but to pay what it costs; aside from flexibility in setting eligibility requirements, states have limited control over either the amount of healthcare or what it costs. At the state level too, rising health-care expenditures are eating away at other important provisions, par-ticularly education and transportation. Medicaid rose from 20.5 percent of state spending in 2008 to an estimated 29.7 percent in 2018, while spending on primary and secondary education fell from 22.0 percent to 19.6 percent. States currently spend half as much again on Medicaid as they do on K–12 education.[49] Such provisions are less important for those who can afford not to rely on public provision.

Ideally, it would be possible to calculate exactly who pays the burden of healthcare, but the sums are so enormous, so dispersed throughout the economy, and so nontransparent that the task is not possible. Yet we are all paying every day, in ways that are more and (often) less obvious. Worse still, little of what we spend is a conscious choice of something we want and are prepared to pay for, in full knowledge of the costs. Instead, the healthcare system is a parasite on the economy, like War-ren Buffett's tapeworm that Americans accidentally swallowed long ago but that has grown to be huge and is sucking the nutrients that the rest of the body needs. Or by our own comparison, the cancer that used to be confined to a small healthcare system has metastasized all over the economy.

Why Is Healthcare So Difficult?

The financing and organization of healthcare is difficult everywhere, not just in the United States. One remedy for most goods and services, but that is no remedy for healthcare, is to leave it to the market. Kenneth Arrow, one of the greatest economists of the twentieth century, proved the master theorems of economics that tell us what the market can and cannot do, and under what circumstances. Arrow's theorems give a more precise account of the arguments made long ago by Adam Smith. It is no accident that Arrow also wrote the key paper in health economics,[50] ex-plaining why a market solution for healthcare would be socially intoler-able. Certainly, as market fundamentalists argue, competitive free markets (together with antitrust enforcement) would almost certainly deliver lower prices than those we see today. But healthcare is not like other services. Patients lack the information that providers possess, which puts us largely in their hands. We are in no position to resist provider-driven overprovision, which can also happen with a garage mechanic, but with less serious consequences.

In the markets for tuna fish, for automobiles, for houses, and for airplane trips, consumers can soon learn which products suit them and which do not, and competition among providers will remove those products that are defective or that suit no one. But try to find out who is the best orthopedic surgeon. When looking for a surgeon for the hip replacement mentioned earlier, we talked to everyone we could and read everything we could, but with no convincing answer; our favorite was, "He's the guy that did the pope, but he's past it now." Immediately after the surgery, a night nurse (appropriately called Cassandra, though the memory of the event may have been affected by the morphine pump) gave the rundown on what *she* thought, but the patient's and the nurse's assessments may not be the same: Cassandra was clearly impressed by speed. Much later, we discovered from an orthopedist friend's own failed knee replacement that even a good orthopedic surgeon can choose badly.

Health insurance works poorly or not at all in an unregulated market. The incentives for both providers *and* patients to spend raise the cost of provision beyond what patients are prepared to pay to be insured, especially so for healthier people. As a result, the healthier patients opt out of expensive insurance that they do not need, leaving an ever sicker and ever more expensive group in the scheme, driving it out of existence, the infamous "death spiral."

Insurance only works when sick and healthy people are pooled together, in America by employment, and in other rich countries by government fiat across the whole population. Without subsidies for those with low incomes, or compulsion to buy it, insurance cannot work, or would be available only to those who are healthy and don't need it. Leaving healthcare to the market, without social support and control, will leave many people without insurance and without access to healthcare when they are sick. What unregulated markets *do* give us is private equity firms holding up sick people at their most vulnerable, when they have a health emergency.

Americans are less inclined than Europeans to accept the sometimes-heavy-handed controls that governments place on healthcare. They like to believe that the system is a free-market one, in spite of the fact that the government is paying half of the costs, is paying the prices demanded by pharmaceutical companies without negotiation (often absurdly described as "market-based pricing"), is granting patents for devices and drugs, is permitting professional associations to restrict supply, and is subsidizing employer-provided healthcare through the tax system. Beyond that, there is the key *political* fact that people do not know how much they are paying. If, at tax time, Americans got an annual bill for $10,739 or if employers showed their contributions to the cost of employees' health insurance as deductions on workers' paychecks, the political pressure for reform would surely be much stronger. That costs are hidden encourages overcharging. Because they are hidden, the problems that such costs bring are not given enough weight, compared with, for example, the fact that almost 10 percent of the population is not covered. The latter is indeed a scandal, and one that we see in no other rich country, but it is the cost explosion that is destroying the ability of the economy to serve less skilled workers as it could and should.

A Protection Racket?

The providers have another important line of defense, and it plays offense too: the healthcare lobby in Washington. Lobbying is far from confined to healthcare, and it is important for our story more generally, so we will come back to it in chapter 15; for the moment we look only at health. In healthcare, as more generally, corporate lobbying has grown dramatically in the last forty years. It is one of the forces redistributing power from labor to capital, and from workers and consumers to corporations and wealthy professionals. Lobbying and rent-seeking are not confined to corporations. Trade associations of small businesses—the American Medical Association (a quarter of a million members) and the American Optometric Society (forty thousand members) are two examples—are geographically widely spread, giving them a voice with each member of Congress and an effective hometown power that backs up their financial clout. The political and financial muscle reinforce each other, acting to increase the profits of the association members at the expense of their patients.[51]

In 2018, the healthcare industry employed 2,829 lobbyists, more than 5 for each member of Congress. More than half of the lobbyists were "revolvers," ex–Congress members or ex-staffers. Some go as far as to describe Congress itself as the "farm league" for lobbying.[52] The industry spent more than $567 million on lobbying in 2018, more than half from pharmaceutical companies.[53] It is the largest-spending industry, larger even than the financial industry, and spends more than ten times as much as the *total* spent by organized labor. The industry additionally spent $133 million on supporting actual or potential members of Congress, $76 million to Democrats and $57 million to Republicans. Much lobbying goes to preserving the status quo, though lobbyists also seize the opportunity to help write and pass favorable legislation when healthcare issues are on the table. Lobbyists are well placed to be the experts that legislators and their staffers turn to for information and analysis; there once was an independent Office of Technology Assessment, not unlike NICE in Britain, but it was abolished (with Newt Gingrich a prime mover) in the 1990s.

We are certainly not claiming that healthcare gets to write its own rules, and lobbyists do not always prevail. Lobbyists oppose one another, but there are no effective lobbyists, or lobbyists of comparable power and size, who are arguing the case for the people who are paying for the enrichment of the healthcare industry or who can act as a countervailing power against it.

During periods of legislative activity, the healthcare lobbyists have sometimes been singularly effective. Obamacare was passed without consideration of a single-payer system or a public option, and the US has nothing like the British system of evaluation. Hospitals, doctors, and pharma companies were effectively paid off in order to support the passage of the Affordable Care Act.[54] This was necessary to get more uninsured people into the system, but it prevented any cost saving, a trade-off that was almost certainly necessary then given the power of the lobbies. Other good examples of legislative protection for the industry are the twin requirements that Medicare pay for any drug that has been approved by the Food and Drug Administration, and that it not negotiate on price. (The industry long opposed a Medicare drug benefit, on the grounds that Medicare would drive down the price of drugs, but as the number and power of its lobbyists increased, they switched sides and secured the favorable [to pharma] arrangements that we have today.)[55]

The historical accident by which most Americans are covered through their employers is a huge source of difficulty and a barrier to reform; that was when the tapeworm was swallowed and the first cell mutated into cancer. But the way the industry is protected in Washington is also key to the enormous incomes and profits that it generates, and its lobbyists are well placed to block any threat. It reminds us of the shopkeeper who, when asked to pay protection, threatened to call the police and was told that the extorter *was* the police. Our government is complicit in extortion by the healthcare industry, an extortion that is an important element of Sheriff of Nottingham–style redistribution in America today. The industry that is supposed to improve our health is undermining it, and Congress, which is supposed to represent our interests, is supporting the shakedown.[56]

14

Capitalism, Immigrants, Robots, and China

AMERICAN CAPITALISM is not working well for less educated Americans. The loss of good jobs and falling real wages over the last half century have made life difficult, not just by lowering living standards but also by undermining the lives of working-class people. For many, the institutions that provided support—marriage, church, and community—no longer do so, identity and status have been challenged, and the meaning of life has been lost. As Emile Durkheim would have predicted, suicides have risen, in this case not only through deliberate self-harm but also by creating an environment in which the diseases of depression and addiction flourish and bring deaths of despair.

What exactly has gone wrong, and how might it be fixed?

We are not against capitalism. We believe in the power of competition and of free markets. Capitalism has brought an end to misery and death for millions in the now rich countries over the past 250 years and, much more rapidly, in countries such as China and India over the last 50 years. Competitive free enterprise has worked to allow people to flourish, historically and around the world today. Trade, innovation, and the movement of people have been key positive elements in this story. But the magic trick is to make sure that markets, trade, innovation, and immigration work for people, not against them, or for some and against many. Working people in America today are too often not benefiting from the market. We have seen the worst face of capitalism—if it can even be called that—in what happened with opioids and the healthcare industry.

In much of the economy, the remedy is not to replace markets but to make them more like the genuinely free and competitive markets that they are supposed to be but increasingly are not. In other cases, government intervention on behalf of the people is needed. Political power has increasingly moved away from working people. Fixing this will take political as well as economic reform.

Inequality is often seen as the central problem of capitalism in America today. President Barack Obama called it "the defining challenge of our time." Many on the left argue that we need a program of redistribution that taxes the rich more heavily in order to transfer to the poor and to spend on public goods that benefit us all. Inequality is indeed a problem, but as we see it, it is really a symptom of a deeper problem. We shall argue that we live in a mirror image of a Robin Hood society, one in which resources are indeed being redistributed, not *downward*, from rich to poor, as Robin Hood was reputed to do, but *upward*, from poor to rich. We saw this Sheriff of Nottingham redistribution in the previous chapter, where we argued that healthcare often works this way. One might at first think that plundering the poor is not very profitable, because they have so little. But they make up in numbers what they lack in resources, while the rich are few, so that the Sheriff of Nottingham and his cronies can live well off the poor.

Transfers to the rich help explain why the working class has done so badly. Upward redistribution is not an inherent feature of capitalism—it does not have to work that way, though the risk is always there—but large parts of the American economy have been captured to serve the wealthy with the consent and connivance of government. The problem with inequality is that so much of the wealth and income at the top is ill-gotten. Or put another way, the problem is not that we live in an unequal society but that we live in an *unfair* society. We have no quarrel with those who became rich in a way that benefited everyone.

Three threats to low-wage workers have received much attention. Less skilled workers face competition from immigrants from low-wage countries. They also must compete with lower-wage workers abroad, who threaten their jobs through the import of goods previously made by American workers. In addition to human competition, workers increasingly must compete with robots, who have quietly taken over many jobs. Robots do not require healthcare or other benefits, or Human Resources representation, or cost-of-living increases; the tax system subsidizes purchases of new machines, but not the cost of labor. We argue that immigration, although it has attracted a great deal of attention, cannot have been the main cause of the long-term stagnation of working-class wages or for the removal of a ladder up to the middle class. Globalization and automation are more important players here; that their effects are worse in the US than elsewhere is because of America's unique history of race, its limited welfare provision, and its absurdly costly healthcare system.

The three threats to less educated workers have come at a time when economic growth has slowed, so people would not be getting ahead as quickly as their parents did, or perhaps as they themselves expected to do, even if growth had been equally shared. From this alone, wages will grow less rapidly than they once did. With unequal sharing, which is what has happened, the less educated have suffered more from the slower growth. Rent-seeking—for example, by the healthcare industry—is perhaps tolerable when everyone is prospering, but it is much less so in an economy that is growing more slowly. Beyond falling growth, the structure of the economy has changed, shifting away from manufacturing and toward services, where jobs are less well paid, even for the same qualifications, and where unions are much less prevalent and workers have less power relative to their employers.

Immigrants and Immigration

Popular accounts of job loss often blame immigrants for stealing jobs. Populist politicians stoke people's fears about immigration, not only in America but also in much of Europe.

We should start with a disclaimer. One of us is a first-generation immigrant. The other was born in America, but her ancestors came from Ireland to northeastern Pennsylvania in the middle of the nineteenth century, and her family remains influenced by their national and religious heritage. Perhaps more relevant, we both have postgraduate degrees and work in an industry—tertiary education—where immigrants have long been common. More than two-thirds of new doctoral degrees in economics in America are earned by people who were not born here, and this has been true for long enough for the same to be true of the faculty. Two-thirds of the Princeton economics faculty were born abroad. Our profession sees this diversity as a great advantage; the different outlooks, experiences, and values that come from different countries are the basis for creative interaction. That said, many of us worry about living and working in communities that, while geographically situated in America, are more like United Nations outposts than other places in America. We are also very poorly placed to use our personal experiences to imagine what less educated Americans feel about immigration when their labor market is under threat.

Immigrants to America are extremely diverse. They have about the same average education as the native population, but this disguises the fact that many have a lot of education, and many have none.[1] The highly educated immigrants, like our Princeton colleagues, may help their co-workers become more productive and actually increase what they earn. Immigrants have a long history of innovation. Alexander Graham Bell was born and raised in Edinburgh. James L. Kraft, who invented a pasteurization process for cheese, emigrated from Canada. Products that were invented by immigrants include the PET scanner, the paddle-controlled video game, and lithium ion batteries. Elon Musk (PayPal, Tesla, SpaceX) is an immigrant, and so is Sergey Brin (cofounder of Google).[2] All six of America's 2016 Nobel Prize winners are first-generation immigrants; in 2015, when one of us was fortunate enough to win, three out of four were, and the other was the son of an immigrant. It is hard to believe that it would be a good idea for America to restrict such immigration—though the transmitting countries might feel differently. Most of the concern is about immigrants with little education, who compete with the less educated Americans whose despair is the topic of this book.

At the time of writing (2019), the percentage of the population that is foreign born is around 13 percent, which is close to its all-time high of a century ago. In the 1980s, around six hundred thousand people legally immigrated each year, rising to eight hundred thousand in the 1990s, and more than a million a year since 2001. Unauthorized inflows were also large, but in recent years, inflows have been similar to outflows, so the total number, estimated to be around eleven million (a quarter of the documented foreign-born), has been constant.[3] If the southern border of the United States were open, there would be many migrants who would come and go, as was the case in the 1970s and early 1980s. Barriers impede this toing and froing, trapping some people in the US while keeping others out.[4] The most rapid increases in foreign-born populations today are not in the traditional receiving states, such as California, New York, Florida, and New Jersey, but in nontraditional states, many of them in the South. It is possible that the reaction to immigrants, even in small numbers, is more negative where people are unfamiliar with the process and do not have friends and neighbors from previous waves of immigration.

Well-off Americans, farmers, and employers like low-skill immigration. They like cheap gardeners, field hands, household servants, and nannies. They may share workers' beliefs that immigrants will reduce wages, but they *like* that outcome because, although workers lose, profits rise. Employers often complain that they are short of labor and, without immigrants, they might have to pay more or increase benefits. Exactly so, say the critics of immigration.[5] Having more workers to compete with at home, like having more cheap workers abroad, or more robots, can certainly reduce wages, at least in principle. Whether they have done so is the crucial question.

To explain the collapse of the working-class labor market, we are looking for factors that might be responsible for a half-century decline in real wages for less educated Americans. Given this, when we think about immigration and jobs, we need to distinguish immediate and longer-term effects. Suppose that the number of jobs is inflexible over a short time period of months or even years; this is the worst possible case for the wages of those already here. Immigrants displace locals or reduce their wages; they also raise profits and the rate of return to capital. Unemployed workers, lower wages, and higher profits present opportunities for entrepreneurs or other employers to expand, though it takes time to open new firms or to build plants and equipment for the workers to use. But in time, albeit perhaps a long time, capital will adjust and the economy will grow. After all, history has seen great population growth together with no long-term increase in unemployment and *rising* real wages. Given a long enough time to adjust, it is simply not true that there are a fixed number of jobs carrying a fixed total paycheck so that more workers must mean fewer available jobs and lower pay for all. Such a long period is more than enough time for capital to adjust to the increased supply, so that it is hard to attribute the long-term decline to immigration. Yet if each wave is followed by another wave, the economy may never get the chance to fully adjust, and the wages of the less educated could be permanently lower, at least until the immigration stops.

The National Academies of Sciences, Engineering, and Medicine, in its 2017 report on immigration, concluded its review of the evidence on wages with the words "Particularly when measured over a period of 10 years or more, the impact of immigration on overall native wage may be small or close to zero."[6] Over shorter periods, there is a range of findings, and some show negative effects on wages, particularly among the previous wave of immigrants. Recall too that many of the immigrants are not unskilled but rather have college degrees. There were periods, the decades of the 1980s and the 2000s, when the college wage premium increased even when immigrants were adding more to the college-educated population than to the population with high school or less. Whatever the results over shorter periods, and in accord with what is to be expected, we judge that immigration did not play an important role in the long-term decline of the wages of less educated Americans. Yet we also recognize that the issue is far from settled, even among academic economists.

Immigrants are not the only way that the population, or the workforce, increases. Population growth brings more people who need jobs. Women, especially women without a college degree, vastly increased their participation in the labor force before 2000 (see figure 11.2). Like immigrants compared with natives, they typically earn less than men. Although there are studies examining whether the increase in working women had negative impacts on men's wages (with indecisive results), the topic attracts none of the sound and the fury that is characteristic of the immigration debate. Which makes us think that the debate here is not primarily about numbers, about new workers taking away jobs from existing workers, about more workers driving down wages, or about there being more people than the country can accommodate, though this last is also a serious topic of debate. It must be about something else, that immigrants are somehow different from "us" and are seen as threatening "our culture." Particularly in places not familiar with immigrants but where jobs are vanishing or being downgraded for other reasons, it is understandable that immigrants would take the blame.

One of us remembers traveling on a crowded train in India, from Ahmedabad to Mumbai. A dozen or so of us were established in what were more like stacked pews than a compartment, half on the upper levels, half beneath. We had all been strangers a few hours before but had become good friends, sharing food, water, and tales about other train trips. At every stop, new passengers would join, and some would try to join our club, only to be met by silent hostility. In the end, we had no choice but to shuffle a little tighter and let a stranger in. By the next stop, the stranger was one of us, ready to repel the next round of immigrants. Of course, we all became a little less comfortable at every station.

Globalization, Trade, Innovation, and Robots

To many it seems obvious that trade and automation are the enemies of American workers. The flood of goods from China and other low-wage countries has cost the jobs of many who used to make these goods in the United States. Workers are being replaced, not just by workers in Shenzhen or Tijuana but also by machines and by computer-assisted processes. Workers in China and Mexico cannot help serve hamburgers, check you in at an airport, or check you out at the grocery, but automatic kiosks can do all of these things. Workers who have the skills and education to work with the new technologies get better jobs and higher wages, while the opposite happens for the less skilled or less educated.

This story invites comparison between less educated Americans today and the handloom weavers in Britain two hundred years ago. Wages fell as the weavers were replaced by machines, and they only stopped falling when handloom weaving was gone. If the parallel holds or is close, wages will fall for all the jobs that can be done by robots, or by less well-paid workers elsewhere, and the decline will stop only when those jobs are gone, or Chinese wages are as high as American wages. And at that point, unless wage policy changes, there will be an even larger fraction of Americans working in service jobs that cannot be outsourced, for wages that barely keep their lives intact. Some service jobs are well compensated; according to *U.S. News and World Report*, the average salary of plumbers in New York State was $78,000 in 2017.[7] But a single person working full time at the federal minimum wage in 2018 ($7.25 an hour) finds him- or herself just $1,400 above the Census Bureau's poverty threshold ($14,500 versus $13,064).[8] This will be a long, bleak process of economic, social, and community destruction.

The rise of China as a manufacturing power and its effects on American workers and their communities have been documented in a series of papers by the economist David Autor and his coauthors.[9] While it is difficult to come up with precise—or noncontroversial—numbers, they estimate that between two and three million American jobs have been lost because of China; there were about eighteen million manufacturing workers in America between 1970 and 1990, and there are about twelve million today (2019). The lost jobs are geographically concentrated in places that used to make the goods that are now being imported, and the effects last for a long time, with elevated levels of unemployment lasting a decade or more.

Marriage rates have fallen in the China-shock-affected communities, and mortality has risen, echoing and supporting the findings of this book.[10] We have emphasized the long, slow erosion of jobs and community destruction, while the work of Autor and his coauthors is more focused on the particular places where and the particular time when Chinese imports were rising rapidly.

More than a story of job loss, the story of globalization is one of tremendous upheaval in the American labor market. Work by Nicholas Bloom and his coauthors[11] shows that in parts of the country (primarily on the coasts) with higher concentrations of college-educated workers, manufacturing jobs sent abroad were offset by new jobs, in research and development, marketing, and management—a large share of which are being generated in the same firms that shed manufacturing workers. As world trade has expanded, America, like China, has exported more, creating new jobs—for example, in the manufacture for export of motor vehicles and semiconductors. Studies by the economist Robert Feenstra and his collaborators have estimated that exports brought two to three million new jobs, similar to the number of jobs lost. But in parts of the country with higher concentrations of low-skilled workers, there was no positive offset to the loss of manufacturing jobs.[12]

The traditional escape route for displaced workers has been to move from cities without jobs to cities that have them, but this route has been limited in recent years by the high costs of living in successful cities. These high costs can be inflated by land-use or other policies imposed by those who live there to protect themselves and keep newcomers out. Successful cities are successful in providing jobs and increasing wages for highly educated workers, but not for the less well educated.[13] Many of the displaced workers have nowhere to go and would likely be even worse off if they moved.

This story of trade and innovation wrecking the economy is compelling but seriously incomplete. It also stands in contrast to the way that economists usually think about trade and technological progress. The conventional account begins with the benefits of cheaper prices; Chinese manufacturers fill the shelves in Target and Walmart at prices that are often a fraction of what they once were. We recently bought a ten-foot stuffed crocodile for our grandson; fifty years ago, such a thing would have attracted crowds, but very few purchasers, in a famous Fifth Avenue toyshop like FAO Schwarz in New York. Indeed, it is precisely lower prices and the benefits that they bring to consumers that are the cause of the difficulty for American manufacturers.

The mistake in the conventional account of gains from trade was to imagine that the transition from the old jobs to the new jobs would be quick and painless, and to suppose, without proposing policies to make it happen, that the gains to consumers would somehow compensate for the losses to (erstwhile) producers.

More broadly, globalization and technological progress are *good*. Both enable us to have collectively higher incomes because they expand the productive capacity of the economy. Yet even the most Panglossian assessment recognizes that trade and innovation bring losers as well as winners. Once upon a time, when unions were larger and stronger than they are today, they could have pressed employers to share the gains from innovation that today accrue to capital, to those who manage it, or to those who operate the new technologies. The famous Treaty of Detroit was a sharing deal between unions and management in the automobile industry; Walter Reuther of the United Auto Workers agreed to a long-term contract with General Motors in which the UAW received health, pension, and other benefits in exchange for a promise not to strike. Globalization, and the fierce competition from abroad that it brought, has undermined such norms. As locally made cars were challenged by cheaper imports, US car manufacturers, in order to compete, needed to develop new ways to hold down costs—by moving tasks abroad to lower their wage bills, for example, and, as we shall see later, by weakening the privately provided safety net. In this way, globalization has contributed to the decline of unions. Consumers benefit from better and cheaper cars, but workers lose. It is only if we prize efficiency over all else that this is an unalloyed good; most of us would argue that at least some inefficiency is an acceptable price for greater fairness. Not only that, but the loss of wages and good jobs has effects on communities beyond those directly affected. Giant stuffed crocodiles are a poor recompense for the loss of a way of life.

Policy and Globalization

If China decimates local industry, and it is true that there are jobs elsewhere or in the near future, albeit different jobs, the state can provide benefits that tide people over—perhaps for many years—or pay for retraining. The US has such a scheme, the Trade Adjustment Assistance program, but it is disliked by conservative politicians, even those who strongly favor trade, so it has been limited in size. Senator Phil Gramm, discussing in 2002 a measure to help those hurt by a trade bill that he strongly favored, remarked disdainfully, "Socialist governments all over the planet are trying to stop doing this sort of thing, and now we're doing it."[14] Helping those who are harmed seems to be unacceptable, even when you are the one doing the harming. Trade Adjustment Assistance and unemployment insurance—which is temporary—played only a minor role in helping displaced workers, less than disability, medical, and retirement benefits that are designed for other purposes. Even taking all this together, there was little compensation.[15]

Yet without the productive expansion that innovation and trade can give, we sacrifice the possibility of becoming collectively richer than we are now. We surely cannot afford to give up growth, and so we must do a better job of making sure that everyone gains from it. The problem is not globalization or innovation; the problem is policies for dealing with them. Economist Dani Rodrik wrote an extraordinarily prescient 1997 book about the effects of globalization in rich countries, *Has Globalization Gone Too Far?*, and answered his own question: "Not if policymakers act wisely and imaginatively."[16] If technological change and globalization have been responsible for hurting the working class, it is not because that is what technological change and globalization must do; it is because policy was neither wise nor imaginative. It is not just employers and corporations that, in the absence of unions, have had little interest in protecting workers, which perhaps makes sense if, as many argue, their primary function is to make profits for their shareholders; governments have also done less than they might, particularly in terms of social protection—which requires a good deal more explanation in a democracy.

As its name tells us, globalization is *global*, as is automation. Computers are found outside America, and all rich countries have to deal with the rise of low-cost manufacturing. Yet many other rich countries have not seen the same negative effects on wages and jobs, nor have they seen deaths of despair, even as they have seen social division and political upheaval. Median real wages in Britain have fallen since the Great Recession, but they grew steadily in the twenty years before the recession, a period over which American wages continued to stagnate. France and Germany also import from China, but there are few deaths of despair in France or Germany. The American experience needs an American explanation. The difficulties of globalization and automation are real enough, and the decline of the working class in America would not have happened without them, but it is American institutions—such as healthcare—and the way that they shaped America's response to the challenges that caused the problems, not the challenges themselves.

American Safety Nets: Globalization and Race

A huge policy difference between the US and other rich countries is the extent to which their governments, much more than the US, provide insurance to their workers through a social safety net. When jobs are lost through recession, through trade, or through technological change, unemployment and other benefits are available to prevent hardship and to aid the change to a new job, often for extended periods. Again, the comparison between Britain and the US is instructive.

From 1994/95 to 2015/16, in both countries, the growth in wages was much slower for those with low wages than for those with high wages; in both countries, the market increasingly favored those with high skills over those with low skills. Family incomes followed a similar trend, with those at the bottom of the distribution doing worse than those at the top. In Britain, family earnings before tax saw no growth over the twenty years for those at the tenth percentile of the distribution, while those at the ninetieth percentile saw 1.4 percent growth a year, or an increase of about a third over the whole period. But there is no such pattern in UK family earnings *after taxes and government benefits*; growth at the bottom and at the top is identical at 1.2 percent a year.[17] In the US, the impact of taxes and benefits is too small to make a difference, and the graph post–tax and benefits looks like that drawn pre–tax and benefits: less at the bottom and more at the top. In both countries, the market has been harder on the less skilled, but in Britain, the tax and benefit system made up the difference.

More generally, countries that are more open to trade have larger governments because they accept, unlike Senator Gramm, that the benefits of trade cannot be fully realized if workers have nothing to break their fall. American workers, in contrast to workers in other rich countries, have to go it alone.

We are not arguing that the British safety net is a panacea; the Brexit catastrophe has exposed stark social divisions that are not so different from those in the US, and as we have seen, deaths of despair are rising in Britain, especially in Scotland. But the numbers are small compared with those in the US, and the safety net has surely helped. Our results in chapter 10 show that there is no simple link between incomes and deaths over the last twenty years, either in the US or in European countries. Rising despair is a cumulative process that has taken many years to develop, and employment in manufacturing in the US reached its peak in the late 1970s and has been declining since. What the safety net does is provide insurance, by sharing risks across all of society and not leaving them to be borne by the least educated. It is this sharing of risk that is lacking in the US, and it is surely one, if only one, of the factors leading to the deaths of less educated Americans.

Why is it that the American safety net is so weak? Many Americans endorse individualism, the doctrine that people should not depend on others, even when they are in trouble. Important too is the history of race and of immigration in the United States. People are less willing to participate in mutual insurance schemes with people whom they do not recognize as being like themselves; even today, state-level benefits are less prevalent and less generous in states whose populations have larger fractions of African Americans.[18] While Britain was building the first modern welfare state after the Second World War, attempts to introduce national health insurance during the Truman administration in the United States foundered on the opposition of Southern Democratic senators.[19]

In a portentous historical accident during the Second World War, American business had taken responsibility for employee healthcare as a way of circumventing wage controls. Business eventually also provided pensions for their workers in the form of postretirement defined benefits that the employer had the responsibility to finance. American business, not the American government, thus provided much of the safety net. This arrangement, like the Treaty of Detroit, worked well enough when healthcare spending was low and business faced little competition from abroad, in the years before 1970. But the import of Japanese and German automobiles in the 1970s, followed by a much more comprehensive globalization, together with rapidly rising healthcare costs, made these arrangements impossible to sustain. Firms could no longer guarantee pensions, and they shifted the responsibility to their employees through 401(k) self-directed saving plans; additionally, as we have seen, the rising cost of healthcare reduced both the quantity and quality of available insurance plans.[20] Yet, even today, the United States' safety net is financed privately to a much greater extent than in any other rich country. According to the Organisation for Economic Co-operation and Development's data for 2013 to 2015, *private* spending on social protection was 9 percent of gross domestic product in the United States, compared with 4.6 percent in Britain and 3.3 percent in France. *Public* spending on social protection, by contrast, was 28 percent of gross domestic product in France, 20.5 percent in Britain, and only 19.8 percent in the United States.[21]

Globalization and competition from abroad made it harder for American firms to provide health insurance, pensions, and other benefits for their workers, and robots need no benefits. These broad global forces underlie our story of stagnant wages, falling benefits, and fewer employment rights. But these forces did not act alone, and their effects would have been different had the American safety net not been so much weaker than that in any other wealthy country. The design of social protection in America, as with much else, owed much to the country's unwillingness to adopt universal protections that included African Americans. Those explanations are long standing. But there is another story that is more recent in origin: the decline in the power of workers relative to corporations, not only in workplaces and markets but also in Congress. It is to this that we now turn.

15

Firms, Consumers, and Workers

IN A FAMOUS PASSAGE in *The Wealth of Nations*, Adam Smith writes that "people of the same trade seldom meet together, even for merriment and diversion, but the conversation ends in a conspiracy against the public, or in some contrivance to raise prices."[1] The use of market power to raise prices remains a concern today, as we have already seen in healthcare. Prices are not the only things at risk from "conspiracy"; so are wages. In one of his last papers, economist Alan Krueger reported his conversation with Jeffrey Suhre, who worked as a nurse in the Critical Care Unit for St. John Providence Hospital in Warren, Michigan. The hospitals in the area wanted to stop nurses from improving their salaries by moving around from one to another, and "the executives would often discuss these issues and exchange pay rates at conferences," no doubt adding to the merriment and diversion. When Suhre became the lead plaintiff in an ultimately successful class action lawsuit, his employer made his life unpleasant enough for him to resign, and other hospitals were reluctant to hire him. He believes that the collusion continues, though less obviously.[2]

That Krueger told this story not to an audience of labor economists or union members but rather to the annual conference of the world's central bankers in Jackson Hole is a testament to the widespread anxiety among policy makers about possible abuse of market power in a world of larger and larger corporations. There are concerns about business in general, about rising concentration in many industries, about business as a creator of inequality, and particularly about its failure to provide good jobs at good wages for many, particularly less educated workers. Yet these concerns are not universally shared. While we know that healthcare is not delivering, if only by comparison with other wealthy countries, there is no similar straightforward argument for the rest of the economy. Business brings large and widely distributed benefits to consumers and employees, and these benefits need to be weighed against harms created and any abuse that exists. Our own view is that the benefits are real, but that the harm, some from legitimate corporate choices and some from anti-competitive behavior, is also real, particularly for less educated workers.

American Capitalism, Then and Now

At the end of the nineteenth century and the beginning of the twentieth, in the first Gilded Age, inequalities in income and wealth were as high as they are today. The United States had become the world's leading industrial economy and, as now, the economy was changing rapidly. Great innovations brought widespread benefits as well as great wealth to some of the innovating entrepreneurs. This is the way that capitalism brings progress, and there is no reason to complain about wealth that comes from activities that benefit so many, as long as those not reaping benefits are treated fairly. In the language of economics, when private incentives are aligned with social incentives, some people get rich in a way that benefits not only themselves but also many others.

Yet there is a second act to the drama. The winners soon face competition, from imitators and from a new generation of disrupters. Some first-act winners are inspired to create new innovations that the newcomers cannot match, but others try to pull up the ladders behind them, using any means at hand to stifle competition. One way is to get help from politicians; ideas and competition were enough in act 1, but political protection becomes useful and sometimes even necessary in act 2.[3] In the first Gilded Age, Standard Oil bought up competitors and set railroad rates that forced others out of business. The meat-packing industry was founded by Gustavus Swift, who figured out how to use refrigerated railroad cars and a system of ice suppliers to bring cheap fresh meat to eastern cities. Later, the industry turned on its competitors using cartels and price-fixing agreements.[4] Private and social incentives were no longer aligned, and businesses got rich on the backs of consumers.

Public benefactors turned into "robber barons," men such as Andrew Carnegie, Andrew Mellon, Henry Clay Frick, John D. Rockefeller, Jay Gould, and John Pierpont Morgan, whom Theodore Roosevelt called "malefactors of great wealth." State and federal politicians served and protected them. Yet the malefactor-versus-benefactor distinction was not always clear. As the economic historian Naomi Lamoreaux has argued,[5] it was often difficult then—as it is now—to tell whether some activities were good or bad. Corporations could get large by innovating, which was good, or by price fixing, which was bad. But what about buying up suppliers or distributors, simultaneously reducing costs and limiting competition? And what if the complaints against the trusts are from their former high-price competitors, whose elimination would be good for everyone else? Determining the balance of the public interest is never easy, even analytically, let alone in the heat of politics.

Today, the counterparts of the benefactors-malefactors are the tech innovators who have become immensely wealthy, and who are joined at the very top of the income distribution by CEOs, business owners, or financiers who are paid many millions of dollars a year. They too have an outsize influence over politics; some, like Google, that initially would have nothing to do with lobbying are now among the largest-spending lobbyists in Washington. Google (Alphabet) spent nothing on lobbying until 2006; in 2018 it spent $21 million, more than any other corporation. There is widespread popular concern not only about inequality but also, as was the case a century ago, about the way that inequality comes about, with business, protected by politicians, making large fortunes for a few at the expense of working people, whose lives are deteriorating. It is not only the radical Left that is concerned about the future of capitalism and democracy as they are practiced in America. There is a recent flood of books not only by long-standing critics but also by erstwhile defenders, successful entrepreneurs, and powerful ex–policy makers.[6]

The first Gilded Age gave way to the Progressive Era, during which laws were passed that limited trusts and monopolies, and most of these laws remain in force today. Yet there is a suspicion, widely debated in the media and among professional economists, that the enforcement of antitrust law has been neglected, allowing the trusts to regrow in modern incarnations. Antitrust policy and its enforcement can and should provide protection to American workers and consumers against the abuse of market power. But we must not expect too much of it. It is designed to promote a competitive environment, not to reduce inequality caused by competition or by the corrupting power of money in Washington.

Many of today's great fortunes came from new high-tech firms in industries that did not exist half a century ago. Google, Apple, Microsoft, Facebook, and Amazon have replaced railroads and steel; bankers and financiers managed to make fortunes in both ages. The new technologies have made our lives better, sometimes spectacularly so; this was also true in the first Gilded Age. A century ago, the possibility of remaining in constant touch with friends and family did not exist. Communication was slow and expensive. People traveled hundreds of miles to hear a rarely performed symphony or to find an out-of-print book; today, we have access to the world's music, films, and literature in an instant. We have entertainment and information at hand, in a way that our parents or grandparents (or indeed our younger selves) could not have dreamed of. Corporations provide great jobs for many Americans, jobs that not only are well paid but also confer dignity and meaning.

Yet Americans without a college degree are not sharing in this progress. Labor market opportunities, especially for those with fewer skills, have dimmed, as firms respond to global competition as well as to the falling prices and rising capabilities of robots. Globalization and automation are ultimately beneficial, but they create disruption, especially in the short run, and many less skilled workers lose out. But as we saw in chapter 14, it is not only globalization and the technology-infused labor market that are working against less educated workers.

The exorbitant price of health insurance has caused firms to shed workers; this is not a natural disaster but rather one based on rent-seeking, politically protected profiteering, and weak enforcement of antitrust in the healthcare sector. Anticompetitive and rent-seeking behavior is not confined to healthcare. Mergers of firms can give employers power to set wages and working conditions in local markets. Large corporations can potentially use market power to raise prices. Such anticompetitive behavior hurts consumers, who face higher prices, and workers, who get hurt twice over, through lower wages and higher prices when they spend those wages. Competition, one of the hallmarks of American capitalism, has faded while (arguably) flourishing elsewhere.[7] Not only in the healthcare industry but also in business more generally, anticompetitive behavior, wherever it exists, is an agent of upward redistribution.

Monopoly and Oligopoly: The Power to Overcharge

One way that a firm can enrich itself at the expense of everyone else is by overcharging. In an ideal (and only slightly simplified) world, people would not have to pay more for something than the additional cost for labor, materials, and a normal rate of profit that it takes to produce it. Consumers are not discouraged from buying things that they can afford and whose cost of production is less than it is worth to them. Competition among producers is supposed to make that happen; if someone is charging more than cost, a competitor will be lured by the potential profit to undercut the price. If the incumbent firm has a monopoly, which might be a license from the state to be the sole seller, or has control over some key ingredient or part of the production process, competition is choked off, and the monopolist can charge whatever suits it. The consumer pays more, for less, and the behavior of the monopolist is unconstrained by competition.

Before its breakup in 1984, the Bell Telephone System (AT&T) was a monopoly, though the main charge against it was less profiteering than failing to innovate. Today, many Americans have only a single cable company or broadband provider; these are local monopolies, even when they have national competition. These local monopolies are today being challenged by internet streaming; long-standing monopolies are often challenged by new technology. More common than monopoly is *oligopoly*, where there are only a few sellers, each of which has some control over price. There may be only one Toyota dealer nearby, but dealers of other brands provide imperfect competition. Apple is not the only producer of cell phones, but it has a large number of loyal customers who are unlikely to switch to Samsung, and this enables Apple to set the price of an iPhone far above what it costs to make. Airlines have frequent-flyer schemes designed to make customers reluctant to switch carriers when prices are raised. Oligopolists sometimes collude to keep prices up, implicitly or explicitly.

Evidence of Pervasive Market Power

There are many indications that something is amiss. Industries are becoming more concentrated, meaning that an increasing fraction of sales is coming from a few large firms, profits rates are rising, the share of labor in gross domestic product is falling, and inequality is growing. Mergers are increasing and the number of startups has fallen. The rate of investment is on a downward trend, especially in the most concentrated industries; investment is a prerequisite for growth, it embodies the latest knowledge and techniques, and it raises productivity, whose rate of growth is low by historical standards. While these broad trends are (mostly) agreed on, there is wide disagreement on how to interpret them, and on how concerned we ought to be.

The share of sales accounted for by the largest firms has increased in most industries. For example, averaged across the retail industry, the largest four firms by sales increased their share of sales from 15 to 30 percent between 1980 and 2015.[8] Along with transportation, retail has seen the largest increase in dominance of large firms. Amazon is a large part in the latter, and the consolidation of the airlines into four major carriers, American, Delta, United, and Southwest, is a large part of the former. The well-known investor Warren Buffett, whose dislike of competition is well attested, and who likes to quote Peter Lynch's maxim that "competition may prove hazardous to human wealth," long refused to invest in the airline industry ("If a capitalist had been present at Kitty Hawk back in the early 1900's he should have shot Orville Wright") and called investing in airlines a "death trap."[9] But he has recently found the industry more to his tastes, and Berkshire Hathaway is now the largest shareholder in Delta and the second largest in Southwest, United, and American.[10] This "horizontal shareholding" poses a threat to competition, especially given that other large shareholders, such as Vanguard, are passive investors.[11] Passengers are unlikely to share Buffett's enthusiasm for the decreased competition; a profitable ride for capital is an uncomfortable ride for passengers herded onto (or even dragged off of) planes and held captive in terminals that have been turned into high-price shopping malls with gates on a distant periphery. Prices have fallen on some routes, but risen on others; in the fall of 2019, a business-class round-trip ticket from Newark to Los Angeles (2,800 miles) was $1,140, to Paris (3,600 miles) was $10,000, and to Hong Kong (8,045 miles) was $7,800. Whatever is determining price, it is not the marginal cost of the service, as would be the case in perfect competition.

Firms less than five years old accounted for half of all firms in 1980 but only a third in 2015; they accounted for a fifth of all employment in 1980 but only a tenth in 2015.[12] Markups (the ratio of price to marginal cost of production) have risen since 1970, with precise estimates depending on (not easily resolved) issues of measurement.[13] The average share of profits in sales, which had been 4 percent in the 1960s, rose from 2 percent in the 1980s to 8 percent in 2015. There is a growing fraction of firms making profits that are more than 15 percent of sales. The share of wages in gross domestic product, long thought to be immutably constant at around two-thirds, has fallen to 60 percent.[14]

These data can be interpreted as showing that American industry is increasingly less competitive; in a currently more popular (populist?) term, the system is seen as increasingly rigged in favor of business. The great British economist Sir John Hicks argued that the best of all monopoly profits is a quiet life.[15] Not only are prices too high, but with irritating competition eliminated, there is no need to improve products, to provide better service, or to invest in finding and implementing new ideas. Instead, the highest returns come from investing the profits not in the business itself but in digging a moat to keep competitors at bay. The monopolist can buy up and eliminate potential competitors or pay for socially unproductive but privately productive lobbying to protect market power and to keep taxes low. There is evidence that many mergers, originally sold on the promise of cost saving and lower prices, have actually resulted in higher prices with no gain in productivity, which suggests that antitrust regulators have been asleep at the switch in the past quarter century.[16]

There is much to these arguments, yet they do not tell the whole story.[17] Much of the growth in markups and in profits has come from a few firms in each industry, usually those that invested heavily in information and communications technology.[18] Think of Amazon and the construction of its platform, or the airlines developing websites and algorithms for pricing, or Walmart, which has constructed an innovative system of logistics, supply, and inventory control. Once the system is in place, the cost of production and delivery falls and margins rise, though profits may not increase until the costs of the system are paid. Over time, these firms expand relative to others in the industry and acquire a larger share of sales. Some other firms find that they cannot compete, so the number of firms in the industry falls and concentration rises. The successful innovators may well acquire some market power, especially if there are few competitors left. Ideally, new firms manage to imitate or even improve the leader's system, and prices fall. When this process works, technological change is socially beneficial for consumers through lower prices and more efficient production methods, though it all takes time, and there are likely many casualties along the way.[19]

In this version of events, the concentration of an industry comes not from malfeasance by firms with market power but from a shift from less to more efficient firms. And indeed, the data show that the increases in margins are happening not to typical firms in each industry but rather to a fringe of profitable firms, especially those with heavy investments in IT. According to this account, these firms are neither criminals nor even robber barons, but superstars.

Evidence that at least part of the increase in concentration is the result of a fringe of especially innovative firms, and not solely the result of firms throwing up unproductive market barriers, comes from the fact that similar changes are happening in Europe. The shares of labor in gross domestic product are declining, and those of capital rising, in most European countries,[20] although Britain is perhaps an exception. Margins are rising and industries are becoming more concentrated in Europe too. All of which tells in favor of the superstar story of rising profits, and against

an account that depends exclusively on American institutions like lobbying, its political system, or a peculiarly American unwillingness to apply
antitrust law.[21] European countries have also seen some recent increases
in income inequality, though less than in the United States, which is consistent with trade and IT pushing up inequality, but with additional,
specifically American forces ramping it up.

Innovation often happens through a process of creative destruction,
or Schumpeterian competition, named after the Austrian economist
Joseph Schumpeter. (He is famous for having declared his wish to be the
greatest economist in the world, the greatest horseman in Austria, and
the best lover in Vienna. He later claimed that only the decline in the
cavalry had thwarted his triple ambition, though not all economists
would agree. There is no surviving evidence on his third ambition.)
According to Schumpeter, technological progress is inherently disrup-
tive. Outsiders with new technologies are a threat to incumbents. Bringing their new ideas to market requires upfront investment and involves
great risk of failure, but with the chance of huge monopoly profits if
they can replace the incumbent. This can be described as competition
for the market, not competition *in* the market. Innovation is a series
of tournaments, challenges for dominance, with rich prizes for the
winners. Justice Antonin Scalia captured this in his judgment that "the
mere possession of monopoly power, and the concomitant charging
of monopoly prices, is not only not unlawful; it is an important element of the free-market system. The opportunity to charge monopoly
prices—at least for a short period—is what attracts 'business acumen'
in the first place; it induces risk taking that produces innovation and
economic growth."[22]

Is Market Power a Current Problem
That Needs to Be Fixed?

In a world of Schumpeterian competition, antitrust regulation needs to
prevent the successful challengers from pulling up the ladders behind

them. A temporary competitive advantage is fine; permanent advantage is not. Regulators should police the sort of competition that eliminates potential competitors—for example, Microsoft eliminating Netscape by building its own browser into its operating system, Facebook buying up Instagram and WhatsApp, or pharmaceutical companies buying up potential generics to prevent them from ever coming to market. Industrial concentration cannot be a target on its own, because concentration can be an indicator of efficiency, not the reverse. And industries are often not the same as markets. Consumers often face a single supplier nearby— cable suppliers, or an airport that is dominated by a single carrier—and may thus face a monopoly even if the industry is competitive. Conversely, the growth of Amazon has *increased* competition in many parts of America, particularly rural and lightly populated areas with little choice of local retail stores.[23]

The extent of market power is one of the most hotly contested areas in economics today, as is the question of how much we should worry. Yet there are key points to take away for our main concern, which is whether monopolies and other forms of market power cause higher prices and lower real wages, setting the stage for deaths of despair. We think that this is true for healthcare, and that there are other industries that are of real concern—for example, the increasing concentration of airlines and airline ownership, or the frequently exploitative behavior of banks. We also worry about dominant firms choking off potential competitors. But we do not believe that it has yet been established that there is any *general* case that American industry has become less competitive and is raising prices to the detriment of consumer welfare.[24] Indeed, the spate of innovation has, for many goods and services, brought ever-lower prices, including much that comes for free. The problem with all the innovation is not that prices are too high; it is that Schumpeterian creative destruction is not only creative but destructive. It eliminates jobs that used to exist, accelerated by the cost of health insurance, throwing workers into an increasingly hostile labor market, and with an inadequate safety net; the lives and communities that were supported by those jobs are put at risk, at the worst leading to despair and death.

Labor Markets and Monopsony:
The Power to Underpay

Just as monopoly exists when there is only one seller, *monopsony* exists when there is only one buyer; here we are particularly concerned with only one buyer of labor. The term *monopsony* was coined by one of economics' most eminent women, Joan Robinson,[25] a pupil and collaborator of John Maynard Keynes in Cambridge, and a major thinker about how competition works. A company town is an example of pure monopsony. As in the case of sellers, there may be only a few employers, each with some power to lower wages; this is *oligopsony*. Monopsony or oligopsony means that firms have power over wage setting, in contrast to perfect competition, where there is a going wage for workers, and anyone who tries to pay less will be unable to hire any employees. The most obvious place where employers might be able to pay less than market wages is in rural areas where there may be little work of any kind, perhaps only at a fast-food restaurant, a chicken-processing plant, or a state prison. Schoolteachers or nurses in rural areas or small towns may find themselves in a similar position. Workers have the option of moving away, but there are always costs and risks to doing so, finding a new job can be costly, and they may have ties to people or the communities where they live, all of which gives employers some power to lower wages. Mobility has decreased in the US, in part because land in many cities has become very expensive, and in part because the opportunities for advancement in urban areas have fallen for the less educated, so there is a possibility that monopsony has become more severe, lowering wages below the competitive level and raising profits at the expense of wages.[26]

When labor markets are competitive, a government-imposed minimum wage that is higher than the going wage will cause employers to lay off workers. This is what the economics textbooks commonly say. There have been many studies that have looked for such outcomes. Although the federal minimum wage has not increased since 2009, many states have raised their state minimum wage since then, providing many opportunities for studying the effects. The most comprehensive and persuasive study to date, by the economists Doruk Cengiz, Arindrajit

Dube, and their collaborators, finds no effects on employment; instead of firing workers or restricting new hires, employers simply shift workers from just below the new minimum to just above it.[27] There is similar evidence from other countries, especially Britain, which, in 1999, went from no minimum to a relatively high minimum wage; dozens of studies there have failed to find any effect on employment levels.[28] None of these outcomes would be possible if employers had no power to set wages. Labor markets are not as competitive as the textbooks would have us believe, and if employers are paying their workers less than they are worth, it is not a surprise that they keep them on when they are forced to pay them more because, at least up to a point, they remain worth more than they cost.

Employees in cities often get paid more than similar employees in rural areas, and places where there are few employers have lower wages than places with many. Yet there are many possible reasons for such differences and, as with the arguments about sellers and market power, it is impossible to know what to make of correlations between employer concentration and wages without understanding *why* there is more or less concentration. Increasing concentration at the national level has come with *decreasing* employer concentration at the local level, which has decreased earnings inequality.[29] Even so, there are specific cases of malfeasance. The account of nurses' wages with which we began shows hospitals colluding to hold down wages—collusion is easier when there are only a few players—and hospitals appear to be skilled at squeezing both their patients and their employees.[30] Holding down nurses' pay generates shortages, and hospitals make up the difference by hiring nurses from contract agencies that are more expensive than their regular nurses but whose hiring does not involve paying more to the much larger number of permanent nurses. Once again, this is evidence that some firms can affect wages against workers.

More Hostile Workplaces and the Decline of Unions

It is common for employers to have employees sign *noncompete agreements*—even in states such as California, where they are unenforceable but perhaps effective as threats—and these agreements limit alternative employment opportunities and make it easier for the employer to hold down wages; a quarter of American workers are covered by some kind of noncompete clause.[31] Noncompetes are understandable when workers acquire trade secrets or other knowledge that is useful to competitors—designing blueprints or writing code—but have no such justification in low-wage jobs, yet one in five below-median-wage workers works under a noncompete. A (very) Panglossian interpretation might be that workers are aware of these clauses when they sign up and are compensated for doing so. More likely, they are not so aware and are unwittingly giving their employers power to hold down their wages.

As we saw in chapter 11, it has become common for firms to contract out a wide range of support services, such as cleaning, security, food provision, and transportation. This allows the firms to specialize in their core business, which is arguably what they are good at, but the outsourcing firms are often less attractive places to work, with poorer benefits, lower wages, fewer employment rights, and little or no chance of promotion.[32] The economists David Dorn, Johannes Schmieder, and James Spletzer write that "domestic outsourcing has thoroughly transformed the nature of the employment relationship for a vast number of jobs, ranging from relatively low skilled tasks like cleaning and security to high skilled tasks like human resources and accounting."[33] They estimate that about a quarter of workers in cleaning occupations and in security worked for business service firms in 2015; more than four times as many workers are employed by business service firms than was the case in 1950. As of March 2019, Google had more temps and contractors than it did employees, even though the former work alongside the latter and sometimes do similar work.[34] The growth of outsourcing and its downgrading of work help undermine working-class lives.

The spread of these practices would surely have been contested by more powerful unions collectively bargaining on behalf of their members. Unions, where they exist, are, or once were, a countervailing power to management in the allocation of the firm's value added between wages and profits, pushing for higher wages, better working conditions, and more benefits and restraining the power of management. In early 2019, 10.5 percent of workers were unionized, compared with 20.1 percent in 1983, when the modern data begin. In the private sector, only 6.4 percent of workers belong to unions. At the peak, in the 1940s and early 1950s, a third of all households had at least one union member.[35]

Weaker unions, whose lobby in Washington has been overwhelmed by business lobbies, are also one reason why the federal minimum wage has remained at $7.25 an hour since July 2009, in spite of the fact that seven out of ten Americans think it ought to be raised. (That said, and as we have noted, many states have raised their minimum wage rates, and twenty-nine states have higher rates, ranging from $8.25 in Illinois to $12.00 in Washington State, so that, weighted by the number of workers, effective minimum wages have actually risen by 10.8 percent from 2007 to 2016.)[36]

Corporate Behavior

As unions faded in importance, firms were run differently. Management moved away from a model in which the firm was seen as serving not only its shareholders but also its employees, its customers, and the community, toward an exclusive attention to the interests of the shareholders, the owners of capital. Perhaps surprisingly, there is controversy over the purpose of the corporation:[37] Who exactly is the board responsible to? The majority view today is that the board's sole obligation is to the shareholders, but there are other interpretations, including that the board is responsible to the corporation itself, or to a wider range of stakeholders, including consumers and employees. States also have jurisdiction, and what they do varies from state to state—for example, California requires that boards have at least one female member. In spite of increased recent questioning, maximization of shareholder value has become the norm in recent years. Of course, shareholders do not directly manage firms, but managers have been increasingly incentivized to act in the shareholders' interest by being paid in stock and stock options, so that their own fortunes become more aligned with the market valuation of the firm. This market value is the value that shareholders assign to the profits that they expect the firm to make in the future, so managers lose out personally if they act so as to benefit other stakeholders, whether employees, customers, or the community, except insofar as treating them well results in higher profits.

The threat that a raider might take over the firm serves to further enforce the exclusive attention to profits. If a well-funded outsider believes that the firm is underperforming in profits, the raider can buy up enough shares to force a change in policy, or to dismiss the management, or even to dismember the firm for the value of its assets. Such attacks have become easier and cheaper in today's world, where a large fraction of shares is held by passive investors (who do not try to influence the board), such as Vanguard or BlackRock, so the raider can gain control with a small fraction of shares.

Many people think that the value of the stock market is a positive indicator of the state of the American economy, and they follow the Dow Jones Index or the S&P 500 in the same way they follow baseball scores, rejoicing in ups and bemoaning downs. While it is true that better future growth prospects will generally lift the market, which everyone agrees is good, it is also true that the market will rise if wages fall or managers replace workers with cheaper robots. The stock market rewards redistribution away from labor and toward capital. As we have seen, managers are increasingly incentivized to make this sort of redistribution happen. But there is another group that is less often discussed in this context: shareholders who hold 401(k) retirement plans, or indeed anyone who has a defined-contribution pension plan. Once upon a time, employees were much more likely to have a defined-*benefit* scheme, which someone else was responsible for funding; the value of the stock market might be relevant to the funder, but not directly to the employee. But employees who have defined-contribution plans, invested in the market, have a direct interest in the market doing well, and thus are rewarded when wages fall or workers are replaced by automation. Yet those holding such assets are predominantly the people with college degrees, whose wages have been doing well. The replacement of defined-benefit by defined-contribution pension schemes has therefore given more-educated and successful Americans an interest in less educated Americans doing badly. We do not suggest that the educated elite agitates against working-class Americans. But they have certainly been well paid for their acquiescence; since 1990, the S&P 500 has risen at more than 7 percent a year.

Corporations and Labor in Washington

A by-product of having very large, profitable firms, and a large number of very wealthy individuals, is the influence that they bring to bear on politics. In particular, we run the risk that those with deep pockets participate more effectively in American politics, and that ordinary people, those with less education whose deaths are the topic of this book, are left as nonparticipants; their interests silenced, they become casualties in the interests of the rich. Democracy in America today is not working well, and its malfunctions have much to do with the way that money works in Washington.[38]

There were 11,654 registered lobbyists in Washington in 2018, who spent $3.46 *billion* on their activities.[39] That is 22 lobbyists for each of the 535 senators and representatives, or $6.5 million available to lobby each one of them. This is in addition to outside money spent on campaign finance; in 2018 this was $1.3 billion. These numbers are large, and have a large effect on politics in Washington, but are small relative to the scale of corporate budgets—for example, relative to the $47 billion that auto manufacturers spent on advertising in 2015.[40]

There have always been lobbyists who tried to persuade government to act in their interests, yet it was not until the regulatory changes of the 1970s that corporations responded by ramping up their lobbying. In 1971, future Supreme Court justice Lewis Powell Jr. wrote in a now famous memo that "the American economic system is under broad attack," and that business must cultivate political power and use it "aggressively and with determination,"[41] a recommendation that was abundantly followed in the subsequent years. Before the 1970s, business was represented in Washington not through lobbying on behalf of individual corporations but by their collective trade associations, which often were (and remain) effective in seeking special favors for their members, such as doctors or realtors.

Most companies do not have lobbyists in Washington, but those that do tend to be large. Ordered by amount spent in 2018, the biggest individual company was Alphabet (Google), followed by AT&T, Boeing, Comcast, Amazon, Northrop Grumman, Lockheed Martin, and Facebook ($12.6 million). Bigger still, ranked by spending, are business associations, the Chamber of Commerce ($94.8 million), the National Association of Realtors, and the associations of pharmaceutical manufacturers, hospitals, insurers, and doctors, whose American Medical Association spent about the same in 2018 as Alphabet. The only non-business group in the top twenty spenders is the Open Society Policy Center, backed by George Soros, which lobbies on national security, civil rights, and immigration, among other issues. The healthcare industry as a whole (including pharma, hospitals, insurers, and doctors) spent more than half a billion dollars in 2018, as did the finance industry; labor groups collectively spent less than one-tenth as much as either, $47 million.[42]

Just as is true within firms, the power of labor in Washington has declined relative to that of corporations, especially large corporations.

The lobbying system, contrary to what is often thought, is not a machine whereby firms and individuals with deep pockets can write their own legislation and have it passed by bought-and-paid-for senators and representatives. There is too much competition and too many lobbyists on all sides of the big issues. Lobbying is important, but it has not rigged the system so that it only works for the paymasters. What it does do is suck up the energy in Washington, so those who cannot or do not lobby have less and less influence. Once-powerful groups, such as unions, have been swamped. If you cannot afford to lobby, you are not represented, and worse, in the oft-used but accurate Washington phrase, if you do not have a seat at the table, you are probably on the menu.

It is around these Washington tables, where working people are rarely represented, that upward redistribution is designed and implemented. The interests of ordinary people are pushed off the table in favor of the matters that corporations care about. Congresspeople and senators, who should be representing the interests of all of their constituents, consistently vote the interests of the wealthier people they represent, ignoring the interests of others.[43] Just as, or more, important is that much of what concerns working people—minimum wages being only one example—is never put to the vote. Democracy plus lobbying is a selective democracy.

Corporations and Workers, in Summary

In chapter 13, we argued that the high and rising cost of healthcare bears much responsibility for the decline in wages and working conditions among less educated workers. Other mandatory benefits to which employers have to contribute, such as Social Security and Medicare payments, unemployment insurance, and compensation insurance for workplace injury, have the same effects, albeit on a smaller scale. Ironically, these benefits were long fought for by unions, but once legislated, they made belonging to a union less attractive. These labor costs also make it more profitable for employers to outsource some of the work, and to reduce the number of direct employees.

Workers are losing out in other ways. While they have shared in the benefits of new technologies, and the goods and services that these have provided, the markets in which they sell their labor have become increasingly hostile. The decline of manufacturing, the threat of being effectively replaced by foreign workers through trade, and the decline of unions in the private sector have all reduced the bargaining power of less educated workers at work,[44] just as the rise of corporate lobbying has deprived them of bargaining power in Washington. Many employers have at least some market power over the wages of their less skilled employees, and they often use it to hold wages below the competitive level. Outsourcing has taken good jobs with good benefits and turned them into precarious jobs with few benefits.[45] The meaning that came from being part of an admirable enterprise, serving the public as well as its shareholders, has been lost for many less educated Americans.

Less educated workers live in a much more hostile world than did less educated workers of half a century ago. Much of this hostility can be seen not only in the United States but also in other rich countries. Wages and working conditions have deteriorated in several of them; they too have experienced a decline in manufacturing in favor of services, slowing rates of economic growth, and a decline in unionization. But these other countries do not face the costs of the American healthcare system, and they have much more comprehensive systems of social protection. None has seen wage stagnation for as long as has the United States. All of which could explain why we do not see epidemics of deaths of despair across the rich world. Yet it remains a real concern that, for all less skilled workers, Western capitalism has a clouded future.

16

What to Do?

WE WOULD LIKE TO see an America that is more just. The problem is that different people have very different and mutually incompatible ideas of justice. But we can go a long way focusing instead on obvious *injustices*, features of society on whose wrongness many people can agree. We do not have to complete the whole jigsaw puzzle of justice to make arguments for reform. This is what the economist and philosopher Amartya Sen calls the comparative approach, which he contrasts with the transcendental approach that begins by describing an ideal society.[1] If we can agree on the identification of a list of injustices, each one removed takes us toward a better world.

To take some concrete examples, there is wide agreement that making money out of human suffering is wrong, and that wealth inequality based on that suffering is unjust. There is also broad agreement, on both right and left, among people with very different political views, that rent-seeking and crony capitalism are unjust. Whatever we think about wealth seeking, we can agree that it is unjust to get rich through special favors, such as those excoriated by Adam Smith as supporting "absurd and oppressive monopolies." By contrast, there is no such agreement that any action that reduces income inequality is thereby automatically desirable.

Many economists who think about income distribution endorse the view, first extensively used in economics,[2] and which philosophers now call "prioritarianism,"[3] that the more people have, the less weight (priority) their wellbeing should be given in policy making. Prioritarians endorse equality, and economic prioritarians design tax systems that aim for income equality while recognizing the limitations that come from the fact that the more heavily people are taxed, the less they will contribute to the economy. The resulting tax system depends on factual issues, particularly on how people respond to taxes, and on how much the rich contribute to the wellbeing of others. It also rests on values, and particularly on prioritarianism, which not everyone endorses; indeed, we suspect that the majority of Americans do not. In particular, it is a controversial ethical position to argue, as economic prioritarians do, that the value to society of giving additional income to those in the top 1 percent of the income distribution is so small that it can be ignored.[4]

We should declare our own values on these matters. We believe that those in distress deserve priority, but not that there should be any decline in priority with income or wealth among those who are not in distress. The anguish associated with deaths of despair is a matter of the greatest importance; reducing inequality by redistributing from the seriously rich to the merely rich, or even to the educated middle classes, does not seem important to us unless it brings other benefits. That is why we are not disturbed by inequality in and of itself, but very concerned with the inequality that comes about through theft and rent-seeking, or through the involuntary upward redistribution that we have described throughout this book. To be clear, we are not denying that inequality can sometimes have consequences that undermine other important social goals—for example, if the rich use their wealth to corrupt democracy, or to agitate against public goods on which most people depend. But we are against the high marginal rates on top incomes that result from prioritarian calculations. Instead, we prefer to fight rent-seeking directly, which, if successful, will do much to reduce inequality.

Opioids

Drug overdoses are the single largest category of deaths of despair. They are part of a broader epidemic that includes death from alcoholism and suicide, a reflection of the social failures that we have described in this book. Yet the behavior of the pharmaceutical companies caused more deaths than would otherwise have happened, showering gasoline on smoldering despair. Stopping the drug epidemic will not eliminate the root causes of deaths of despair, but it will save many lives and should be an immediate priority.

Addiction is extremely hard to treat, even with the cooperation of the addict. There appears to be wide agreement that medication-assisted treatment can be effective, but it is not available to everyone, often because of cost. There are accounts of substantial reductions in drug deaths in some places—for example, in Dayton, Ohio, where there was a statewide Medicaid expansion under Governor John Kasich, and where the police and public health officials worked together to focus on treatment over policing.[5] Further expansion of Medicaid would be helpful, for drug problems as well as other medical care.

The dangers of opioid prescriptions are much better understood by physicians than was true early in the epidemic, and the prescribing rate peaked in 2012. But as late as 2017 there were still fifty-eight opioid prescriptions for every hundred Americans, three times the rate in 1999, with the average prescription for an eighteen-day supply.[6] As we have seen, this two-decade expansion in prescriptions of opioids has done nothing to decrease reports of pain, and while we are sympathetic to those who are suffering, we believe that opioids are still being wildly overprescribed for chronic pain. The healthcare system needs to explore better options, including the wide range of alternative treatments that were used before 1999. Insurers should pay for such treatments, even if they are more expensive than prescribing a pill.

The American pharmaceutical industry is currently dysfunctional, as is healthcare more generally. OxyContin should not have been approved without consideration of the likely consequences of a large-scale release of an addictive drug into the population. As part of healthcare reform more generally, America needs an agency such as Britain's National Institute for Health and Care Excellence (NICE) that assesses the benefits and costs of treatments and has the power to prevent the adoption of treatments whose benefits fail to exceed their costs. This is, of course, an example of government interference in the market. Yet, as we have already argued, the market for pharmaceuticals is nothing like a free market, nor could it ever be.

Healthcare

The generally powerful arguments for the social benefits of free markets do not apply to healthcare.[7] Unregulated markets for health are not socially beneficial, and regulated markets can work well; in Britain, NICE appears to have resisted the political pressures that could have either closed it or turned it into a magnet for rent seekers.[8] America should follow other rich countries in providing universal insurance and in controlling healthcare costs; the former is important, and the latter even more so. America currently has the worst of both worlds, where government interference, instead of controlling costs, creates opportunities for rent-seeking that inflate costs. It is not possible for an unregulated market to provide a socially acceptable degree of coverage; as Kenneth Arrow noted long ago, "The *laissez-faire* solution for medicine is intolerable."[9] Some amount of compulsion is required, as are subsidies for those who cannot pay. Reforms that deny those facts are doomed.

While there are many difficulties, there is a hugely positive aspect to a better healthcare system, at least in principle. Because the current American system is so wasteful, it is possible to have a better, more efficient system that will improve health while saving immense sums of money and improving fairness of access. Such a system not only could cover the 28.5 million Americans (as of 2017) without insurance[10] but also could increase the take-home pay of typical employees. Many unionists and politicians fear the removal of the present system on the grounds that less educated workers have had no or less than no increase in earnings for many years, and that removing their employer-provided healthcare would be a further insult. It needs to be more widely understood that the employer-provided healthcare is one of the main reasons why wages have not done better.

It need not be true, as is often stated by the alarmists, that universal healthcare is unaffordable and, if provided by the government, would require enormous additional taxes for the indefinite future. We know that what may sound like a utopian dream is far from utopian, because other countries do it. Yet it is true that getting there will be far from easy. What we would do if we were designing a system from the ground up is very different from what we will have to do today to improve today's mess. Even so, the huge benefits that are possible need to be constantly kept in mind and should set both a goal and an inspiration.

No viable scheme can work without compulsion to prevent those who do not need insurance from refusing to pay, nor without cost control, which will cut the incomes of providers, not all of whom are extremely rich. It would also deny some people some of the insurance products or treatments that they currently have and like. No one likes compulsion, perhaps especially Americans, who hate the idea that healthcare should be rationed, although apparently not when the rationing is done by money, excluding those who cannot pay. They also want mutually contradictory outcomes, such as having coverage for preexisting conditions without having to buy insurance before those conditions exist. Every cent we spend on healthcare shows up as someone's income, and those someones will fight to preserve the status quo. But it needs to be understood that they are fighting to preserve their incomes, not fighting for health, or to preserve the mythical free market for health that pharmaceutical firms like to talk about when threatened with price controls.

We are not endorsing any of the several plans that are currently being discussed; there are many options in play, including variants of what other countries do, which themselves differ from one country to another. It is not true, for example, that the only alternative to what currently exists is the British system, where the government actually delivers care, paying doctors and hospitals. There are also many alternatives to the extremely expensive idea that the federal government should provide Medicare for all, opening the scheme to those under age sixty-five and bearing the total cost out of taxes. Other countries work with a smaller and tightly regulated insurance sector and with private providers, but all have some way of ensuring that everyone is in the system, that there are subsidies for some, and that costs are controlled.[11] What works for other countries may not work in the United States, where people have different incomes, different traditions, and different expectations. The economist Victor Fuchs, who has devoted much of his life to thinking about healthcare, writes, "The United States can learn from the experience of others, but must fashion a system consistent with US history, circumstances, and its values."[12] He has developed a detailed plan using vouchers that is not a single-payer system.[13] It does have a cost-control board like Britain's NICE, and it is financed through a dedicated value-added tax. Other plans work to extend Medicare in a way that does not immediately switch the total cost to the government,[14] requiring employers to continue to provide insurance or, if they do not, pay toward a federal scheme.

It will almost certainly be necessary to increase government expenditure at the rollout, while controlling the escalation of costs over time so that providers, instead of facing reductions of income at once, would slowly gain less than they would otherwise have done. The healthcare lobby is the most powerful in Washington, and it is almost certainly impossible to have reform without paying them off at the time of the reform. The alternative is to keep paying them off forever, and a well-designed reform, with cost control, will slowly reduce the tribute we have to pay them by controlling the diffusion of ever more expensive treatments that do little. Again, we emphasize that while the questions involved in designing and financing an alternative scheme are challenging, the problem is not one of finding a large amount of new money to fund a new entitlement program. The money that is already being spent is more than enough. The problem is in part one of technical and financial engineering, of finding ways to reallocate money, and in part a political one, of doing the engineering in a way that buys off the opposition of those who are currently benefiting, while recouping this buy-off over time. The Labour Party minister of health, Nye Bevan, when he opened the British National Health Service in 1946, was asked how he dealt with the doctors' lobby, which had compared him to a Nazi medical *führer*. His response was that he succeeded "by stuffing their mouths with gold."[15]

Corporate Governance

The decline of unions has tipped power away from employees and toward managers and the owners of capital. Although we would like to see a reversal of the decline in unions, or at least a restoration of the services that unions used to provide, we think a rebirth of unions is unlikely or, if it does happen, is likely to be slow.

A comprehensive reform of US corporations, in which employees are represented on corporate boards, as occurs in many parts of Europe, is also unlikely. A less attractive but still useful reform would be to regulate some of the harmful practices in which firms now engage. For example, it should be possible to ensure that outsourcing firms do not exist simply to cut benefits or to undercut wages using undocumented immigrants. Noncompete clauses could be outlawed everywhere, as is the case today in California.

Tax and Benefit Policies

European safety nets were, for many years, strong enough to prevent any increase in inequality in take-home incomes, in spite of increases in inequality in incomes before tax.[16] We have already seen a recent example in Britain where the safety net effectively offset the more rapid growth of incomes at higher percentiles of the income distribution. Even so, there is currently no smoking gun that links deaths of despair to a lack of safety nets, either within countries or between them. In particular, the white less educated men and women in America who are at the epicenter of the epidemic are far from the poorest people in America, and we have documented that neither their poverty status nor fluctuations in their incomes through the 1990s, the 2000s, and the Great Recession have any obvious link to the mortality rates.

Rewinding the clock forty years, a more generous safety net would have made the transitions wrought by globalization and automation less painful for those who lost their jobs and their incomes. So would have universal healthcare. Unconditional benefits would also have eased the downward pressure on wages, because people would have found it less urgent to find work in the short term, and universal healthcare would have reduced the incentives for firms to shed workers. Some benefits that do exist, such as the Earned Income Tax Credit, can only be obtained conditional on work. The active labor-market policies that are favored by

Scandinavian countries would have helped by stemming the outflow of workers from the labor market.

Yet it would be wise not to rely too heavily on a stronger safety net. If Michael Young's division into the "populists" and the "hypocrisy" is ongoing, with educational success dividing the US population, as well as populations in Europe, the safety net is something of a Band-Aid, useful but incapable of addressing the fundamental problem. That said, we have no recipe for policies that *would* address that issue. The philosopher Kwame Anthony Appiah has argued that we need to valorize a wider range of talents beyond the passing of meritocratic exams, but it is unclear, at least to us, how that might be implemented.[17]

The idea of a universal basic income (UBI) has many adherents, and it would make sense that, in a world in which robots have replaced many or even most workers, something of the kind would be required to ensure that all of the national income did not go to the owners of and inventors of the robots. But we are still a long way from such a dystopia. Yet even today, there are powerful and persuasive arguments for a UBI, just as there are arguments for universal healthcare and universal education; people in a free society should have a free basic allocation of time to use as they choose. We particularly recommend the eloquent and persuasive argument by Philippe van Parijs and Yannick Vanderborght,[18] that a UBI would enhance freedom for everyone. Many believe that politics and democracy would work much better with a UBI, and may not work at all without it, especially in places where subsistence is not guaranteed.[19] There is also a powerful ethical argument about the source of earnings in rich countries, which, although they are certainly dependent on current efforts, are to a much larger extent supported by our national patrimony—the infrastructure of education and jobs, as well as the physical and social capital that we owe to earlier generations.[20] We are all entitled to a share of our patrimony.

Yet we are not in favor of a UBI under current circumstances. The oft-cited support on both right and left dissolves in the face of arithmetic. On the right, the benefit replaces all other government transfers, including pensions and disability payments, so that many elderly and disabled people would be worse off than now. On the left, the UBI is seen as an addition to the current system, which makes it extraordinarily expensive;

a universal benefit of $10,000 per person a year would approximately double the amount of taxes that are currently collected. More realistic possibilities lie between those two extremes, and they could be implemented by tinkering with current benefits and taxes to make the system more like a UBI—for example, by designing benefits so that poor people do not face high taxes on anything extra that they earn. Even this, it turns out, is extraordinarily hard to do at a feasible cost.[21]

A deeper issue with UBI is what to think about work. Defenders of the UBI are split between, on the one hand, those who want to demonstrate that a UBI would not make people less likely to work and, on the other hand, those who see the freedom not to work as a feature, not a bug. There is little doubt that for many taxpayers, some of whom are unhappy about paying for others' healthcare, or the education of other people's children, paying for their leisure is a step too far. The economist Robert Frank has conjured up an image of a hardworking dentist in Indianapolis who drives through the snow to spend his day treating bad-tempered patients who begrudge his fees and care not at all about his varicose veins, and who sees on television a commune of adults, reading poetry and cultivating the arts, all bankrolled from their pooled UBIs.[22] Many Americans believe that work is essential if one is to fully participate in life, and that if a UBI reduces people's willingness to work and takes pressure off them to find gainful employment, it will diminish their life chances. Which makes the political feasibility of the UBI depend on its effects on labor supply. It is possible that a UBI would give people whose jobs have been lost the freedom to train for new jobs, undertake new activities, and contribute to their communities, as well as to participate more fully in democratic political activity and, in the long run, rebuild their own lives. For us, who are concerned about deaths of despair and the loss of meaning and status that has come with job destruction, we find it hard to see a UBI as the best way forward.

Antitrust

Antitrust enforcement is a hugely controversial topic in economics and law today. One side sees increasing concentration, market power, and exploitation while the enforcers sleep, or have been put to sleep. Others see no evidence of harm and see much benefit, especially to consumers. We reviewed these debates in chapter 15. We agree that there are real problems in some industries, such as healthcare and finance, but we are not persuaded that there is a general issue of monopoly. Market power in labor markets—monopsony—is another matter, and there is good evidence of employers finding ways of paying their workers less than the competitive wage.

Even so, it is important that the debate take place. Industry is changing rapidly with technological change and with trade, and even if current policies work today, that may not continue to be the case. It is also good that European regulators and politicians think differently, so we get practical experience of alternatives, even if they are sometimes inspired by protectionism against American companies. Monopsony is illegal but is difficult to prosecute and to police; work needs to be done to figure out ways of doing this better. We also think it would be a good idea if antitrust policy were more active in scrutinizing mergers and, in particular, in preventing already large firms from acquiring potential competitors. Perhaps the burden of proof should be moved more firmly from the regulatory agency to the firms proposing the merger. We also endorse the idea of making Amazon, Facebook, and Google pay every time they use the information that they acquire from their users.[23] This is a good example of making capitalism stronger by extending markets, rather than by undermining them.

Wage Policies

A main argument of this book is that the loss of good jobs for less educated Americans not only is hurting those who are directly affected but is also hurting others, through the devastation of many communities and the destruction of a way of life. There is then a strong case for public policy that props up wages because, left to themselves, labor markets do not take account of the external effects. This could be done through a system of wage subsidies, or by raising the minimum wage. Wage subsidies create jobs and raise both wages and profits; among others, they have long been advocated by the Nobel Prize–winning economist

Edmund Phelps, and more recently by the conservative commentator Oren Cass.[24] Raising the minimum wage also increases wages. Whether it costs jobs will depend both on the size of the increase and on whether labor markets are competitive; either way, firm profits will likely fall. Those on the right tend to favor subsidies and oppose increases in the minimum wage; those on the left take the opposite view.

We are not opposed to wage subsidies; for us the key is to restore jobs. But we think the recent work on the minimum wage in the United States provides compelling evidence that small increases do not cost jobs but simply shift people from below the minimum to above it, with knock-on effects for workers originally above the minimum, presumably to restore pay differentials in occupations where they are important. We are also impressed by what happened to low pay in Britain after the introduction of a minimum wage in 1999. Both sets of evidence are discussed in chapter 15. It is also relevant that so many Americans are in favor of an increase in the minimum wage, as this means that implementing it is likely to be politically easier than implementing a wage subsidy.

We are therefore in favor of a modest increase in the minimum wage and support the campaign to gradually raise the federal minimum to $15.00 from $7.25 an hour today. We see an increase in the minimum wage as part of our more general aim to redistribute power and money from corporations to labor. In 2017, according to the Bureau of Labor Statistics, about two-thirds of the 1.8 million Americans who earned at or below the minimum wage worked in service occupations, mostly preparing and serving food.[25] These are not the good jobs that less educated Americans have been losing but rather the jobs that they risk having to turn to after losing their job. Raising the minimum wage, similar to extending the safety net, would help cushion that transition.

Rent-Seeking

Joan Robinson described what she called the *paradox of patents*, that they obstruct diffusion so as to make more of it.[26] Patents are publicly granted licenses to acquire rents, but their terms are not set in stone, and they are the subject of intense lobbying. Brink Lindsey and Steven Teles[27] argue that copyright laws and patents, as well as licensing requirements and local land-use rules, have grown rapidly in favor of rent-seekers, for incumbents and against challengers, and are slowing down innovation and economic growth. As software has replaced physical capital in much of industry, copyright has become much more aggressively applied; buildings can be protected with fences and guards, but code is easily duplicated. There are sound arguments for the existence of copyrights, patents, land-use regulations, and licensing but, when abused to redistribute upward, from those who are competing and innovating to those who are already established and are trying to protect their lucrative positions, they need to be reined in. There are good arguments that much of patent protection is unnecessary and against the public interest,[28] that in current practice the costs far outweigh the benefits.

In chapter 15, our discussion of lobbying focused mostly on corporate lobbying by large businesses like Google, AT&T, or Boeing. But small businesses often spend even more, not directly but through their associations, such as the US Chamber of Commerce, the National Association of Realtors, and the American Medical Association. These organizations are powerful not just because of the money they spend but also because their members are scattered around the country, represented in every community, or more relevantly, in every state and every congressional district. They lobby for special treatment for small businesses, such as exemptions from regulations that bigger businesses face, or for special tax breaks—for example, for realtors.[29] Car dealers are protected by state laws that prevent manufacturers from selling directly to consumers. Physicians and their associations control access to medical schools, keeping the number of doctors down and keeping their salaries high. They enforce residency requirements that effectively exclude foreign doctors; professionals in the elite are much better than less educated workers at preventing challenges from foreign workers.

Rent-seeking and protection for small businesses are two keys to understanding inequality in America. The economists Matthew Smith, Danny Yagan, Owen Zidar, and Eric Zwick have examined tax data on firms and their owners, and find that entrepreneurs who actively manage their firms are key contributors to top income inequality. For top inequality, these rich owners are much more important than corporate CEOs, both in amounts of income and in numbers of people; they are "in professional services (e.g., consultants, lawyers, specialty tradespeople) or health services (e.g., physicians, dentists). A typical example owned by the top 0.1% is a regional business with $20M in sales and 100 employees, such as an auto dealer, beverage distributor, or a large law firm."[30] Nearly all of these businesses are protected by lobbying in Washington or in state houses through licensing requirements, the "laws that may be said to be written in blood," according to Adam Smith.[31] The lawyers advise the rent seekers on what laws to target for writing or amendment, and help keep them out of jail.

There is nothing to stop trade associations or corporations from lobbying elected officials for protection. The weight that federal and state lawmakers give to these solicitations may depend on what voters know about the protections being granted, and how much they would care if they did know. We suspect that voters are generally unaware that they are being nickel-and-dimed (or worse). Increasing the flow of information on who is lobbying, for what, and the consequences might provide a brake on the effectiveness of this activity.

Education

Over and again in this book, we have seen the divide between those with and without a four-year college degree, with a whole range of bad outcomes, up to and including death, being visited on those with less education. Would the world be a better place if everyone had a bachelor's degree?

Perhaps so. The United States led the world in universal primary schooling and, when technology changed to require it, provided universal high school education to everyone. With the current revolution in information and communication, perhaps it is time to up our game to make college the norm?

We think that many of those who do not have a bachelor's degree today could have obtained one, or could obtain one now, and that they, and the rest of us to a lesser extent, would be better off as a result. That is especially true of those who have talent and who cannot go to college, either for financial reasons or, even worse, because they do not realize that people like them can go on to tertiary education. Many people argue that educational access for such people is tougher today than it once was, with fewer low-cost opportunities for high school graduates to get back into school and go to college. The financial returns on a bachelor's degree are high enough to support the investment in college, even today, but there are real risks, and about half of those entering college today do not graduate, and so can be left with debt and no qualifications. The fraction of young people entering college has continued to rise, but the fraction graduating with a bachelor's degree has nearly stalled, which is unfortunate in many ways. Having had some college but not graduating appears to provide relatively few benefits, so the current situation is extremely wasteful. Any policy that addresses these issues would help, although free college for everyone would be extremely expensive and would distribute most of the benefits to those who need them least.

More broadly, there is obviously nothing in a bachelor's degree that insulates the holder against being replaced by a machine or outcompeted by cheaper labor in the rest of the world. A bachelor's degree is not a suit of armor that protects you against change. It is entirely possible that, just as African Americans were the first to suffer from job loss and community destruction fifty years ago and whites without a college degree are suffering today, many of those with a college degree will be next in line. Educating everyone will not prevent such an outcome.

The sharp division between those with and without a college degree does not characterize other rich countries. In Britain, fewer people go to college, although the numbers are rising rapidly, in spite of rising costs. Germany has its famous apprenticeship system, which many people choose over going to college, and which fosters great pride of work and craftsmanship among people without college degrees. One argument against apprenticeships is that they tie people into specific skills, as opposed to providing them with the flexibility and adaptability that is supposed to come with a liberal arts education. Yet German workers do not seem to suffer from this, and retraining in the face of change is routine.

We think that the US must consider alternatives. The sharp bachelor's degree cutoff in America is divisive and unproductive. The K–12 educational system is largely designed to prepare people to go to college, although only a third succeed in doing so, something that is both wasteful and unjust.[32] Those who do not make it risk being branded as failures and left feeling either that they themselves are at fault or that the system is rigged, or both.[33]

Lessons for Other Rich Countries

We have spent a good deal of space on what the US can learn from other countries so that we might undo the epidemic of deaths of despair. But what about the threat to other countries? While we do not believe that the American experience must, in time, spread elsewhere, there is much for other countries to learn from what has happened in the US, much of it negative—what *not* to do.

The most obvious and immediate lesson is to maintain the controls on opioids that are currently in place. European (including British) doctors are much more conservative about prescribing for pain in the first place, and the evidence suggests that their patients do not suffer as a result. There is certainly no sign of the midlife pain epidemic in European countries. Opioids, such as OxyContin, are used in hospitals immediately after surgery but are rarely prescribed in the community. Yet the opioid manufacturers have taken a page out of the book of the tobacco companies and are pushing their drugs as remedies for pain relief around the world. Purdue Pharmaceutical has a set of international subsidiaries called Mundipharma that pay doctors and other advocates to tout opioids and encourage doctors to overcome their "opioidphobia."[34] Pieces by doctors arguing for the relaxation of prescription regulations pop up regularly in European medical journals. The American example should not be followed; rather, it should act as a terrible warning to other countries of what happens when people's lives are sacrificed to corporate profits.

Politics in Europe today are almost as fraught as politics in America. Many of the people who voted for Brexit, or for right-wing or populist parties in Europe, feel as disenfranchised from the political process as do many less educated Americans. As in the United States, the traditional social democratic parties that represented labor are no longer seen as very different from the parties representing capital. At the same time, and perhaps as a consequence, ordinary people in some (but not all) European countries, including Britain, have suffered a decade of stagnant wages and austerity, which brought a decline in public services, including healthcare.[35] Our story of American distress is that, at a time when working people were increasingly vulnerable to automation and trade, politicians and corporations, instead of working to cushion the harm, seized the chance to benefit themselves, redistributing upward from labor to managers and shareholders. In Britain, austerity is playing a similar role, weakening the safety net at a time when it is most needed.

There has been no sustained decrease in life expectancy in Britain, but the previously long-established and sustained increase has slowed or ceased. A decade of lost wage growth in Britain is very different from half a century of wage decline in America, but there are surely enough warning signs to undermine complacency. It would be ironic if Britain, whose Labour government built the first modern welfare state after 1945, was one of the first to destroy it, causing young people in Britain, like many young people in America, to see capitalism as their enemy.

Future, Not Failure

If we are to stop deaths of despair, we must somehow stop or reverse the decline of wages for less educated Americans. Pessimists might argue that we are looking at the inevitable consequences of disruptions in trade and technology about which nothing can be done. If so, we will just have to wait until the tide turns, and accept that many will be lost in the meantime.

Perhaps the troubles of the working class have nothing to do with wages and jobs, or any other external circumstance, but rather, as argued by the political scientist Charles Murray, come from a loss of industriousness and other American virtues among less educated white Americans.[36] If so, it is not clear that policies can help; a moral or religious revival is needed. We do not share this view. In chapter 11 on the labor market, we saw that both labor force participation and wage rates were declining for less educated whites, for men for many years, and more recently for women. That participation and wages should decline together is a clear indication that employers want fewer less skilled workers; there are fewer jobs, and workers are reacting either by withdrawing from the market (lower participation) or by taking worse jobs (lower wages). If lower participation is to be explained by falling industriousness—a lower willingness to work—wages should *rise* as employers compete for the smaller number of available workers. That is not what happened.

The deaths neither were nor are inevitable. They are not happening at anywhere near this scale in any other wealthy country. We believe that the extent of despair and of deaths in America reflects specific American policies and circumstances. The organization of the American healthcare system is a disaster for the harm it does to health, but even more because it is draining the livelihoods of Americans in order to make a rich minority richer. Pharmaceutical companies are reaping enormous profits from their patients' addictions, and from pricing strategies that deny ordinary people access to decades-old medical advances. Elsewhere in the economy, as trade and automation have made working-class people more vulnerable, corporations and legislators have not taken the opportunity to strengthen the safety net to minimize the harm. If anything, they have taken the opportunity to exploit labor's weaknesses, reducing wages and distributing income upward, away from labor and toward capital, and away from ordinary people and toward the elite. The political system, strangled by lobbying and by legislators' need for deep-pocketed backers, has increasingly become a battleground for competing commercial and professional interests. Congress, which in a better-functioning democracy would have protected the interests of the majority, has mostly ignored them. The law, which ought to have protected the weak against rent-seeking by the strong, has increasingly moved to support the shakedown. The Sheriff of Nottingham has taken up residence in Washington, DC, and the good cops have left town. Robin Hood is nowhere to be seen.

Yet we are optimistic. We considered using the phrase "the *failure* of capitalism" in our title but opted instead for "the *future* of capitalism," a future that we hope will be better. We believe that capitalism is an immensely powerful force for progress and for good, but it needs to serve people and not have people serve it. Capitalism needs to be better monitored and regulated, not to be replaced by some fantastical socialist utopia in which the state takes over industry. Democracy can rise to the challenge. The state can do more than it does, and do it well, but we are acutely aware of the risks of government and the danger that larger government means more rent-seeking and yet more inequality.[37] Many of the reforms above are pro-market, not anti-market, and should command support from both Right and Left, from market fundamentalists on the right, and from the critics of excessive inequality on the left. We favor a fairer tax system than the present one, but we do not prioritize higher taxes on the rich, because we do not see inequality as the fundamental problem. The fundamental problem is *unfairness*, that the great wealth at the top is seen as ill-gotten in a system that gives no chance to many. We argue that limiting rent-seeking and reducing plunder will rein in the rich and reduce unfair top incomes without high taxes on income or wealth that is widely seen as fairly earned.

Democracy is fully capable of serving people better than it now does. Democracy in America is not working well, but it is far from dead, and it can work again if people push hard enough, just as it was made to work better in the Progressive Era a century ago and in the New Deal of the 1930s.

For readers who have persisted with us this far, our recommendations will have come as no surprise. They mostly follow from our account of what has gone wrong. Even so, it is useful to put them in one place. We cannot describe policies in detail, and it is neither our purpose nor within our competence to choose among the many varieties of healthcare reform and safety net design that have already been comprehensively described by others. Yet we hope that the sheer awfulness of the epidemic of deaths, as well as the extremes of inequality that have been generated by rent-seeking and upward redistribution, will generate an opportunity where schemes that have been long thought about might be put into place. It is past time.

ACKNOWLEDGMENTS

Many people have contributed to this book, and we are grateful to them for their advice, suggestions, and comments. In particular, we would like to acknowledge Orley Ashenfelter, Lisa Berkman, Tim Besley, Eric Caine, Dave Card, Susan Case, Daniel Chandler, Andrew Cherlin, Jim Clifton, Francis Collins, Janet Currie, David Cutler, Jason Doctor, Bill Easterly, Janice Eberly, Hank Farber, Vic Fuchs, Jason Furman, Leonard Gelosa, Debbi Gitterman, Dana Goldman, Oliver Hart, Susan Higgins, Joe Jackson, Danny Kahneman, Arie Kapteyn, Lane Kenworthy, Jenna Kowalski, Nancy Krieger, Ilyana Kuziemko, Anna Lembke, David Lipton, Adriana Lleras-Muney, Trevon Logan, Michael Marmot, Sara McLanahan, Ellen Meara, Alice Muehlhof, Frank Newport, Judith Novak, Barack Obama, Sam Preston, Bob Putnam, Julie Ray, Leonard Shaeffer, Andrew Schuller, Jon Skinner, Jim Smith, Joe Stiglitz, Arthur Stone, Bob Tignor, John van Reenen, Nora Volkov, David Weir, Gil Welch, Miquelon Weyeneth, Dan Wikler, Norton Wise, Martin Wolf, Owen Zidar, and Luigi Zingales.

We are particularly grateful to those noneconomists who were prepared to help us think and to avoid at least some of the blunders that we would otherwise have made. We hope they will forgive any errors and misinterpretations that remain, all of which are our own. It is impossible to treat the topics in this book from a single discipline, and it has been a humbling experience for two economists to learn just how much our subject neglects or how often it is mistaken. We got invaluable help from a range of sociologists, demographers, philosophers, political scientists, historians, physicians, and epidemiologists.

We presented some of the material in the book as the Tanner Lectures in Human Values at Stanford University in April 2019. We are grateful to the Tanner Foundation for its support and Stanford for its hospitality, the formal discussants, and many useful conversations.

Both of us have taught and researched at Princeton University's Woodrow Wilson School for many years. Princeton University provides an ideal environment for scholarship; the Woodrow Wilson School does the same for bringing scholarship to bear on policy issues. We also have a long association with the National Bureau of Economic Research, whose directors, Jim Poterba and the late Marty Feldstein, have supported and encouraged our work over many years. Deaton is also a presidential professor at the University of Southern California, and he is grateful to his colleagues there in the Center for Self-Report Science, the Center for Economic and Social Research, and the Leonard D. Schaeffer Center for Health Policy and Economics. He is also a senior scientist with Gallup, whose people have been a boundless source of material support, data, enthusiasm, and good ideas.

Princeton University Press is the ideal publisher. We would like to thank Jackie Delaney, Joe Jackson, Terri O'Prey, Caroline Priday, James Schneider, and the many others who helped bring the book into the world.

We have been generously supported by the National Institute on Aging of the National Institutes of Health; work supported by several different grants is synthesized into the story that we tell. The late Richard Suzman at the National Institute on Aging, a research entrepreneur of the highest class, was largely responsible for our interest in health. We acknowledge grants to one, the other, or both of us from the National Institute on Aging through the National Bureau of Economic Research (Grants R01AG040629, P01AG05842, R01AG060104, R01AG053396, P30AG012810-25), through Princeton (Grant P30AG024928) and through the University of Southern California (Grant R01AG051903).

NOTES

Introduction

1. Emile Durkheim, 1897, *Le suicide: Etude de sociologie*, Germer Baillière, but the link with education goes back further. See Matt Wray, Cynthia Colen, and Bernice Pescosolido, 2011, "The sociology of suicide," *Annual Review of Sociology*, 37, 505–28.

2. Sara McLanahan, 2004, "Diverging destinies: How children are faring under the second demographic transition," *Demography*, 41(4), 607–27; Andrew Cherlin, 2014, *Labor's love lost: The rise and fall of the working-class family in America*, Russell Sage Foundation; Robert D. Putnam, 2015, *Our kids: The American dream in crisis*, Simon and Schuster; David Goodhart, 2017, *The road to somewhere: The populist revolt and the future of politics*, Hurst; Charles Murray, 2012, *Coming apart: The state of white America, 1960–2010*, Crown.

3. Michael Young, 1958, *The rise of the meritocracy*, Thames and Hudson.

4. Michael Sandel, 2018, "Populism, Trump, and the future of democracy," openDemocracy, May 9, https://www.opendemocracy.net/en/populism-trump-and-future-of-democracy/.

5. William Julius Wilson, 1987, *The truly disadvantaged: The inner city, the underclass, and public policy*, University of Chicago Press, 39.

6. Carol Anderson, quoted in Susan B. Glasser and Glenn Thrush, 2016, "What's going on with America's white people?," *Politico Magazine*, September/October 2016.

7. Martin Luther King Jr., 1965, "Address at the conclusion of the Selma to Montgomery march," March 25, Martin Luther King, Jr. Research and Education Institute, Stanford, https://kinginstitute.stanford.edu/king-papers/documents/address-conclusion-selma-montgomery-march.

8. Daniel Cox, Rachel Lienesch, and Robert P. Jones, 2017, "Beyond economics: Fears of cultural displacement pushed the white working class to Trump," PRRI/*Atlantic* Report, April 9, https://www.prri.org/research/white-working-class-attitudes-economy-trade-immigration-election-donald-trump/.

9. Anderson, quoted in Glasser and Thrush, "What's going on."

10. Wilson, *Truly disadvantaged*; Charles Murray, 1984, *Losing ground: American social policy 1950–1980*, Basic Books.

11. Murray, *Coming apart.*

12. Bureau of Labor Statistics, 2015, "Table A-4: Employment status of the civilian population 25 years and over by educational attainment," Data Retrieval: Labor Force Statistics (CPS), July 8, https://www.bls.gov/webapps/legacy/cpsatab4.htm.

13. Nicholas Bloom, 2017, "Corporations in the age of inequality," The Big Idea, *Harvard Business Review*, https://hbr.org/cover-story/2017/03/corporations-in-the-age-of-inequality.

14. Neil Irwin, 2017, "To understand rising inequality, consider the janitors at two top companies, then and now," *New York Times*, September 2, https://www.nytimes.com/2017/09/03/upshot/to-understand-rising-inequality-consider-the-janitors-at-two-top-companies-then-and-now.html.

15. Emily Guendelsberger, 2019, *On the clock: What low-wage work did to me and how it drives America insane*, Little, Brown; James Bloodworth, 2018, *Hired: Six months undercover in low-wage Britain*, Atlantic Books.

16. Durkheim, *Le suicide.*

17. Dani Rodrik, 1997, *Has globalization gone too far?*, Institute for International Economics.

18. Sam Quinones, 2015, *Dreamland: The true tale of America's opiate epidemic*, Bloomsbury.

19. Adam Smith, 1776, *The wealth of nations*, bk. 4.

20. Matthew Smith, Danny Yagan, Owen M. Zidar, and Eric Zwick, 2019, "Capitalists in the 21st century," *Quarterly Journal of Economics*, 134(4), 1675–745.

21. Kenneth Scheve and David Stasavage, 2016, *Taxing the rich: A history of fiscal fairness in the United States and Europe*, Princeton University Press.

22. Charles Jordan Tabb, 2007, "The top twenty issues in the history of consumer bankruptcy," *University of Illinois Law Review*, 1, 9–30, 29.

23. Jacob S. Hacker and Paul Pierson, 2011, *Winner-take-all politics: How Washington made the rich richer—and turned its back on the middle class*, Simon and Schuster; Martin Gilens, 2012, *Affluence and influence: Economic inequality and political power in America*, Princeton University Press; Larry M. Bartels, 2008, *Unequal democracy: The political economy of the new gilded age*, Princeton University Press.

24. Walter Scheidel, 2017, *The great leveler: Violence and the history of inequality from the Stone Age to the twenty-first century*, Princeton University Press.

25. David Cannadine, *Victorious century: The United Kingdom, 1800–1906*, Penguin.

26. Robert C. Allen, 2017, *The Industrial Revolution: A very short introduction*, Oxford University Press.

Chapter 1: The Calm before the Storm

1. Quoted in Paul Farmer, 1999, *Infections and inequalities: The modern plagues*, University of California Press, 202.

2. William F. Ogburn and Dorothy S. Thomas, 1922, "The influence of the business cycle on certain social conditions," *Journal of the American Statistical Association*, 18(139), 324–40; Christopher J. Ruhm, 2000, "Are recessions good for your health?," *Quarterly Journal of Economics*, 115(2), 617–50.

3. John Komlos and Benjamin E. Lauderdale, 2007, "Underperformance in affluence: The remarkable relative decline in U.S. heights in the second half of the 20th century," *Social Science Quarterly*, 88, 283–305, https://doi.org/10.1111/j.1540-6237.2007.00458.x.

Chapter 2: Things Come Apart

1. Brookings Institution, 2017, *Policy approaches to the opioid crisis, featuring remarks by Sir Angus Deaton, Rep. Ann McLane Kuster, and Professor Bertha K. Madras: An event from the USC-Brookings Schaeffer Initiative for Health Policy, Washington, DC*, November 3, https://www.brookings.edu/wp-content/uploads/2017/11/es_20171103_opioid_crisis_transcript.pdf.

2. Unless otherwise noted, throughout the book, we will refer to white non-Hispanics as "whites," black non-Hispanics as "blacks," and Hispanics of all races as "Hispanics."

3. See Katherine Baicker, Amitabh Chandra, and Jonathan S. Skinner, 2005, "Geographic variation in health care and the problem of measuring racial disparities," *Perspectives in Biology and Medicine*, 48(1), supplement (Winter), S42–53.

4. Another question is whether the pause or reversal is in part a result of people getting older over this stretch of time within this midlife age-group. Indeed, the average age within the age band from forty-five to fifty-four increased by four-tenths of a year (from 49.2 to 49.6) be tween 1990 and 2017, and we would expect mortality to rise (if slightly) just because of the aver-age increase in age. But the graph makes an adjustment that takes this into account. Without the adjustment, the mortality line for the US whites rises a little more, but the difference be-tween the US whites and citizens of other countries, or between the US whites and what would have been expected had late twentieth-century progress continued, remains starkly obvious independent of any such adjustments. See Andrew Gelman and Jonathan Auerbach, 2016, "Age-aggregation bias in mortality trends," *Proceedings of the National Academy of Sciences*, 113(7), E816–17.

5. At the time we go to press, we do not know what has happened to US life expectancy in 2018, and it is not clear which way it will move.

Chapter 3: Deaths of Despair

1. *PBS Newshour*, 2017, "'Deaths of despair' are cutting life short for some white Ameri-cans," February 16, video, 8:19, https://www.pbs.org/newshour/show/deaths-despair-cutting-life-short-white-americans.

2. Nicole Lewis, Emma Ockerman, Joel Achenbach, and Wesley Lowery, 2017, "Fentanyl linked to thousands of urban overdose deaths," *Washington Post*, August 15, https://www.washingtonpost.com/graphics/2017/national/fentanyl-overdoses/.

3. Robert L. DuPont, 2008, "Addiction in medicine," *Transactions of the American Clinical and Climatological Association*, 119, 227–41.

4. Robert L. DuPont, 1997, *The selfish brain: Learning from addiction*, American Psychiatric Association.

5. Alcoholic liver disease mortality rates fell slightly over this period in Maryland and Mississippi, and rose slightly in New Jersey. In a number of small states, data were not reported in some years. These are Alaska, Delaware, Hawaii, North Dakota, South Dakota, Vermont, and Wyoming. In all of these states, with the exception of Delaware, rates increased over the period that data were reported.

6. Ellen Meara and Jonathan Skinner, 2015, "Losing ground at midlife in America," *Proceedings of the National Academy of Sciences*, 112(49), 15006–7.

7. These statistics are for white non-Hispanics and white Hispanics together; before 1990, ethnicity is not fully available.

8. Yulia Khodneva, Paul Muntner, Stefan Kertsesz, Brett Kissela, and Monika M. Safford, 2016, "Prescription opioid use and risk of coronary heart disease, stroke, and cardiovascular death among adults from a prospective cohort (REGARDS study)," *Pain Medicine*, 17(3), 444–55, https://www.ncbi.nlm.nih.gov/pmc/articles/PMC6281131/; American Heart Association, 2018, "Opioid use may increase risk of dangerous hearth rhythm disorder," meeting report, poster presentation, November 5, https://newsroom.heart.org/news/opioid-use-may-increase-risk -of-dangerous-heart-rhythm-disorder?preview=303c; L. Li, S. Setoguchi, H. Cabral, and S. Jick, 2013, "Opioid use for noncancer pain and risk of myocardial infarction amongst adults," *Journal of Internal Medicine*, 273(5), 511–26, https://www.ncbi.nlm.nih.gov/pubmed/23331508.

9. Andrew Stokes and Samuel H. Preston, 2017, "Deaths attributable to diabetes in the United States: Comparison of data sources and estimation approaches," *PLoS ONE*, 12(1), e0170219, https://doi.org/10.1371/journal.pone.0170219.

10. Jay Olshansky, Douglas J. Passaro, Ronald C. Hershow, et al., 2005, "A potential decline in life expectancy in the United States in the 21st century," *New England Journal of Medicine*, 352(11), 1138–45.

11. For England, see NHS Digital, 2018, "Health Survey for England 2017," December 4, https://digital.nhs.uk/data-and-information/publications/statistical/health-survey-for -england/2017; for Australia, see Australian Institute of Health and Welfare, 2018, "Overweight and obesity rates across Australia 2014–15," June 7, https://www.aihw.gov.au/reports/overweight -obesity/overweight-and-obesity-rates-2014-15/data.

Chapter 4: The Lives and Deaths of the More (and Less) Educated

1. Statistics are from Thomas D. Snyder, ed., 1993, *120 years of American education: A statistical portrait*, Center for Education Statistics, US Department of Education, table 3, https://nces.ed .gov/pubs93/93442.pdf.

2. The earnings premium is calculated as the ratio of median hourly wages for full-time, full-year workers with a four-year degree and median hourly earnings for those with a high school diploma but no additional education. Jonathan James, 2012, "The college wage premium," *Economic Commentary*, 2012-10, August 8, Research Department of the Federal Reserve Bank of Cleveland.

3. Statistics are for the civilian population. American Community Survey 2017.

4. Lawrence Mishel and Julia Wolfe, 2019, "CEO compensation has grown 940% since 1978," Economic Policy Institute, August 14, https://www.epi.org/publication/ceo-compensation -2018/.

5. Thomas Piketty and Emmanuel Saez, 2003, "Income inequality in the United States, 1913–1998," *Quarterly Journal of Economics*, 118(1), 1–39; Thomas Piketty, 2013, *Capital in the 21st century*, Harvard; Matthew Smith, Danny Yagan, Owen M. Zidar, and Eric Zwick, 2019, "Capitalists in the 21st century," *Quarterly Journal of Economics*, 134(4), 1675–745.

6. Robert D. Putnam, 2015, *Our kids: The American dream in crisis*, Simon and Schuster; Charles Murray, 2012, *Coming apart: The state of white America, 1960–2010*, Crown; Sara McLanahan, 2004, "Diverging destinies: How children are faring under the second demographic transition," *Demography*, 41(4), 607–27.

7. Authors' calculations using Gallup's tracking poll.

8. Alex Bell, Raj Chetty, Xavier Jaravel, Neviana Petkova, and John van Reenen, 2019, "Who becomes an inventor in America? The importance of exposure to innovation," *Quarterly Journal of Economics*, 134(2), 647–713.

9. Michael Young, 1958, *The rise of the meritocracy*, Thames and Hudson.

10. Young, 152.

11. Michael Sandel, 2018, "Populism, Trump, and the future of democracy," openDemocracy, May 9, https://www.opendemocracy.net/en/populism-trump-and-future-of-democracy/.

12. Kim Parker, 2019, "The growing partisan divide in views of higher education," Pew Research Center, August 19, https://www.pewsocialtrends.org/essay/the-growing-partisan-divide-in-views-of-higher-education/.

13. Dana Goldstein and Jugal K. Patel, 2019, "Need extra time on tests? It helps to have cash," July 30, *New York Times*, https://www.nytimes.com/2019/07/30/us/extra-time-504-sat-act.html.

14. Christopher Hayes, 2012, *Twilight of the elites: America after meritocracy*, Crown.

15. See also Daniel Markovits, 2019, *The meritocracy trap: How America's foundational myth feeds inequality, dismantles the middle class, and devours the elite*, Penguin.

16. Samuel H. Preston, 1996, "American longevity: Past, present, and future," Syracuse University Center for Policy Research, Policy Brief No. 7, 8; Samuel H. Preston and Michael R. Haines, 1971, *Fatal years: Child mortality in late nineteenth-century America*, Princeton University Press.

17. Michael Marmot, 2004, *The status syndrome: How social standing affects our health and longevity*, Times Books.

18. Authors' calculations from the Behavioral Risk Factor Surveillance System and National Health and Nutrition Examination Survey data.

19. Our data on mortality by educational attainment go back only to 1992, by which time most states were including education on death certificates. Four states—Georgia, Oklahoma, Rhode Island, and South Dakota—were slow to comply, so the 5 percent of the total US population who live in those states is excluded from all of our results on deaths and education.

20. From the late 1990s to 2017, the fraction of forty-five-to-fifty-four-year-olds with a bachelor's degree remained nearly constant at around one-third. If the fraction with and without a bachelor's degree had changed dramatically since the late 1990s, there would be a worry that what we are seeing in the figure are not changes in death rates but rather changes in the kind of people who do and do not have a bachelor's degree. The stability of the shares of the population makes such an account unlikely.

21. Emile Durkheim, 1897, *Le suicide: Etude de sociologie*, Germer Baillière; Matt Wray, Cynthia Colen, and Bernice Pescosolido, 2011, "The sociology of suicide," *Annual Review of Sociology*, 37, 505–28.

Chapter 5: Black and White Deaths

1. Gary Trudeau, 2017, *Doonesbury, Washington Post*, March 26.

2. Mortality rates are for all whites, including Hispanic whites, and all blacks, including Hispanic blacks. Before 1968, death certificates categorized decedents as "white" and "other race," so we limit the series to the period 1968–2017.

3. Emile Durkheim, 1897, *Le suicide: Etude de sociologie*, Germer Baillière.

4. George Simpson, introduction to *Suicide, a study in sociology*, by Emile Durkheim, trans. John A. Spaulding and George Simpson, ed. George Simpson, Free Press, 1951, loc. 367 of 7289, Kindle.

5. William Julius Wilson, 1987, *The truly disadvantaged: The inner city, the underclass, and public policy*, University of Chicago Press, 39.

6. Wilson, 254.

7. Raghuram Rajan, 2019, *The third pillar: How markets and the state leave the community behind*, Penguin.

8. William N. Evans, Craig Garthwaite, and Timothy J. Moore, 2018, "Guns and violence: The enduring impact of crack cocaine markets on young black males," NBER Working Paper 24819, July.

9. Daniel Patrick Moynihan, 1965, *The negro family: The case for national action*, US Department of Labor.

10. Charles Murray, 1984, *Losing ground: American social policy 1950–1980*, Basic Books; Charles Murray, 2012, *Coming apart: The state of white America, 1960–2010*, Crown.

11. Wilson, *Truly disadvantaged*, 14.

Chapter 6: The Health of the Living

1. Amartya K. Sen, 1985, *Commodities and capabilities*, Elsevier.

2. World Health Organization, n.d., "Constitution," accessed October 15, 2019, https://www.who.int/about/who-we-are/constitution.

3. Centers for Disease Control and Prevention, 2019, "Behavioral Risk Factor Surveillance System," last reviewed August 27, https://www.cdc.gov/brfss/index.html.

4. National Center for Health Statistics, 2019, "National Health Interview Survey," last reviewed August 22, https://www.cdc.gov/nchs/nhis/index.htm.

5. The BRFSS (a telephone survey) is an order of magnitude larger than the NHIS (administered in-home), which is, in turn, an order of magnitude larger than the National Health and Nutrition Examination Survey, a program that collects data through a mix of interviews, physical examinations, and lab work on five thousand people each year. For information on the National Health and Nutrition Examination Survey, see National Center for Health Statistics, 2019, "National Health and Nutrition Examination Survey," last reviewed September 17, https://www.cdc.gov/nchs/nhanes/index.htm.

6. Majid Ezzati, Hilarie Martin, Suzanne Skjold, Stephen Vander Hoorn, and Christopher J. L. Murray, 2006, "Trends in national and state level obesity in the USA after correction for self-report bias: Analysis of health surveys," *Journal of the Royal Society of Medicine*, 99, 250–57, https://doi.org/10.1177/014107680609900517; Duncan Thomas and Elizabeth Frankenberg, 2002, "The measurement and interpretation of health in social surveys," in *Summary measures of population health: Concepts, ethics, measurement and applications*, World Health Organization, 387–420.

7. Amartya K. Sen, 2002, "Health: Perception versus observation: Self reported morbidity has severe limitations and can be extremely misleading," *British Medical Journal*, 324, 860–61.

8. Ellen L. Idler and Yael Benyamini, 1997, "Self-rated health and mortality: A review of twenty-seven community studies," *Journal of Health and Social Behavior*, 38(1), 21–37.

9. To cross-check that the results are not driven by some peculiarity of the BRFSS, we have used the other large national survey, the NHIS, to replicate the results in figure 6.1, and we find the same results.

10. Nicholas Eberstadt, 2016, *Men without work: America's invisible crisis*, Templeton.

11. Jeffrey B. Liebman, 2015, "Understanding the increase in disability insurance benefit receipt in the United States," *Journal of Economic Perspectives*, 29(2), 123–50.

Chapter 7: The Misery and Mystery of Pain

1. Naomi I. Eisenberger, 2015, "Social pain and the brain: Controversies, questions, and where to go from here," *Annual Review of Psychology*, 66, 601–29, https://doi.org/10.1146/annurev-psych-010213-115146.

2. National Academies of Sciences, Engineering, and Medicine, 2017, *Pain management and the opioid epidemic: Balancing societal and individual benefits and risks of prescription opioid use*, National Academies Press, https://doi.org/10.17226/24781.

3. Rob Boddice, 2017, *Pain: A very short introduction*, Oxford; Antonio R. Damasio, 2005, *Descartes' error: Emotion, reason, and the human brain*, Penguin.

4. Margo McCaffery, 1968, *Nursing practice theories related to cognition, bodily pain and man-environmental interaction*, University of California, Los Angeles, Students' Store, quoted in American Pain Society, n.d., *Pain: Current understanding of assessment, management, and treatments*, 4.

5. Anne Case and Angus Deaton, 2005, "Broken down by work and sex: How our health declines," in David A. Wise, ed., *Analyses in the economics of aging*, National Bureau of Economic Research Conference Report, University of Chicago Press for NBER, 185–212.

6. This map is drawn with an age range from twenty-five to sixty-four, rather than for forty-five-to-fifty-four-year-old whites, which allows us to use a larger sample to estimate pain by small area.

7. Anne Case and Angus Deaton, 2017, "Suicide, age, and well-being: An empirical investigation," in David A. Wise, ed., *Insights in the economics of aging*, National Bureau of Economic Research Conference Report, University of Chicago Press for NBER, 307–34.

8. Gallup World Poll, accessed September 18, 2019, https://www.gallup.com/analytics/232838/world-poll.aspx.

9. These are Australia, Austria, Belgium, Canada, Denmark, Finland, France, Germany, Ireland, Italy, Japan, the Netherlands, New Zealand, Norway, Portugal, Spain, Sweden, Switzerland, and the UK.

272 NOTES TO CHAPTER 8

10. The question asked in the Gallup surveys pertains to "yesterday," while the questions asked in the NHIS pertain to the last three months, which may explain the higher fraction reporting pain in the NHIS. That said, the patterns observed, of faster increases before age sixty than after sixty, are similar in the two surveys. We have no explanation for the high pain levels among elderly Europeans in figure 7.2.

11. Authors' calculations using annual Behavioral Risk Factor Surveillance System surveys.

12. Case and Deaton, 2005, "Broken down."

13. Greg Kaplan and Sam Schulhofer-Wohl, 2018, "The changing (dis)-utility of work," Journal of Economic Perspectives, 32(3), 239–58.

Chapter 8: Suicide, Drugs, and Alcohol

1. Emile Durkheim, 1897, Le suicide: Etude de sociologie, Germer Baillière.

2. Robert L. DuPont, 1997, The selfish brain: Learning from addiction, American Psychiatric Association, Kindle.

3. Zachary Siegel, 2018, "I'm so sick of opioid disaster porn," Slate, September 12, https://slate.com/technology/2018/09/opioid-crisis-photo-essays-leave-out-recovery.html.

4. DuPont, Selfish brain, loc. 2093 of 8488, Kindle.

5. Kay Redfield Jamison, 2000, Night falls fast: Understanding suicide, Vintage, 128.

6. Ian R. H. Rockett, Gordon S. Smith, Eric D. Caine, et al., 2014, "Confronting death from drug self-intoxication (DDSI): Prevention through a better definition," American Journal of Public Health, 104(12), e49–55, e50.

7. Daniel S. Hammermesh and Neal M. Soss, 1974, "An economic theory of suicide," Journal of Political Economy, 82(1), 83–98; Gary S. Becker and Richard A. Posner, 2004, "Suicide: An economic approach," unpublished manuscript, last revised August, https://www.gwern.net/docs/psychology/2004-becker.pdf.

8. Norman Kreitman, 1976, "The coal gas story: United Kingdom suicide rates, 1960–71," British Journal of Preventive Social Medicine, 30, 86–93.

9. Kyla Thomas and David Gunnell, 2010, "Suicide in England and Wales 1861–2007: A time-trends analysis," International Journal of Epidemiology, 39, 1464–75, https://doi.org/10.1093/ije/dyq094.

10. John Gramlich, 2018, "7 facts about guns in the U.S.," Fact Tank, Pew Research Center, December 27, https://www.pewresearch.org/fact-tank/2018/12/27/facts-about-guns-in-united-states/.

11. National Research Council, 2005, "Firearms and suicide," in Firearms and violence: A critical review, National Academies Press, 152–200.

12. Robert D. Putnam, 2000, Bowling alone: The collapse and revival of American community, Simon and Schuster.

13. CDC Wonder, average suicide rates over the period 2008–17.

14. Across the fifty US states, the correlation coefficient is .4.

15. Anne Case and Angus Deaton, 2017, "Suicide, age, and well-being: An empirical investigation," in David A. Wise, ed., Insights in the economics of aging, National Bureau of Economic Research Conference Report, University of Chicago Press for NBER, 307–34.

16. The fractions of the birth cohorts of 1945 and 1970 who finish a four-year degree are not very different, so these results are unlikely to be attributable to changing compositions of those with and without a bachelor's degree between the cohorts.

17. Eric Augier, Estelle Barbier, Russell S. Dulman, et al., 2018, "A molecular mechanism for choosing alcohol over an alternative reward," *Science*, 360(6395), 1321–26, https://doi.org/10.1126 /science.aao1157.

18. Christopher Finan, 2017, *Drunks: An American history*, Beacon, 41.

19. Keith Humphreys, 2003, *Circles of recovery: Self-help organizations for addictions*, Cambridge University Press.

20. National Institute on Alcohol Abuse and Alcoholism, n.d., "Alcohol's effects on the body," accessed September 18, 2019, https://www.niaaa.nih.gov/alcohol-health/alcohols -effects-body.

21. Global Burden of Disease Alcohol Collaborators, 2018, "Alcohol use and burden for 195 countries and territories, 1990–2016: A systematic analysis for the Global Burden of Disease Study 2016," *Lancet*, 392, 1015–35, http://dx.doi.org/10.1016/S0140-6736(18)31310-2.

22. We are grateful to Frank Newport at Gallup for sending us these data.

23. Jay Bhattacharya, Christina Gathmann, and Grant Miller, 2013, "The Gorbachev anti-alcohol campaign and Russia's mortality crisis," *American Economic Journal: Applied Economics*, 5(2), 232–60, http://dx.doi.org/10.1257/app.5.2.232.

24. Pavel Grigoriev, France Meslé, Vladimir M. Shkolnikov, et al., 2014, "The recent mortality decline in Russia: Beginning of the cardiovascular revolution?," *Population and Development Review*, 40(1), 107–29.

25. Robert T. Jensen and Kaspar Richter, 2004, "The health implications of social security failure: Evidence from the Russian pension crisis," *Journal of Public Economics*, 88(1–2), 209–36.

26. Angus Deaton, 2008, "Income, health and wellbeing around the world: Evidence from the Gallup World Poll," *Journal of Economic Perspectives*, 22(2), 53–72.

Chapter 9: Opioids

1. Stephen R. Platt, 2018, *Imperial twilight: The opium war and the end of China's last golden age*, Knopf.

2. Platt, 202.

3. Richard J. Grace, 2014, *Opium and empire: The lives and careers of William Jardine and James Matheson*, McGill-Queen's University Press.

4. Tom M. Devine, 2018, *The Scottish Clearances: A history of the dispossessed, 1600–1900*, Allen Lane, 3.

5. National Institute on Drug Abuse, 2019, "Overdose death rates," revised January, https://www.drugabuse.gov/related-topics/trends-statistics/overdose-death-rates.

6. Amy S. B. Bohnert, Maureen A. Walton, Rebecca M. Cunningham, et al., 2018, "Overdose and adverse drug event experiences among adult patients in the emergency department," *Addictive Behaviors*, 86, 66–72. Twenty-one percent of patients surveyed in a level 1 trauma center in Flint, Michigan, following an overdose reported that they were unsure of their intent.

7. Substance Abuse and Mental Health Services Administration, 2017, *Key substance use and mental health indicators in the United States: Results from the 2016 National Survey on Drug Use and Health*, HHS Publication No. SMA 17-5044, NSDUH Series H-52, Center for Behavioral Statistics and Quality, Substance Abuse, and Mental Health Services Administration, https://www.samhsa.gov/data/sites/default/files/NSDUH-FFR1-2016/NSDUH-FFR1-2016.pdf.

8. Dionissi Aliprantis, Kyle Fee, and Mark Schweitzer, 2019, "Opioids and the labor market," Federal Reserve Bank of Cleveland, Working Paper 1807R; Alan B. Krueger, 2017, "Where have all the workers gone? An inquiry into the decline of the U.S. labor force participation rate," *Brookings Papers on Economic Activity*, Fall, 1–87.

9. Jared S. Hopkins and Andrew Scurria, 2019, "Sacklers received as much as $13 billion in profits from Purdue Pharma," *Wall Street Journal*, October 4.

10. Sam Quinones, 2015, *Dreamland: The true tale of America's opiate epidemic*, Bloomsbury.

11. David T. Courtwright, 2001, *A history of opiate addiction in America*, Harvard University Press, Kindle.

12. Courtwright, loc. 604 of 4538, Kindle.

13. Beth Macy, 2018, *Dopesick: Dealers, doctors, and the drug company that addicted America*, Hachette.

14. Ronald Melzack, 1990, "The tragedy of needless pain," *Scientific American*, 262(2), 27–33.

15. Dana Guglielmo, Louise B. Murphy, Michael A. Boring, et al., 2019, "State-specific severe joint pain and physical inactivity among adults with arthritis—United States, 2017," *Morbidity and Mortality Weekly Report*, 2019(68), 381–87, http://dx.doi.org/10.15585/mmwr.mm6817a2.

16. James M. Campbell, 1996, "American Pain Society 1995 Presidential Address," *Journal of Pain*, 5(1), 85–88.

17. Chris McGreal, 2019, "US medical group that pushed doctors to prescribe painkillers forced to close," *Guardian*, May 25, https://www.theguardian.com/us-news/2019/may/25/american-pain-society-doctors-painkillers; Damien McNamara, 2019, "American Pain Society officially shuttered," Medscape, July 2, https://www.medscape.com/viewarticle/915141.

18. Mayo Clinic, 2019, "Hydrocodone and acetaminophen (oral route)," last updated October 1, https://www.mayoclinic.org/drugs-supplements/hydrocodone-and-acetaminophen-oral-route/description/drg-20074089.

19. Mayo Clinic Staff, 2018, "How opioid addiction occurs," Mayo Clinic, February 16, https://www.mayoclinic.org/diseases-conditions/prescription-drug-abuse/in-depth/how-opioid-addiction-occurs/art-20360372.

20. Jason Doctor, Andy Nguyen, Roneet Lev, et al., 2018, "Opioid prescribing decreases after learning of a patient's fatal overdose," *Science*, 361(6402), 588–90.

21. Macy, *Dopesick*, 60.

22. Quinones, *Dreamland*.

23. Quinones.

24. Scott Gottlieb, 2019, "The decline in opioid deaths masks danger from designer drug overdoses in US," CNBC, August 22, https://www.cnbc.com/2019/08/21/decline-in-opioid-deaths-masks-new-danger-from-designer-drug-overdoses.html.

25. For African Americans aged twenty-five to sixty-four, age-adjusted mortality rates increased by 20.8 per 100,000 between 2012 and 2017. Mortality implicating other synthetic (nonheroin, nonmethadone) opioids—i.e., fentanyl—increased by 15 per 100,000 over this period.

26. Anna Lembke, 2016, *Drug dealer, MD: How doctors were duped, patients got hooked, and why it is so hard to stop*, Johns Hopkins University Press.

27. Travis N. Rieder, 2016, "In opioid withdrawal, with no help in sight," *Health Affairs* 36(1), 1825.

28. Lee N. Robins, 1993, "Vietnam veterans' rapid recovery from heroin addiction: A fluke or a normal expectation?," *Addiction*, 88, 1041–54, 1049.

29. We are grateful to Daniel Wikler for discussion of this episode. The ideas of his father, Abraham Wikler, were important in the design of the Vietnam detox program.

30. Ken Thompson, personal communication, September 13, 2018.

31. Benjamin A. Y. Cher, Nancy E. Morden, and Ellen Meara, 2019, "Medicaid expansion and prescription trends: Opioids, addiction therapies, and other drugs," *Medical Care*, 57(3), 208–12, https://www.ncbi.nlm.nih.gov/pmc/articles/PMC6375792/; Andrew Goodman-Bacon and Emma Sandoe, 2017, "Did Medicaid expansion cause the opioid epidemic? There is little evidence that it did," *Health Affairs*, August 23, https://www.healthaffairs.org/do/10.1377/hblog20170823.061640/full.

32. Energy and Commerce Committee, US Congress, 2018, *Red flags and warning signs ignored: Opioid distribution and enforcement concerns in West Virginia*, December 19, 4, https://republicans-energycommerce.house.gov/wp-content/uploads/2018/12/Opioid-Distribution-Report-FinalREV.pdf.

33. Brit McCandless Farmer, 2019, "The opioid epidemic: Who is to blame?," 60 Minutes Overtime, February 24, https://www.cbsnews.com/news/the-opioid-epidemic-who-is-to-blame-60-minutes/; Scott Higham and Lenny Bernstein, 2017, "The drug industry's triumph over the DEA," *Washington Post*, October 15.

34. Peter Andrey Smith, 2019, "How an island in the antipodes became the world's leading supplier of licit opioids," *Pacific Standard*, July 11, updated July 24, https://psmag.com/ideas/opioids-limiting-the-legal-supply-wont-stop-the-overdose-crisis.

35. Katie Thomas and Tiffany Hsu, 2019, "Johnson and Johnson's brand falters over its role in the opioid crisis," *New York Times*, August 27.

36. District of Massachusetts, US Attorney's Office, Department of Justice, 2019, "Founder and four executives of Insys Therapeutics convicted of racketeering conspiracy," May 2, https://www.justice.gov/usao-ma/pr/founder-and-four-executives-insys-therapeutics-convicted-racketeering-conspiracy.

37. Lembke, *Drug dealer, MD*. Of course, once the drug was approved, there was no such exclusion in prescribing, so the population who are given the drug are different from those on whom it was tested.

38. National Academies of Sciences, Engineering, and Medicine, 2017, *Pain management and the opioid epidemic: Balancing societal and individual benefits and risks of prescription opioid use*, National Academies Press, https://doi.org/10.17226/24781.

39. Allen Frances, quoted in Patrick Radden Keefe, 2017, "The family that built an empire of pain," *New Yorker*, October 23.

40. Keefe.

41. We are grateful to John van Reenen for this sentence.

42. Devine, *Scottish Clearances*, 3.

Chapter 10: False Trails: Poverty, Income, and the Great Recession

1. Raj Chetty, Michael Stepner, Sarah Abraham, et al., 2016, "The association between income and life expectancy in the United States, 2001–2014," *Journal of the American Medical Association*, 315(16), 1750–66.

2. Irma Elo and Samuel H. Preston, 1996, "Educational differences in mortality: United States, 1979–85," *Social Science and Medicine*, 42(1), 47–57.

3. Kathryn Edin and H. Luke Shaefer, 2015, *$2.00 a day: Living on almost nothing in America*, Houghton Mifflin; Matthew Desmond, 2016, *Evicted: Poverty and profit in the American city*, Crown; United Nations Human Rights Office of the Commissioner, 2017, "Statement on visit to the USA, by Professor Philip Alston, United Nations rapporteur on extreme poverty and human rights," December 15, https://www.ohchr.org/EN/NewsEvents/Pages/DisplayNews .aspx?NewsID=22533; Angus Deaton, 2018, "The US can no longer hide from its deep poverty problem," *New York Times*, January 24. The World Bank, which is the official keeper of the global poverty counts, estimates that there are 5.3 million people in the US who are poor judged by the global poverty line. Recent work, using administrative data, has argued that the surveys used by the World Bank (and the Census Bureau) to calculate poverty understate the amounts that poor Americans receive from the safety net. See Bruce D. Meyer, Derek Wu, Victoria R. Mooers, and Carla Medalia, 2019, "The use and misuse of income data and extreme poverty in the United States," NBER Working Paper 25907, May. The same is almost certainly true of the developing country surveys used by the World Bank, so the truth of the comparison remains unresolved. The ethnographic work by Edin and Shaefer, Desmond, and, on a smaller scale, Alston, documents the grotesque poverty that exists in the US.

4. Richard Wilkinson and Kate Pickett, 2009, *The spirit level: Why greater equality makes societies stronger*, Bloomsbury. See also the wide range of claims at the Equality Trust's website, https://www.equalitytrust.org.uk/.

5. Bureau of Labor Statistics, 2015, "Table A-4: Employment status of the civilian population 25 years and over by educational attainment," Data Retrieval: Labor Force Statistics (CPS), https://www.bls.gov/webapps/legacy/cpsatab4.htm.

6. Census Bureau, n.d., "Poverty," accessed September 19, 2019, https://www.census.gov /topics/income-poverty/poverty.html; authors' calculations using the March Current Population Survey.

7. Authors' calculations from the March Current Population Survey.

8. An excellent interactive mapping tool for drug overdoses and poverty is available at https://overdosemappingtool.norc.org/.

9. Richard Wilkinson, 2000, *Mind the gap: An evolutionary view of health and inequality*, Darwinism Today, Orion, 4.

10. Raj Chetty, Nathaniel Hendren, Patrick Kline, and Émmanuel Saez, 2014, "Where is the land of opportunity? The geography of intergenerational mobility in the United States," *Quarterly Journal of Economics*, 129(4), 1553–623.

11. David M. Cutler, Edward L. Glaeser, and Karen E. Norberg, 2001, "Explaining the rise in youth suicide," in Jonathan Gruber, ed., *Risky behavior among youths: An economic analysis*, University of Chicago Press, 219–79; Julie A. Phillips, 2014, "A changing epidemiology of suicide? The influence of birth cohorts on suicide rates in the United States," *Social Science and Medicine*, 114, 151–60.

12. Kyla Thomas and David Gunnell, 2010, "Suicide in England and Wales 1861–2007: A time trends analysis," *International Journal of Epidemiology*, 39, 1464–75.

13. William F. Ogburn and Dorothy S. Thomas, 1922, "The influence of the business cycle on certain social conditions," *Journal of the American Statistical Association*, 18(139), 324–40.

14. Christopher J. Ruhm, 2000, "Are recessions good for your health?," *Quarterly Journal of Economics*, 115(2), 617–50.

15. Ann H. Stevens, Douglas L. Miller, Marianne Page, and Mateusz Filipski, 2015, "The best of times, the worst of times: Understanding pro-cyclical mortality," *American Economic Journal: Economic Policy*, 7(4), 279–311.

16. A more comprehensive analysis of income and mortality patterns by race and education is in Anne Case and Angus Deaton, 2017, "Mortality and morbidity in the 21st century," *Brookings Papers on Economic Activity*, Spring.

17. Ben Franklin, Dean Hochlaf, and George Holley-Moore, 2017, *Public health in Europe during the austerity years*, International Longevity Centre, UK, https://www.bl.uk/collection-items /public-health-in-europe-during-the-austerity-years.

18. There is another, more recent, mystery about life expectancy in Europe. In the years after 2010, mortality improvements have been slowing in the healthiest countries, and between 2014 and 2015, at least twelve countries saw life expectancy *fall*. Although it is tempting to think so, this is *not* continental Europe catching up with events in the United States. In Europe, the fall in life expectancy comes from increased mortality among the elderly, while in the United States, the fall comes from increased mortality in midlife or before. In Europe, there was a very bad flu season in the early months of 2015, the vaccine turned out not to be a good fit for the virus, and many elderly people died. To compensate, there were fewer deaths than usual in the early months of 2016, because many of those who were frail had already been "harvested" (yes, it is a standard term among demographers), and life expectancy bounced back in 2016 over 2015. An exception was Britain, where there was no bounce back, and where the deaths have fed into the bitter debate over austerity and its effects. An excellent account is given by Simon Wren-Lewis, 2017, "Austerity and mortality," *Mainly macro* (blog), November 25, https://mainlymacro.blogspot .com/2017/11/austerity-and-mortality.html.

19. Rob Joyce and Xiaowei Xu, 2019, *Inequalities in the 21st century: Introducing the IFS Deaton Review*, Institute for Fiscal Studies, May, https://www.ifs.org.uk/inequality/wp-content /uploads/2019/05/The-IFS-Deaton-Review-launch.pdf.

20. Public Health England, 2018, *A review of recent trends in mortality in England*, December, https://assets.publishing.service.gov.uk/government/uploads/system/uploads/attachment _data/file/762623/Recent_trends_in_mortality_in_England.pdf; Office of National Statistics,

2018, "Changing trends in mortality: An international comparison: 2000 to 2016," August 7, https://www.ons.gov.uk/peoplepopulationandcommunity/birthsdeathsandmarriages /lifeexpectancies/articles/changingtrendsinmortalityaninternationalcomparison/2000to2016; Jessica Y. Ho and Arun S. Hendi, 2018, "Recent trends in life expectancy across high income countries: Retrospective observational study," *BMJ*, 362, k2562, https://doi.org/10.1136/bmj.k2562.

21. David Autor, David Dorn, and Gordon Hansen, 2018, "When work disappears: Manufacturing decline and the falling marriage market-value of young men," NBER Working Paper 23173, revised January; Justin R. Pierce and Peter K. Schott, 2016, "Trade liberalization and mortality: Evidence from U.S. counties," NBER Working Paper 22849, November.

22. Amy Goldstein, 2017, *Janesville: An American story*, Simon and Schuster.

Chapter 11: Growing Apart at Work

1. Benjamin M. Friedman, 2005, *The moral consequences of economic growth*, Vintage; Thomas B. Edsall, 2012, *The age of austerity: How scarcity will remake American politics*, Doubleday.

2. Loukas Karabarbounis and Brent Neiman, 2013, "The global decline of the labor share," *Quarterly Journal of Economics*, 129(1), 61–103.

3. Compensation (wages and benefits) is measured for the median production or nonsupervisory workers (80 percent of payroll employment) in the private sector. Economic Policy Institute, 2019, "The productivity–pay gap," updated July, https://www.epi.org/productivity -pay-gap/.

4. In 1980, the college wage premium for women was higher than that for men (50 percent versus 30 percent). In 2000 and beyond, there is an 80 percent premium for both men and women. Authors' calculations from the Current Population Survey.

5. Authors' calculations from the Current Population Survey. Some adults continue to work toward a bachelor's degree into their late twenties. In 2008, at age thirty, the fraction having completed a bachelor's degree was 30 percent in 2008, rising to 36 percent in 2017. Authors' calculations from the American Community Survey.

6. Stephen Machin, 2015, "Real wage trends," Understanding the Great Recession: From Micro to Macro Conference, Bank of England, September 23 and 24, https://www.ifs.org.uk /uploads/Presentations/Understanding%20the%20recession_230915/SMachin.pdf.

7. White House, 2019, *Economic Report of the President*, March, https://www.govinfo.gov /features/erp.

8. Robert D. Putnam, 2000, *Bowling Alone: The collapse and revival of American community*, Simon and Schuster, 196–97.

9. Nikki Graf, 2016, "Most Americans say that children are better off with a parent at home," Pew Research Center, October 10, https://www.pewresearch.org/fact-tank/2016/10/10/most -americans-say-children-are-better-off-with-a-parent-at-home/.

10. Katharine G. Abraham and Melissa S. Kearny, 2019, "Explaining the decline in the US employment to population ratio: A review of the evidence," NBER Working Paper 24333, revised August.

11. Not everyone sees a ratchet effect in figure 11.2. Nicholas Eberstadt of the American Enterprise Institute argues that "there is a remarkable linearity of the decline in labor-force participation

rates for prime-age American men over the past fifty years. This great male flight from work has been almost totally un-influenced by economic fluctuations." Eberstadt, 2018, "Men without work," *American Consequences*, January 30, http://www.aei.org/publication/men-without-work-2/.

12. Other reasons include the aging of the labor force and the greater fraction of covered female workers, given that women have more sickness than men. See Jeffrey B. Liebman, 2015, "Understanding the increase in disability insurance benefit receipt in the United States," *Journal of Economic Perspectives*, 29(2), 123–50.

13. Henrik Jacobsen Kleven, 2014, "How can Scandinavians tax so much?," *Journal of Economic Perspectives*, 28(4), 77–98.

14. Lane Kenworthy, 2019, *Social democratic capitalism*, Oxford University Press.

15. Bertrand Russell, 1935, *In praise of idleness and other essays*, Routledge.

16. Michele Lamont, 2000, *The dignity of the working man*, Harvard University Press.

17. Andrew Cherlin, 2014, *Labor's love lost: The rise and fall of the working class family in America*, Russell Sage Foundation.

18. Richard B. Freeman and James L. Medoff, 1984, *What do unions do?*, Basic Books.

19. Henry S. Farber, Daniel Herbst, Ilyana Kuziemko, and Suresh Naidu, 2018, "Unions and inequality over the twentieth century: New evidence from survey data," NBER Working Paper 24587, May.

20. Bureau of Labor Statistics, 2019, "Union members summary," Economic News Release, January 18, https://www.bls.gov/news.release/union2.nr0.htm.

21. Cherlin, *Labor's love lost*.

22. Emily Guendelsberger, 2019, *On the clock: What low-wage work did to me and how it drives America insane*, Little, Brown.

23. James Bloodworth, 2018, *Hired: Six months undercover in low-wage Britain*, Atlantic Books, 57.

24. Guendelsberger, *On the clock*.

25. Neil Irwin, 2017, "To understand rising inequality, consider the janitors at two top companies, then and now," *New York Times*, September 3.

26. Nicholas Bloom, 2017, "Corporations in the age of inequality," The Big Idea, *Harvard Business Review*, https://hbr.org/cover-story/2017/03/corporations-in-the-age-of-inequality.

27. Cherlin, *Labor's love lost*, 172.

28. Daniel Cox, Rachel Lienesch, and Robert P. Jones, 2017, "Beyond economics: Fears of cultural displacement pushed the white working class to Trump," PRRI/*Atlantic* Report, April 9, https://www.prri.org/research/white-working-class-attitudes-economy-trade-immigration-election-donald-trump/.

Chapter 12: Widening Gaps at Home

1. An early statement is in David T. Ellwood and Christopher Jencks, 2004, "The uneven spread of single-parent families: What do we know? Where do we look for answers?," in Kathryn M. Neckerman, ed., *Social inequality*, Russell Sage Foundation, 3–77.

2. We present three-year averages for each time period, 1980–82, 1990–92, 2000–02, 2010–12, and 2016–18.

3. Claudia Goldin and Lawrence F. Katz, 2002, "The power of the pill: Oral contraceptives and women's career and marriage decisions," *Journal of Political Economy*, 110(4), 730–70.

4. Robert D. Mare and Christopher Winship, 1991, "Socioeconomic change and the decline of marriage for blacks and whites," in Christopher Jencks and Paul F. Peterson, ed., *The urban underclass*, Brookings Institution, 175–202.

5. William Julius Wilson and Kathryn Neckerman, "Poverty and family structure: The widening gap between evidence and public policy issues," in Sheldon H. Danziger and Daniel H. Weinberg, ed., *Fighting poverty: What works and what doesn't*, Harvard University Press, 232–59.

6. Ansley J. Coale and Susan Cotts Watkins, 1986, *The decline of fertility in Europe*, Princeton University Press; E. Anthony Wrigley and Roger Schofield, 1981, *The population history of England 1541–1871: A reconstruction*, Edward Arnold.

7. Sara McLanahan, 2004, "Diverging destinies: How children are faring under the second demographic transition," *Demography*, 41(4), 607–27.

8. McLanahan; Kathleen Kiernan, Sara McLanahan, John Holmes, and Melanie Wright, 2011, "Fragile families in the US and the UK," https://www.researchgate.net/profile/Kathleen _Kiernan3/publication/254446148_Fragile_families_in_the_US_and_UK/links /0f31753b3edb82d9b3000000/Fragile-families-in-the-US-and-UK.pdf; Kelly Musick and Katherine Michelmore, 2018, "Cross-national comparisons of union stability in cohabiting and married families with children," *Demography*, 55, 1389–421.

9. Andrew Cherlin, 2014, *Labor's love lost: The rise and fall of the working-class family in America*, Russell Sage Foundation, 145.

10. Guttmacher Institute, 2017, "Abortion is a common experience for U.S. women, despite dramatic declines in rates," news release, October 19, https://www.guttmacher.org/news-release /2017/abortion-common-experience-us-women-despite-dramatic-declines-rates.

11. Kathryn Edin and Timothy J. Nelson, 2013, *Doing the best I can: Fathers in the inner city*, University of California Press.

12. Andrew Cherlin, 2009, *The marriage-go-round: The state of marriage and the family in America today*, Vintage Books/Random House, loc. 2881 of 4480, Kindle.

13. Robert D. Putnam, 2000, *Bowling alone: The collapse and revival of American community*, Simon and Schuster.

14. Authors' calculations from Gallup tracking polls. For a general description, see Gallup, "How does Gallup Daily tracking work?," accessed September 20, 2019, https://www.gallup.com /174155/gallup-daily-tracking-methodology.aspx.

15. Larry M. Bartels, 2008, *Unequal democracy: The political economy of the new gilded age*, Princeton University Press; Martin Gilens, 2012, *Affluence and influence: Economic inequality and political power in America*, Princeton University Press.

16. Robert D. Putnam and David E. Campbell, 2010, *American grace: How religion divides and unites us*, Simon and Schuster.

17. Gallup tracking poll, authors' calculations.

18. Putnam and Campbell, *American grace*.

19. Robert P. Jones and Daniel Cox, 2017, *America's changing religious identity*, PRRI, https:// www.prri.org/research/american-religious-landscape-christian-religiously-unaffiliated/.

20. Robert Wuthnow, 1998, *After heaven: spirituality in America since the 1950s*, U of California.

21. Cherlin, *Marriage-go-round*, loc. 485 of 4480, Kindle.

22. Kathryn Edin, Timothy Nelson, Andrew Cherlin, and Robert Francis, 2019, "The tenuous attachments of working-class men," *Journal of Economic Perspectives*, 33(2), 211–28.

23. David G. Myers, 2008, *A friendly letter to skeptics and atheists: Musings on why God is good and faith isn't evil*, Jossey-Bass/Wiley.

24. Richard Layard, 2005, *Happiness: Lessons from a new science*, Penguin.

25. Authors' calculations from questions on each of the feelings, using Gallup tracking data.

Part IV: Why Is Capitalism Failing So Many?

1. Kaiser Family Foundation, 2018, "Key facts about the uninsured population," December 7, https://www.kff.org/uninsured/fact-sheet/key-facts-about-the-uninsured-population/.

2. Victor R. Fuchs, 2019, "Does employment-based health insurance make the US medical care system unfair and inefficient?," *Journal of the American Medical Association*, 321(21), 2069–70, https://doi.org/10.1001/jama.2019.4812; Victor R. Fuchs, 1976, "From Bismarck to Woodcock: The 'irrational' pursuit of national health insurance," *Journal of Law and Economics*, 19(2), 347–59.

3. John Maynard Keynes, 1919, *The economic consequences of the peace*, Macmillan.

4. Charles P. Kindleberger, 1986, *The world in depression, 1929–1939*, University of California Press, 17–26.

5. Max Hantke and Mark Spoerer, 2010, "The imposed gift of Versailles: The fiscal effects of restricting the size of Germany's armed forces, 1924–29," *Economic History Review*, 63(4), 849–64.

6. Authors' calculations using the American Community Survey.

7. Frank Newport, 2013, "In U.S., 87% approve of black-white marriage, vs. 4% in 1958," Gallup, July 25, https://news.gallup.com/poll/163697/approve-marriage-blacks-whites.aspx.

8. Andrew J. Cherlin, *Love's labor lost: The rise and fall of the working-class family in America*, Russell Sage Foundation, 54.

9. Ilyana Kuziemko, Ryan W. Buell, Taly Reich, and Michael I. Norton, 2014, "'Last-place aversion': Evidence and redistributive implications," *Quarterly Journal of Economics*, 129(1), 105–49.

10. Alan S. Gerber, Donald P. Green, and Edward Kaplan, 2003, "The illusion of learning from observational research," September 10, https://www.researchgate.net/profile/Donald_Green4/publication/228755361_12_The_illusion_of_learning_from_observational_research/links/0046351eaab43ee2aa000000/12-The-illusion-of-learning-from-observational-research.pdf.

Chapter 13: How American Healthcare Is Undermining Lives

1. Anne B. Martin, Micah Hartman, Benjamin Washington, Aaron Catlin, and the National Health Expenditure Accounts Team, 2019, "National health care expenditure in 2017: Growth slows to post-Great Recession rates; share of GDP stabilizes," *Health Affairs*, 38(1), 96–106, https://doi.org/10.1377/hlthaff.2018.05085.

2. Adam Smith, 1776, *The wealth of nations*, bk. 4. See our introduction.

3. Robert E. Hall and Charles I. Jones, 2007, "The value of life and the rise in health spending," *Quarterly Journal of Economics*, 122(1), 39–72, https://doi.org/10.1162/qjec.122.1.39.

4. Kenneth J. Arrow, 1963, "Uncertainty and the welfare economics of medical care," *American Economic Review*, 53(5), 941–73.

5. Authors' update of Max Roser, 2017, "Link between health spending and life expectancy: US is an outlier," Our World in Data, May 26, https://ourworldindata.org/the-link-between -life-expectancy-and-health-spending-us-focus. The underlying data used for extension are from the World Bank's World Development Indicators, http://data.worldbank.org/data-catalog /world-development-indicators; and Organisation for Economic Co-operation and Development data, data https://stats.oecd.org/.

6. Victor Dzau, Mark B. McClellan, Michael McGinnis, et al., 2017, "Vital directions for health and health care: Priorities from a National Academy of Medicine initiative," *Journal of the American Medical Association*, 317(14), 1461–70, https://doi.org/10.1001/jama.2017.1964.

7. William H. Shrank, Teresa L. Rogstad, and Natasha Parekh, 2019, "Waste in the US health care system: Estimated costs and potential for savings," *Journal of the American Medical Association*, 322(15), 1501–9, https://doi.org/10.1001/jama.2019.13978.

8. Elizabeth Arias and Jiaquan Xu, 2019, "United States life tables, 2017," *National Vital Statistics Reports*, 68(7), https://www.cdc.gov/nchs/data/nvsr/nvsr68/nvsr68_07-508.pdf.

9. OECD.Stat, 2019, "Health status," last updated July 2, https://stats.oecd.org/Index.aspx ?DatasetCode=HEALTH_STAT.

10. Jonathan Skinner and Amitabh Chandra, 2018, "Health care employment growth and the future of US cost containment," *Journal of the American Medical Association*, 319(18), 1861–62.

11. Irene Papanicolas, Liana R. Woskie, and Ashish K. Jha, 2018, "Healthcare spending in the United States and in other high-income countries," *Journal of the American Medical Association*, 319(10), 1024–39, https://doi.org/10.1001/jama.2018.1150; Ezekiel J. Emanuel, 2018, "The real cost of the US healthcare system," *Journal of the American Medical Association*, 319(10), 983–85.

12. James Banks, Michael Marmot, Zoe Oldfield, and James P. Smith, 2006, "Disease and disadvantage in the United States and in England," *Journal of the American Medical Association*, 295(17), 2037–45.

13. Authors' calculations, Gallup World Poll.

14. Karen Davis, Cathy Schoen, Stephen Schoenbaum, et al., 2007, *Mirror, mirror on the wall: An international update on the comparative performance of American Health Care*, Commonwealth Fund, https://www.commonwealthfund.org/publications/fund-reports/2007/may/mirror -mirror-wall-international-update-comparative-performance.

15. Papanicolas et al., "Healthcare spending."

16. Emanuel, "Real cost."

17. Dean Baker, 2016, *Rigged: How globalization and the rules of the modern economy were structured to make the rich richer*, Center for Economic Policy Research.

18. Jon Bakija, Adam Cole, and Bradley T. Heim, 2012, "Jobs and income growth of top earners and the causes of changing income inequality: Evidence from U.S. tax return data," April, https://web.williams.edu/Economics/wp/BakijaColeHeimJobsIncomeGrowthTopEarners.pdf.

19. Papanicolas et al., "Healthcare spending."

20. Michelle M. Mello, Amitabh Chandra, Atul A. Gawande, and David M. Studdert, 2010, "National costs of the medical liability system," *Health Affairs*, 29(9), 1569–77, https://doi.org/10.1377/hlthaff.2009.0807; Martin et al., "National health care expenditure."

21. Emanuel, "Real cost," 983.

22. Baker, *Rigged*.

23. Danielle Ofri, 2019, "The insulin wars: How insurance companies farm out their dirty work to doctors and patients," *New York Times*, January 18.

24. *Economist*, 2019, "Why America's biggest charities are owned by pharmaceutical companies," August 15.

25. Nicholas Timmins, 2009, "The NICE way of influencing health spending: A conversation with Sir Michael Rawlins," *Health Affairs*, 28(5), 1360–65, 1362, https://doi.org/10.1377/hlthaff.28.5.1360.

26. Emanuel, "Real cost."

27. Zack Cooper, Stuart V. Craig, Martin Gaynor, and John van Reenen, 2019, "The price ain't right? Hospital prices and health spending on the privately insured," *Quarterly Journal of Economics*, 134(1), 51–107, https://doi.org/10.1093/qje/qjy020.

28. Zack Cooper, Fiona Scott Morton, and Nathan Shekita, 2017, "Surprise! Out-of-network billing for emergency care in the United States," National Bureau of Economic Research Working Paper No. 23623, July; Eileen Appelbaum and Rosemary Batt, 2019, "Private equity and surprise medical billing," Institute for New Economic Thinking, September 4, https://www.ineteconomics.org/perspectives/blog/private-equity-and-surprise-medical-billing; Jonathan Ford, 2019, "Private equity has inflated US medical bills," *Financial Times*, October 6.

29. Steven Brill, 2015, *America's bitter pill: Money, politics, backroom deals, and the fight to fix our broken healthcare system*, Random House.

30. David Robinson, 2016, "Top 5 highest paid New York hospital officials," Lohud.com, June 2, https://www.lohud.com/story/news/investigations/2016/06/02/hospitals-biggest-payouts/85049982/.

31. NewYork-Presbyterian Hospital, 2017, "Amazing things are happening," https://www.nyp.org/amazingthings/.

32. Shefali Luthra, 2018, "Playing on fear and fun, hospitals follow pharma in direct-to-consumer advertising," Kaiser Health News, November 19, https://khn.org/news/hospitals-direct-to-consumer-health-care-advertising-marketing/.

33. Katie Thomas and Charles Ornstein, 2019, "Top cancer doctor, forced out over ties to drug makers, joins their ranks," *New York Times*, January 7, https://www.nytimes.com/2019/01/07/health/baselga-sloan-kettering-astrazeneca.html.

34. Katie Thomas and Charles Ornstein, 2018, "Memorial Sloan Kettering's season of turmoil," *New York Times*, December 31, https://www.nytimes.com/2018/12/31/health/memorial-sloan-kettering-conflicts.html.

35. Patrick Thomas, 2018, "Ever heard of Iqvia? Its CEO made $38 million," *Wall Street Journal*, June 12, https://www.wsj.com/articles/ever-heard-of-iqvia-its-ceo-made-38-million-1528801200.

36. Matthew Smith, Danny Yagan, Owen M. Zidar, and Eric Zwick, 2019, "Capitalists in the twenty-first century," *Quarterly Journal of Economics*, 134(4), 1675–1745.

37. Centers for Medicare and Medicaid Services, 2018, "National health expenditure data," last modified April 17, https://www.cms.gov/Research-Statistics-Data-and-Systems/Statistics-Trends-and-Reports/NationalHealthExpendData/index.html.

38. Ezekiel J. Emanuel and Victor R. Fuchs, 2008, "Who really pays for health care? The myth of 'shared responsibility,'" *Journal of the American Medical Association*, 299(9), 1057–59.

39. Martin et al., "National health care expenditure."

40. Yi Chin, Maurizio Mazzocco, and Béla Személy, 2019, "Explaining the decline of the U.S. saving rate: The role of health expenditure," *International Economic Review*, 60(4), 1–37, https://doi.org/10.1111/iere.12405.

41. Sara R. Collins, Herman K. Bhupal, and Michelle M. Doty, 2019, "Health insurance coverage eight years after the ACA," Commonwealth Fund, February 7, https://www.commonwealthfund.org/publications/issue-briefs/2019/feb/health-insurance-coverage-eight-years-after-aca.

42. Martin et al., "National health care expenditure."

43. Collins et al., "Health insurance coverage."

44. David I. Auerbach and Arthur L. Kellerman, 2011, "A decade of health care cost growth has wiped out real income gains for an average US family," *Health Affairs*, 30(9), 1630–36.

45. Jonathan Gruber, 2000, "Health insurance and the labor market," in Anthony J. Culyer and Joseph P. Newhouse, ed., *Handbook of Health Economics*, Elsevier Science, vol. 1, pt. A, 645–706, https://doi.org/10.1016/S1574-0064(00)80171-7.

46. Joint Committee on Taxation, 2018, "Estimates of federal tax expenditures for fiscal years 2017–2021," May 25, https://www.jct.gov/publications.html?func=select&id=5.

47. Victor R. Fuchs, 2019, "Does employment-based health insurance make the US medical care system unfair and inefficient?," *Journal of the American Medical Association*, 321(21), 2069–70, https://doi.org/10.1001/jama.2019.4812.

48. Leslie Josephs, 2017, "FedEx says US roads are so bad it's burning through tires twice as fast as it did 20 years ago," Quartz, February 1, https://qz.com/900565/fedex-says-us-roads-are-so-bad-its-burning-through-tires-twice-as-fast-as-it-did-20-years-ago/.

49. National Association of State Budget Officers, 2018, *Summary: NASBO state expenditure report*, November 15, https://higherlogicdownload.s3.amazonaws.com/NASBO/9d2d2db1-c943-4f1b-b750-0fca152d64c2/UploadedImages/Issue%20Briefs%20/2018_State_Expenditure_Report_Summary.pdf.

50. Arrow, "Uncertainty."

51. Robert D. Atkinson and Michael Lind, 2018, *Big is beautiful: Debunking the myth of small business*, MIT Press.

52. Lawrence Lessig, 2015, *Republic, lost: version 2.0*, Hachette.

53. All data from https://www.opensecrets.org/, accessed August 2019.

54. Brill, *America's bitter pill.*

55. Lee Drutman, 2015, *The business of America is lobbying: How corporations became politicized and politics became more corporate*, Oxford University Press.

56. Zack Cooper, Amanda E. Kowalski, Eleanor N. Powell, and Jennifer Wu, 2019, "Politics and health care spending in the United States," NBER Working Paper 23748, revised February.

Chapter 14: Capitalism, Immigrants, Robots, and China

1. National Academies of Sciences, Engineering, and Medicine, 2017, *The economic and fiscal consequences of immigration*, National Academies Press, https://doi.org/10.17226/23550. We draw on this compendium of evidence extensively in this section.

2. Ufuk Akcigit, Salomé Baslandze, and Stefanie Stantcheva, 2016, "Taxation and the international mobility of inventors," *American Economic Review*, 106(10), 2930–81, http://dx.doi.org/10.1257/aer.20150237.

3. National Academies of Sciences, Engineering, and Medicine, *Economic and fiscal consequences*.

4. Douglas S. Massey, 2017, "The counterproductive consequences of border enforcement," *Cato Journal*, 37(3), https://www.cato.org/cato-journal/fall-2017/counterproductive-consequences-border-enforcement.

5. Tom Cotton, 2016, "Fix immigration. It's what voters want," op-ed, *New York Times*, December 28.

6. National Academies of Sciences, Engineering, and Medicine, *Economic and fiscal consequences*, 247.

7. *U.S. News and World Report*, n.d., "How much does a plumber make?," accessed July 28, 2019, https://money.usnews.com/careers/best-jobs/plumber/salary.

8. Census Bureau, "Poverty thresholds," accessed February 18, 2019, https://www.census.gov/data/tables/time-series/demo/income-poverty/historical-poverty-thresholds.html.

9. David Autor, David Dorn, and Gordon H. Hansen, 2013, "The China syndrome: Local labor market effects of import competition in the United States," *American Economic Review*, 103(6), 2121–68, http://dx.doi.org/10.1257/aer.103.6.2121. For a later review, see also David Autor, David Dorn, and Gordon H. Hansen, 2016, "The China shock: Learning from labor-market adjustment to large changes in trade," *Annual Review of Economics*, 8, 205–40, https://doi.org/10.1146/annurev-economics-080315-015041.

10. David Autor, David Dorn, and Gordon H. Hansen, 2017, "When work disappears: Manufacturing decline and the falling marriage market of men," NBER Working Paper 23173, February, https://www.nber.org/papers/w23173.

11. Nicholas Bloom, Kyle Handley, André Kurman, and Phillip Luck, 2019, "The impact of Chinese trade on US employment: The good, the bad, and the apocryphal," July, https://nbloom.people.stanford.edu/sites/g/files/sbiybj4746/f/bhkl_posted_draft.pdf.

12. Robert Feenstra, Hong Ma, Akira Sasahara, and Yuan Xu, 2018, "Reconsidering the 'China shock' in trade," VoxEU, January 18, https://voxeu.org/article/reconsidering-china-shock-trade.

13. David Autor, 2019, "Work of the past, work of the future," *American Economic Association Papers and Proceedings*, 109, 1–32.

14. Quoted in Steven Brill, 2018, *Tailspin: The people and forces behind America's fifty-year fall—and those fighting to reverse it*, Knopf, 181.

15. Autor, Dorn, and Hansen, "China shock."

16. Dani Rodrik, 1997, *Has globalization gone too far?*, Institute for International Economics, loc. 178 of 1486, Kindle.

17. Robert Joyce and Xiaowei Xu, 2019, *Inequalities in the 21st century: Introducing the IFS Deaton Review*, Institute for Fiscal Studies, May, https://www.ifs.org.uk/inequality/wp-content/uploads/2019/05/The-IFS-Deaton-Review-launch_final.pdf.

18. Alberto Alesina and Edward Glaeser, 2006, *Fighting poverty in the US and Europe: A world of difference*, Oxford University Press; Alberto Alesina, Reza Baqir, and William Easterly, 1999, "Public goods and ethnic divisions," *Quarterly Journal of Economics*, 114(4), 1243–84.

19. Michael A. McCarthy, 2017, *Dismantling solidarity: Capitalist politics and American pensions since the New Deal*, Cornell University Press, 51.

20. Jacob S. Hacker, 2008, *The great risk shift: The new economic insecurity and the decline of the American dream*, Oxford University Press; McCarthy, *Dismantling solidarity*.

21. Organisation for Economic Co-operation and Development data quoted by Jacob S. Hacker, 2019, "The economy is strong, so why do so many Americans still feel at risk?," *New York Times*, May 21.

Chapter 15: Firms, Consumers, and Workers

1. Adam Smith, 1776, *The wealth of nations*, bk. 1.

2. Alan B. Krueger, 2018, "Reflections on dwindling worker bargaining power and monetary policy," luncheon address at the Jackson Hole Economic Symposium, August 24, https://www.kansascityfed.org/~/media/files/publicat/sympos/2018/papersandhandouts/824180824kruegerremarks.pdf?la=en.

3. Luigi Zingales, 2017, "Towards a political theory of the firm," *Journal of Economic Perspectives*, 31(3), 113–30.

4. Naomi Lamoreaux, 2019, "The problem of bigness: From Standard Oil to Google," *Journal of Economic Perspectives*, 33(3), 94–117.

5. Lamoreaux.

6. Joseph Stiglitz, 2019, *People, power, and politics: Progressive capitalism for an age of discontent*, Norton; Thomas Philippon, 2019, *The great reversal: How America gave up on free markets*, Harvard University Press; Raghuram Rajan, 2019, *The third pillar: How markets and the state leave the community behind*, Penguin; Paul Collier, 2018, *The future of capitalism: Facing the new anxieties*, Harper; Jonathan Tepper and Denise Hearn, 2018, *The myth of competition: Monopolies and the death of competition*, Wiley; Steven Pearlstein, 2018, *Can American capitalism survive? Why greed is not good, opportunity not equal, and fairness won't make us poorer*, St. Martin's; Tim Wu, 2018, *The curse of bigness: Antitrust in the new gilded age*, Columbia Global Reports; Elizabeth Anderson, 2017, *Private government: How employers rule our lives (and why we don't talk about it)*, Princeton University Press; Dean Baker, 2016, *Rigged: How globalization and the rules of the modern economy were structured to make the rich richer*, Center for Economic Policy Research; Tim Carney, 2019, *Alienated America: Why some places thrive while others collapse*, Harper; Lane Kenworthy, 2019, *Social democratic capitalism*, Oxford University Press. For an unapologetic defense, see Tyler Cowen, 2019, *Big business: A love letter to an American anti-hero*, St. Martin's.

7. Philippon, *Great reversal*.

8. David Autor, David Dorn, Lawrence F. Katz, Christina Patterson, and John van Reenen, 2019, "The fall of the labor share and the rise of superstar firms," NBER Working Paper 23396, revised May 2, figure 4, https://economics.mit.edu/files/12979.

9. Buffett quoted in Tepper and Hearn, *Myth of competition*, 2, 198.

10. Numbers from CNN Business online, February 19, 2019: for United, see https://money .cnn.com/quote/shareholders/shareholders.html?symb=UAL&subView=institutional; for Delta, see https://money.cnn.com/quote/shareholders/shareholders.html?symb =DAL&subView=institutional; for Southwest, https://money.cnn.com/quote/shareholders /shareholders.html?symb=LUV&subView=institutional; for American, https://money.cnn .com/quote/shareholders/shareholders.html?symb=AAL&subView=institutional.

11. Einar Elhauge, 2019, "How horizontal shareholding harms our economy—and why antitrust law can fix it," SSRN, revised August 4, http://dx.doi.org/10.2139/ssrn.3293822; José Azar, Martin C. Schmalz, and Isabel Tecu, 2018, "Anticompetitive effects of common ownership," *Journal of Finance*, 73(4), 1513–65.

12. Tepper and Hearn, *Myth of competition*.

13. Susanto Basu, 2019, "Are price-cost markups rising in the United States? A discussion of the evidence," *Journal of Economic Perspectives*, 33(3), 3–22; Chad Syverson, 2019, "Macroeconomics and market power: Context, implications, and open questions," *Journal of Economic Perspectives*, 33(3), 23–43.

14. Jan De Loecker, Jan Eeckhout, and Gabriel Unger, 2018, "The rise of market power and the macroeconomic implications," November 22, http://www.janeeckhout.com/wp-content /uploads/RMP.pdf.

15. John R. Hicks, 1935, "Annual survey of economic theory: The theory of monopoly," *Econometrica*, 3(1), 1–20.

16. Carl Shapiro, 2019, "Protecting competition in the American economy: Merger control, tech titans, labor markets," *Journal of Economic Perspectives*, 33(3), 69–93.

17. Carl Shapiro, 2018, "Antitrust in a time of populism," *International Journal of Industrial Organization*, 61, 714–48.

18. De Loecker et al., "Rise of market power."

19. John Van Reenen, 2018, "Increasing differences between firms: Market power and the market economy," prepared for the Jackson Hole conference, https://www.kansascityfed.org /~/media/files/publicat/sympos/2018/papersandhandouts/jh%20john%20van%20 reenen%20version%2020.pdf?la=en.

20. Autor et al., "Fall of the labor share"; International Labor Organization and Organisation for Economic Co-operation and Development, 2015, *The Labor share in G20 economies*, report prepared for the G20 Employment Working Group, Antalya, Turkey, February 26–27, https:// www.oecd.org/g20/topics/employment-and-social-policy/The-Labour-Share-in-G20 -Economies.pdf.

21. For a contrary view, see Philippon, *Great reversal*.

22. Verizon Communications Inc. v. Law Offices of Curtis V. Trinko LLP, 540 U.S. 398 (2004), https://www.law.cornell.edu/supct/html/02-682.ZO.html.

23. Esteban Rossi-Hansberg, Pierre-Daniel Sarte, and Nicholas Trachter, 2018, "Diverging trends in national and local concentration," NBER Working Paper 25066, September.

24. For an argument to the contrary, see Philippon, *Great reversal*.

25. Joan Robinson, 1933, *The economics of imperfect competition*, Macmillan.

26. David G. Blanchflower, 2019, *Not working: Where have all the good jobs gone?*, Princeton University Press; David Autor, 2019, "Work of the past, work of the future," *American Economic Association Papers and Proceedings*, 109, 1–32.

27. Doruk Cengiz, Arindrajit Dube, Attila Lindner, and Ben Zipperer, 2019, "The effect of minimum wages on low-wage jobs," *Quarterly Journal of Economics*, 134(3), 1405–54.

28. David Metcalf, 2008, "Why has the British national minimum wage had little or no impact on employment?," *Journal of Industrial Relations*, 50(3), 489–512; David Card and Alan B. Krueger, 2017, "*Myth and measurement* and the theory and practice of labor economics," *ILR Review*, 70(3), 826–31.

29. Kevin Rinz, 2018, "Labor market concentration, earnings inequality, and earnings mobility," US Census Bureau, CARRA Working Paper 2018-10, September, https://www.census.gov/content/dam/Census/library/working-papers/2018/adrm/carra-wp-2018-10.pdf.

30. Krueger, "Reflections."

31. Krueger.

32. David Weil, 2014, *The fissured workplace: Why work became so bad for so many and what can be done to improve it*, Harvard University Press.

33. David Dorn, Johannes Schmieder, and James R. Spletzer, 2018, "Domestic outsourcing in the United States," January 31, 1, https://www.dol.gov/sites/dolgov/files/OASP/legacy/files/Domestic-Outsourcing-in-the-United-States.pdf.

34. *New York Times*, 2019, "Senators urge Google to give temporary workers fulltime status," August 5.

35. Henry Farber, David Herbst, Ilyana Kuziemko, and Suresh Naidu, 2018, "Unions and inequality over the 20th century: New evidence from survey data," NBER Working Paper 24587, May, https://www.nber.org/papers/w24587.

36. Kathryn Abraham and Melissa Kearney, 2018, "Explaining the decline in the US employment to population ratio: A review of the evidence," NBER Working Paper 24333, February, https://www.nber.org/papers/w24333.

37. We are grateful to Oliver Hart for discussion of these issues.

38. The following draws on Lee Drutman, 2015, *The business of America is lobbying: How corporations became politicized and politics became more corporate*, Oxford University Press; Jacob S. Hacker and Paul Pierson, 2011, *Winner-take-all politics: How Washington made the rich richer—and turned its back on the middle class*, Simon and Schuster; and Brink Lindsey and Steven M. Teles, 2017, *The captured economy: How the powerful enrich themselves, slow down growth, and increase inequality*, Oxford University Press.

39. Data from https://www.opensecrets.org, accessed August 5, 2019.

40. Stephanie Hernandez McGavin, 2016, "Volkswagen Group leads automotive spending on advertising," *Automotive News*, December 9, https://www.autonews.com/article/20161209/RETAIL03/161209824/volkswagen-group-leads-automotive-spending-on-advertising.

41. Lewis F. Powell Jr., 1971, "Attack of American free enterprise system," confidential memorandum to Eugene B. Sydnor Jr., August 23, Supreme Court History: Law, Power, and

Personality, PBS, accessed August 14, 2019, https://web.archive.org/web/20120104052451 /http://www.pbs.org/wnet/supremecourt/personality/sources_document13.html.

42. Data from https://www.opensecrets.org, accessed August 5, 2019.

43. Martin Gilens, 2014, *Affluence and influence: Economic inequality and political power in America*, Princeton University Press; Larry M. Bartels, 2008, *Unequal democracy: The political economy of the new gilded age*, Princeton University Press.

44. Dani Rodrik, 1997, *Has globalization gone too far?*, Institute for International Economics.

45. Weil, *Fissured workplace*.

Chapter 16: What to Do?

1. Amartya K. Sen, 2009, *The idea of justice*, Harvard University Press; Amartya K. Sen, 2006, "What do we want from a theory of justice?," *Journal of Philosophy*, 103(5), 215–38.

2. Anthony B. Atkinson, 1970, "The measurement of inequality," *Journal of Economic Theory*, 2, 224–63.

3. Derek Parfit, 1997, "Equality and priority," *Ratio*, 10(3), 202–21.

4. Peter Diamond and Emanuel Saez, 2011, "The case for a progressive tax: From basic research to policy recommendations," *Journal of Economic Perspectives*, 25(4), 165–90.

5. Abby Goodnough, 2018, "This city's overdose deaths have plunged. Can others learn from it?," *New York Times*, November 25, https://www.nytimes.com/2018/11/25/health/opioid -overdose-deaths-dayton.html.

6. Centers for Disease Control and Prevention, 2019, "Prescription opioid data," last reviewed June 27, https://www.cdc.gov/drugoverdose/data/prescribing.html.

7. Kenneth J. Arrow, 1963, "Uncertainty and the welfare economics of medical care," *American Economic Review*, 53(5), 941–73.

8. Nicholas Timmins, 2009, "The NICE way of influencing health spending: A conversation with Sir Michael Rawlins," *Health Affairs*, 28(5), 1360–65, https://doi.org/10.1377/hlthaff.28.5.1360.

9. Arrow, "Uncertainty," 967.

10. Edward R. Berchick, Emily Hood, and Jessica C. Barnett, 2018, *Health insurance coverage in the United States: 2017*, report no. P60-264, US Census Bureau, September, https://www .census.gov/library/publications/2018/demo/p60-264.html.

11. Victor R. Fuchs, 2018, "Is single payer the answer for the US health care system?," *Journal of the American Medical Association*, 319(1), 15–16, https://doi.org/10.1001/jama.2017.18739.

12. Victor R. Fuchs, 2018, "How to make US health care more equitable and less costly: Begin by replacing employment-based insurance," *Journal of the American Medical Association*, 320(20), 2071–72, 2072, https://doi.org/10.1001/jama.2018.16475, 2072.

13. Ezekiel J. Emanuel and Victor R. Fuchs, 2007, *A comprehensive cure: Universal health care vouchers*, Discussion Paper 2007-11, Brookings Institution, July, http://www.hamiltonproject .org/assets/legacy/files/downloads_and_links/A_Comprehensive_Cure-_Universal_Health _Care_Vouchers.pdf.

14. Dylan Scott, 2019, "How to build a Medicare-for-all plan, explained by somebody who's thought about it for 20 years," Vox, January 28, https://www.vox.com/policy-and-politics/2019

/1/28/18192674/medicare-for-all-cost-jacob-hacker. See also Jacob S. Hacker, 2018, "The road to Medicare for everyone," *American Prospect*, January 3.

15. BBC News, 1998, "Making Britain better," July 1, http://news.bbc.co.uk/2/hi/events/nhs _at_50/special_report/119803.stm.

16. Anthony B. Atkinson, 2003, "Income inequality in OECD countries: Data and explanations," *CESifo Economic Studies*, 49(4), 479–513.

17. Kwame Anthony Appiah, 2018, *The lies that bind: Rethinking identity*, Liveright.

18. Philippe van Parijs and Yannick Vanderborght, 2017, *Basic income: A radical proposal for a free society and a sane economy*, Harvard University Press.

19. Emma Rothschild, 2000, "A basic income for all: Security and laissez-faire," *Boston Review*, October 1, http://bostonreview.net/forum/basic-income-all/emma-rothschild-security-and -laissez-faire.

20. Herbert Simon, 2000, "A basic income for all: UBI and the flat tax," *Boston Review*, October 1, http://bostonreview.net/forum/basic-income-all/herbert-simon-ubi-and-flat-tax.

21. Hilary W. Hoynes and Jesse Rothstein, 2019, "Universal basic income in the US and advanced countries," NBER Working Paper 25538, February, https://www.nber.org/papers /w25538.

22. Robert H. Frank, 2014, "Let's try a basic income and public work," *Cato Unbound*, August 11, https://www.cato-unbound.org/2014/08/11/robert-h-frank/lets-try-basic-income -public-work.

23. Eric A. Posner and E. Glen Weyl, 2018, *Radical markets: Uprooting capitalism and democracy for a just society*, Princeton University Press.

24. Edmund Phelps, 2009, *Rewarding work: How to restore participation and self-support to free enterprise*, Harvard University Press; Oren Cass, 2018, *The once and future worker: A vision for the renewal of work in America*, Encounter Books.

25. Bureau of Labor Statistics, 2018, "Characteristics of minimum wage workers, 2017," BLS Reports, Report 1072, March, https://www.bls.gov/opub/reports/minimum-wage/2017 /home.htm.

26. Joan Robinson, 1956, *The accumulation of capital*, Macmillan, 87.

27. Brink Lindsey and Steven M. Teles, 2017, *The captured economy: How the powerful enrich themselves, slow down growth, and increase inequality*, Oxford University Press.

28. Lindsey and Teles. See also Dean Baker, 2016, *Rigged: How globalization and the rules of the modern economy were structured to make the rich richer*, Center for Economic Policy Research.

29. Robert D. Atkinson and Michael Lind, 2018, *Big is beautiful: Debunking the myth of small business*, MIT Press.

30. Matthew Smith, Danny Yagan, Owen M. Zidar, and Eric Zwick, 2019, "Capitalists in the 21st century," *Quarterly Journal of Economics*, 134(4), 1675–1745, 1677.

31. Adam Smith, 1776, *The wealth of nations*, bk. 4.

32. Cass, *Once and future worker*.

33. Michael J. Sandel, 2018, "Populism, Trump, and the future of democracy," openDemocracy, May 9, https://www.opendemocracy.net/en/populism-trump-and-future-of -democracy/.

34. Harriet Ryan, Lisa Girion, and Scott Glover, 2016, "OxyContin goes global—'We're only just getting started,'" *Los Angeles Times*, December 18, https://www.latimes.com/projects /la-me-oxycontin-part3/.

35. Ellen Barry, 2019, "'Austerity, that's what I know': The making of a young UK socialist," *New York Times*, February 24, https://www.nytimes.com/2019/02/24/world/europe/britain -austerity-socialism.html.

36. Charles Murray, 2012, *Coming apart: The state of white America, 1960–2010*, Crown.

37. Angus Deaton, 2017, "Without governments would countries have more inequality, or less?," *Economist*, July 13.

INDEX

abortion, 169, 171

Abraham, Katharine G., 278n10, 288n36

Abraham, Sarah, 276n1

accidental poisonings, 2, 38, 39, 97, 113. *See also* drug overdoses; opioids

acetaminophen, 117

Achenbach, Joel, 267n2

addiction, x, 2, 4, 37, 95–96, 115–16, 120, 261; black market and, 124; characteristics of, 39; costs of, 104; cures for, 129; depression and, 212; developing, 117; hangover of, 69; to heroin, 122, 123; medication-assisted treatment for, 109; opioids and, 112, 122; pain and, 4; people predisposed to, 192; risk for, 118; seen as moral weakness, 28; suicide and, 84; treating, 247

Advil, 117

advocacy organizations for pain sufferers, 124

Affordable Care Act, 210. *See also* Obamacare

Afghanistan, 125

African Americans, 5, 8, 38, 68, 140, 148, 172–73, 174, 224, 275n25; black culture, 189; contrasting outcomes for, 183; drug overdoses and, 119; exclusion of, 166; fentanyl and, 114, 188; happiness and, 181; heart disease and, 44; improvements in lives of, 186; inner-city, 67; job loss and, 258; life expectancy of, 27; misfortunes of, 69; mortality rates and, 6, 31, 62; mortality rates for white Americans and, 64–65; pain and, 90–91; poverty

and, 137; religion and, 178; social protection and, 225

age effects, 35; deaths of despair and, 59; drinking and, 106; life evaluation and, 182; mental health and, 78; pain and, 87–89; poor health and, 76

aging, 84, 88, 90

Aid to Families with Dependent Children program, 172

airlines, 231, 233; increasing concentration of, 235

Akcigit, Ufuk, 285n2

Alabama, 43, 100, 140, 268n5

Al-Anon, x

alcohol: average drinks per occasion, 106; social life and, 103; in Soviet Union, 106–7; taxes on, 104–5. *See also* binge drinking

alcoholic liver diseases, 2, 38; China and, 58; common features of, 97; mortality rates from, 40, 268n5; rising, 106

Alcoholics Anonymous (AA), x, 104

alcoholism, 4, 28, 31, 36, 37, 65–66, 71, 96, 104, 138, 185; drug overdoses and, 246; high-functioning, 39; National Institute on Alcohol Abuse and Alcoholism, 105, 273n20; white Americans and, 38

Alesina, Alberto, 286n18

Aleve, 117

Aliprantis, Dionissi, 274n8

Allen, Robert C., 266n26

Alston, Philip, 276n3

Alzheimer's, 24

suicides (cont.)
99; in United States, 98; upper-class, 28; white Americans and, 38; white non-Hispanics and, 98, 102; women and, 58
surveys, 74–75, 166, 272n10; patient satisfaction, 117
Suzman, Richard, 264
Sweden, 22, 163
Swift, Gustavus, 227
Switzerland, 193, 194, 195
Sydnor, Eugene B., Jr., 288n41
synthetic narcotics, 67. *See also* fentanyl; heroin
Syverson, Chad, 287n13
Személy, Béla, 284n40

Tabb, Charles Jordan, 266n22
Tanner Lectures in Human Values, 263
Target, 220
Tasmania, 10, 120
Tasmanian Alkaloids, 125
taxation, 12, 104–5, 158, 246, 252–53, 256; confiscatory, 13; health-related, 204; income after, 206; lobbying and, 232
technological change, 9, 222, 254; socially beneficial for consumers, 233. *See also* automation; robots
Tecu, Isabel, 287n11
Teles, Steven, 255–56, 288n38, 290n27, 290n28
Tepper, Jonathan, 286n6, 287n9, 287n12
terminal illnesses, 95
Texas, 33, 110
Thomas, Dorothy, 141–42, 266n2, 277n13
Thomas, Duncan, 271n6
Thomas, Katie, 275n35, 283n33, 283n34
Thomas, Kyla, 272n9, 277n12
Thomas, Patrick, 283n35
Thompson, Ken, 275n30
Thrush, Glenn, 265n6, 265n9
Tignor, Bob, 263
Timmins, Nicholas, 283n25, 289n8
Tolstoy, Leo, 71

Toyota, 230
Trachter, Nicholas, 287n23
Trade Adjustment Assistance program, 221–22
trade secrets, 238
"Tragedy of Needless Pain, The" (Melzack), 116
Treaty of Detroit, 221, 224
trente glorieuses, Les, 20
Trudeau, Gary, 63, 270n1
Truly Disadvantaged, The (Wilson, W.), 67
Trump, Donald, 13, 87, 124
tuberculosis, 23
Twain, Mark, 103
Tylenol, 83, 117
typhus, 25

unemployment, 134, 159; doubling of, 142; insurance, 222, 243; rates of, 51, 87, 102, 135, 144, 147
unfairness, 12, 14, 166, 213, 221, 227, 262
Unger, Gabriel, 287n14, 287n18
unintended pregnancies, 169
unions, 161, 221; decline of, 174–75, 244, 250; less prevalent, 214; power of, 238–39; restoration of, 251; wages and, 4, 164
United Airlines, 231
United Auto Workers (UAW), 221
United Kingdom, 145. *See also* Britain
United Nations, 215
United States (US), 20, 25, 29, 41, 108, 186, 193, 199, 218, 249; Britain and, 223; church membership in, 176; consolidation of industries in, 9; fentanyl and, 38; four-year college degrees and, 3; healthcare costs in, 197; immigration and, 215; labor in, 165; level of inequality in, 151; life expectancy in, 23, 194, 195; lobbying in, 234; mobility in, 236; pain, in comparison countries and, 87; pain in, 93; safety net in, 133; social safety net and, 223, 225; suicides in, 98; Trade Adjustment Assistance program, 221–22